Convers

Conversation analysts have begun to challenge long-cherished assumptions about the relationship between gender and language, asking new questions about the interactional study of gender and providing fresh insights into the ways it may be studied empirically. Drawing on a lively set of audio- and video-recorded materials of real-life interactions, including domestic telephone calls, children's play, mediation sessions, police-suspect interviews, psychiatric assessments and calls to telephone helplines, this volume is the first to showcase the latest thinking and cutting-edge research of an international group of scholars working on topics at the intersection of gender and conversation analysis. Theoretically, it pushes forward the boundaries of our understanding of the relationship between conversation and gender, charting new and exciting territory. Methodologically, it offers readers a clear, practical understanding of how to analyse gender using conversation analysis, by presenting detailed demonstrations of this method in use.

SUSAN A. SPEER is a Senior Lecturer in Psychology at the University of Manchester. She is the author of *Gender Talk: Feminism, Discourse and Conversation Analysis* (2005).

ELIZABETH STOKOE is Professor of Social Interaction in the Department of Social Sciences at Loughborough University. She is the co-author of *Discourse and Identity* (2006).

Conversation and Gender

Edited by

Susan A. Speer and Elizabeth Stokoe

CAMBRIDGE
UNIVERSITY PRESS

CAMBRIDGE UNIVERSITY PRESS
Cambridge, New York, Melbourne, Madrid, Cape Town, Singapore,
São Paulo, Delhi, Dubai, Tokyo, Mexico City

Cambridge University Press
The Edinburgh Building, Cambridge CB2 8RU, UK

Published in the United States of America by Cambridge University Press, New York

www.cambridge.org
Information on this title: www.cambridge.org/9780521696036

© Cambridge University Press 2011

First published 2011

Printed in the United Kingdom at the University Press, Cambridge

A catalogue record for this publication is available from the British Library

ISBN 978-0-521-87382-6 Hardback
ISBN 978-0-521-69603-6 Paperback

Contents

Contributors

WAYNE A. BEACH is Professor in the School of Communication at San Diego State University, Adjunct Professor in the Department of Surgery, School of Medicine, and Member of the Moores Cancer Center, University of California San Diego, USA. His research focuses on the interactional organization of everyday conversation, as well as how family members, providers, physicians, oncologists and patients communicate about a wide variety of illness dilemmas. He is currently principal investigator of a grant funded by the National Cancer Institute (NCI) examining how cancer patients and oncologists orient to hopes, fears and uncertainties about cancer. Recently completed books are *A Natural History of Family Cancer* (2006) and the first *Handbook of Patient–Provider Interactions* (2006).

CARLY W. BUTLER is a Lecturer in Social Psychology in the Department of Social Sciences at Loughborough University, UK. Her research interests include ethnomethodology, conversation analysis, children's interaction and play, and helpline interactions. She is author of *Talk and Social Interaction in the Playground* (2008) in the Directions in Ethnomethodology and Conversation Analysis series.

JAKOB CROMDAL is Professor in Child Studies at Linköping University, Sweden. His research focuses on talk and social interaction among children and youth in a variety of mundane and institutional settings, including classrooms, detention homes and calls to the emergency services.

LISA M. FISHER is a doctoral candidate in the Department of Sociology at the University of Cincinnati, USA. She is primarily interested in social psychology in small-group and organizational settings, as well as work–family issues. Her research examines structural and cultural contexts and the ways in which they influence identity, communication and behaviour. She is currently studying flexible work arrangements.

ANGELA CORA GARCIA is an Associate Professor of Sociology at Bentley University, USA. Her conversation analytic research includes studies of mediation hearings, emergency phone calls to the police, computer-mediated communication, and gender in talk. In addition she is currently engaged in ethnographic research on voluntary organizations and leisure activities.

PHILLIP GLENN is Professor of Communication Studies at Emerson College, Boston, USA. He is the author of *Laughter in Interaction*, which received the Outstanding Scholarly Publication Award from the Language and Social Interaction Division of the National Communication Association. He was co-editor of *Studies in Language and Social Interaction* (2003) and serves on the editorial board of *Research on Language and Social Interaction*. Besides continuing studies of laughter, his research interests include interaction in mediation/negotiation settings and in employment interviews. He has held Fulbright appointments in the Czech Republic and Republic of Moldova, and he was a Visiting Scholar at the Program on Negotiation at Harvard Law School.

MARJORIE HARNESS GOODWIN is Professor of Anthropology at the University of California, Los Angeles, USA. Her work focuses on how people build their cognitive and social worlds through the use of language in interaction in a range of natural settings. An extended ethnographic study of an African American peer group formed the basis of her book *He-Said-She-Said: Talk as Social Organization Among Black Children* (1990). She has also investigated interaction in the workplace (as part of the Xerox PARC Workplace Project), daily life in families (as a core faculty member of the UCLA Center for Everyday Lives of Families) and interaction in the home of a man with severe aphasia, and is continuing to look in detail at the lives of preadolescent girls. Her most recent book is *The Hidden Life of Girls: Games of Stance, Status, and Exclusion* (2006).

ALEXA HEPBURN is a Reader in Conversation Analysis in the Department of Social Sciences at Loughborough University, UK. She has studied school bullying, issues of gender, violence against children and interaction on child protection helplines, as well as writing about the relations of the philosophy of Derrida to the theory and practice of social psychology. Currently she is applying conversation analysis to core topics in interaction. She has written two recent books, *An Introduction to Critical Social Psychology* (2003) and *Discursive Research in Practice* (2007), as well as co-edited a special issue of *Discourse and Society* on developments in discursive psychology.

CLARE JACKSON is a Teaching Fellow in the Department of Sociology at the University of York, UK. She is using conversation analysis to explore gender and person references in mundane talk-in-interaction for her doctoral research.

CELIA KITZINGER is Professor of Conversation Analysis, Gender and Sexuality and Director of the Feminist Conversation Analysis Unit at the University of York, UK. She researches basic structures of talk-in-interaction as well as exploring the reproduction of culture – including power and oppression – in mundane interaction.

NOA LOGAN KLEIN is a lecturer in the Department of Sociology at the University of California, Santa Barbara, USA. Hir current teaching and research focuses on genders, sexualities and the socialization of bodies. Ze is working on a book entitled *Loving Touch: Therapeutic Massage, the Socialization of the Body and the Healing of US Culture.*

VICTORIA LAND was a Research Associate in the Digital World Research Centre, University of Surrey, UK, studying patterns of interaction across written, spoken and electronic media for a cross-media communications project in partnership with British Telecommunications plc, prior to beginning her maternity break. She is also a member of the Feminist Conversation Analysis Unit at the University of York, UK. Victoria's research interests include conversation analysis, gender and sexuality research, feminism, mediated communications, and sociological understandings of the everyday world.

JONATHAN POTTER is Professor of Discourse Analysis at Loughborough University, UK. He has studied racism, argumentation, fact construction, and topics in social science theory and method. His most recent books include *Representing Reality*, which attempted to provide a systematic overview, integration and critique of constructionist research in social psychology, postmodernism, rhetoric and ethnomethodology, and *Conversation and Cognition* (2005, with Hedwig te Molder), in which a range of different researchers consider the implication of studies of interaction for understanding cognition. He is one of the founders of discursive psychology.

JACK SIDNELL is an Associate Professor of Anthropology at the University of Toronto, Canada. His current research focuses on the structures of social interaction with special emphases on the organization of turn-taking and repair. He has conducted long-term ethnographic fieldwork in two Caribbean communities (Guyana and Bequia) and is currently studying repair and understanding in the talk of children between the ages of 4 and 8. His other publications include *Talk and Practical Epistemology: The Social Life of Knowledge in a Small Caribbean Community* (2005) and an edited collection, *Conversation Analysis: Comparative Perspectives* (Cambridge University Press, 2009).

SUSAN A. SPEER is a Senior Lecturer in Psychology at the University of Manchester, UK. Her research uses conversation analysis to study psychiatrist–patient interaction, and how gender is produced and oriented to in talk and embodied action. She recently completed an ESRC-funded project investigating interaction in a gender identity clinic, and is the author of *Gender Talk: Feminism, Discourse and Conversation Analysis* (2005).

ELIZABETH STOKOE is Professor of Social Interaction in the Department of Social Sciences at Loughborough University, UK. Her research interests are in conversation analysis and social interaction in various ordinary and institutional settings, including neighbour mediation, police interrogation, speed-dating and talk between friends. She is the author of *Discourse and Identity* (with Bethan Benwell, 2006).

ANN WEATHERALL is a Reader in the School of Psychology at Victoria University of Wellington, New Zealand. Her interests include conversation analysis, discursive psychology, feminist psychology, gender and language, and language and social psychology. She is the author of *Gender, Language and Discourse* (2002) and an editor of *Language, Discourse and Social Psychology* (2007, with Bernadette Watson and Cindy Gallois).

SUE WILKINSON is Professor of Feminist and Health Studies in the Department of Social Sciences at Loughborough University, UK. She is the founding editor of the international journal *Feminism and Psychology*, and her publications encompass six books – including *Feminist Social Psychologies* (1996), *Feminism and Discourse* (1995) and *Heterosexuality* (1993) – and more than eighty articles in the areas of gender/sexuality, feminism, health and qualitative methods. She has a longstanding academic interest in the social construction of inequality and is also a campaigner for equal marriage rights for same-sex couples. She (re)trained in conversation analysis (CA) at the University of Los Angeles, California, USA, in 2001–2, and her recent work uses CA to study helpline interaction. She is also particularly interested in technical specifications of repair.

Data and transcription

The system of transcription used throughout the book is that developed by Gail Jefferson (2004a) for conversation analysis (see also Schegloff, 2007a).

Aspects of the relative placement/timing of utterances

=	Equals sign	Immediate latching of successive talk
(0.8)	Time in parentheses	The length of a pause or gap, in tenths of a second
(.)	Period in parentheses	A pause or gap that is discernible but less than a tenth of a second
[overlap]	Square brackets	Mark the onset and end of overlapping talk
//	Double obliques	In older transcripts mark the onset of overlapping talk

Aspects of speech delivery

.	Period	Closing, usually falling intonation
,	Comma	Continuing, slightly upward intonation
?	Question mark	Rising intonation
¿	Inverted question mark	Rising intonation weaker than that indicated by a question mark
Underline	Underlining	Talk that is emphasized by the speaker
Rea::lly	Colon(s)	Elongation or stretch of the prior sound – the more colons, the longer the stretch

<u>c</u>:	Underline preceding colon	When letters preceding colons are underlined, the pitch rises on the letter and the overall contour is 'up-to-down'
<u>:</u>	Underlined colon	Rising pitch on the colon in an overall 'down-to-up' contour
!	Exclamation mark	Animated tone
-	Hyphen/dash	A sharp cut-off of the just-prior word or sound
↑	Upward arrow	Precedes a marked rise in pitch
↓	Downward arrow	Precedes a marked fall in pitch
thē	Macron above a vowel	Indicates a long vowel pronunciation (e.g. 'thee')
<	'Less than' sign	Talk that is 'jump-started'
>faster<	'Greater than' and 'less than' signs	Enclose speeded up or compressed talk
<slower>	'Less than' and 'greater than' signs	Enclose slower or elongated talk
LOUD	Upper case	Talk that is noticeably louder than that surrounding it
°quiet°	Degree signs	Enclose talk that is noticeably quieter than that surrounding it
huh/hah/heh/hih/hoh		Various types of laughter token
(h)	'h' in parentheses	Audible aspirations within speech (e.g., laughter particles)
.hhh	A dot before an h or series of h's	An in-breath (number of h's indicates length)
hhh	An h or series of h's	An out-breath / breathiness (number of h's indicates length)
#	Hash	Creaky voice
$ or £	Dollar or pound sign	Smile voice
*	Asterisk	Squeaky vocal delivery

( )	Empty single parentheses	Non-transcribable segment of talk
(talk)	Word(s) in single parentheses	Transcriber's possible hearing
(it)/(at)	A slash separating word(s) in single parentheses	Two alternative transcriber hearings
((laughs))	Word(s) in double parentheses	Transcriber comments or description of a sound

Other symbols

| → | Arrow | Placed in the margin of a transcript to point to parts of data the author wishes to draw to the attention of the reader |

1 An introduction to conversation and gender

Susan A. Speer and Elizabeth Stokoe

This book showcases cutting-edge research and current thinking by researchers writing on topics at the intersection of conversation analysis and gender. Work in this area has advanced rapidly over the past decade, and this edited collection provides the first comprehensive, book-length treatment of the field. Bringing together an international group of scholars, the chapters illustrate authors' perspectives on the operation of gender in interaction. Each chapter examines real-life audio or video interactions recorded across a range of ordinary and institutional settings, including face-to-face conversation, domestic telephone calls, children's play, mediation sessions, police–suspect interviews, psychiatric assessment and calls to telephone helplines.

The aims of this collection are both theoretical and methodological. At a theoretical level, we push forward the boundaries of our understanding of the relationship between conversation and gender, charting new territory as we present the most incisive and sophisticated thinking in the field. At a methodological level, the book offers readers a clear and practical understanding of precisely how gender is analysed using conversion analysis and related methodologies, by presenting detailed demonstrations of these methods in use. Although conversation is typically understood as referring to '*talk*-in-interaction', several contributors analyse and reflect on the inextricable relationship between talk, gender and embodied conduct. This introductory chapter is divided into four sections. First, to contextualize the book's chapters and convey their distinctive analytic position, we provide a critical overview of *conversation and gender research* grounded in studies of either sex/gender 'difference' or gender identity 'construction'. We explain the background, key questions for and criticisms of both traditional studies of linguistic features and interactional styles, and contemporary studies of the construction, enactment or performance of gender identities. Second, we contrast studies of difference and construction with *conversation analytic research on gender* and other categorial topics. We provide a brief introduction to conversation analysis itself, before discussing how researchers with an interest in gender have used its techniques. Third, we provide a concise *overview of the chapters*, which have been grouped into sections according to the key analytic questions they address. Finally, we discuss some of the *implications and issues* that emerge from the reported findings and set out some possible trajectories for the field as it moves forward over the next decade.

Conversation and gender research: From difference to construction

We start our introduction by considering two broad strands of gender and language research that have, since their inception in the 1970s and 1980s, theorized and demonstrated, with particular empirical flavours, the links between gender and language (for overviews see Speer, 2005a; Weatherall, 2002a). Methodologically diverse and interdisciplinary in orientation, research spans not just linguistics, but also sociology, psychology, anthropology and communication studies. Any attempt to categorize this large body of work inevitably disguises areas of cross-over and overlap. However, we will discuss the two types of work that represent often competing theoretical and methodological assumptions about the nature of gender and how it might best be grasped analytically: *sex differences in language* and *the construction of gender and gender identities*.

Sex differences in language

The first body of research we examine focuses on sex differences in language, in terms of both the way men and women are represented *in* language, with a focus on the encoding of sexism, and the way men and women *use* language, with a focus on the features and function of speech styles (note that the terms 'sex' and 'gender' are often used interchangeably despite their differing etymologies and theoretical baggage). Sex/gender difference research has had a significant impact on the larger trajectory of gender and language studies, not least because it took seriously the role of language in the instantiation and maintenance of sex/gender inequality. Researchers working within this tradition have addressed several key questions.

- Do women and men talk and interact differently? If women and men talk differently, what features characterize men's talk and women's talk? Since Lakoff (1973; 1975) wrote her pioneering account of difference, hundreds of studies have identified and tested a cluster of linguistic variables (e.g., tag questions, hedges, vocabulary) and interactional patterns (e.g., interruptions, topic control, verbosity, politeness) and correlated their use with the sex/gender of speaker (for overviews see Aries, 1996; Bucholtz, 2004; Cameron, 1998a; 2007; Cheshire & Trudgill, 1998; Christie, 2000; Coates, 1998a; 2004; Coates & Cameron, 1988; Conrick, 1999; Freed & Greenwood, 1996; Graddol & Swann, 1989; Litosseliti, 2006; Mills, 2003; Swann, 1992; Talbot, 1998).

- If women and men talk differently, how do we best account for such differences? Do linguistic disparities reflect women's deficiency as speakers and their subordinate status in society (the 'deficit' model, cf. Lakoff, 1975), a patriarchal reality (the 'dominance' model, e.g., Fishman, 1978; Spender, 1980; Thorne & Henley, 1975; Thorne et al., 1983; Zimmerman & West, 1975), subcultural, socialized differences between men and women (the 'difference' model, e.g., Holmes, 1995; Maltz & Borker, 1982; Tannen, 1990; 1994), or different interactional goals such as competition, conflict or affiliation (e.g., Coates, 1996; 2003; M. H. Goodwin, 1990; 2006)?
- How do other cultural categories, such as age, class, religion, ethnicity or sexuality, mediate sex/gender as a key variable in speech styles? For example, in the field of queer linguistics, what are the features of 'gay men's English' (e.g., Leap, 1996) or lesbian women's speech (e.g., Moonwomon-Baird, 1997; see Koch, 2008)?
- Does language encode and perpetuate a patriarchal, sexist reality? If language is sexist, how is sexism realized directly and indirectly (e.g., Spender, 1980; Mills, 2008)? How is sexist language used 'ironically' to subvert prejudice (e.g., Benwell, 2004; Christie, 2000) and how may it be challenged through policy and the practice of language reform (see Litosseliti, 2006; see also Cameron, 1992; Gibbon, 1999; Goddard & Patterson, 2000; Henley & Kramarae, 1991; Pauwels, 1998)? What are people's attitudes to sexist language (e.g., Parks & Roberton, 2008)?

When taking the development of sex/gender difference literature as a whole, consistent claims about difference have proved elusive. Despite this, and despite its often being presented as an outmoded line of investigation, many researchers still ask questions about sex/gender difference in language (e.g., Drescher, 2006; Menz & Al-Roubaie, 2008; Precht, 2008; Schleef, 2008). This is unsurprising when one considers the sheer unquestioned dominance of sex/gender difference research throughout both academia and popular culture, including hundreds of studies examining the neurological basis of sex/gender differences in language (e.g., Burman et al., 2008; G. S. Harrington & Farias, 2008). Sex/gender difference studies – of language and all other aspects of human biology, action, cognition and emotion – continue relentlessly despite sustained criticism about methodological flaws, the reification of binaries, essentialism and so on (e.g., Bohan, 1993; Lorber, 1994; 2000). In research about difference, researchers treat sex/gender, usually implicitly, as pre-discursive, pre-theorized, natural categories which are biologically determined or socialized from birth and trait-like. This essentialist notion means that human action varies according to the independent variable of sex/gender (e.g., Uchida, 1992).

Difference studies were therefore criticized for committing what Cameron (1997a) calls the *correlational fallacy*, whereby particular linguistic features

are attributed unproblematically to one sex/gender or the other. The tempta-
tion to 'see' gender where it might not be relevant is discussed by Jefferson
(2004b: 117):

Working with interactional data, one sometimes observes that a type of behavior seems
to be produced a great deal by one category of persons and not all that much by another
category. But when put to the test of a straightforward count, the observation does
not hold up: Category X does not after all do this thing significantly more often than
Category Y does. It may then be that the apparent skewing of the behavior's distribution
across categories is the result of selective observation; noticing with greater frequency
those cases which conformed to some biased notion held by the observer of how these
categories behave.

For many feminists and other critically oriented researchers, 'difference' studies
are both theoretically and methodologically circular, and politically unproductive.
It is perhaps inevitable that such studies, which prioritize the analyst's taken-for-
granted assumptions about sex/gender difference, will prevent them from seeing
sex/gender as anything other than a reified, dualistic category. Indeed, they start
out '"knowing" the identities whose very constitution ought to be precisely the
issue under investigation' (Kulick, 1999). This means that analysts are in the business of *reproducing* rather than *studying* gendered 'facts' (see Hammersley, 2001;
Jefferson, 2004b). As Lorber (2000: 79) points out, 'it is the ubiquitous division
of people into two unequally valued categories that undergirds the continually
reappearing instances of gender inequality'. Järviluoma *et al.* (2003: 2) similarly
conclude that 'gender should be understood as a concept requiring analysis, rather
than as something that is *already* known about' (emphasis in original).

Throughout the 1990s, researchers began to challenge the focus on difference
in the language and gender literature (e.g., Bergvall *et al.*, 1996; Cameron,
1996; Crawford, 1995; Hall & Bucholtz, 1995; Mills, 1996). Freed (1996: 69)
reflected that 'as researchers, we now realize, perhaps with some reluctance,
that we need to abandon a number of our early and fairly simplistic feminist
ruminations about the role of gender in language'. These sorts of criticisms
appeared hand in hand with a new breed of studies that followed the 'performative' or 'constructionist' turn or the 'turn to discourse' that was pervading
academia and paving the way for new methodologies and research questions
(see Benwell & Stokoe, 2006). Within language and gender research, Crawford
(1995: 18) proposed that adopting a constructionist framework would prompt
analysts to ask different questions about the links between language and gender,
such as 'how people come to have beliefs about sex differences in speech style'
and 'how those beliefs are encoded and enacted in one's self-presentation'. In
stark contrast to 'difference' studies, then, researchers began to ask questions
about how sex/gender and sex/gender identities are 'constructed' in language,
and how 'gender is an effect of language use, rather than a determinant of
different uses of language' (Litosseliti, 2006: 44).

Constructing gender

During the 1990s, the language of 'difference' began to be replaced with the language of 'construction' and 'performance'; indeed, as Holmes (2007: 52) puts it, 'the field of language and gender was engulfed in a wave of social constructionism' (see also Cameron, 2009). This second strand entailed a radical paradigmatic shift in thinking about the ontological status of sex/gender (and sex/gender difference). Like other identity categories, sex/gender was understood as 'the emergent product rather than the pre-existing source of linguistic and other semiotic practices' (Bucholtz & Hall, 2005: 588).

Much of this second strand of work has its 'social constructionist' roots in postmodernism, poststructuralism and literary theory, drawing heavily on the language of discourse and performativity in, for example, Foucault (1972), J. Butler (1990a) and Bauman (2004). It is also somewhat rooted in ethnomethodology, in Garfinkel's (1967) groundbreaking work on the social production of gender. Through a case study of Agnes, a 19-year-old male-to-female transsexual, Garfinkel analysed the practices involved in 'passing' and the 'managed achievement of sex status' (1967: 116). Thus Garfinkel's task was to 'understand how membership in a sex category is sustained across a variety of practical circumstances and contingencies, at the same time preserving the sense that such membership is a natural, normal moral fact of life' (Zimmerman, 1992a: 195). These ideas were developed by Kessler and McKenna (1978) and West and Zimmerman (1987), who coined the phrase 'doing gender' to refer to the idea that gender is a social accomplishment (see Jurik & Siemsen, 2009; West & Zimmerman, 2009). From this perspective, sex, like gender, is not a biological or socialized essence or trait that exists prior to and outside of discourse. The male–female dualism is not 'natural'. Instead, both sex and gender are things that one *does* rather than things that one *has*; they are activities rather than attributes, socially constructed belief systems rather than natural, inevitable and timeless facts.

There are now numerous studies that examine the 'multiple', 'contradictory', 'fluid', 'fragmentary' and 'dynamic' 'construction', 'performance', 'production' or 'enactment' of gender 'identities' or 'subject positions'; femininities and masculinities; or the 'doing' of gender (for an overview, see Benwell & Stokoe, 2006). In constructionist-informed analyses, the focus of inquiry shifts away from correlating linguistic variables with demographic variables, and away from claims that 'men talk like this' and 'women talk like that', towards a 'focus on the process of gendering, the on-going accomplishment of gender, as well as the dynamism and fluidity of the process' (Holmes, 2007: 55). Thus, instead of concentrating 'on the results of seeing someone as female or male' (Kessler & McKenna, 1978: 163), analyses progress by treating the 'natural' coherence of gender as a performance, or an accomplishment which is locally produced and 'shaped moment by moment through the details of discourse' (Bucholtz, 1999: viii). Central to constructionist work is the view that gender and sexism are 'best analysed at the level of discourse' (Cameron, 1998a: 87). This focus on discourse and the discursive has, in turn, led to a gradual shift away from research which analyses sexist word forms and decontextualized sentences, or which searches for the linguistic or cultural correlates of gender difference, towards a more detailed qualitative analysis of extended sequences of language use, and its role in producing and naturalizing specific understandings of gender and gender difference (see K. Harrington *et al.*, 2008; Pichler & Eppler, 2009; Sunderland, 2006; Weatherall, 2002a). Key questions asked by researchers in this tradition include:

- How do people construct and use gender identities in talk? How do men perform masculinity and how do women perform femininity? How are multiple and contradictory gender identities taken up across stretches of talk (e.g., Benor *et al.*, 2002; Bucholtz *et al.*, 1999; Buzzanell *et al.*, 2004; Coates, 1997; 1999; Johnson & Meinhof, 1997; Kendall, 2008; Korobov & Bamberg, 2004; Pichler, 2009; Wetherell & Edley, 1999)?
- What is the relationship between gender, discourse and sexuality? How do people construct their own and others' gendered or sexual identities? How is desire produced and regulated as a discursive, social accomplishment (e.g., P. Baker, 2008; Bucholtz & Hall, 2004; Cameron, 2005a; Cameron & Kulick, 2003a; 2003b; Livia & Hall, 1997)?
- How do people position themselves and each other as male and female at the 'micro' level within dominant gendered macro-level 'discourses'? How do discourse and ideology make available and limit the subject positions that may be occupied by men and women, and how are such positions challenged, resisted or subverted (e.g., Baxter, 2003; Hollway & Jefferson, 2000; Koller, 2004; Lazar, 2005; 2007; Mullany, 2007; Remlinger, 1999; Sunderland, 2004; Walsh, 2001; Wodak,1997)?
- How are gendered 'communities of practice', or speech communities, constructed within the contexts of their social engagement? How do people participate in multiple communities of practice and how are gendered institutional contexts shaped and negotiated (e.g., Eckert & McConnell-Ginet, 1998; 2003; Holmes & Meyerhoff, 1999; Tannen, 1993; Walsh, 2001)?

On the surface, at least, the theoretical and methodological assumptions that underpin this list of questions overcame problems associated with the essentialist, sex-difference research outlined earlier, by emphasizing the ongoing and often contradictory production of the meaning of gender. Within this framework people can intervene in and subvert solidified gender discourses, creating new configurations and meanings, and, in so doing, generate ideological shift.

Despite the radical potential of constructionist approaches, however, they suffer a number of problems in their empirical translation. The first problem is for work particularly influenced by poststructuralist and Foucauldian models of discourse. From this perspective, speakers and their talk are conceived as shaped, constrained, 'positioned' or otherwise determined by abstract discourses, ideologies or forces of power 'from above' or 'beyond' the talk (e.g., Hollway & Jefferson, 2000; Sclater, 2003; Wetherell, 1998). This 'top-down', 'macro'-level understanding of discourse has a tendency to reify abstract societal discourses, ideologies and norms concerning appropriate masculine and feminine behaviour, investing them with agency to shape and constrain what (gendered) speakers say at the discursive, micro level of 'local' interactions (e.g., Sunderland, 2004; Wetherell, 2007; Wodak, 2001). The problem of reification is also relevant to the practical analytic moves made by the very process of ascribing discourse labels to stretches of text or interaction. For Wooffitt (2005), talk and texts are too complex to reduce to discourses. This kind of analysis, therefore, offers 'an impoverished view of human conduct' (p. 179). Attributing gross discourse labels to chunks of talk is problematic because there is rarely an evidential basis for that attribution.

A second problem for constructionist approaches focuses on another type of empirical translation. Despite the fact that the *theory* of gender is different, studies about the 'construction of gender identity' often end up making essentialist-sounding claims, particularly those that collect the talk of women or men, in interviews or natural settings, and then look at how *women* perform *femininities* and *men* perform *masculinities*. There is rarely a notion in such work of people *not* performing gender. If the data do not 'look like' recognizable femininity or masculinity, the 'finding' is that gender identity is not what we thought it was, or that it is variable, inconsistent, multiple or fragmentary (Edwards & Stokoe, 2004: 4; see also Cameron, 2009; Lorber, 2000; Swann, 2009). Thus the performance of gender is explained or accounted for in a somewhat circular fashion, leaving what Velody and Williams (1998) call a 'realist residue'. This type of 'constructionist' research, therefore, buys back into the sex-difference framework that it was originally designed to replace, and inadvertently reintroduces essentialism and determinist understandings of gender identity construction 'by the back door' (see Stokoe, 2005; 2008a). As Sidnell (2003: 347) notes:

There is an underlying tension here in so far as many researchers advance anti-essentialist, theoretical conceptions of gender (suggesting that gender emerges through the practices of talk) but at the same time employ the very same categories in their analysis. The theoretical notion of 'performativity' offered as an anti-essentialist antidote, is problematic in so far as it presupposes some 'real' set of actors who inhabit the roles of the dramatis personae.

Finally, there are problems with the way 'social constructionism' is (mis)understood in some language and gender research. Such misunderstandings are revealed in criticisms that, while constructionism is generally regarded as a 'good thing', it is also regarded as 'dangerous' for ignoring 'facts [*sic*] about gender and language which have been repeatedly pointed out in the language and gender literature over the decades, and which, as socially responsible academics, we cannot and do not want to ignore' (Holmes & Meyerhoff, 2003: 9). In everyday life, Holmes and Meyerhoff (2003) argue, people treat gender as 'real', as a social category that matters, as a distinction that is 'crucial' and 'vital', and as a stable, essential distinction to which any threat is extremely disturbing (pp. 9–10). However, such appeals to the 'actual' world of facts and reality contradict basic constructionist premises. Here, social constructionism (vs. essentialism) is conflated with social/ cultural (vs. biological) understandings of gender: it is treated as a construction *rather than* as biological, or as *only* a construction rather than real. The idea that 'construction' means that gender identities are 'only' constructions rather than real is itself a reiteration of essentialism (Edwards, 1997).

The issue for many constructionists is not whether gender is actually 'real' or 'true'; rather, it is the business of analysis to 'analyze the workings of those categories, not to merely use them as they are used in the world' (Jefferson, 2004b: 118). Social constructionist analysis is about the investigation of knowledge production: how people maintain a sense of a commonly shared, objectively existing world (see Lynch, 1993; Potter, 1996). In everyday life, people generally treat 'gender' as a real thing that they can know about themselves and other people, and are not generally sent into a 'metaphysical spin' about 'real' or 'constructed' statuses (Francis, 1994). And if people do question their or someone else's membership of a gender category – that is, make it accountable – then this is something we can study (see Speer, 2005b; this volume). This version of constructionism is also consonant with the ethnomethodological perspective that underpins the concept of 'doing gender', which explores the way people constitute themselves as recognizably, taken-for-grantedly gendered, or hold each other accountable for membership in a category (e.g., West & Zimmerman, 1987).

Having set out the two main traditions in gender and language research, we now move on to the substantive background for the current edited collection. Our brief discussion of ethnomethodology in the previous paragraph partly sets up the 'theoretical' basis of conversation analysis, and its relevance for understanding gender. In the next section, we start by explaining the discipline of conversation analysis, before moving on to describe the way it has enriched gender and language research by opening new doors for the field.

Conversation analytic research on gender

We start with a brief explanation of conversation analysis before outlining its procedures for studying 'gender' as an analytic topic. We will then examine the bodies of work that have used conversation analysis to make claims about gender, and reflect critically on some of the key questions each strand of work has addressed.

What is conversation analysis?

Conversation analysis (CA) emerged in the 1960s and 1970s in the work of the American sociologist Sacks and his colleagues Schegloff and Jefferson. Sacks's aim was to develop an alternative to mainstream sociology: an observational science of society and social action that could be grounded in the 'details of actual events' (Sacks, 1984a: 26). It has developed into an influential programme of work with many findings about how conversation works. CA's roots are in ethnomethodology (EM), a programme developed by another sociologist, Garfinkel (1967), which was, in turn influenced by the phenomenological philosophy of Schütz (e.g., 1962) and Goffman's (e.g., 1959) work on the interaction order. Garfinkel's basic idea was that people in society, or *members*, continuously engage in making sense of the world and, in so doing, methodically display their understandings of it: making their activities 'visibly-rational-and-reportable-for-all-practical-purposes' (Garfinkel, 1967: vii). Language was central to the EM project of explicating members' methods for producing orderly and accountable social activities. For Schegloff (1996a: 4), talk is 'the primordial scene of social life … through which the work of the constitutive institutions of societies gets done'. It is through talking that we live our lives, build and maintain relationships, and establish '*who we are to one another*' (Drew, 2005: 74; emphasis added).

CA involves the study of transcripts of recordings of ordinary and institutional talk of various kinds, focusing on the turn-by-turn organization of talk and embodied conduct in interaction. CA is primarily concerned to describe the methods and procedures speakers use to coordinate their talk to produce orderly and meaningful conversational actions. These procedures are not idiosyncratic, but display relatively stable patterns and organized regularities that are oriented to by participants. Examples of patterns and topics studied include how people take turns in conversation, what it means to overlap with another speaker or produce a delayed response, how conversations are opened and closed, how people make reference to themselves and each other, how actions (e.g., complaining, questioning, assessing, inviting, etc.) are accomplished, how turns at talk are designed and formulated, how people solve problems in hearing, speaking and understanding, and a range of other conversational phenomena (Sacks, 1992; Schegloff, 2007a; for introductions see Ten Have, 2007; Hutchby & Wooffitt, 2008). The goal of CA is to establish the structural frameworks that underpin and organize such regularities in interaction: 'the structures of social action' (Atkinson & Heritage, 1984).

Conversation analysis and the relevance of gender

With regard to gender (or any categorial or identity topic) conversation analysts invert what previous language and gender researchers have done when they either rush to explain differences in language use, or examine, in a circular way, the construction of gender identities, in some stretch of data. LeBaron (1998; quoted in Tracy, 1998: 15) summarizes the basic CA position:

we should not ... say 'oh, look, here's a man and a woman talking; ... oh, we can make these conclusions about gendered communication'. But rather we should say, 'gender only becomes an issue when the participants themselves make it one and we can point to different things about that'.

For CA, any analysis of social categories is based on what participants do and say, rather than on what analysts take to be relevant as a function of their hypotheses, research questions, politics or theory. From this perspective, then, in order to warrant an analytic claim that a particular category is relevant to any stretch of interaction, the analyst must be able to demonstrate that such identities are linked to specific actions. There are two key issues here for conversation analysts:

1   *The problem of relevance*: Given the indefinitely extendable number of ways any person may be categorized, how should we decide which from a range of potential identities is relevant? The answer is to go by what is demonstrably relevant to participants 'at the moment that whatever we are trying to produce an account for occurs' (Schegloff, 1991: 50).
2   *The issue of procedural consequentiality*: If we can establish that a particular identity category is relevant, can we see that it is consequential for participants, in terms of its trajectory, content, character or organizational procedures? Does it have 'determinate consequences for the talk' (Heritage, 2005: 111)?

In his classic paper, Schegloff (1997) provides an empirical demonstration of these two issues, challenging what he sees as the classic mistake often made by discourse analysts: using gender as an *a priori* lens through which to analyse data. The materials that Schegloff bases his arguments on include a conversation in which one male speaker appears to interrupt a female speaker on several occasions. Studies of interruption have a long history within language and gender studies. In fact, the 'dominance' studies of sex difference mentioned earlier used a broadly CA approach to identify the micro-interactional techniques by which men dominate and control talk (e.g., Ainsworth-Vaughn, 1992; Conefrey, 1997; Davis, 1986; 1988; DeFrancisco, 1991; Edelsky, 1981; Fishman, 1978; 1983; S. Shaw, 2000; West, 1984; 1995; West & Garcia, 1988; Zimmerman & West, 1975; for criticisms see D. James & Clarke, 1993; D. James & Drakich,

1993; McMullan *et al.*, 1995). Schegloff (1987a: 214) criticized these early CA studies of gender and interruption for the way they aimed 'to link an asymmetrical outcome in the talk to differential attributes of the participants of a macrorelevant type'.

In his analysis of one male speaker's supposed interruption of a female speaker, Schegloff shows that the 'beating down' of the female speaker can be explained in terms of the way turns at talk are accomplished, rather than in terms of male dominance and power over women. As Schegloff notes elsewhere, 'the rules of conversation operate in ways that are, in principle at least, independent of the extradiscursive identities of the participants ... the turn-taking rules themselves operate in terms of locally constructed discourse statuses rather than, for example, position in a social hierarchy' (1992a: 480). More recently, Kitzinger (2008b) has shown how, in work that purportedly shows how much more men interrupt other speakers than women, the identification of turns as 'interruptions' is often erroneous and does not take into account 'what is being said and why, the projectability of the utterance under way, and the nature of the interaction between the people concerned' (p. 123).

Thus, to the extent that identity is relevant to the analysis of the extract at all, it is in terms of the participants' 'activity-relevant identities' (Schegloff 1997: 180). In Schegloff's data, it is activity, rather than power or gender, which accounts for what the participants are doing. Nevertheless, Schegloff suggests that this 'technical' analysis does not necessarily 'undercut' critical discourse analysis. It is not that interruptions can never be explained in terms of power, dominance or gender. Rather, within Schegloff's framework, there must be explicit grounds for characterizing the parties as 'male' and 'female'. Without this linkage, claims about the relationship between gender and interruption, along with the results of any research which proceeds in this way, are, for Schegloff, 'profoundly equivocal' (2001a: 309; see also Kitzinger, 2008b) and a matter of 'theoretical imperialism' (1997). This is because speakers are not just men and women but members of an indefinitely extendible number of categories. Just because all of these descriptions of identity are *potentially* available, it does not mean that they are actually *consequential* for any piece of interaction: there is no automatic causal relationship between language and demographic variables. Rather, in order to claim a link there needs to be some 'analytic criteria on the basis of which a speaker can legitimately be heard to be speaking as a member of one category rather than another' (Land & Kitzinger, this volume).

Conversation analysts, then, must be able to show that and how 'participants' production of the world was itself informed by ... particular categorization devices ... that the parties were oriented to that categorization device in producing and understanding – moment-by-moment – the conduct that composed its progressive realization' (Schegloff, 2007b: 475; see also Schegloff,

2009). If the participants do orient to gender, then that gives us grounds, as analysts, for making the claim that gender is 'procedurally consequential' for (that is, has a direct influence on) what is going on in the interaction. Conversely, if the participants do not orient to gender, then we do not have grounds for claiming that gender is relevant or consequential for the participants in the interaction at that moment. Once a formal analysis has been conducted, we can begin to know what kind of political issues our data will allow us to address (Schegloff, 1997). In doing so, we may find that the social and political is already 'a constitutive element of the object in the first instance' (1997: 170) and that we do not, therefore, need to import or 'add in' a sociopolitical analysis at all.

Schegloff's (1997) paper provided a clear set of criteria for judging whether a piece of discourse is gendered. It generated enormous interest amongst feminists and other critically oriented researchers, who began to work through the implications of Schegloff's arguments for their own research and interrogate their own analytic practices. It has generated considerable (and heated!) debate in the field in recent years. Some argued that although Schegloff's 'exclusive' focus on participants' orientations may be 'extremely revealing' such an approach is restrictive and impractical (Wetherell, 1998; 2007), and cannot account for the invisible workings of power, the unsaid or what is not oriented to (Frith, 1998), the pervasive 'omnirelevance' of gender (Weatherall, 2000), or the fact that very few features of (English) language explicitly index gender (Ochs, 1992). Indeed, some feminists suggest that Schegloff's approach 'limits admissible context so severely that only the most blatant aspects of gendered discursive practice, such as the overt topicalizing of gender in conversation, are likely candidates for Scheggloffian analysis' (Bucholtz, 2003: 52; see also Enfield, 2007, on going beyond the 'Members'-Only Filter'). Many language and gender researchers reject CA on this basis, preferring to recruit 'wider' contexts, politics and ideology to make claims about what is happening in a piece of data.

Others argued that the 'symmetrical', seemingly 'neutral' form of analysis is apolitical, 'invites missed opportunities' and 'risks a form of ideological complicity' (Edley, 2001: 137). Billig (1999: 554–6), for example, claims that CA's 'participatory rhetoric' encourages the analyst to treat participants' contributions equally, thus ignoring the power differential between, say, 'rapist' and 'victim'. Finally, some researchers suggest that, contrary to Schegloff's injunction that the analyst must bracket their politics, CA is already ideologically loaded and relies on the analyst's unacknowledged cultural and commonsense understandings (Billig, 1999; Edley, 2001; Stokoe & Smithson, 2001; 2002). It is 'imbued with politics' (McIlvenny, 2002a: 18) and, despite its claims to neutrality, is an example of male dominance and sexism within the academy (Lakoff, 2003; and see Stokoe, 2005, for a critique).

It is clear that the use of CA for the study of gender and language is controversial. Its impact and location in the wider field of gender and language are also somewhat contentious, being embraced only recently as a valid strand of contemporary theorizing. We move on now to consider some of the key, gender-relevant questions that analysts have addressed.

Conversation analysis, gender and feminism

In contrast to the early CA studies of gender and dominance mentioned above, since the late 1990s a second type of conversation analytic studies of gender has emerged. These studies employed the technical machinery of CA to analyse gender, whilst embracing the 'problem of relevance' and the need to demonstrate 'procedural consequentiality' discussed earlier. Practically, this meant showing *that and how* speakers 'orient' to, or make relevant, gender as they accomplish a course of action. Furthermore, instead of presupposing that such a focus on 'participants' orientations to gender' would necessarily be limited, or apolitical, or that it would require external explanations of why participants say what they do, researchers set about exploring just how far an approach which begins with an analysis of members' perspectives can take us in advancing our understanding of 'what counts' as gender in interaction (see papers in McIlvenny, 2002b; Stokoe & Weatherall, 2002a; 2002b).

Key antecedents of contemporary gender and CA work included not just Schegloff's (1997) position piece but Sacks's (1992) original observations about the study of categories more generally. The position articulated in Schegloff's article resonates with Sacks's argument that any study of members' categories should be made 'in the activities in which they're employed' (1992: 27). For Sacks, any study of categorial topics must consider how categories – in our case, gender – 'might be relevant for the doing of some activity'. Several key empirical and theoretical studies published in the late 1990s paved the way for the work showcased in this book. These included Hopper and LeBaron's (1998) demonstration of the stepwise process through which 'gender creeps into talk'; that is, how gender gets 'noticed' and becomes focal, rather than peripheral, in talk. In a related study, Stringer and Hopper (1998: 213) analysed 'repair sequences' initiated by speakers' use of the generic 'he' when referring to 'sex-unspecified incumbents of traditionally male social categories'. In Edwards's (1998: 15) study of 'identity categories in use', he showed how gender is picked out as 'the relevant thing' about participants in marriage guidance counselling interaction, again often within a repair operation (see Stokoe, this volume). Finally, in our own work we promoted the importance for language and gender researchers of examining gender as a participants' category (Stokoe, 1997; 1998) and the possibility of a *'feminist conversation analysis'* (Speer, 1999).

Current work is often referred to, then, as comprising an 'emerging field' (Wowk, 2007: 132) of 'feminist conversation analysis' (see articles in Kitzinger, 2007c; and also Kitzinger, 2000a; 2002; 2006; 2008a; Speer, 1999; 2002a; 2005a; Stokoe, 1998; 2000; 2008a; Wilkinson & Kitzinger, 2003; 2007), although not all authors would position themselves underneath this banner. Key questions asked by researchers representing this second strand of work on gender and CA include:

- How do people interact so as to make a world of two sexes appear natural and inevitable, and what practices are involved in 'passing' as male or female in interaction? How do members produce 'gender attributions' – that is, claims that someone is male or female – and what are the procedures through which they manage trouble in making a gender attribution (e.g., Fenstermaker & West, 2002; Garfinkel, 1967; Kessler & McKenna, 1978; Speer, 2005b; in press; Speer & Green, 2007)?
- How is gender 'done', or accomplished and rendered accountable in situated interaction, and how do speakers manage their conduct 'in relation to normative conceptions of appropriate attitudes and activities for particular sex categories' (West & Fenstermaker, 1993: 156; see also Nilan, 1995; West & Fenstermaker, 2002a; 2002b; West & Zimmerman, 1987; Wickes & Emmison, 2007; Wowk, 1984)?
- What counts as 'gender', or an 'orientation to gender' in an interaction? How can claims that gender is relevant to talk-in-interaction be analytically warranted? In what interactional environments do 'gender noticings' occur (e.g., Hopper, 2003; Hopper & LeBaron, 1998; Schegloff, 1997, Speer, 2001; Stokoe & Smithson, 2001)?
- What sorts of actions are accomplished as speakers invoke, reformulate and repair gendered membership categories and person references (e.g., 'girl', 'woman', 'mother', 'slut', 'lady', 'whore', 'bitch', etc.)? Does the use of gender categories provide one way 'into' studying how speakers orient to gender, produce it as a solid feature of the world, and invoke it as part of conversational action? How do speakers move between practices of description and categorization in courses of action, displaying a shared understanding of gender categories in their accomplishment (e.g., Evaldsson, 2004; 2007; Kitzinger & Rickford, 2007; Speer, 2005b; 2009; Stockill & Kitzinger, 2007; Stokoe, 2003; 2004; 2006; 2008a; 2009)?
- How do speakers refer to themselves and others in interaction? How do different forms of person reference implement different types of social action? If parties to an interaction index terms that are gendered linguistically (e.g., 'woman', 'girl' or 'gentleman') does this automatically mean that gender is relevant to the interaction? Conversely, if gender is not indexed, does this mean gender is not relevant to the interaction? Can words which are

linguistically gender-neutral (e.g., 'we' or 'people') none the less be oriented to as gendered by their speakers? What might 'implicit' orientations to gender look like (e.g., Kitzinger, 2005a; 2007b; Kitzinger & Rickford, 2007; Land & Kitzinger, 2005; 2007; Stockill & Kitzinger, 2007)?

- How do 'macro' issues of power, resistance, harassment, prejudice and social change get played out through recurrent patterns in interaction, in ways that reproduce or transcend gender norms? Are these issues analytically tractable? Can we find participants orienting to their own talk, or that of others, as potentially sexist or heterosexist? If, when people produce what analysts see as prejudiced statements, speakers themselves display no such awareness, can analysts make claims – on any grounds – that sexism, heterosexism or some other form of prejudice has occurred (e.g., Beach, 2000; Berard, 2005; Eglin, 2002; Eglin & Hester, 1999; Kitzinger, 2000a; 2005b; Kitzinger & Peel, 2005; Land & Kitzinger, 2005; Speer, 2002b; Speer & Potter, 2000; 2002; Stokoe & Smithson, 2001; 2002; Tainio, 2003; Widdicombe, 1998)?
- How is talk organized to accomplish conflict and cooperation, affiliation or gatekeeping, power and exclusion, in ways that are relevant to gender (e.g., M. H. Goodwin, 1990; 2006; Speer, 2010; Speer & Parsons, 2006, 2007)?
- How does talk-in-interaction combine with other semiotic conduct and features of the material environment and embodied conduct to construct and orient to gender (e.g., Evaldsson, 2003; M. H. Goodwin, 1990; 2006; M. H. Goodwin *et al.*, 2002; Speer & Green, 2007; Stokoe, 2006; 2008a; Toerien & Kitzinger, 2007)?

Although the *questions* above may seem to 'start' with gender as an analysts' category or interest, the *analyses* that address them deal only with participants' productions of such categories and the actions they accomplish in those productions. So CA shows how 'even though a woman may be speaking, that does not mean that she is always speaking "as a woman"' (McElhinny, 2003: 33; see also Kitzinger, 2005a; 2007b).

Those that subscribe to the 'Schegloffian' (1997) position argue that if political levels of analysis have any place, they must come after technical analyses of data. At the technical level, analysts can investigate whether and how participants treat a prior turn at talk as derogatory, offensive, acceptable and so on. At the political level, analysts may argue about the wider ideological meaning of the interactions under examination. If the two levels are confused, and political agendas are imposed prematurely, then analysts will obscure the very sociopolitical features of talk that they seek to explain and produce analyses (and politics) that are not empirically grounded, that do not 'bind' to the data and, as such, risk 'ending up merely ideological' (Schegloff, 1997: 183). In a 'manifesto' for feminist CA, Toerien and Kitzinger (2007: 658) write that

Such work seeks to remain true to the CA principle that analytic claims must be grounded in participants' practices. At the same time, the aim is to go beyond the 'basic science' of how interaction works, using CA to say something of political relevance. In blending these aims, feminist CA should offer something to feminists and conversation analysts... Seeking to understand both the mechanics of social action and the socio-political consequences thereof is, in our view, a hallmark of an adequate feminist CA.

Although there is a commitment in this work to 'bracket' one's politics initially, it would be a mistake to claim that ('non-feminist') CA has no interest in matters of politics and social change (see Heap, 1990). Indeed Sacks's lectures were littered with references to the empirical study of social change (e.g., Sacks, 1979: 7–14), often in his writings about membership categorization (Sacks, 1992). This has led some to suggest that CA is already compatible with a political, feminist agenda (e.g., Speer, 1999; 2005a), and that one does not need to 'subsidize' CA with feminism, or invent a new field of inquiry called 'feminist CA' in order to ask questions, and produce findings, that have political relevance. Others, including Wowk (2007), doubt that the politically informed union of feminism and CA is genuinely identifiable *as* CA. Wowk challenges Kitzinger's (2000a; 2002; 2005a) argument that 'feminist CA' solves the 'micro–macro debate' by examining concepts such as oppression and power ('macro') in the details of talk ('micro'), because to not examine such concepts makes CA 'unbearably limiting' (Kitzinger, 2002: 57). As Wowk points out, any analysis that *starts* with (analysts') concepts such as these, claiming to track their empirical realization, raises the same problem that using *anything other than members' categories* in analysis does. Wowk reiterates what amounts to the Schegloffian 'stricture' that the 'requirement (to not go beyond participants' own demonstrable orientations) is fundamental rather than limiting' (2007: 142). With regard to topics like heterosexism and heteronormativity, Kitzinger (2005b) has shown how, in out-of-hours calls to doctors, call-takers reveal their assumption that patients are heterosexual through their use of particular family reference terms. Wowk glosses Kitzinger's argument that 'an absence of an explicit (or implicit) orientation to sexism/heterosexism', such as was found in these calls, 'would not be unexpected and in such cases we would hardly expect to find members orienting to the phenomenon (or if they were then these orientations would be buried far too deep to be accessible to CA)' (2007: 143). Wowk's problem, however, is that Kitzinger labels '*what in her opinion* are situations where oppression is taking place and where it is so routinised that members don't refer to it or even necessarily realise it' (2007: 143, emphasis added; see also Schegloff, 2009, for criticisms of Kitzinger's analysis of heterosexism).

  This debate (see Kitzinger, 2008a, for a rebuttal), like the debate between Schegloff (1997), Wetherell (1998) and Billig (1999), throws up theoretical and methodological issues which are clearly central to any study of gender and conversation analysis, but particularly with studies that have an explicitly feminist agenda. Some of the chapters in this book work with such an agenda; more do not. Having spent some time laying out the field of conversation analysis and gender, we now turn to the scope of the current volume.

Overview of the chapters

This book represents authors' thinking at a key moment in the development of gender and CA studies. Each of the contributors has engaged to varying degrees with the debates discussed above. What unites them is the view that gender is best analysed as a *members' phenomenon* as it crops up in everyday, naturally occurring interaction, looking at the regular, situated practices through which gendered identities and categorizations are *realized*. There are some subtle differences in emphasis among our contributors, with some conducting sequential CA, others combining CA with related approaches such as discursive psychology or anthropology, and still others attending particularly to membership categorization practices. Hence the book provides a comprehensive, integrated collection of the most exciting work on conversation and gender currently available.

The chapters are organized loosely into four parts, reflecting the themes or questions that they address: (I) gender, person reference and self-categorization; (II) gender, repair and recipient design; (III) gender and action formation; and (IV) gender identities and membership categorization practices. All chapters deal, to a great or lesser extent, with the issue of 'gender relevance'; that is, the analytic warrants for making claims about how gender is relevant to the interaction under investigation.

Part I: Gender, person reference and self-categorization

The first three chapters address the issue of how people refer to themselves and other people. In particular, they focus on whether linguistically *gender-neutral* terms used for self-reference on the one hand, and linguistically gendered terms used to self-categorize on the other, automatically do (or do not) convey gender in the interaction. In Chapter 2, and in a persuasive challenge to Schegloff's (1996c) claims that 'I' is neutral with respect to indexing categorical information about the speaker, Clare Jackson demonstrates how it may none the less convey such information in gendered (and age-related) terms. Using data from telephone calls between young women and girls, Jackson shows that 'I' becomes 'interactionally gendered *for participants*' (p. 32) in the environment of talk that explicitly discusses, or obliquely invokes, gender norms, and where the speaker resists (or embraces) the relevance of those norms for themselves as individuals. Jackson argues that 'although each speaker *is* a member of a gendered category (as well as others), it is in part with and through the use of a gendered "I" that … [speakers] become *relevantly* gendered in the talk' (p. 45). Jackson concludes by suggesting that since 'this sort of categorized self-reference appears to be occasioned by talk about normative conduct and its implications for individuals, then the practice may illuminate social-scientific debates about the relationship between self (or selves) and society' (p. 46).

In Chapter 3, drawing on data from ordinary telephone conversations in which at least one of the participants identifies as lesbian, Victoria Land and Celia Kitzinger examine instances of 'first person categorization' in which speakers explicitly label themselves as members of particular social categories (e.g., 'I'm a schizophrenic', 'We're all queer') in order to explore 'how people orient to and deploy categorization in the course of their mundane social activities' (p. 49). In an extension of Schegloff's (1997) claims about gender relevance, Land and Kitzinger argue that 'evidence of category membership is not in and of itself sufficient to claim its relevance for the participants' (p. 62). Analysing sequences in which speakers self-categorize as, variously, 'schizophrenic', 'student' or 'committee member', these contributors argue that 'it is not only that speakers *can* self-categorize in multiple ways, but also that they *do* self-categorize in multiple ways' depending on the interactional goal they are pursuing. Land and Kitzinger make the point, relevant to 'difference' studies in language and gender research, that if analysts treat female and male speakers *only as* women and men, they risk disregarding such alternative, non-gendered, local interactional explanations. Likewise, if there is evidence of gender in the talk it does not mean that gender is omnirelevant, or the most salient or relevant category.

In Chapter 4, Noa Logan Klein furthers our understanding of the ways in which gender can be made relevant to interaction by examining how and why speakers do 'gender categorization in non-recognitional person reference' (p. 64). Unlike recognitional person reference, by which speakers display to recipients that the person being referred to is known to them, non-recognitional references tell the recipient that they do not know them. Klein argues that since they are not designed to achieve recognition of the person referred to, non-recognitional person references 'can act as information-free placeholders' (p. 66) or, simultaneously, achieve another interactional task such as 'the placement of people as members of social groups by characteristics such as race, gender, occupation, and relationship to the speaker' (p. 66). Klein suggests it is gender categorization that 'constitutes a minimum basic form of non-recognitional reference, making gender a – perhaps even *the* – central mechanism for classifying people in English-speaking cultures' (p. 66). To illuminate the way gender categorization is omnirelevant to non-recognitional person reference, Klein draws a distinction between 'action' and 'system' relevance. Gender categorization is *action* relevant when 'gender can aid recipients in understanding the meaning of speakers' stories by cueing recipients to draw on their prior knowledge about gender' (p. 67). By contrast, gender categorization is *system* relevant when it is used as 'a feature of grammar that helps connect initial and subsequent references to the same person' (p. 78). Klein demonstrates how listeners can exploit the system relevance of 'simple non-recognitional reference' for a variety of interactional purposes and concludes, contrary to Land and Kitzinger, that 'the normative inclusion of gender categorization as a minimum basic form of non-recognitional reference makes gender an omnipresent category of persons in talk' (p. 81).

Part II: Gender, repair and recipient design

Two key conversational practices are addressed in the following three chapters: repair (in particular, self-initiated self-repair in which a speaker marks some aspect of their ongoing talk as problematic and repairs it within the same turn) and recipient design (the way speakers orient to and monitor their recipients and design or reshape their talk accordingly: see C. Goodwin, 1979; Sacks *et al.*, 1974). In Chapter 5, Elizabeth Stokoe focuses on the way repair and reformulation of consecutive references to third parties broaden our understanding of the interactional circumstances under which gender may (or may not) be oriented to. In particular, and drawing on Edwards's (2005) notion of the way speakers design talk to deal with the 'subject' and 'object sides' of description, Stokoe identifies four different formats for producing consecutive alternate gender categories and considers what each format might display about speakers' orientation to gender. She argues that these repairs (e.g., 'girl' – 'woman') cannot be explained in terms of fixing some 'category-formed errors', or of repairs on person reference preferences. Rather, these repairs appear to be interactionally motivated by a range of factors bound up with issues of recipient design, and the management of various forms of 'trouble'. This trouble includes the adequacy of the reference for characterizing the object of the description, and the speaker-identity issues that may be invoked by using particular forms of gender categories (e.g., being a 'gender aware' speaker). Stokoe concludes that, despite the appeal of the intuitive notion that speakers must be oriented to gender when they explicitly replace one category with another, such repairs may not be 'oriented to gender' in the feminist, political sense that this interest in conversation stems from.

In Chapter 6, Sue Wilkinson also considers how gender relevance is or is not bound up with speakers' practices of recipient design, by examining the way call-takers on a fibromyalgia helpline use 'prefabricated talk', what Wilkinson calls their 'signature formulation', in multiple, similar versions across a series of conversations with callers. Yet despite its being routinized, formulaic and apparently almost scripted, Wilkinson shows that such talk is none the less expertly recipient-designed in ways that deliver a solution to a problem that comes off as uniquely designed for the particular caller. Wilkinson argues that although call-takers do not explicitly invoke gender in this script-like talk, gender is none the less oriented to in the way they select 'as designated recipients' of their 'signature formulation' 'only those callers [they take] to be women' (p. 133). This approach initially appears to reproduce just the kind of variables-and-effects approach to discourse associated with the 'sex difference' perspective criticized earlier. However, Wilkinson argues that because the production of the scripted talk attends to 'the presumed gender of the participants', gender remains 'endogenous to the interaction rather than imposed upon it by the analyst' (p. 133). As she concludes, 'the key challenge for comparative work of this type is to specify exactly *how* an orientation to gender (or some other category set) is consequential for the content and course of the interaction' (p. 133).

In Chapter 7, Alexa Hepburn and Jonathan Potter also address the issue of recipient design in relation to the use of 'tag questions' (e.g., 'You're coming home early that night, *aren't you*?'). The background for their study is the classic, widely criticized, research by Robin Lakoff (1975), who claimed that, as a symptom of their relative powerlessness, lack of assertiveness and general deficiency as speakers, women use more tag questions than men. Hepburn and Potter 'bracket off' arguments about whether or not there are actually gender differences in the use of tags, and whether their use is a symptom of psychological states that drive interaction. Instead, drawing on discursive psychology as well as conversation analysis, they focus 'on the way psychological states are sequentially and publicly invoked as parts of practices' (p. 135). Using data from various sources, they demonstrate that, far from representing some intrinsically weak or strong psychological state, tag questions can be 'systematically exploited to press subtly and rather indirectly for a course of action that has already been resisted' (p. 135). They argue that tag questions can be *invasive* in the sense that they attempt to reconstruct recipients' 'desires, beliefs, knowledge or other "psychological" matters' (p. 150), and *coercive* 'in the sense that they indirectly build a course of action (that has already been resisted) as desirable for, and desired by, the recipient' (p. 136). The contributors conclude that 'the challenge for sociolinguistic or other approaches that link forms of talk with social categories such as gender and inequality is to do so in a way that is sensitive to the specific conversational practices that we have started to show are operating' (p. 152). In the same way that Kitzinger's (2008b) work on interruption de-genders what has often been a solid assumption about how women and men talk, Hepburn and Potter similarly de-gender stereotypical notions of the gendered, unassertive tag.

In Part II, both Stokoe and Hepburn and Potter consider the embodied conduct that works in aggregate with talk to accomplish, say, the production of

to during the ensuing interaction, and either supported or challenged by his classmates. They identify three methods through which his female identity is produced, including the management of epistemic status, person reference practices, and explicit reference to gender categorizations and category-bound features. Butler and Weatherall demonstrate how these methods, taken together, establish and maintain the 'production and recognition of the fictional identity' (p. 236), and thus established a temporary cross-gender category membership. But, in particular, they note how a 'quite remarkable claim of a change in identity and gender was accomplished by rather ordinary conversational procedures' (p. 249).

Chapter 12 also examines how children invoke gender identities in the course of their everyday interactions. Marjorie Harness Goodwin examines video-recorded materials of children's peer groups, arguing that the participants' formulations of gender are critical in building affiliative and adversarial alignments, or stances, that can be articulated through prosody, embodied action and talk. She suggests that by examining such 'stance-taking' we can understand 'the concerns that deeply animate participants' (p. 251). For example, Goodwin demonstrates how children take for granted and work to maintain a heteronormative social order. Furthermore, during adversarial encounters, children use gendered categories (as well as age) to accomplish 'borderwork'; that is, to maintain and defend the boundaries of their own gendered group or space. Goodwin also shows how the gender categories 'girl' and 'boy' may be mobilized in the midst of disputes as well as in, say, mutual congratulatory exclamations during affiliative assessment sequences. The latter function provides further evidence that, echoing Land and Kitzinger (this volume), 'the very same term ("girl") can be used to produce a stance that displays either heightened affiliation or derision' (p. 270). Goodwin concludes, therefore, that 'the same person formulation can have very different meanings depending on the interactive context in which it emerges, as it takes its meaning from the activity-in-progress being produced through its utterance' (p. 268).

In Chapter 13, Angela Cora Garcia and Lisa M. Fisher focus explicitly on gender identity and inequality in a divorce mediation session. Like Sidnell, and Butler and Weatherall, they produce a single case analysis, here of talk between a divorcing heterosexual couple and two female mediators. Garcia and Fisher combine CA 'with an interpretive analysis of the interaction based on shared cultural knowledge', putting their politics alongside fine-grained analysis. Like other authors in Part IV, Garcia and Fisher consider the issue that gender, while always potentially relevant, is not always explicitly evident on the surface of the interaction. They argue that analysts should pay attention to the 'unseen, unnoticed, background assumptions and routine practices and procedures through which we construct and reconstruct our shared social worlds' (p. 293). These background assumptions include participants' understandings of 'gendered spousal and parental roles' which enable them 'to make arguments based on gender-differentiated parental roles without necessarily referring to gender' (p. 275). The contributors observe that divorce mediation is a particularly rich site for the study of gender because of the salience of topics like family and parenting. Garcia and Fisher's analysis shows how the participants, through the strategic use of gendered categories and moral accounts of each other's parenting, create a situation of gender inequality where the wife is disadvantaged in the interaction relative to the husband, and the wife's position in the struggle over residential custody of the children is compromised. The contributors conclude that 'while our analysis supports the notion that participants collaboratively create local gender orders, this does not mean that all parties' interests are equally well served by their creation' (p. 291).

In the final chapter, Jakob Cromdal draws on membership categorization analysis alongside sequential analysis to examine how children invoke, use and exploit gender categories and stereotypes in the course of their mundane play activities. He shows how such categorizations not only manage participation in activities with peers, as Goodwin demonstrates in Chapter 12, but how 'social and moral orders are invoked and locally produced in children's mundane interaction' (p. 295). He contrasts this ethnomethodological approach with current, more traditional sociological work on childhood and children's play, by providing an empirically grounded demonstration of children's understandings of the gendered social order. Drawing on video-recorded play activities of groups of children, Cromdal demonstrates how girls invoke and exploit normative gender-category attributes (and specifically gender stereotypes) to highlight the non-normative, 'gender-incongruity' of the boys' behaviour. In doing so, the girls 'undercut the actions of their male peers' and constrain 'the options available to them in the continuing interaction' (p. 308). Cromdal's analysis reveals that the boys deal with this by disattending to the girls' turns at talk or by removing themselves from the scene altogether. In other words, they adopt a form of 'motivated noticing' of gender (p. 308).

Implications and issues

The empirical chapters in this collection significantly develop our understanding of the relationship between conversation and gender. In particular, they extend our understanding of the 'explicit' ways in which gender can be made relevant, through person reference and categorization practices, as well as the more 'implicit' ways, through gender-resonant descriptions and accounts that accomplish a variety of social actions, across a variety of conversational contexts.

We conclude this introduction by touching briefly on what we take to be some of the key issues and questions arising from the chapters in this book, and, perhaps, for conversation analytic work more generally, that future research may address. These are both methodological and theoretical in orientation, including issues of data collection and analysis; of gender's 'omnirelevance'; of the coherence of gender and conversation analysis as a 'field'; and of the policy relevance and 'usefulness' of the work itself.

Conversation analysis, data and analysis

What kind of data should analysts collect to 'access' and analyse gender in talk to best access? Across this book, we have encountered numerous data sources, almost exclusively 'naturally occurring' ordinary or institutional talk, but also written materials and scripted dramatic dialogue. Some discourse and conversation analysts take a position against the use of 'contrived' data (e.g., interview materials, focus groups), whereas others use both researcher-elicited data and field-notes to analyse the workings of gender (for an overview of the debate about natural and contrived data see Speer, 2007). Speer (2007) argues that it actually makes little theoretical or practical sense to map the 'natural/contrived' distinction onto discrete 'types' of data or to treat the researcher as a potentially contaminating force. Rather, *all* data can be natural or contrived depending on what one wants to *do* with them. It follows that decisions about data should be taken reflexively with an awarenesss of whether and in what ways the mode of data collection is procedurally consequential for the research question, as well as the issue or phenomenon under investigation. Issues of generalizability are also relevant here. In order to make our claims about the operation of gender in interaction persuasive, it is fruitful if the researcher is able to show how the same (gendered) phenomenon operates across a range of settings and sequential environments, thereby controlling for the idiosyncratic specificities of any one setting (e.g., Stokoe, 2009).

It is also the case that, with technological advances, researchers can fully embrace the multiple modalities of interaction: the embodied, semiotic conduct that works with spoken language to accomplish social action. M. H. Goodwin (1990; 2006) pioneered the multimodal analysis of gender and interaction and has proceeded to influence many other researchers (e.g., Evaldsson, 2002; Speer & Green, 2007; Stokoe, 2006; 2008a; Toerien and Kitzinger, 2007). However, the issue – which is relevant to CA more generally – is how to *describe* matters of gaze, body orientation and so on in ways that remain true to the notion of 'participants' orientations'. That is, spoken talk's activities are designed to be understood, and have procedures for fixing misunderstandings, as conversation analysts have readily shown. However, conduct that is not linguistic is nevertheless rendered as linguistic description: it cannot 'stand alone' or go uninterpreted. The challenge for conversation and gender researchers is to produce robust, endogenous descriptions of embodied conduct that do not build heavy layers of interpretation into the process of 'mere description'.

The omnirelevance of gender?

The issue of 'omnirelevance' is addressed in this volume by several of the contributors, in rather contradictory ways. Whereas Land and Kitzinger argue that 'gender is not omnirelevant. Even when evidence of gender is in the talk it does not mean that this is the most salient or relevant category' (p. 63), Klein discusses 'the omnirelevance of gender as a daily performance and a social institution' (p. 65). Some authors mention the 'seen but unnoticed' omnirelevance of gender, or the idea that gender is always possibly, if not focally relevant (Speer, this volume; see also Heritage, 2005: 111). Schegloff himself appears to hold contrary positions, arguing, on the one hand, that one must make claims about relevance by attending to what is demonstrably relevant to participants 'at the moment that whatever we are trying to produce an account for occurs' (Schegloff, 1991: 50), but, on the other, that 'explicit mention of a category term ... is by no means necessary to establish the relevant orientation by the participants ... orientation to gender can be manifested without being explicitly named or mentioned' (1997: 182; see Stokoe & Smithson, 2001). For conversation and gender researchers the key question is what counts as an 'inexplicit' orientation to gender that is none the less 'demonstrably relevant' for the participants.

'Feminist conversation analysis'?

Some of the contributors to in this volume claim allegiance to the 'feminist conversation analysis' agenda of Kitzinger and her colleagues (e.g., Jackson, Land & Kitzinger, Wilkinson, all this volume). Others question the necessity of a subfield or subdiscipline (e.g., Cromdal, this volume). The issue, as Wowk (2007) also discusses, is whether for language and gender researchers CA needs to be supplemented or imbricated with feminist politics, or whether CA already meets the needs of these researchers in its own terms (Speer, 1999; 2005a). One problem with the label 'feminist conversation analysis', and, indeed, with a book of this sort, is that the explicit focus on matters of gender (and, to a lesser extent, sexuality) is vulnerable to the criticism that it re-essentializes gender by prioritizing it. In this sense 'feminist CA' may overlook those interactional patterns and practices that are, in the first instance, 'identity' practices more generally. For example, the practices of person reference, repair, compliments, affiliation and so on can all be studied (and have been) without gender being a relevant concern. The challenge for future research is to show that and how gender is a focal or subsidiary aspect of these broader social actions.

The policy relevance of gender and conversation analysis

In an academic environment that prioritizes research funding, being able to demonstrate the real-world relevance of analysis is an increasing concern (or, as some might say, a distraction). However, within conversation analysis in general, and work on gender within CA, there is plenty of applied work that is impacting on the working practices and policies of numerous professionals across a variety of institutions (see chapters in Antaki, in press, and see also Antaki, 1999; Drew *et al.*, 2001; Edwards & Stokoe, 2007; Heritage & Maynard, 2006; Heritage *et al.*, 2007; Maynard, 2003; Maynard *et al.*, 2002; Robinson & Heritage, 2006; Stivers *et al.*, 2003). Some of this work is directly relevant to issues of gender. Kitzinger and Kitzinger (2007) and Kitzinger and Wilkinson (in press), for example, have worked with call-takers on birth crisis helplines. In this volume, Garcia and Fisher's chapter on divorce mediation, like Garcia's other work (1991; 1995; 1996; 1998; see also Speer & Parsons, 2006; 2007; Stokoe, 2003), provides materials for practitioners to use to reflect on their own practice, and not least on the gender inequalities a 'no-side' approach may foster.

We hope you enjoy the book.

Part I

Gender, person reference and
self-categorization

2   The gendered 'I'

Clare Jackson

Introduction

In English, the word 'I' does not contain any categorical information about the speaker; neither gender, age, class nor race. It is what Schegloff (1996c: 440) calls 'reference *simpliciter*'; it does simple self-reference and its use 'masks the relevance of the referent and the reference for the talk' (Schegloff, 1996c: 446) because it is 'opaque with respect to all the usual key categorical dimensions – age, gender, status and the like' (Schegloff, 2007c: 123). Building on Schegloff's cogent analysis, the key claim I wish to make in this chapter is that there *are* instances where a speaker's self-referential 'I' can be rendered hearably gendered in the context of its production. In other words, my data show instances in which the ordinary, unremarkable form of self-reference is itself hearably gendered, without the speaker's categorical membership being explicitly linguistically produced. I call this use of 'I' the gendered-I. Drawing on extracts from the CTS corpus,[1] I show how the self-reference 'I' can be gendered.

I locate my work in the emerging discipline of feminist conversation analysis (see Kitzinger, 2000a; 2007a; Speer, 2002a; 2005a; Stokoe & Weatherall, 2002a) in which gendered identities (and others) are seen as emergent, locally occasioned and routinely constituted in interaction. Feminist conversation analysis resonates with ethnomethodological feminisms (Kitzinger, 2000a: 166), in which men/boys and women/girls are *not* regarded as always-and-forever talking as gendered beings, but rather may produce themselves or be produced as gendered in the taken-for-granted, routinized details of interaction (see Garfinkel,

I am very grateful to the editors, Susan A. Speer and Elizabeth Stokoe, and to Celia Kitzinger for their insightful comments on earlier drafts of this chapter. I should also like to thank participants in a data session hosted by the Feminist Conversation Analysis Unit, University of York, 1 November 2007, at which I presented the data extracts included here. The lively discussion was invaluable. Special thanks must also go to Galina Bolden, Danielle Jones, Victoria Land and Merran Toerien for their encouragement and contributions to the development of my analysis of gendered self-reference. Any errors are, of course, mine alone.

[1] This is a corpus of telephone calls that I am collecting for my PhD research. The calls are all made or received by young women, aged between 12 and 19. There are, so far, over 100 calls in the corpus, amounting to some 30 hours of mundane talk-in-interaction. All participants are pseudonymized in the transcripts.

31

1967; Kessler & McKenna, 1978:136; West & Zimmerman, 1987:13–14). Accordingly, feminist conversation analysis requires detailed analysis of the local features of naturalistic interaction as they are oriented to by participants.

One key finding to emerge from this kind of work is that use of terms that are gendered linguistically (such as 'man', 'woman', 'gentleman', 'lady') are not necessarily analysable as interactionally gendered *for participants* in talk-in-interaction (e.g., Kitzinger, 2007b:43; Stockill & Kitzinger, 2007:230). Conversely, terms which are gender-neutral in their abstract, linguistic sense are not necessarily gender-neutral for participants. For example, Stockill and Kitzinger (2007: 230) show how, in context, a particular use of the linguistically gendered term 'man' was not relevantly gendered in the interaction; on the other hand, deployment of the linguistically gender-neutral 'people' in the same conversation was clearly hearable as referring to a gendered category. Stockill and Kitzinger (2007: 233) conclude that 'deployment of a linguistically gendered term is not sufficient evidence for analysts to claim the relevance of gender to interactional participants... and... deployment of a linguistically gendered term is not necessary for gender to be interactionally relevant'. This chapter extends the scope of the second component of this claim by exploring how the linguistically non-gendered term 'I' *can* be interactionally gendered for the participants.

This chapter contributes to feminist analyses of gender and language by showing where and how speakers are oriented to themselves as gendered. It also contributes to conversation analytic work on person reference, particularly self-reference in talk, where 'I' has so far been viewed as obscuring rather than indexing categorical information (Schegloff, 2007c: 123). In order to provide some context for this last claim, I next provide a summary of what is known about self-reference in talk from the perspective of conversation analysis (CA).

A review of conversation analytic explication of self-reference

The domain of conversation analysis of relevance here is known as 'person reference', and analysis seeks to explicate practices for referring to selves and others in talk. Person reference is potentially central to any sociological project analysing the ways that people are individuated and classified in a given society (Stivers *et al.*, 2007: 2). It is through person reference (and other practices, including deployment of membership category devices; Schegloff, 1996c; 2007c) that traditional sociological variables such as kinship, gender, race, class, professional status and so on are made live and relevant in talk-in-interaction. Yet, leaving aside the separate literatures on membership categorization devices (MCD) – many of which are not concerned with self-reference or which do not clearly differentiate between MCD and referring (Schegloff, 2007c) – there has been what Stivers *et al.* (2007) describe as a curious neglect of empirical study of conversationally grounded ways of referring to self and others. Lerner and Kitzinger (2007a) make a similar point, showing there have been, in a sense, two false dawns in person reference research: the first in the 1970s with the publication of Sacks and Schegloff's (1979) germinal work on the normative organization of person reference, and then another almost twenty years later with Schegloff's (1996c) analysis of its sequential organization. Given the potential social-scientific import of person reference, and the inspirational early analyses of both Sacks and Schegloff, it is perhaps surprising that it has taken until the mid-2000s for research in the area really to take off. With the publication of Enfield and Stivers's (2007) edited collection and a special issue of *Discourse Studies* (see Lerner & Kitzinger, 2007a) dedicated to the topic, there is now a new dawning of interest. Interestingly, and of relevance here, much of the new work focuses on self-reference. Here is some background.

One centrally organizing feature of person reference rests on a distinction between default and marked (or alternative[2]) practices (Schegloff, 1996c: 439; see also Enfield, 2007: 97). There are various ways that a speaker can refer to themselves (and/or others) in talk-in-interaction. For example, I can refer to myself using 'I' (or a grammatical variant such as 'me'); or by name – 'Clare' (or some of its variants – 'Ms Jackson'); or by some relevant descriptor – 'the author'. These options are not equivalent. That is, the design of each reference has its own local contingencies and consequences (consider, for example, the difference between 'I' and 'the author') and the task of recipients (and analysts) is to make sense of why any particular person reference gets used; in Schegloff's terms, 'why that now' (1996c: 439).

In his classic paper on person reference, Schegloff (1996c: 438–9) begins with a basic puzzle to be solved: how do people 'do reference to persons so as to accomplish, on the one hand, that nothing but referring is being done, and on the other hand that something else in addition to referring is being done'? He shows that there are systematic, standard ways of doing reference that convey that nothing special is intended. These default practices can be contrasted with alternative practices, which are less typical and therefore hearable as inviting recipients to inspect the talk for what else is being specially done in *addition* to reference (Schegloff, 1996c: 439).

Schegloff (1996c: 442) shows that in English, the default practice for doing self-reference is use of the dedicated pronoun 'I'[3] (or its grammatical variants).

---

[2] 'Marked' is a somewhat contentious term because of its multiple uses and meanings in literatures outside of CA. Some writers (e.g., Land & Kitzinger, 2007; Lerner & Kitzinger, 2007b; Stivers, 2007) use 'alternative' to refer to less typical usage where more than one option is available to speakers in a given context.

[3] Schegloff (1996c: 442), citing Sacks (1992), cautions against 'pronoun' as a term because in linguistic terms, pronoun means standing in place of the noun. However, as Schegloff observes, first person pronouns 'I' and 'me' and second person pronoun 'you' are default ways of referring

He has patently clear grounds for this: 'I' is the most numerically common form of self-reference (Schegloff, 1996c: 442), and it is uncomplicated in that its basic form, 'I', remains unaffected by its sequential position in talk. This contrasts with referring to non-present persons, where an initial reference is usually done as a name, or a descriptive phrase (e.g., 'Vicky', 'my best friend'), whereas subsequent references to the same person are normally done as pronouns (e.g., 'she'), as in Extract 1.

Extract 1 CTS36
```
01   Ell:   Hum .HHH C- I saw Vicky drunk last
02          night.
03   Kar:   Oh:: was she piss:ed.
```

By contrast, in Extract 2, a teenage boy, Stan, self-deprecatorily tells his girl-friend that he cannot visit her until his mother has made his travel arrangements. Across this short spate of talk, Stan refers to himself six[4] times. Of these self-references, five take the form 'I' (the remaining one being a grammatical variant, 'me', at line 2), each is produced in default terms and its form does not change across the turn (except, of course, in the case of 'me', due to grammatical necessity).

Extract 2 CTS05
```
01   Sta:   I'm just waiting I just want my mum to
02          sort out this t- ticket and tell me what I'm
03          doing because like I'll just stuff it up won't I.
```

Default *self*-reference, then, takes the standard form of 'I' (and its grammatical variants) no matter what form of self-reference precedes or follows it. Extract 3 also illustrates that 'I' masks categorical information about the speaker; Stan does not talk here as a relevantly gendered male. Though he is male, and is known by his recipient to be so, *he is not talking relevantly as* a male (Schegloff, 1997: 165), because he is many other things as well – a musician, a writer, a British citizen, an atheist, a feminist and so on. As we might expect, following Schegloff (1996c; 2007b), most of these categorical memberships (with the possible exception of his maleness, which is available from the quality of his voice, though not here relevantly so) are obscured in Stan's uses of 'I' in extract 2 – here his uses of 'I' (and 'me') mean simply 'I the speaker'.

In comparison to self-reference, references to third parties are often categorically loaded. For example, names and locally subsequent terms are often

---

to speaker and recipients. Third person pronouns 'he' and 'she' are default locally subsequent reference terms. In all cases, if nouns (e.g., names) are used then they are being used in place of the pronoun and not the other way round.

[4] Putting aside the complication of the implied self-reference contained in what is actually a reference to a non-present third party, 'my mum'.

linguistically gendered and *can* make available inferences (or reveal assumptions) about such things as sexuality (Land & Kitzinger, 2005: 408) and national, ethnic or religious heritage (Sacks, 1992: 338) *even when speakers are not designing them to do so.* That is, even though gender may not be interactionally *relevant*, it is interactionally *available* as a resource when speakers use prototypical male and female names, descriptors and locally subsequent third person terms such as 'he' and 'she'. By contrast, 'I' is used by men and women, heterosexual and LGBT (lesbian, gay, bisexual or transgender) persons, Jews and Gentiles alike and is not inflected with age, status, gender, race and the like.

The relative abstruseness of 'I' as revealing categorical information ordinarily means that when speakers wish to draw specific attention to their own categorical membership (or some aspect of their identity) through talk-in-interaction, they do so designedly, through use of alternative forms of self-reference.

One practice speakers use to highlight a particular aspect of their identity is self-description using the basic format 'I am an X' or a grammatical variant, as in extracts 3 and 4, in which speakers say such things as 'I'm a girl' and 'I'm really girly.' In Extract 3, Penny's declaration that she is a girl occurs at line 7, constitutes a tease (note the laughter, and the soft delivery) and is occasioned by boyfriend Stan's lengthy complaint about the sorts of comments he receives about his hair (over-complaining provides a common sequential context for teasing; Drew 1987: 242).

Extract 3 CTS01

```
01   Pen:         [I sa(h)y that thou(hh)gh:
02   Sta:    No but that shouldn't- why- why would
03             you say that, you- you've got
04             [longer] hair than me::
05   Pen:    [.hh   ]
06                  (.)
07   Pen:    Huh huh I'm a °girl° [haHAHAHA .hhhh ]
08   Sta:                         [Yeah ye- d- what    ]
```

We might note in passing here the force of the other person references in this extract, which are also not gendered. So, at line 1, Penny's 'I' simply means 'I, the speaker'. At lines 2–3, Stan uses 'you' multiply in the course of his turn to refer to his recipient, and at line 4, he uses 'me' to refer to himself. Evidence that these simple, straightforward references are not hearably gendered, at least for the recipient, is provided by Penny's invocation of gender as a tease in her turn at line 7. Here, it is apparent that Penny has not oriented to 'you' and 'me' as possibly gendered.

In Extract 4, Sophie describes herself as 'really girly' (line 5) in order to highlight a contrast with a friend of her recipient. The non-present friend is referred to in line 1 using (a locally subsequent) 'she' and so is also hearably a girl, but that she is clearly not 'girly' is given by virtue of her membership of the here contrastive category 'Mosher.'[5]

Extract 4 CTS02

```
01   Sop:    But is she a Mosher.
02                   (0.7)
03   Emm:    Yeah
04                   (0.8)
05   Sop:    But I'm really gir:ly huhuhu=
06   Emm:    =↑Wh:at?
07   Sop:    .hhh but I'm really gir:ly.
08                   (1.4)
09   Emm:    Well she's turning me into a Mosher so
10           (0.9) better get used to it hhh.hhh
```

Using such formulations as 'I am an X', speakers describe themselves as gendered persons. However, it is not the self-reference – 'I' – that achieves this. 'I' is simply a person reference that refers to the speaker (see Schegloff, 1996c: 441; 2007c: 123). The person reference in such statements is produced *independently* of the descriptive component – even when that descriptive component is a category, as it is in Extract 3, or an adjective built off categorical membership, as in Extract 4 (see Schegloff, 2007d: 434). When a speaker *describes* themselves as belonging to a category (see Land & Kitzinger, this volume, for an analysis of this sort of formulation) it is the categorical component of the utterance that conveys the gendered nature of the speaker and *not* the person reference. My interest in this chapter is specifically in the self-reference and its localized, context-specific capacity for conveying categorical information without having to name the category.

Speakers do have practices for referring to themselves other than using 'I' (Schegloff, 1996c: 442–5). These include use of a generic 'you' which often seems to mean 'I' (see Extract 5, line 11, in which a generic 'you' refers to the speaker, as well as to her recipient and to an unspecified collectivity of others, in accounting for her behaviour as normative[6]); use of kinship names when talking to small children (as in a mother telling her child that 'Mummy is tired'); use of 'we' to convey speaking on behalf of an institution or collectivity of persons (see also Lerner & Kitzinger, 2007a); and even use of prototypical (locally initial) third person references (e.g., I might refer to myself as 'the author').

---

[5] A Mosher is a UK term for a member of a youth culture that involves dancing (or 'head-banging') to rock/punk music and often dressing in dark clothes.

[6] Compare Mary's use of 'I' as agent of the 'being naughty' with her use of 'you' in her account of why she told her boyfriend she was on her period. In both cases, Mary means to refer to herself, though with the 'you', Mary is characterizing herself as a member of a group of people who do not 'rush into things'.

Extract 5 CTS33

```
01   Mar:        [( ) like. And then (0.9) I was
02               a little naughty hhhhhhhhh
03   Kar:        Wh(h)at d(h)id you do::.
04                    (.)
05   Mar:        Erm well I tol- I don't know why
06               but I told him I was on my period.
07                    (0.5)
08   Mar:        I think that was like kind of
09               like a barrier thing wasn't it.
10   Kar:        Oh right. [Yeah.
11   Mar:                  [Because you don't
12               want to rush into anything. So
13               I told him I was on my period so
14               that like I sort of °did stuff to
15               him.°
```

In the matter of designing self-reference to invoke a particular relevancy of self, Land and Kitzinger (2007) show how speakers sometimes use terms ordinarily reserved for references to absent/non-addressed third parties in order to do self-reference (e.g., Land & Kitzinger, 2007: 498, have data in which a speaker refers to herself as 'the woman he fell in love with', where 'he' is her male partner: the speaker is engaged in presenting herself as if from the perspective of her husband). In many of the data extracts presented by Land and Kitzinger (2007) the third party self-reference terms are descriptive rather than names.[7] This is perhaps not surprising, since in using third party terms for self-reference, speakers need to 'select such terms as display (or constitute) the current relevance with which the referent figures in the talk' (Schegloff, 1996c: 447). This contrasts with situations where third party descriptors are necessary in order to achieve recognition of a non-addressed or absent referent (see Sacks & Schegloff, 1972a; Schegloff, 1996c). The key point about this difference is that when third-party descriptive terms appear in their normative environment, they may convey a stance or categorical information about a referent even if they are not designed so to do (Stivers *et al.*, 2007: 4), but in self-reference, the inferences available in a third party descriptor are specifically designed to be there and are fitted to (indeed may constitute) whatever course of action is under way (Land & Kitzinger, 2007: 521). In the words of Land and Kitzinger (2007: 521), third party self-references are 'selected to make available in the talk those

---

[7] Sacks and Schegloff (1979) and Schlegoff (1996c) distinguish between recognitional and non-recognitional reference. A recognitional person reference is used when speakers assume their recipients know (about) a particular referent. Typical recognitional references are names or descriptors. Non-recognitional person reference is used when the identity of the referent is (assumed to be) unavailable or not known to speaker, recipient or both. Typical non-recognitional references are such things as 'this guy' or 'someone'.

aspects of "I" or "me" that are otherwise submerged in an English pronoun that conveys nothing about gender, nationality, relationship with recipient, etc.'.

Previous conversation analytic work (particularly Land & Kitzinger, 2007; Schegloff, 1996c; 2007c) treats 'I' as reference *simpliciter* and shows the extra work required of speakers if they are designedly to convey the local relevance of a particular feature of their identity through use of an alternative practice for referring (as opposed to naming a category). I want to turn now to work that extends the analysis of uses of 'I' beyond its status as a self-reference *simpliciter*, particularly the recent work of Lerner and Kitzinger (2007b) and Turk (2007). Both papers resonate with my work on the gendered 'I' by showing that there is more to be said about 'I' than that it is a term dedicated to doing self-reference.

Is there more to be said about uses of 'I'?

The preceding section explored canonical uses of 'I' as a self-reference and ended with the observation that speakers have to do something special in order to convey how the self figures relevantly in the talk. Does this mean that uses of 'I' are unworthy of analytical attention? To date, only two papers have examined participants' uses of 'I': Lerner and Kitzinger (2007b) and Turk (2007). Both articles are empirically persuasive that there is more to be said about 'I'.

Lerner and Kitzinger (2007b: 551) extend the scope of canonical self-reference to include 'we' as well as 'I'. That is, they show that, in referring to themselves, speakers have a choice between two equally viable (or equally unremarkable) forms of self-reference: 'I' and 'we'. However, speakers are sensitive to the consequences of selecting one over the other, as demonstrated in the instances examined by Lerner and Kitzinger where speakers halt the progressivity of talk in order to deal with (or more formally, repair) some ostensible trouble in relation to self-reference. Citing Schegloff's (1996c: 446) argument that 'I' masks the relevance of the referent for the talk, they observe that 'when its use is the result of a repair operation that explicitly selects it over another form of self-reference (i.e., collective self-reference), then its local relevance may be partially unmasked' (Lerner & Kitzinger, 2007b: 531). They show that 'I' and 'we' are both possible selections in many turns at talk and that recipients can inspect either of them for what they might be doing given that the other could have been used. Repairs make visible precisely the import of these issues *for the participants*. Given participants' concerns with forms of self-reference, *any* use of 'I' (or 'we') may be analysed for ways in which its selection is informed by considerations beyond simple referral. Lerner and Kitzinger's insightful work opens up a potentially rich seam of analytic scrutiny of the use of 'I' on a case-by-case, turn-by-turn basis in order to explicate its sequential fit for the speaker, recipient and action.

A beginning to this analytic scrutiny is made by Turk (2007), who examines self-referential gestures (e.g., bringing the hand to the chest) in data where the participants are co-present. Turk's analysis focused on those self-referential gestures that coincided with the speakers' production of a prosodically stressed 'I' in speech. Turk shows how this combination of self-referential activities (i.e., of speech and gesture) accomplishes more than simple reference. Specifically, Turk develops Lerner and Kitzinger's analysis of repairs in which speakers extract themselves from a collectivity (e.g., some variant of 'we' to 'I'), showing how these repairs may be embodied in gesture. For example, in one of Turk's extracts (Extract 3, 2007: 565) the speaker repairs (in third turn) 'the first day' to 'the first time I was there' and places prosodic stress on the self-reference 'I'. Here the combination of gesture and prosodic stress accomplishes extraction of the speaker from a collectivity (of students in her class). Turk informs us that the gesture was produced just before the production of the stressed 'I', which is important because it suggests that the gesture itself projects the extraction and is not a simple reference to self.

The work of Lerner and Kitzinger (2007) and Turk (2007) shows there is more to be said about uses of 'I' beyond its use as a reference *simpliciter*. I turn now to my own work in the same vein, which shows that the normatively non-gendered self-reference 'I' can sometimes be hearably gendered by virtue of the context of its production.

The gendered 'I'

The vast majority of uses of 'I' in my data are reference *simpliciter*s; they do nothing but self-referral. Here are some examples. In Extract 6, 16-year-old Penny is building a claim to have 'real depression' rather than mere and temporary low mood.

Extract 6 CTS05

```
01   Pen:   Yeah: .hhh No I- I've been feeling this
02          for ages. I've been feeling it coming on
03          for like wee:ks: now. .hh I've been feeling
04          really down you know because I've been
05          crying a lot. And everything.
```

In Extract 7, 15-year-old Sophie has invited her older sister Penny to the cinema.

Extract 7 CTS20

```
01   Pen:   There's a couple of films I want
02          to see. I haven't got any money though.
03                  (.)
04   Sop:   Yea::h. I'll pay and you can pay
05          me back
```

In Extract 8, 16-year-old Ellie is telling her friend Karen about a party she went to the night before.

Extract 8 CTS36

```
01   Ell:   I dran_k_::: quite a lot.
02                 (.)
03   Ell:   But .HHHHH I didn't (.) get drunk.
04          hhh As such .hhh
05                 (0.7)
06   Kar:   Oh you're so used to it now eh
07   Ell:   .HH I don't know. It's just it didn't
08          really seem to effect me. Really.
```

In each of these extracts, speakers' self-references are produced using the canonical form of 'I' or its grammatical variant 'me'. In each case, the 'I' simply refers to the current speaker and does nothing to invoke particular categorical membership. However, I have observed instances in my own data where the self-reference 'I' does invoke categorical membership (particularly of gender and age) by virtue of the context of its production. I next present three instances from this collection where the speaker uses 'I' to invoke a gendered identity.

The first instance of a gendered 'I', Extract 9, is taken from earlier in the same call as Extract 3. This is a call between girlfriend and boyfriend – Penny and Stan – and the candidate gendered 'I' occurs on line 8. Stan is complaining about the sorts of comments people feel free to make about the length of his hair. He patently resents the sorts of gender stereotypes that cast him as deviant for having long hair and, at the opening of the extract, asks rhetorically 'what's the big deal' (line 1).

Extract 9 CTS01

```
01   Sta:   What what's the big de_a_l. .hhh
02          It's l- it's like when people come
03          up to you and go [uh ((mimics))=
04   Pen:                    [Huh=
05   Sta:   =['↓<Are you hot in with that hair] cut>'.=
06   Pen:   =[Huh huh huh huh              ]
07   Sta:   =Are y- No. Why woul- why the he_ll
08          would I be h_o_t? Gi_r_ls have long hai:r.
09   Pen:   Are you a what. .hh
10   Sta:   Wh- 'are you h_o_t'.
11                 (0.3)
12   Pen:   °I-(h) [.hhhhhhhh=              ]
13   Sta:          [(Isn't) Aren't you hot with that]
14          hair [cut.
```

Following his rhetorical question at line 1, Stan illustrates the sort of comment he typically receives and emphasizes its silliness by mimicking the voice and style of a possibly male, possibly stupid person (i.e., he noticeably lowers the pitch of his voice, and slows the pace of delivery) when he says at line 5, 'Are you hot in with that hair cut.' Note that the generic person references 'people' (line 2) and 'you' (for 'me', line 3) make this a reporting of a scripted event (Edwards, 1994); something that typically happens to Stan rather than a specific one-off occurrence. Later (lines 7–8), Stan challenges the basis of this typical comment and does so with an insertion repair that upgrades its force – that is, after 'Why woul-', Stan cuts off and reproduces 'why' and what was clearly hearable as 'would', but with new words, 'the hell', inserted between them. This changes 'Why woul-' to 'why the hell would'. Two analytical points are noteworthy about how Stan presents this turn as a challenge, before we get to the matter of self-reference. First, note that Stan's comment is formulated as a 'why' interrogative. Sacks (1992: 4) observes that 'why' questions 'propose about some action that it is an accountable action'.[8] That is, Stan's use of 'why' here renders the comments he receives, and not his hair length, as the accountable matter. Second, Stan deploys the modal verb 'would', which, following Edwards (2006), works to invoke normative, scripted and timeless knowledge of the world such that one can hardly imagine the precise circumstances in which Stan may be caused to be hot by the length of his hair. It is the self-reference 'I' as it appears in this robust challenge (line 8) to his critics that is now the focus of my analysis.

At the moment the self-reference 'I' is uttered at line 8, it is not specifically gendered. That is, it is spoken as the default form of speaker self-reference by a speaker who is male but who is equally twenty-something, a Virgo, a guitarist and so on. Despite the fact that Stan's story is all about discrimination he experiences as a male person with long hair, this 'I' does not, then, specifically, relevantly invoke gender, or make gender hearably relevant at the point of its production. To use Schegloff's phrase, the relevance of the reference and the referent for the talk is 'masked' by self-reference with 'I', since this is 'opaque' with respect to gender. At the moment of its use, it means 'I the speaker'. It is only in the production of the contrastive category 'girls' in his next turn constructional unit (TCU) at line 8 that 'I' is, retrospectively, gendered. In effect, Stan's challenge amounts to asking why he, a boy, would have a different physiological response to having long hair from members of the category 'girl'. Here, then, 'I' is hearably gendered by virtue of the contrast category 'girls', which make relevant Stan's membership of the category 'boys'.

In Extract 10, the candidate gendered 'I' occurs in line 16, and here it also displays an orientation to normative heterosexual relations. Fifteen-year-old Emma is telling her older brother Michael about a Valentine's Day date the week before. Just before this extract starts, Michael has teasingly requested an account from

---

[8] My thanks to Galina Bolden for alerting me to Sacks's analytical observation on 'why'.

Emma for having ended up on the back row at the cinema with her boyfriend. As we join the call, Emma is explaining that, having gone for a pizza first, she and her date arrived late at the cinema, 'and it was absolutely packed in there' (lines 3–4), thereby implying that they had little option about where to sit.

Extract 10 CTS41

```
01   Emm:    .HHh 'Cause we went to Pizza Hut
02           first and then we were late.
03           And we walked in. .hh And it was
04           it was absolutely packed in there
05                   (1.0)
06   Mic:    Oh right. So he treated you to a me-
07           for a tea then.
08                   (.)
09   Emm:    Yeah. He normally does pay for
10           most of my stuff.
11                   (.)
12   Mic:    Good. That's how it should be eh?
13   Emm:    Heh heh heh heh .HH hhh
14           .hhh pt Yea[h  but  ]
15   Mic:               [Unless] Unless it's when
16           I am taking a girl out, then she should pay
17   Emm:    Huh huh huh huh huh .HHH
18           #That's how it's always been with you:
19           huh huh [huh huh ]
20   Mic:            [Yeah.   ] I know.
21                   (0.3)
22   Mic:    Y- you gotta s- see whether they
23           like you though at first don't you
24           before you start splashing
25           your ca:sh.
26   Emm:    Huh huh huh huh huh huh huh
```

Michael topicalizes part of Emma's account with 'so he treated you to a me-for a tea then' (lines 6–7). There are a number of interesting observations about the design of this turn; the 'so' preface acts as an upshot marker – as in 'from what you just said, I am surmising the following … '; the self-initiated replacement repair of 'meal' to 'tea' perhaps reveals a stance on the choice of eating establishment, 'tea' here referring to food eaten in the evenings at home; a mundane, non-celebratory occasion. By replacing 'meal' with 'tea', Michael is downplaying its significance as an appropriate Valentine's Day treat. The turn as a whole is what Labov (1972a: 301) characterizes as a B-statement – that is, a statement about a recipient's domain of knowledge, which requires (dis)confirmation (hence, 'then' at the end of the TCU). However, I wish to focus more fully on the selection of 'treated' (line 6) to characterize the respective roles of Emma and her boyfriend. When Emma tells of going to Pizza Hut (a popular and relatively inexpensive chain of pizza restaurants), she describes it simply as something they did together – 'we went to Pizza Hut' – there is no hint here about who paid for the meal (Emma does not say 'he took me to Pizza Hut'). Yet, at lines 6–7, Michael guesses (correctly as it turns out) that Emma's boyfriend paid for the food. It may be tempting here to suggest that Michael is invoking an unnamed hetero-gendered norm for the organization of dating behaviour, namely that boys/men pay for girls/women. However, it might equally be that Michael is drawing on his personal knowledge of his sister – perhaps she would not pay for meals in any event. It is not until after Emma constructs her boyfriend's 'treat' as something he does typically (lines 9–10) that Michael names (line 12) the hetero-gendered norm he *may*[9] have earlier obliquely invoked. Certainly, by the end of line 12, hetero-gendered relations are firmly on the table (so to speak). As a (heterosexual) male, Michael is included in the category of persons who normatively cover the expenses of a date with a girlfriend, a fact which is obviously not lost on him as he makes it the subject of a joke at lines 15–16. The gendered 'I' is produced as part of this joke (line 16), and it serves to extract him from the collectivity of heterosexual males in order to produce himself as the exception. Here, then, 'I' means more than just 'I the current speaker'. It is instead hearable as 'I as a male'.

In Extract 11, the candidate gendered 'I' occurs at line 9. In this call, two-15-year-old girls, Mary and Amy, are discussing boyfriends. Mary has recently come out of what she implies was a 'long relationship' with Dan (lines 2–3), a breakup that had caused her some heartache, but she is 'better' now because she has a new boyfriend, Tom. Her ex-boyfriend, Dan, is reported as also having 'moved on' to form a relationship with new girlfriend, Tess.

Extract 11 CTS33

```
01   Mar:   Libby made me feel better ʼcause
02          she said (.) well boys after a long
03          relationship they [tend to     ]kind of (.)=
04   Amy:                      [((coughs)) ]
05   Mar:   =go downhill with girls whereas
06           girls go uphill.
07               (0.4)
08   Amy:   [Mm::::
09   Mar:   [So I've gone for Tom who's uphill.
10               (0.5)
11   Mar:   Dan's gone for Tess who's downhill
```

---

[9] The invocation of a gendered norm is ambiguous here, as Michael could mean something like 'it should always be the case that other people pay for our meals'.

```
12          huh huh
13               (0.3)
14   Amy:   Huh huh huh
15   Mar:   #I fe(h)el like an absolute cow for
16          saying this, but it makes me feel better
17               (0.3)
18   Amy:   We:ll it's true.<Like (.) like er (1.0)
19          Terry went for (.) Samantha after Emma.
```

As the extract opens, Mary is describing the sympathetic words of a friend, Libby, who made her 'feel better'. Libby's reported words have a proverbial feel about hetero-gendered relationships: 'boys after a long relationship... tend to... go downhill whereas girls go uphill' (lines 2–6). Exactly what is meant by 'downhill' and 'uphill' is not specified except in terms of persons known in common to Mary and Amy, as Mary shows how she and Dan exemplify Libby's reported claim (lines 9–11), and later, Amy provides an example of her own (lines 18–19). We might speculate that its meaning is something roughly equivalent to 'upmarket' and 'downmarket'; that is, that boys subsequently have female partners who are widely considered less desirable in the heterosexual marketplace, and girls subsequently have male partners considered more desirable. Mary later acknowledges the insult contained within her remarks directed at Dan and/or Tess (line 15).

So the 'I' at line 9 does not simply mean 'I the speaker' but 'I as a (presumed heterosexual) girl'. Using this 'I', Mary extracts herself from the category 'girl' named at line 5 in order to display that, in choosing Tom, who is 'uphill', her conduct is normative for her categorical membership. Note that Mary's turn at line 9 is 'so' prefaced – an upshot marker, conveying that it is *because* she is a girl that she has gone 'uphill' (and because Dan is a boy, he has gone 'downhill').

Discussion

Looking across these extracts and others like them in the collection, it is possible to offer tentative observations common to them all. First, it is evident in all cases that the gendered 'I' occurs in an environment in which gender has already 'crept into' the talk (Hopper & LeBaron, 1998: 59). In Extract 9, gendered norms underpin the basis of Stan's complaint about comments on his long hair. In Extract 10, gender is obliquely present, though not yet explicitly, when Michael comments on how the norms of dating behaviour 'should' be. In Extract 11, gender is explicitly invoked in the reported words of comfort of a friend following Mary's breakup. In each case speakers are producing and managing gendered norms – and particularly the relevance these have for themselves as individuals.

- Stan (Extract 9) is resisting gender stereotypes in relation to hair-length.
- Michael (Extract 10) is (jokingly) reproducing and resisting hetero-gendered norms in relation to paying for dates with girls.
- Mary (Extract 11) is reporting and embracing for herself a gendered claim – that girls choose better male partners after a breakup.

The gendered world reflected and produced by these social members is a world in which hair is a contested site of gendered identity (see Toerien & Wilkinson, 2003), women and girls are not expected to pay their own way on heterosexual dates, and boys are (see Rose & Frieze, 1989), and girls apparently learn from the mistakes of past heterosexual relationships, and boys do not. All these rely upon and reproduce a common understanding of what it means to be a gendered male or female in a social world. The gendered identities produced by each speaker are emergent, locally occasioned features of ongoing talk-in-interaction. That is, although each speaker *is* a member of a gendered category (as well as others), it is in part with and through the use of a gendered 'I' that Stan, Michael and Mary (Extracts 9, 10 and 11 respectively) become *relevantly* gendered in the talk.

This finding contributes to the feminist conversation analytic distinction between terms in language that are gendered by virtue of their linguistic definition and those that are gendered interactionally by and for the participants in talk. The self-reference 'I' is linguistically gender-neutral, but I have shown instances where its use is hearably interactionally gendered; where it means 'I as a male' or 'I as a female'.[10]

The gendered 'I' also shows that there is more to be said about uses of 'I' than as a self-reference *simpliciter*. It demonstrates that, far from 'masking' categorical information about the speaker (Schegloff, 1996c), 'I' *can* hearably and relevantly convey categorical information – here gender – by virtue of the context of its production. Furthermore, it is likely that speakers can use 'I' to refer to themselves as members of categories other than gender, such as class, race, professional status and so on. My collection includes at least one example of an age-relevant 'I' (reproduced as Extract 12), in which a speaker uses 'I' to produce herself as an older person. In this extract, an age norm gets produced as part of a complaint by Penny about her stepmother, Mandy, and occasions a speaker – Mum – to produce herself as an exception to the reported 'rule' that older people do not find the British comedian and presenter Russell Brand amusing. In this instance, the self-reference 'I' at line 25 hearably conveys the speaker's *age* category.

---

[10] In developing this argument, it is my intention to explore uses of gendered 'you'. As a preliminary to this work, I was pleased to notice the following occurrence of a 'female you' in the by-line on the cover of the March 2008 UK edition of the women's magazine *Cosmopolitan*, which read: 'The truth! The sex advice men wish you knew'.

Extract 12 CTS29

```
01   Pen:      Yeah she's just like it it was just
02             unbelie:vable what she what she-
03             You know that Russell Brand Mum.
04   Mum:      Yeah::
05   Pen:      She said the same thing about him.
06             He came on after after it[and] I=
07   Mum:                              [W- ]
08   Pen:      went(0.6)erm me and Stan were saying=
09             like 'Oh he's funny' and everything.
10   Mum:      [Yeah      ]
11   Pen:      [She was go]ing 'YOU only think that
12             becau::se (0.4)
13   Mum:      Oh[hhhh::::          ]
14   Pen:        [He's- he's a bit diff]eren[t   ]=
15   Mum:                                    [Ha]=
16   Pen:      =[But when you're young] (0.5)
17   Mum:      =[Ha ha               ]
18   Pen:      [them kind of things     ] do appeal to you.
19   Mum:      [.hhhhhh                  ]
20   Pen:      [When you- ] But when you get ol:d=
21   Mum:      [#Right     ]
22   Pen:      you sort of think (0.4)No:: you wa-
23             you like a bit more of a mature humour and
24             stuff' and I'm like 'fuck o:ff:.'
25   Mum:      Well I: think he's really funn↑y::
```

In this extract Mum resists the suggestion that 'old' people would necessarily view Russell Brand as performing a style of comedy for the young or immature by producing herself as an 'old' person who nevertheless finds the broadcaster 'really funny' (note the upgrade in assessment here from Penny's 'funny' at line 9, signalling agreement; Pomerantz, 1984a). Mum accomplishes this, in part, through the use of the singular self-reference 'I'. As a whole, the turn at line 25 produces Mum as a co-member (with Mandy) of the category 'old' but conveys her views as contrastive to Mandy's. Note that Mum is not claiming that she is somehow young at heart, because to do so would be to support Mandy's reported position. Rather Mum is challenging the reported claim that it is normative for the category of 'older people', of which she is one, to find appreciation of Russell Brand's humour immature.

It is worth noting that in three of the four instances of a categorised 'I', the speakers appear to be extracting themselves from a category in order to resist category-relevant norms. Given, however tentatively, that this sort of categorized self-reference appears to be occasioned by talk about normative conduct and its implications for individuals, then the practice may illuminate social-scientific debates about the relationship between self (or selves) and society.

As Goffman (1961:175) observes, if every social category 'implies a broad conception of the person tied by it, we should go on to ask how the individual handles this defining of himself'. I have shown how speakers handle this by resisting (or in one example, embracing) category-normative conduct in relation to gender (and age) as a situated practice.

Finally, then, the work in this chapter contributes to conversation analytic understanding of self-reference by showing that this reference *simpliciter* can convey categorical information about the speaker. This work also extends the literature on gender and language by showing just one of the resources speakers have to produce themselves as gendered without having to name the category.

3   Categories in talk-in-interaction: Gendering speaker and recipient

Victoria Land and Celia Kitzinger

Introduction

Social scientists and linguists have sometimes written about 'men's talk' (Coates, 2003), 'women's talk' (Coates, 1996), 'lesbians' talk' (Morgan & Wood, 1995) or 'gay men's talk' (Leap, 1996) as though the fact that the speakers whose talk is being analysed *are* men, or women, or gay is sufficient warrant for analysing their talk as such. But, as Schegloff (1997, following Sacks, 1972) has famously pointed out, any given individual can be characterized by a wide range of category terms taken from many different category sets, including, for example, gender, sexuality, political alignment, ethnicity, age, nationality, religion, occupation, place of residence, health status, family position and so on. One consequence of this is that we cannot explain the selection of any given category term simply 'by saying that they are, after all, such a one' (Schegloff, 1997: 165). The speaker who *is* a 'woman' is also, for example, a lesbian, a Pagan, an environmentalist, a diabetic, a sister and so on. There is always a range of different characterizations of any one person, all of which are equally 'true'.

Since Schegloff (1997) highlighted the analytical implications of speakers' multiple category memberships, there has been a concerted effort to locate analytic criteria on the basis of which a speaker can legitimately be heard to be speaking as a member of one category rather than another (e.g., Antaki & Widdicombe, 1998; Kitzinger, 2000a; 2006; 2007b; Speer, 2005b; Stokoe, 2005; Wilkinson & Kitzinger, 2003; 2007). This chapter makes three key contributions to that area.

First, ever since Sacks's early work (1972) analysing 'The baby cried. The mommy picked it up', most research across conversation analysis (CA), membership categorization analysis (MCA) and discursive psychology (DP) has focused on the categorization of non-present third parties (e.g., Edwards, 1998; Kitzinger & Rickford, 2007; Stockill & Kitzinger, 2007; Stokoe, 2004; Wilkinson & Kitzinger, 2003; but see Kitzinger, 2007b; Land & Kitzinger, 2007; Lerner & Kitzinger, 2007b, for work focusing on speaker and/or recipient). This is because third persons are often described or referred to using non-recognitional forms which take the form of categories ('the old guy', 'the white woman', 'the teenager', etc.), whereas first and second person reference is normally done without naming a category (e.g., 'I', 'we', 'you'; Schegloff, 1996c). Here, by contrast, we focus on first person categorization, that is, on the ways in which speakers explicitly label themselves as members of particular categories in the course of talk-in-interaction. The limited amount of research that has addressed this mostly deals with institutional talk, in settings in which particular categorical identities are made relevant by context and topic (e.g., Berard, 2005; West & Fenstermaker, 2002b; see also Kitzinger, 2006; 2007b).

Second, a great deal of the research on identity categories has used interviews, focus groups or other forms of research-generated material as its database – for example, Watson and Weinberg's (1982) study of how male interviewees produced themselves as 'homosexual' and 'bisexual' over the course of interviews with a 'straight' interviewer, and Widdicombe's (1998) study of how people who are potentially visibly analysable as members of specific youth subcultures come to categorize themselves – or not – in response to interviewers' questions. Similarly, Speer (2005b) used pictorial prompts of people engaged in leisure activities conventionally not associated with their gender 'as a resource to provoke and facilitate discussion of gender issues' (p. 70),[1] and Edley and Wetherell (2001) examined focus-group talk in which they found competing repertoires for the way in which feminism and feminists are constructed. Although these studies are influenced by MCA and CA, the data that they use are to a greater or lesser extent manipulated by the researcher through the use of questions and prompts. We cannot know in advance whether or not – and how – the use of non-naturalistic data is procedurally consequential for participant self-categorisation. Our own study is based on naturalistic data and explores how people orient to and deploy categorization in the course of their mundane social activities (see also Stokoe, 2008a; 2009; Stokoe & Edwards, 2007).

Third, a key contribution is that we show how – and in the interests of what interactional goals – the same person self-categorizes at different interactional moments. Crucially, it is not just that people *can* produce themselves as members of diverse different categories but that they *do* so. Although there are undoubtedly other ways in which speakers produce themselves as categorical members (e.g., see Wilkinson & Kitzinger, 2003), our focus here is on occasions on which speakers *name* these categories (such as 'woman', 'student' and 'gay male'), and in most of the examples we cite, speakers are oriented specifically to the action of locating themselves in those categories: that is, they say things like 'I'm a schizophrenic' (Extract 2) or 'We're all queer' (Extract 3).

The data extracts used in this chapter are taken from the Land corpus, a collection of more than 150 recorded ordinary telephone conversations in which at least one participant is lesbian. The data were collected by advertising for

---

[1] Note that this research was completed as part of Speer's PhD, supervised by Celia Kitzinger, who explicitly advised the use of picture prompts.

volunteers who self-identified as lesbian, gay, bisexual or transgender (LGBT) and who were willing to record the everyday telephone conversations to and from their homes for conversation analytic research.[2] As it happened, all the volunteers were women and lesbians: the resulting sample of participants comprised five lesbian volunteers and their lesbian, gay and heterosexual co-conversationalists – along with some whose sexuality never becomes apparent. Traditionally, research in the interdisciplinary field of gender studies has analysed talk by women for what it reveals about 'women's talk', irrespective of whether or not the speakers are oriented to speaking as such (Coates, 2004; Fishman, 1978; Lakoff, 1975; Maltz & Borker, 1998; Spender, 1980; Tannen, 1997; 1998). Likewise, talk by men has been analysed as 'men's talk' (Coates, 2003). Here we treat participants' own orientations to their own and each other's category memberships as crucial and show that the women (and the man) in our data set are not necessarily speaking *as* women (or a man): sometimes they are relevantly women (or a man) and sometimes they are not.

Categorizing the self

Rebecca: 'Woman' and 'schizophrenic'

The following two data extracts involve the same speaker, Rebecca. In the first extract, she produces herself as a woman; in the second, as a schizophrenic. In Extract 1, Rebecca is relevantly a 'woman'. At line 1 she is launching a new sequence, telling her mother about the name proposed for her putative painting and decorating company: its name, pseudonymized as 'Joy about your House', is a pun on her surname, pseudonymized as 'Joy'. After some interactional difficulty caused by Mum having apparently not remembered Rebecca's plans to launch a company, Rebecca elaborates on these plans, describing how she proposes to advertise her services. In so doing, she produces herself as a member of the category 'woman': elderly women, she says, 'might rather have a woman doing .hh doing their hou:ses up' (lines 29–30).

Extract 1 Rebecca: woman
[Land:SW76]
```
01  Reb:  .hhhh An' names- uh (na-/m-) Steve has already
02        named my company
03               (0.5)
04  Mum:  'As 'e?
05  Reb:  Ye:s.
```

[2] Consent forms were completed by each of the people who volunteered to record their calls. The consent form allowed participants to specify the ways in which they were happy for the data to be used. The form also reminded participants of the legal obligation to seek permission from their co-conversationalist to tape the calls (also explained in the accompanying letter). The co-conversationalists gave oral consent.

```
06                    (.)
07   Mum:    [ (Wh-) ]
08   Reb:    [For me.]
09   Mum:    Who?
10   Reb:    Steve.=My psychologis[t.
11   Mum:                        [Yeah what's he named
12   Reb:    JOY ABOUT YOUR HOUSE
13                    (1.2)
14   Mum:    °Joy about your house.°
15   Reb:    Yeah. B'cause I'll be doing painting an'
16           decorat[ing won't I?]
17   Mum:           [Of cou:rse y]eah. That's right. Yeah
18   Reb:    That's (a) good one i'n't it?
19   Mum:    Yeah that is a good. O[ne.
20   Reb:                          [Yeah.
21   Mum:    Yea[h. Mm (right)
22   Reb:       [((sniff)) ((cough)) So that's what I'm gonna
23           call it
24   Mum:    Good. Oh we[ll that's-]
25   Reb:               [ Make li]ttle cards up and
26           pu[t through]
27   Mum:    [ Y e a h ] Yeah. [That's right]
28   Reb:               [ .h h h    ]'Specially
29           for like elderly women because they might rather
30           have a woman [doing .hh [doing their hou:]ses up=
31   Mum:                 [ Yes  yes [ That's °true°   ]
32   Mum:    =Yeah that's true yeah pensioners and
33           [people] like that
34   Reb:    [ Mm ]
35   Mum:    Oh well that's g[ood then.]
36   Reb:                    [ .h h h  ] Do it cheap if they
37           buy the paint. An' I'll do [it chea]p for 'em.
38   Mum:                               [ Yeah ]
39   Mum:    Yeah. That's right love. Y[eah oh well [( )
40   Reb:                              [ .h h h     [So uh:
41   Reb:    So yeah so no other news. I'm going to do
42           Lorraine's housework today ((continues))
```

Rebecca's sequence-opening turn (lines 1–2) embodies two presuppositions: that her proposed 'company' is not news to Mum and that Mum knows who Steve is. As it turns out, it is not clear that Mum has remembered anything about Rebecca's putative company, and despite her forwarding action in line 4 (which claims adequate understanding of the prior turn), she subsequently initiates repair three times before grasping that Rebecca is talking about her proposed painting and decorating company. Rebecca treats Mum's first repair initiation ('who', line 9) as a failure in recognizing the person referred to as

'Steve' (not unreasonably, since 'who' targets a person, and Steve is the only person referred to in Rebecca's immediately prior talk). However, Mum's second repair initiation ('what's he named', line 11) clearly targets the 'company' as the trouble source and this turn is hearable as a redone repair targeting, more precisely, the same trouble source as the first. When Rebecca responds by reporting the name Steve has invented for her putative company, and not with a repair solution such as a repeat of 'my company' or some more elaborate version such as 'the painting and decorating company I'm going to set up, remember?', Mum produces a third repair initiation which targets the whole of Rebecca's prior turn ('Joy about your house', line 14), displaying she has heard it, and can accurately repeat it, but claiming that it makes no sense to her. Only when Rebecca reminds her what kind of business she is planning ('painting and' decorating', lines 15–16), does Mum apparently 'get it'. Once Mum has grasped Rebecca's telling (that is, the name Steve has suggested for her prospective painting and decorating business), an assessment of the name is due, but Mum has to be prompted to provide this (line 18).

Rebecca's subsequent topic talk about her proposed company is, then, produced in an environment of scepticism from her interlocutor. She is describing her business plans so as to make her putative company plausible to Mum, who – as we can see from her multiple repair initiations – had evidently taken her daughter's proposals to launch a new company so lightly as to have forgotten them entirely and, even when reminded, has to be prompted to display enthusiasm of any kind. It is in the course of this topic talk, and in service of highlighting a promotional aspect of the business to a less-than-enthusiastic recipient, that Rebecca makes relevant her categorical membership as a woman (line 30). She does not label herself directly as a 'woman', but rather begins with reference to another category of people, 'elderly women' (line 29), who she claims 'might rather have a woman doing … their houses up' (lines 29–30). Rebecca uses the term 'woman' (line 30) to allude to herself by invoking a category of which she is relevantly a member, ' "relevantly" given what is going on at that moment in the interaction' (Schegloff, 2007d: 36). That is, Rebecca produces elderly women as preferring as a decorator not herself as an individual but rather any incumbent of the category 'women', and it is only because of the context that Rebecca *in particular* is alluded to. Rebecca deploys this category here in service of promoting a selling point of her proposed business in comparison with the (presumed male) competition, and in particular to building up her customer base, especially given her mother's apparent failure to take seriously Rebecca's proposition (as displayed through her lack of recollection and lack of enthusiasm). Mum de-genders and therefore broadens the category to include all elderly people (suggesting it is their age that is salient to preferring a woman decorator and not their gender). Mum, however, does not contest the relevance of Rebecca's production of herself as a woman.

In Extract 2, Rebecca produces herself as a schizophrenic. Feminist and other critical analyses of diagnostic categories have focused on the use of mental illness labels as a form of social control, to stigmatize and invalidate persons so labelled (e.g., Chesler, 1972; Smith, 1978), but here Rebecca adopts that label for herself. She has called the Benefit Enquiry Line[3] to request information to help her make a claim for Disability Living Allowance (DLA),[4] and speaks to a call-taker (Ctr). At line 25 she states: 'I'm a schizophrenic.'

Extract 2 Rebecca: schizophrenic

[Land: SW53]

```
01   Reb:   I- I'm not actually su:re what I'm entitled to.=
02          Uhm .hh On uhm uhm tcht off: work now. >I have
03          been off work since< Novembe:r. .hh A:nd (.)
04          they've signed me off uhm on indefinite
05          sick until uhm (.) October the twenty
06          ninth two thousand and fou:r.
07   Ctr:   [Ri:ght.]
08   Reb:   [ .hhhh ] I'm only gettin' income suppo:rt a:nd
09          my- I've been to my psychologist today and I see
10          a psychiatrist. .hh But >the thing is< I
11          can't go out alone, I have to get taxis
12          everywhere and I'm finding it very hard
13          .hhhh to li:ve. On the mone:y. .hh And they-
14          they('ve) said that I should be entitled to
15          disability living allowance?=But I (.)
16          y'know I don't know what I'm entitled to:.
17   Ctr:   Oh okay yeah. <Disability living
18          allowance is paid to people who 'ave
19          problems either wi:th >y'know< mobility
20          getting about o:r their personal ca:re needs.
21   Reb:   Yeah=
22   Ctr:   =An' it- it can be paid to people who
23          'a:ve u:h y'know mental health [prob[lems.]
24   Reb:                                   [.hhh[ Well]
25          that's it.=I'm a schizophre:ni[c:.  hh]
26   Ctr:                                  [°Yeah°]
27   Ctr:   So I- D'you want me to send the forms out for
28          you?=
29   Reb:   =Yes plea:se
```

---

[3] An information helpline provided for people wishing to make enquiries about which UK government-ment benefits (if any) they may be entitled to receive.
[4] A government allowance paid to people with disabilities in the UK.

In this extract, Rebecca does not request information about benefits directly: rather, she instead describes her circumstances (at lines 1–16) thereby making relevant an offer of information from her recipient (produced at lines 27–8). Although Rebecca subsequently labels herself as 'a schizophrenic' (line 25), in formulating her circumstances she does not initially produce herself in categorical terms, but describes her individual circumstances: being on 'indefinite sick' leave (lines 4–5), being unable to go out alone (lines 10–11), her dependence on taxis (lines 11–12) and finding it 'hard to live on the money' (lines 12–13). Through mentioning her 'psychologist' (line 9) and 'psychiatrist' (line 10), she makes available the inference that she has mental health problems, but without categorically so defining herself.[5] In response, the call-taker explains DLA-eligibility criteria with reference to *categories* of people: first 'people who 'ave problems either with … mobility getting about or their personal care needs' (line 18–20) (recipient-designed for a caller who has described not being able to 'go out alone' (line 11) and the necessity of her 'hav[ing] to get taxis' (line 11)); and second, 'people who 'ave … mental health problems' (lines 22–3) as a subset of this first category (i.e., eligibility criteria permit a claimant's mobility problems to be of a psychological rather than purely physical nature). Rebecca treats this latter category as one to which she belongs and labels herself as 'a schizophrenic' (line 25). By positioning herself as a member of a category included under the umbrella category of 'people who 'ave … mental health problems' (lines 22–3) she makes a bid to forward the action she is pursuing (i.e., being accepted as someone who is entitled to make a claim for DLA). Rebecca's production of herself as a member of the category 'schizophrenics' displays her understanding that it is under these auspices that she is eligible to make a claim. It has been argued that '[t]he danger of the insanity ascription for the would-be rational actor is that it removes the agency from the actor's acts' (Eglin & Hester, 1999: 259) – and that is undoubtedly true in many cases. Yet, here, Rebecca is acting agentically and claiming this mental illness category in her own self-interest.

In sum, then, although Rebecca is known to be a woman (by herself, by her recipients and by us as analysts), she is not *relevantly* a woman in this interaction. The call-taker may be able to discern her membership in the category 'women' from the quality of her voice but he does not display any orientation to this in the talk. The fact that she is a woman is not demonstrably interactionally relevant to Rebecca (or to the call-taker) in this interaction, presumably because it has no bearing on her eligibility for DLA. Here, then, Rebecca's relevant categorizations are 'person with mobility problems' and 'schizophrenic'.

---

[5] Similarly, Sacks (1992: 47) analyses an instance in which a caller to a helpline uses indirect references to lifestyle choices in a bid to make available the inference of his homosexuality to his interlocutor.

Note that in overtly labelling herself ('I'm a schizophrenic', line 25) 'schizophrenic' is not used here as a person reference term. Person reference is achieved with 'I', and 'schizophrenic' is 'doing describing' (see Schegloff, 2007d: 27) in so far as it describes the relevant feature of the person referred to. By contrast, in Extract 1 Rebecca's self-categorization was more subtle – a form comparable to that used in Extract 2 would have been 'I'm a woman' – but it was not attended to as troublesome by either speaker or recipient. It is the interactional context and the attention to recipient design that contribute to this being heard unproblematically as indexing Rebecca's membership in the category 'women'. This understanding is dependent on the participants' shared, taken-for-granted knowledge that Rebecca *is* a woman. This method for categorizing requires a recipient to hear a statement about a category (or categories) of people and then work out that the speaker is invoking her membership in that category. So, when Rebecca says ''specially for like elderly women because they might rather have a woman doing … their houses up' (lines 28–30) she is requiring Mum to achieve the logical conclusion; that is, 'Rebecca is a woman', therefore 'elderly women might rather have Rebecca (than a man) doing their houses up'. In the remainder of this chapter we will be examining only categories that (like 'schizophrenic' in Extract 2) are being used to describe (rather than refer to) the speaker.

Finally, notice that in Extract 1 it is clear that Mum already knew why Rebecca meets with a psychologist, so that when Rebecca mentions her psychologist in the course of this sequence (lines 1 and 10) she refreshes this information and thereby makes available her membership in the category 'schizophrenics'. However, even though there is evidence of this in the talk, Rebecca is not oriented to her membership in this category as relevant here – unlike in Extract 2. Foregrounding her as a person with schizophrenia in Extract 1 would not achieve the same interactional outcome in this talk as her production of herself as a woman does. Although the suggested business name is built off Rebecca's surname and it was she who invoked her membership in the category 'women' (rather than its being incorporated into the name), her psychologist could have suggested 'Mad about your house' as an alternative name for her painting and decorating business. In this case, the emphasis would have been on her mental illness. Having a woman about the house is built as a promotional point for a painting and decorating business, particularly one that is aimed at the elderly. It is perhaps unlikely that having a schizophrenic around the house (even though this would also be the case – Rebecca does not stop being 'a schizophrenic' just because some other category is made salient) would be produced as a selling point. The invocation of this category membership in this interaction would have been potentially detrimental to the business under way – that is, promoting her business to her mother.

Karen: 'Woman' and 'queer'; 'committee member'; and 'student'

In the following three data extracts the same speaker, Karen, categorizes herself in three different ways; as 'queer', as 'a committee member' and as 'a student'. In Extract 3, we show that even though there is reference to Karen's (and her interlocutor's) membership in the category 'women', she is oriented to and produces herself and her co-conversationalist, Becky, as 'queer'. Karen and Becky are talking about Peter, a tutor they both like at the college where both are studying for a social work qualification. Pondering the question of why other students are 'quite down on 'im' (line 2) or even 'really pissed off' (line 3) with him, Karen explains this with reference to the fact that three of the people who 'find him really good to work with' (herself, her co-conversationalist and a third person, Paula, lines 26–7) are 'all queer' (line 29), whereas it may be that those who are complaining about him are 'straight' (line 34).

Extract 3 Karen: queer
[Land:NE21]

```
01  Kar:   Some people 'ave- I mean some people are
02         quite down on 'im.=Some thee other day
03         were really pissed off abou' 'im.=
04         I thou- I thought I ca- I don't get
05         this at all 'cause 'e's only ever
06         been 'elpful wi' me.
07  Bec:   I think 'e's lovely:.
08  Kar:   Mm.
09  Bec:   'E's really really ni:ce.
10  Kar:   °I do°=(Act-) <To be honest [y'know I-]
11  Bec:                           [He's yer ]
12         personal tutor i'n't 'e?
13  Kar:   Mine.=Ye[ah. ]
14  Bec:       [ Ye]ah. [(  )]
15  Kar:              [An'] 'e's [yours as well]=
16  Bec:                    [ An'  mine  ]=
17         [ yea:h. ]
18  Kar:   [i'n't 'e¿] An' Paula's.
19  Bec:   Yes. Huh huh huh huh [.hhhh (  (h)      (h)      )]=
20  Kar:                        [D'yih know what I wonder?]
21  Bec:   =on pur(h)pose. [huh huh huh]
22  Kar:                   [ D'yih know] what I wonder wi' 'im
23  Bec:   [Wha(h)t.]
24  Kar:   [Well if  ] yih think about it.=I mean
25         'cause I know y- you ged on wi' 'im.=
26         An' you find 'im really good to work
27         with.=S[o does Paula. .hhh =Well=
28  Bec:          [°'Eah°
29  Kar:   =we're all queer.
```

```
30  Bec:   Ye(h)ah heh heh [heh heh     ]
31  Kar:                   [W- Hah ha]h hah .hh Well (.)
32          y'know wha' I wonder is if the other
33          women who I've heard complainin' they're
34          straight.
35                  (0.2)
36  Kar:   .hhh An' (.) an' I'm- it's got nothing tuh do
37          wi'- I don't mean tha' I don't think- I'm
38          not saying that it's a straight gay thing
39          [ bu::t (.) ] Peter's that far down t'roa:d=
40  Bec:   [('tis a bit)]
41  Kar:   =of understanding particular feminis:t
42          (.) uh pract[ices.=Right into feminist
43          ((continues))
```

Initially those who do not get on with Peter are produced only in the most general category 'some people' (line 1) and their attitude is contrasted with the speaker (Karen, lines 4–6), her co-conversationalist (Becky, who agrees that he is 'lovely', line 7, and 'really really nice', line 9) and – by implication – that of a third party (Paula, line 18), all of whom have Peter as a personal tutor. Becky treats the mention of Paula as another of Peter's tutees as laughable (line 19) and (although Karen does not display any grasp of it at this point) from what transpires next it is very likely that Becky is here orienting to the categorical membership that she, Karen and Paula have in common (as 'queers'), adopting a stance towards it without naming the category. What Becky says after laughing is lost in overlap but it appears that she is providing an account for her laughter (the laughter continues through this turn) and alluding to something that the three of them (Becky, Karen and Paula) share in common such that their all being Peter's students may have been arranged 'on purpose' (line 21). That categorical membership that all three share in common is what Karen then undertakes to expound in her next turn.

After a redone pre-telling (line 22, redone version of line 20) and preface 'well if yih think about it' (line 24), Karen restates that Becky 'ged[s] on wi' 'im' (line 25) and 'so does Paula' (line 27). She does not reiterate her liking for Peter but she includes herself in the connection she produces between them: 'well we're all queer' (lines 27 and 29). Similar to the way in which Rebecca produced herself as 'a schizophrenic' in Extract 2, Karen's deployment of 'queer' is here 'doing describing' (Schegloff, 2007d: 27). The inference is that membership in the category 'queer' is the solution to the puzzle regarding why some people get on with him and others do not. Becky's 'yeah' and laughter (line 30) confirm Karen's connection and in so doing she aligns with Karen about the relevance of the category 'queer' on this occasion.

Despite Becky's response Karen continues by spelling out precisely what it would take for their sexuality to partition effectively those who like Peter from those who do not. That is, Karen speculates about the sexuality of those who have complained about him, suggesting that they may be straight (lines 31–4). In so doing, Karen transforms the 'people' (line 1) who do not get on with Peter into 'women' (line 33) – although it is not clear that 'women' is relevantly gendered at this point in the interaction (see Kitzinger, 2007b). That is, although they are referred to using a gendered term – which also produces the speaker (and her recipient and the non-present third person, Paula) as a gendered female – it is not (at this point in the interaction) treated as relevant to the course of the action undertaken at this point; that is, solving the puzzle regarding why some of their fellow students do not like a particular tutor that they (Karen, Becky and Paula) find likeable and inspiring. The relevant contrast is at this point analysably 'a straight gay thing' (line 38) – an analysis that the speaker herself displays in the act of disclaiming it. However, the selection of 'women' rather than the gender-neutral 'people' (used earlier, line 1) may be relevant to the subsequent claim about Peter's understanding of 'feminist practices' (and indeed the question of whether it is as 'women' or as 'gays' that people like or dislike Peter's course becomes overt later in this conversation (data not shown)).

In Extract 4, the same speaker, Karen, labels herself as a 'student'. This extract is taken from 45 minutes into a call between Karen and another friend, Cheryl. Karen launches a new sequence with a bid to close the call (line 1) and an account for the proposed action (lines 1–3). The sequence analysed here is a repair sequence that follows. Karen's turn accounting for wanting to close the conversation – that is, she was reprimanded by the telephone company (BT[6]) for being on the telephone too long – contains the trouble source.

Extract 4 Karen: student

[Land:NE4]

```
01   Kar:   Anyway I better ger off me 'cause I got told
02          off by Bee Tee t'other day.=Being on t'phone.
03          .hhh for a length of time so hh
04   Che:   By Bee Tee?
05   Kar:   .hhh Well I've got one of them limit things=
06          Y'know well 'cause of being a stu:dent I mean
07          it- it's sometime it's just bloody 'ard to pay
08          your phone bill y'know so=
09   Che:   =What you on w[i- free after six o'clock one
10   Kar:                 [(  )
11   Kar:   No: I 'aven't got onto that yet
```

Cheryl's repair initiator (line 4) marks 'by Bee Tee' as a trouble source in Karen's prior turn. Implicitly, Cheryl is treating being on the telephone for a long time

---

[6] BT is a UK telephone company (previously known as British Telecom).

as something that might warrant reprimand but the source of the reproach as unusual or problematic. Karen treats it this way too since she does not merely confirm that it was BT but, rather, explains why the telephone company is in a position to reprimand her about the length of time that she spends making telephone calls. That is, she has arranged a limit with the company to prevent her bill from being too expensive.[7] She immediately continues with an account for why she has arranged a limit on her telephone bill: that is, 'being a student' (line 6) makes it 'bloody 'ard to pay your phone bill' (lines 7–8). In this talk Karen invokes her membership in the category 'student' – explicitly naming it, and then using a generic 'your' (where 'my' could have been deployed) – to display that she is indexing the attributes of 'students' in general to account for her financial position. Like Extracts 2 and 3, the category term is not being used to do person reference but, rather, it is 'doing describing'. Research on the economic position of women vis-à-vis men suggests that, because of the gender gap in wages (Fawcett Society, 2005) and discrimination in the workplace (Macpherson & Hirsch, 1995) women have a relatively poor economic position. Here, then, it could be argued that Karen's gender is a relevant factor in her difficult financial position: however, this is not what she is orienting to and making interactionally relevant in her account. This is not to suggest that Karen is able to provide the definitive explanation for her economic situation, but by the same token it should not be assumed that the external observer should be allowed to specify what category from the many of which Karen is a member is relevant here. The concern is not the 'actual' cause of Karen's economic position; rather, it is relevant that in this interaction being a student is treated as a reasonable and understandable account for having difficulty paying a telephone bill. It is this category membership that Karen is producing as relevant in the ongoing interaction. None the less, Karen does not cease to be a woman simply because she is not displaying any orientation to her gender.

In Extract 5, Karen has phoned her uncle, Alfred, to make a request for him to give a presentation to the LGBT students at the university where Karen is a student. She is asking him to talk to the LGBT students about what it was like to be gay when Alfred was younger (apparently many years ago). Extract 5 is taken from the beginning of this call, immediately after the ethics exchange.

Extract 5 Karen: committee member
[Land:NE5b]
01   Kar: .hhhh Wh- what I'm ringing abou:t
02   actually mainly .hh is uhm y'know

---

[7] BT provide a service for their customers who may experience difficulty paying their telephone bill by allowing them to set a limit on the cost of each bill. Before customers reach their arranged limit, BT telephone them with a warning that the limit has almost been reached.

```
03   .       at Greentown Uni again.
04   Alf:    Yes.=
05   Kar:    =.hhh Well uh I've just been (.)
06           nominated onto thei:r uh (.) committee
07           uh which is for the lesbian gay bisexual
08           and transgendered students[:.
09   Alf:                              [Yeah.
10   Kar:    So it's what they call the Ell Gee Bee
11           Tee committee.
12   Alf:    Ye[:s.
13   Kar:      [.hhh An' anyway uhm what they do is
14           they meet on Tuesdee ni:ghts an' that's
15           just fer all: (.) y'know kind'v (        )
16           .hhhhh (.) y'know hh talks on either coming
17           ou:t or y'know [a- any kind'v Ell Gee=
18   Alf:                  [Yea:h.
19   Kar:    Bee Tee issues.=Anything l[ike that.
20   Alf:                              [Yeah.
21   Kar:    .hhhh An' then afterwards they go tuh
22           t'pub an' 'ave a social an' wha' 'ave
23           yih.=So I've been to quite a few'v
24           'em.
25   Alf:    Y[eah.
26   Kar:     [An' as I say I'm also a committee
27           member no:w. .hhhh Uhm <An' I 'ad this
28           idea I do(h)n't know- I just want tuh run it
29           by yih but .hhh do say 'no' obviously if
30           it dun't suit yih or- or- or wha'ever. .hh
31           But I- a lot of 'em are younger than me
32           obviously 'cause >they don't-< They're
33           like between twenny three twenny sixish
34           an' that.=But I've got to say they're
35           generally a really nice bunch of people.
36           .h[hh uhm An' the students who've=
37   Alf:      [Yeah.
38   Kar:    =been coming tuh t'meetings are y'know
39           quite friendly an' everything. .h[hhh
40   Alf:                                      [Mm.
```

This is a request sequence. At the outset Karen marks the main business of the call with 'what I'm ringing about actually mainly is ...' (lines 1–2), although she does not produce the request until much later in the conversation. Karen announces she has 'just been nominated onto their committee which is for the lesbian, gay, bisexual and transgendered students' (lines 5–8). Her concern is to ensure Albert is aware of what the LGBT committee is and she also explains what the committee does (lines 13–17, 19 and 21–3) and reports her attendance at these events (lines 23–4). Although Karen has already announced her new role on the LGBT committee earlier in the interaction (lines 5–6), she produces herself as 'a committee member' (lines 26–7), and therefore this is not news to Alfred at this interactional point but, rather, marks a return to the business of the call.

The categorization of herself as 'a committee member' (lines 26–7), which is 'doing describing', comes just after Karen has reported that she has attended many of the events organized by the LGBT committee (lines 23–4). Karen's production of 'now' after she describes herself as a committee member highlights her new role. This is an important distinction for Karen in this interaction since she is now in a position where she is required to organize events. The categorization of herself as a committee member is relevant in this interaction since this indicates that it is under these auspices that she is asking Alfred to come to the university to give a talk. Therefore, it is her role on the committee – rather than her role as an attendee – that is relevant on this occasion.

Of the three extracts (3–5) in which Karen is a participant, it is only in Extract 4 that Karen has labelled herself as a member of the category 'student'. However, in Extracts 3 and 5 her membership of this category is evident: in Extract 3 she is talking about people who are *students* who do and do not get on with Peter (a university tutor), and in Extract 5 Karen is a committee member on the committee for LGBT *students* – being a student is a prerequisite for being a committee member. Even though Karen is not always interactionally oriented to her membership in the category 'student', she does not cease being a student just because she is explicitly invoking some other category: the fact that she *is* a student remains available in the talk. Similarly, Karen's lesbianism is available since, in the same way that being a committee member (of the university's LGBT committee) is predicated on her being a student, it also requires her to be self-identified as lesbian, gay, bisexual or transgender. It is known from elsewhere in the data that Alfred is aware of Karen's lesbianism and here this information is refreshed in the talk. However, although it is available and necessary for her to be a member of the category she is producing herself as ('a committee member'), this is not sufficient for her lesbianism to be the most relevant category membership in the interaction (just as in Extract 1 Rebecca's schizophrenia was available in the talk without being the most relevant category). Clearly, then, the availability of a category membership is not necessarily sufficient warrant to claim that this membership is directly relevant to the participants at that particular interactional location. It may be simply presumed as known-in-common – part of the 'backdrop' of the conversation rather than a focal action.

In Extracts 1–5, speakers invoke their membership in some category ('woman', 'schizophrenic', 'queer', 'student' and 'committee member') by naming the category and positioning themselves as a member of that group.

In Extract 1 categorization is achieved through Rebecca's use of the term 'woman' to allude to herself, and in Extracts 2–5 speakers' deployment of category terms are 'doing describing' (Schegloff, 2007d: 27). Speakers orient to different category memberships as relevant on different interactional occasions depending on the action being pursued in the local context. So it is not only that speakers *can* self-categorize in multiple ways, but also that they *do* self-categorize in multiple ways. The gender of these speakers is not always treated as relevant by the participants, who instead invoke alternative category memberships. The risk for analysts who treat female speakers always and only as 'women' is, then, that they may be disregarding what – for the speakers themselves – is their most salient identity at that moment ('schizophrenic', 'student', 'committee member', etc.).

Finally, we have shown that there is often evidence of alternative category memberships in talk in which some other category is being oriented to as part of the focal action. For example, in Extract 1, in which Rebecca alluded to herself with the category term 'woman' to promote her proposed painting and decorating business, the speaker's schizophrenia is also available through her reference to her psychiatrist (at least to Mum as a knowledgeable recipient). Likewise, in Extract 5, in which Karen is building up to requesting her uncle to give a talk, there is evidence of Karen's lesbianism in her claim to be 'a committee member' (of the LGBT committee). These alternative categories are presumed to be known-in-common and made available as part of the recipient design of the talk, without being recruited for the focal action. For us as analysts, then, evidence of category membership is not in and of itself sufficient to claim its relevance for the participants (see Kitzinger, 2005a, for examples of instances in which evidence of heterosexuality is available in talk but not oriented to as significant for the participants).

Conclusion

In this chapter, we have analysed instances in which speakers are engaged in self-categorization. Previous membership categorization and conversation analytic work on categorization has tended to focus on the categorization of third parties. Moreover, this existing research has overwhelmingly focused on the implication of categorization through the use of category terms to do person reference. That is, a category term such as 'the doctor' or 'the racist' is deployed to reference and categorize a person concurrently. By contrast, in this chapter person reference is almost always achieved independently from categorization. We have shown not only that categorization occurs in these naturalistic fragments of mundane conversation, but also *how* categorization is produced. Categorization has mostly been achieved (see 'schizophrenic', 'queer', 'student' and 'committee member') through the use of category terms to 'do describing' (see Schegloff, 2007d: 27), but see Land and Kitzinger (2007) for an analysis of descriptive self-reference, as in Extract 2.

We have shown that there are multiple layers of categories. People move between categories across stretches of interaction. In Extract 1, for instance, Rebecca's mention of her psychologist hints at her membership in the category 'schizophrenics' (for a knowing interlocutor such as Mum), but this is subsumed by Rebecca's subsequent direct categorization of herself as a 'woman'. Categories remain in the background when others rise to the surface, as has been illustrated in the analysis of Extract 3, in which Karen's (and Becky's) membership in the category 'student' is a prerequisite for a discussion of a relationship with one of their tutors even though this is background to her (and Becky's) categorization as 'queer', upon which the discussion is based. We have demonstrated that gender is not omnirelevant. Even when evidence of gender is in the talk it does not mean that this is the most salient or relevant category.

We have shown how – for specific local interactional goals – speakers locate themselves as gendered and as members of other social categories. The interactional aims of the participants in our data extracts are diverse: producing a selling point for a proposed business ('woman'); producing oneself as eligible for a government disability allowance ('schizophrenic'); providing an account for liking someone who is disliked by others ('queer'); accounting for difficulty paying a telephone bill ('student'); and establishing the auspices under which an upcoming request is being made ('committee member'). At least in our data (but see Stokoe, 2006), there is no correlation between the category that is invoked and the action that it is being used to do: rather, categories can be deployed to do any number of actions. However, on each occasion the category invokes and reinforces the category-bound attributes associated with that particular category. So, for example, that 'student' can be used unproblematically to account for difficulty paying a telephone bill displays that 'not having very much money' is an attribute associated with being a student – and it is reproduced in this usage. So, although particular categories do not have a predetermined set of actions they can be deployed to implement, the selection of a category must be culturally relevant and, therefore, this is one way in which culture can be available in talk.

This chapter, while not inherently 'political' per se, provides a rationale for exploring participant orientations *on their own terms*. In so doing, it demonstrates that we *can* do politically informed research *and* be sensitive to participants' orientations. We can see here that participants do spontaneously orient to category membership in their talk and this provides a justifiable warrant for us to represent them in these terms.

4   Doing gender categorization:
     Non-recognitional person reference and
     the omnirelevance of gender

Noa Logan Klein

Introduction

The questions of whether and how analysts of conversation should deal with
the genders of conversational participants and whether and how conversation
analytic methods can contribute to feminist research have recently been much
debated (on gender: Billig, 1999; Schegloff, 1997; 1998a; 1999; Stokoe &
Smithson, 2001; Wetherell, 1998; on feminism: Kitzinger, 2000a; Speer, 1999;
2005a). Ethnomethodologists and gender scholars have asserted that gender
is 'omnirelevant' in interaction at least since Garfinkel's (1967: 118) classic
study of 'Agnes' (see Weatherall, 2000; 2002b; West & Fenstermaker, 1995).
Because the primary interest of conversation analysis has been to explicate the
context-free organizations that enable interaction, conversation analysts have
only more recently begun to address the context-specific ways in which gender is consequential for talk-in-interaction (see Jefferson, 2004a; Kitzinger,
2005a; 2005b; Land & Kitzinger, 2005). This chapter works to bridge the divide between gender theory and conversation analytic method by explicating
how and why speakers do gender categorization in non-recognitional person
reference. I explain why non-recognitional reference is a particularly important site for the classification of persons, and I argue that doing gender categorization at this site is normative. To understand how gender categorization
comes to be 'relevant' in interaction, I introduce a distinction between action
relevance – where a categorization is warranted by its 'inference-rich' (Sacks,
1992: 40) contribution to a speaker's meaning – and system relevance – where
a categorization is warranted by the organization and interactional contingencies of person reference itself. I argue that gender categorization, in addition to
being action relevant, is uniquely system relevant in non-recognitional reference, and I illustrate the procedural consequences of these dual relevances for
conversational interaction. Finally, I suggest that the systematic relevance of

I would like to thank Karl Bryant, Mary Bucholtz, Sarah Fenstermaker, Gene Lerner, Leila
Rupp, Verta Taylor and especially Geoff Raymond for commentary on earlier drafts of this chap-
ter. Thanks also to Jeff Robinson, Barbara Fox and the Language Use and Social Interaction
(LUSI) Museum for making data available to me. All shortcomings are, of course, my own.

gender categorization in non-recognitional person reference has far-reaching implications for the omnirelevance of gender as a daily performance and a social institution.

Data collection

The data analysed here are excerpts taken from existing video- and audio-taped collections of naturally occurring conversations. Instances of person reference were collected from seven video-tapes, each approximately one hour in length, and several shorter audio-tapes of telephone conversations. Video- and audio-tapes used were collected between the 1970s and the 2000s in various parts of the USA. Most participants knew one another prior to the recorded interactions, others did not. One hundred and five instances of non-recognitional person reference were catalogued, in addition to twenty-four cases of recognitional person reference.

Categorization and person reference

Schegloff (1996c: 439) provides the most comprehensive available overview of the domain of person reference, focusing on how speakers and hearers accomplish person references such that on the one hand 'nothing but referring is being done, and/or on the other hand that something else in addition to referring is being done by the talk'. Speakers and hearers use the systematic organization of conversation to negotiate what counts as a 'simple' reference (Schegloff, 1996c: 440) where 'nothing but referring is being done', and this also allows them to produce and recognize person references that do something 'more than just' referring. According to Schegloff, the most basic way to divide up the realm of person reference is according to who is being referred to. A speaker can refer to (1) herself or himself, (2) one or more recipients of the talk or (3) a third party or parties. References to third parties can be further subdivided into references to (3a) present or (3b) non-present parties, and non-present parties can be referred to in two very different ways, with (3b1) recognitional or (3b2) non-recognitional references.

By using a recognitional person reference, a speaker can 'convey to the recipient that the one being referred to is someone that they know (about)', whereas non-recognitional references tell the recipient 'you don't know this person' (Schegloff, 1996c: 459). All references to (1) speakers, (2) recipients or (3a) third parties present in the conversation are recognitional references, in the sense that recipients can locate or 'know (about)' the person being talked about. Non-recognitional references to non-present parties (3b2) are of special analytic interest because they may or may not provide descriptive information about the person(s) referred to. Since achieving recognition by the recipient is not a relevant project for this type of person reference, non-recognitionals can act as information-free placeholders. A non-recognitional reference can simply say to its recipient, 'insert human being here'. Or, more commonly, some other conversational task may be accomplished simultaneously through the person reference.

One important outcome speakers can achieve within and through person references is the placement of people as members of social groups by characteristics such as race, gender,[1] occupation and relationship to the speaker. The English language furnishes speakers with a range of terms and practices for referring to people, many of which locate persons within such category sets. Through the interaction between these linguistic resources and the management of conversation as a moment-by-moment construction of shared meaning, speakers doing person reference demonstrate what kinds of people are believed to exist within their culture (Sacks, 1972; 1992: 40–8; Schegloff, 1996c). In what follows, I propose that gender categorization constitutes a minimum basic form of non-recognitional reference, making gender a – perhaps even the – central mechanism for classifying people in English-speaking cultures, both in talk-in-interaction and in the social world built from these interactions (see J. Butler, 1990a; Hawkesworth, 1997; Lorber, 1994; Scott, 1986). To illuminate the omnirelevance of gender categorization in non-recognitional person reference, I distinguish between two kinds of relevance: action relevance and system relevance.

Action relevance

The simple fact that someone can be accurately labeled as a member of a social category, such as women or men, is not grounds for referring to her or him in this way (Schegloff, 1997). Any one person is at the same time a member of multiple social groupings and can be categorized in a number of different ways, so some grounds other than accuracy must be operative when referring to a person as a member of one category rather than another. Social categories are 'inference-rich' (Sacks, 1992: 40), meaning that they can convey

[1] Much previous work dealing with gender categorization has used the term 'sex categorization' (e.g., West & Zimmerman, 1987). Sex and gender have been importantly separated by social scientists, but in everyday practice most people do not distinguish between sex and gender (Speer, 2005a: 62). Judith Butler (1990a: 7) notes that sex is 'always already' gender, being itself socially constructed (Fausto-Sterling, 2000). I use the terms 'gender' and 'gender categorization' to discuss how society members categorize one another because these categorizations are based on the social processes of 'doing gender' (Garfinkel, 1967; West & Zimmerman, 1987) and attributing gender (Devor, 1989; Kessler & McKenna, 1978; Speer, 2005b) rather than a person's sex assignment. Although members infer sex category from gender attribution and gender categorization, it is possible that the two do not 'match'; what members are actually aware of is gender, not sex.

a whole constellation of cultural information about members of the category, in addition to non-recognizability. Many possible categorizations – such as occupation, race/ethnicity and age – are voiced most often or only when the cultural inferences carried by the category are demonstrably relevant to the action accomplished through the reference. In practice, this usually means the categorization is essential to a listener's ability to make sense of the speaker's utterance. What I will call 'action relevance', then, is one ground for choosing among various category sets. Most categorizations are introduced into non-recognitional reference only when action relevant.

As an 'inference-rich' and action-relevant category, gender can aid recipients in understanding the meaning of speakers' stories by cueing recipients to draw on their prior knowledge about gender. For example, gender categorization is action relevant in the following excerpt, in which Bonnie relates 'another one of these horrible "my life sucked when I was growing up" stories' over pizza. Bonnie's only reference to the story's antagonist is 'some guy' (line 9). Her stretch on the word 'guy' and pauses before and after 'said' (line 9) serve to emphasize the word 'guy', suggesting that the guy's gender is action relevant to the story.

Extract 1 MP3 (00:48:25)

```
1   Bon:   We had to take Spanish and I picked for my Spanish na:me
2          the most- (.) close- (.) translation from mBonnie (.)
3          Bonita-
4   Dav:   Mmhm=
5   Bon:   =And that means prettyhh
6          (.)
7   Fay:   [Mm      ]
8   Bon:   [(h)And th]e teacher sa:id oh Bonita that means
9          pretty:, and some gu:y (.) said (.) THAT'S A STUPID
10         NAME FOR HER SHE AIN'T PRETTY
```

'She ain't pretty' (line 10) is an insult, regardless of who utters it. But in order to grasp the full import of this story as an instance of how 'my life sucked when I was growing up', recipients are invited to treat gender as critical for heightening the injury. Bonnie makes gender relevant by emphasizing 'guy'. While it could be argued that Bonnie's prosody is simply indicative of disdain, rather than a foregrounding of gender, Faye's response (transcript not shown) suggests that she understands gender as relevant to Bonnie's story.

Faye demonstrates her understanding of Bonnie's story first by expressing horror ('oh my god, that's terrible'), then by telling a second story fitted to the details of the first (Jefferson, 1978). Faye tells that 'this one boy' repeatedly asked out her best friend, a 'very pretty girl'. Faye's friend tried to rid herself of this nuisance by suggesting the boy ask out someone else, like Faye ('cause [she] was just over there'). The punchline of Faye's story is the boy's response: 'I only ask out the good looking girls.' This is an insult to Faye's appearance, done by a boy, and done in a way that makes gender specifically relevant. Faye thus treats both the insult to appearance and the genders of the persons giving and receiving the insult as relevant for understanding Bonnie's story (i.e., action relevant).

The introduction of many different categories, in addition to gender, can be warranted by their action relevance. In the following excerpt, Shane uses the relational occupational categorization 'muh boss' (line 4). The status of the referred-to person as a member of the category 'boss', and in particular as Shane's boss, is critical for understanding the significance of the interaction Shane describes.

Extract 2 Chicken dinner (00:19:49)
```
1   Sha:   I been (0.6) I- ruh- r'member I calledju up the other
2          night (.) Toosday n-uh la- uh: las' night. (0.2) I
3          called you up. From work? en I wz on the'phone f'r a
4          long ti:me? (0.5) Muh boss says ju know (1.2) watch
5          those: (.) pers'nal phone cal[ls
```

The job categorization 'muh boss' is essential for understanding the meaning of the boss's actions. A co-worker does not have the right to say 'watch those pers'nal phone calls', so this statement by a co-worker would be likely to be taken as a joke. In contrast, a boss has the right to make this kind of statement and be taken seriously; bosses have authority over workers' time and actions while at work, bosses have an interest in worker productivity, and bosses can fire workers who don't meet their requirements. The meaning of Shane's story depends on his reference to his boss as his boss. In this case, by using an occupational category to introduce his boss, Shane has also effectively omitted a gender categorization from his initial reference. However, there are also cases in which gender and another categorization are simultaneously present in a non-recognitional reference, where the other categorization is most action relevant, or necessary for conveying the meaning of the utterance.

In Extract 3, we see a more complex example of multiple-set categorization in person reference. Alex is describing a radio show that follows the lives of several strangers as they live together in a house, where the goal is to see who can endure living with the others the longest. Alex provides three descriptive non-recognitional references to people living in the house: a 'total neo-Nazi guy', 'a big fat redneck' and 'some black girl from the inner city' (lines 17–18; overlapping conversations going on in the room have been omitted from the transcript).

Extract 3 Hanging out (00:05:59)
```
1   Gav:   Ha' you guys ever watched those internet things (1.0)
2          that are like this that have cameras all over the house
3                   (1.0)
4   Reg:   No
```

5   (1.0)
6   Ale: There's a (1.0) some uh: (1.0) some radio station in
7   Columbus Ohio (   ) they have their their own kind of
8   like real world survivor type thing
9   Gav: Yeah
10   Ale: >And they just pick like< (0.5) four of the weirdest
11   people that they could possibly (   ) house and it's
12   actually a contest to see who (could) (0.5) who can
13   stay there the longest and (>have it like<) they have
14   updates on the radio (   ) and shit
15   Gav: (   ) good idea for (   )
16   (3.0)
17   Ale: Total neo-Nazi guy (1.5) a big fat redneck (2.0) some
18   (0.5) black g(hh)irl from the inner cit(h)y(h) she's
19   like all (   ) out (1.0) so funny

Alex describes these three as examples of 'the weirdest people that they could possibly [get/find]' (lines 10–11). It is clear that 'weirdest' is a proxy for most incompatible; the reason it is entertaining to 'see … who can stay there the longest' (lines 12–13) on 'real world survivor type' shows (line 8) is that the people are chosen specifically so that they will not get along well. What makes these person references understandable as a three-part list is the contrasts that would create tension between the referred-to people. The reference 'total neo-Nazi guy' categorizes the referred-to person racially (he can be assumed to be white), by reference to his racist beliefs, and by gender. Similarly, 'black girl from the inner city' categorizes the referred-to person by race, gender and urban location (which may be a proxy for socioeconomic class). The gender categorizations of these two do not explain why they won't get along. However, the white supremacist hatred and violence invoked by 'neo-Nazi' *are* meaningful to listeners in juxtaposition with the racial category 'black' in 'black girl from the inner city'. 'From the inner city' contrasts with 'big fat redneck' in terms of urban/rural location, but 'redneck' also suggests whiteness and conservatism, pointing to another possible racial-ideological ground for conflict. Although it is arguable that gender may play a part in the incompatibility of these three people, racial and racial-ideological categorizations are clearly most important. If gender categories are not action relevant, how do they come to be included in such references?

System relevance

Gender categorizations often appear in 'simple' non-recognitional references, where both the speaker and the recipient treat the reference as doing 'nothing but referring'. The following cases are typical of 'simple' non-recognitional person reference. In each case, the speaker uses an initial reference form that gender categorizes the person referred to as part of the reference.

Extract 4 Kara (00:20:58)

```
1   Deb:   The first five minutes of the- (.) trip was like
2          Everyone's in the vhan, like we all pile in there,
3          y'(h)all excited (0.2) then we started on the roa[d
4   Stn:                                                    [Hahha
5   Deb:   An' we're all like (1.2) oh my gosh (h)an this one guy
6          was kinda outspoken of the group he's like
7          'you gu:ys we've got twenty-four hours to go'
```

Extract 5 NB II.2 (00:16:36)

```
1   Emm:   Eh theh no:w we (.) ne:xt sutuh Saturdee this girl's
2          comin' in with'er (0.3) [two dau: (.) liddle]=
3   Nan:                           [(              )]
4   Emm:   =dau:ghters 'n I=
5   Nan:   =[°(Y  a :  h,)°]
6   Emm:   =[j's wanna ha]ve it kahna nea:t? 'n thin[k God< .hhhh]hhh
7   Nan:                                            [ W'l ↑su↓:re. ]
```

These gendered references – 'this one guy' (Extract 4, line 5), 'this girl' (Extract 5, line 1) – are treated by recipients as simple, in Schegloff's (1996c) sense, and unproblematic. Although gender categorization is included in both cases, the gender of the referred-to person is not directly relevant to what is being told about them (i.e., not action relevant). Gender categorizations uniquely and frequently appear in 'simple' non-recognitional references when they are not action relevant, but are instead what I will call 'system relevant'.[2] The fact that pronouns are gendered in English,[3] along with the practices of initial and subsequent reference, supplies a systematic basis for the relevance of gender categorization in non-recognitional reference to persons. As we shall see, system relevance makes the inclusion of gender categorization in both initial and subsequent 'simple' non-recognitional references normative.

'Locally initial' and 'locally subsequent' refer separately to both (1) conversational locations and (2) linguistic formats for doing person reference (Schegloff, 1996c: 450). Initial references are ordinarily done in full noun

---

[2] Whitehead and Lerner (2009) note that racial categorizations also appear in non-recognitional references when they are not action relevant. However, racial categorizations do not seem to be system relevant in the way that gender categorizations are, and so are not nearly as ubiquitous.

[3] Only about one third of the world's languages have sex-based systems of grammatical gender (Corbett, 2005) and personal pronouns are correspondingly gendered in only about one third of world languages (Siewierska, 2005). The systematic relevance of gender categorization in person reference, which I am suggesting is supported by gendered pronouns, may appear quite differently or not at all in languages lacking pronominal gender.

phrase format and subsequent references are ordinarily done using pronouns. To use a locally subsequent form (pronoun) in a locally initial location is to claim that your turn is a continuation of some prior talk. Inversely, using a locally initial form (full noun phrase) in a locally subsequent location can be a way of constituting your utterance as the beginning of 'a new spate of talk' about the same person (Schegloff, 1996c: 452). Gender categorization is often done in locally initial reference forms even when it is not action relevant. One important reason for speakers to make gender available in an initial reference is to help listeners manage subsequent references, which are usually done with gendered pronouns.

Gender categorization as a resource for recipient understanding

Because pronouns are gendered, they provide a resource speakers can use to show that they are referring to the same person previously referred to, if the initial reference also implicates gender. The following illustrates the use of initial and subsequent gendered reference forms and the importance of using pronouns when re-referring to the same person. Jennifer is telling her house-mates about a problem at work: her boss ('he', line 1) wants to raise the rent for the apartments Jennifer manages, but Jennifer has already promised one to a prospective tenant at the original price.

Extract 6 Housemates (00:42:22)
```
1   Jen:   .hh And he:- like a- this girl's waiting: (.) to hear,
2          (0.3) like can she rent it or not. And I promised it to
3          her. (0.5) And now I have to be like Well, (0.2) I don't
4          know
```

Jennifer shows that she is re-referring to the same person ('this girl', line 1) by using the locally subsequent forms 'she' (line 2) and 'her' (line 3). In this case, Jennifer includes a gender categorization of the person referred to in the initial reference form, 'this girl'. The repetition of the same gender categorization in 'this girl', 'she' and 'her' provides a resource to aid listeners in connecting the subsequent references back to the initial reference.

Tracking non-recognizable parties through a story using pronouns can be complicated, and it is essential that speakers gender categorize each party consistently in order to be understood. Prior to the following extract, Tyrone has been telling a story about his friend ('he', line 2) who was given $2,000 by 'this girl' ('her', line 1) in order to buy cocaine but instead kept the money. In line 4, Tyrone is referring again to his friend who stole the money as the one who is in danger of being killed, so he must correct the pronoun from 'her' to 'him' in order to maintain the integrity of his storyline.

Extract 7 Hanging out (01:22:09)

```
1  Tyr:  But it wasn't e(n) her money it was like her friend's
2         money >and then< he was like afraid to come in town for
3         a whi:le >cuz like< (0.2) s- he said the dude was trying
4         to kill her and shit (.) kill him and shid >bu'like<
5         (0.2) nothing ever happened(h)
```

Tyrone's friend, 'this girl' and 'her friend' (line 1) are all introduced as non-recognizable parties, then tracked through the precise use of initial and subsequent references. 'Her friend' (line 1) is the same person as 'the dude' (line 3). 'The dude' is a (1) gender-marked, (2) locally initial, (3) recognitional form. This alerts listeners to the fact that 'the dude' refers to (1) a masculine-gendered person and therefore not 'this girl', (2) someone other than Tyrone's friend, who is the protagonist of the story ('he' in lines 2 and 3), and (3) someone listeners 'know (about)'. The only possible already known character who is neither 'this girl' nor Tyrone's friend is 'her ['this girl's'] friend'. Listeners can understand from the reference form 'the dude' that 'the dude' is in fact the person to whom the stolen money belonged ('her friend'). It is necessary for Tyrone to correct 'her' to 'him' (line 4) in order to be understood as re-referring to his friend – rather than to the girl his friend took the money from – as the person 'the dude' was trying to kill. The inclusion of gender categorizations in Tyrone's person references is system relevant – it is his immediate production of a correctly gendered subsequent reference form ('him', line 4) that allows his listeners to understand the outcome of his story.

Gender categorization as a resource
for recipient production

By including gender categorization in the initial reference, speakers provide resources not only for recipients to hear and recognize the appropriate subsequent reference, but also to enable recipients to produce a subsequent reference themselves. For example, here Alex makes the initial reference, and Gavin produces the first subsequent reference.

Extract 8 Hanging out (00:11:01)

```
1  Ale:  I'm going down to Texas to visit my brother ((crunch))
2         couple weeks ((crunch))
3  Gav:  Oh eh (0.5) what's he doing in Texas
```

Gavin is able to use the correctly gendered subsequent reference form 'he' (line 3) precisely because Alex has provided gender categorization in the initial reference 'my brother'.

If the first speaker uses an initial reference form that does not convey the gender of the referred-to person, the recipient may encounter trouble in producing the first subsequent reference. In the next extract, Gavin tells a story about his 'teacher' (line 1) – using a person reference that does not do gender categorization.

Extract 9 Hanging out (00:13:15)

```
1   Gav:   My teacher called me on (the) sleeping yesterday
2   Tyr:   hhhh[hih
3   Ale:        [(hh)Y(h)ou g(h)o(t) c(h)all(h)ed [   out f'    ]=
4   Gav:                                          [There's two]=
5   Ale:   =[sn(h)oozin]
6   Gav:   =[ people   s]leeping in the back me and this dude next
7          to me er (0.3) go:ne
8   Reg:        (1.5) ((crunch crunch))
9   Ale:   .hh khhhhihhhi[hhhi
10  Reg:                 [He actually said something to you
11  Gav:   Yes:(h)
```

Since gender category is not provided in the reference 'my teacher', Reggie must select the gender to use for subsequent pronominal reference. He uses his knowledge of the category 'teachers' (here, college professors) to select the gendered pronoun 'he' (line 10). This is consistent with Stringer and Hopper's (1998: 213) finding that 'speakers do occasionally select *he* when referring to sex-unspecified incumbents of traditionally male social categories'. Similarly, Stokoe and Smithson (2001: 232–5) found that a gender-unspecified parent is likely to be categorized by second speakers as a woman (i.e., a mother). Second speaker selection of gender categories reveals cultural 'default assumptions' associated with various occupational and familial roles (Stringer & Hopper, 1998: 213). In this case, Reggie happens to have chosen the correct gender categorization of Gavin's teacher. Gavin's affirmative and type-conforming response ('yes', line 11) to Reggie's question ('He actually said something to you', line 10) indicates that Gavin accepts the terms in which the question is formulated (Raymond, 2003). In other words, by continuing the action sequence rather than interrupting it to do a repair, Gavin tacitly confirms that Reggie has correctly assumed the teacher's gender.

When the pronoun selected by the second speaker is correct, all goes smoothly and the machinery of conversation is invisible. However, in so far as a gender is being inferred on the basis of another category membership, recipients can gender-categorize incorrectly, exposing the contingencies involved. This happens in Extract 10, in which Shane is telling Michael about what happened after some long phone conversations the two had while Shane was at work.

Extract 10 Chicken dinner (00:19:53)

```
1   Sha:   Muh boss says ju know (1.2) watch thosse: (.) pers'nal
2          phone cal[ls
3   Viv:            [uhh!
```

```
4   Mic:   Oh did'e? Yeah,
5          (0.7)
6   Sha:   u-She- one a'the- one a'my bosses cuz she sid thet (0.4)
7          she said she didn't ca:re. °yihknow.°
```

In this case, because Shane's initial reference to his boss (line 1) does not convey gender, Michael has to select a pronoun for his subsequent reference. As it happens, Michael chooses the wrong pronoun (''e' for 'he', line 4). When a recipient uses a locally subsequent form, she or he is making a claim that the pronoun refers to the same person referenced by the first speaker. The first speaker can assess whether the second speaker has used the proper gendered pronoun, on the basis of her or his knowledge of the referred-to party. Shane sees that a problem has arisen, from his knowledge of his boss's feminine gender and Michael's claim to be re-referring to her with the masculine pronoun 'he' (line 4). Shane corrects the gender categorization of his boss in the next turn (lines 6–7), a preferred site for repair (Schegloff, 1992b; Schegloff, *et al.*, 1977).

Not correcting at this spot would serve as tacit confirmation of the gender categorization done by Michael. Shane does not know how the conversation will unfold, so it is risky to pass up this first opportunity to signal trouble (Land & Kitzinger, 2005). If Shane did not correct Michael's pronoun use but made reference to his boss again, his use of the correct pronoun would cause confusion; the two differently gendered pronouns would not be seen to be pointing to the same referent. In this case, system relevance makes gender categorization just as important for conveying meaning as it would be if gender were action relevant. The difference is that here meaning is preserved through gender categorization as an aide to talk's coherence rather than introduced through the use of gender as an inference-rich category.

By including gender categories in initial reference forms, speakers provide (1) an interpretive key for hearing subsequent references by them and (2) a resource for next speakers to re-refer to the same party. Extracts 9 and 10 involve speakers telling stories which make uptake by a recipient, and the need for the recipient to produce a subsequent person reference, systematically relevant. The organization of person reference shapes how these references will be formulated: in locally subsequent forms. Although initial references may not involve gender categorization, subsequent references (pronouns) do. The fact that recipients are constrained by action sequences and the organization of person reference to re-refer to an unknown party using gendered pronouns promotes the system relevance of gender categorization in initial reference forms. It is the system relevance of gender categorization that makes the inclusion of gender categories in non-recognitional person references normative. One procedural consequence of this is that when gender is not there, listeners treat it as missing. In the next section, I examine multi-reference sequences (those with at least one subsequent reference) where gender is accountably missing.

Procedural consequentiality 1: Subsequent reference without gendered pronouns

McConnell-Ginet (2003: 91) states that 'it is actually very difficult in English … to talk about a third person without ascribing sex [gender; see footnote 1] to them – and virtually impossible to do so over an extended period'. However, I find that this is not the case; looking to instances of naturally occurring conversation, it is entirely possible, and not necessarily difficult, for speakers to refer to a person continually without using a gendered pronoun. It is, however, quite unusual to do so, at least within my collection of examples. This kind of avoidance seems to be practised in a circumscribed set of situations, because it indicates that something special is going on. The first speaker either (1) does not know the referred-to person's gender, (2) is withholding information about the person's gender from recipients, or (3) knows the person's gender but cannot or will not fit that gender into the available dichotomy. Avoiding gendered pronouns can be accomplished in three ways, corresponding to these three situations: by (1) using 'they' as a singular pronoun, (2) avoiding pronouns altogether or (3) using a gender-neutral pronoun.

Gender: Unknown

I have come across two circumstances in which people use the pronoun 'they' to refer to individuals and in both cases the speaker does not know the referred-to person's gender. One type of case occurs when the speaker can infer the presence of a person, but has had no contact with the person and so cannot know her or his gender. A second is 'prospective' person reference, or reference to an as yet unspecified person whose gender therefore cannot be known. The following two extracts provide examples of how speakers manage reference when they do not know the gender of the person they are talking about. In the first instance, Dave describes the details of a skiing accident in which he was impaled by the end of a skiing pole. The circumstances Dave describes – being hit on the back of the head and passing out – make comprehensible why an unseen and unknown person is memorable and worthy of being talked about.

Extract 11 MP3 (00:16:19)

```
1   Dav:   Well (0.5) someone must have been (0.3) °khuh° an idiot
2          or- like- actually wanted to inflict pain on me
3   Fay:   °hmuhuhuh [uh°
4   Dav:             [Cause they had thuh- thee thee (0.2) it's not
```

5   sha:rp- but thee less blunt side (.) facing forward (.)
6   and hit me in the back of the head

Dave's initial reference 'someone' (line 1) is a prototypical way of 'doing nothing but referring' that does not include gender categorization. In my collection of instances, speakers beginning with 'someone' often proceed to include gender in their subsequent references. In this case, Dave uses the pronoun 'they' (line 4) to do subsequent reference. As Dave's story continues, it becomes clear that he was knocked unconscious by the blow to the back of his head, so there was no way he could have seen his assailant. Since gendered pronouns are the norm for subsequent reference, Dave's use of 'they' reinforces for his recipients the lack of information available about the person he is referring to.

Prospective person references are handled similarly. In Extract 12, Mary is describing a person ('somebody', line 1) who has yet to be hired for a particular job, so she cannot know if this person will be a woman or a man.

Extract 12 Stringer and Hopper (1998: 217)

1   Mary: Ah- well see this is *it* they'll bring somebody i:n
2   who's this complete dummy: who just thinks oh my god I've
3   gotta jo:b you know and- .hhh and It'll t*a*ke them a year
4   before they realize how much they hate it
5   Kate: That's ri::ght.

Her subsequent use of the pronouns 'them' (line 3) and 'they' (line 4) preserves the lack of gender information appropriate to this prospective reference. (Note that 'they' in line 1 refers to the hiring committee, not an individual.) Stringer and Hopper (1998: 211) assert that 'the unmarked form for referring to gender-unknown singular referents is *they*'. The fact that speakers so rarely use 'they', and do so only under special circumstances that explain why gender cannot be known, suggests that gender category membership is considered the minimal information one could have about a person. That is, if one has ever seen, heard or met a person and knows nothing else about her or him, one will at least know her or his gender. Thus, it is not in most cases problematic for speakers to select a gendered pronoun for subsequent reference. On the other hand, there are cases in which a speaker may wish to avoid using pronouns that disclose a referred-to person's gender when it is known.

Avoiding pronouns

Where a speaker has some knowledge of the person she or he is referring to, which is the case most of the time, the use of gendered pronouns is normative. By contrast, avoiding gendered pronouns produces one of many possible 'marked forms which … invite a recipient/hearer to examine them for what they are doing other than simple reference' (Schegloff, 1996c: 449). A well known case of pronoun avoidance occurs when a gay or lesbian person wishes to maintain a presumed heterosexual identity (remaining 'in the closet'). Liang (1999) suggests that this kind of withholding of gender information may occur frequently in non-recognitional references regarding 'a person' of romantic interest. Morrish (2002: 186) offers the following example of 'syntactic convolutions performed' in the service of guarding her own lesbian identity:

Extract 13 Morrish (2002: 186)
1   I once managed to dislodge my partner's hyoid bone when
2   kissing.

She argues that the meaning of this sentence would be more smoothly conveyed by, '… when I was kissing her'. Such circumlocutions allow gay and lesbian individuals to remain closeted without being dishonest through the use of inaccurate gender pronouns. Ironically, the avoidance of gendered pronouns functions both to keep homosexuality hidden and simultaneously as 'a recognizably gay tactic' (Morrish, 2002: 186). Because normative gender categorization is missing, listeners can find that what these references are doing 'other than simple reference' is avoiding a display of sexuality. As Kitzinger (2005a: 258) puts it, 'given the pervasiveness of heterosexual self-display … the failure to display oneself as heterosexual must also be an indicator of possible homosexuality'.[4] In most other cases of pronoun avoidance I have come across, gender disclosure is avoided as part of withholding the referred-to's identity rather than hiding her or his gender itself. Knowing someone's identity without knowing their gender is considered to be impossible, and gender can function as a clue to identity, so the avoidance of pronouns is hearable as withholding information (rather than a lack of knowledge) about the referred-to person's gender.

Respecting non-binary genders

In order to select a gendered pronoun, not only must a speaker know the referred-to person's gender but this gender must be interpretable within the binary model that corresponds to the available pronouns. If the speaker knows that the referred-to person's gender does not fit within this binary scheme and wishes to respect this, she or he (or otherwise)[5] is in a bit of a bind. Using 'they' as a singular pronoun or avoiding pronouns will, as we have seen, send up red flags for listeners that there is something problematic about the referred-to person's

---

[4] The imperative for heterosexual self-display produces the opposite effect as well. See appendix to this chapter for an example.

[5] Note here that 'she or he', although it is intended to be inclusive language, implicitly excludes people whose genders are not represented by these pronouns.

gender – it is unknown or is being hidden for some reason. In order to avoid these interpretations, some people with non-binary gender identities, as well as those who wish to demonstrate respect for these individuals and their identities, currently promote various gender-neutral third person singular pronouns (Bornstein, 1998; Feinberg, 1998). In Feinberg's (1998: 71) words, 'We need a gender-neutral pronoun that honors us as unique human beings.' Ze prefers the pronoun 'ze' for this purpose and considers the inanimate pronoun 'it' a poor choice because it functions as 'an epithet meant to strip us [transgender people] of our humanity' (Feinberg, 1998: 70–1). An(other) example of use would look like this:

Extract 14 Boenke (2003)
1   When talking with Leslie Feinberg, noted transgender
2   author, I asked Leslie which pronouns to use. Ze shrugged
3   hir shoulders and said ze didn't care.[6]

Although these are examples of recognitional reference, gender-neutral pronouns can be similarly incorporated into non-recognitional reference (as in, 'This person walks into a bar, and ze says …'). While there is a long history of attempts to introduce various third gender and/or epicene pronouns into English, none has yet succeeded in gaining wide usage (Baron, 1986: 190–216). This matters, of course, because one's success at using a gender-neutral or third gender pronoun in conversation – as measured by listeners' continued comprehension – is dependent upon speaking within a language community that accepts the existence of such a pronoun and, by extension, such an ungendered or third gendered category of persons.

Procedural consequentiality 2: The exploitation of gender's omnipresence

Gender is clearly an important resource for speakers both as an inference-rich categorization of persons (action relevance) and as a feature of grammar that helps connect initial and subsequent references to the same person (system relevance). We have seen when and how speakers violate the norm of including gender in person references and what consequences this has. The normative presence of gender categorization in simple non-recognitional reference can also be pressed into service, or exploited, by listeners for a variety of ends. The following conversation takes place among a group of friends (composed of two heterosexual couples: Shane and Vivian, Michael and Nancy) in southern California. They have been talking about calling friends on the East Coast during winter storms and telling them how nice the weather is in California.

---

[6]   'Ze' is pronounced 'zee' and 'hir' is pronounced 'here' (Feinberg, 1998: 71). Other forms of this pronoun are 'hirs' (possessive) and 'hirself' (reflexive).

Vivian designs her references to 'this guy' (line 13) or 'one guy' (line 16) as simple non-recognitionals. Vivian's boyfriend (Shane) treats these gender-categorizing reference forms as potentially indicative of romantic interest, and therefore, as problematic (lines 23–34).

Extract 15 Chicken dinner (00:14:32)

```
 1  Viv:    Wir gunnuh call[up     ]
 2  Sha:                   ['T's in]sa[:ne.    ]
 3  Viv:                        [Wir g'n]nuh[call up sm]=
 4  Mic:                                   [    (s'p    ]=
 5  Viv:    =[ friends ]=
 6          =[thA::d'). ]=
 7  Sha:    =hih hh[Wz ↑eigh]d[y degrees here the oth]uh ]=
 8  Viv:           [ en   say] [eighty    degrees    ]ihh]=
 9  Sha:    =[day. ih hih]    [he
10  Viv:    =[hnhh heh-hu]h-h[uh
11  Nan:    Oh they hate tih hear that.
12  Sha:    I kno:w. En[then hang up](°they go°)=
13  Viv:               [Well this gu]y
14  Sha:    =↑Who was tha[t (     )
15  Mic:                 [mn nah ah[hah
16  Viv:                           [One guy thet I[wanna caw:ll=
17  Mic:                                          [(         )
18  Viv:    =he usually comes ↑ou:t. yihknow[so weyou jus tell'm
19  Nan:                                     [Mmhm,
20  Viv:    =it's eighdy degree:s hi'll get onna pla:n[e
21  Nan:                                              [hhh[Yheh ]=
22  Sha:                                                  [Woah]=
23  Viv:    =[n a h-ha-ha]
24  Nan:    =[heh heh heh]
25  Sha:    =[w a i' w e e way:o[ee-
26  Viv:                        [ih hih hehh he[h
27  Sha:                                       [Wu wai'a wai'a wu.
28          (0.4)
29  Sha:    One: gu::y you usually ca(h)a(h)ll? W'd['z's
30  Mic:                                           [mm-hm-m-h[m
31  Viv:                                                     [No we
32          [↑ca:ll.    ]
33  Sha:    [W'd is this]::.
34          (0.5)
35  Sha:    Oh:.Okay it wz: a friend a'mi:ne t[oo.Aw] rig[ht.
36  Nan:                                      [Oh:  ]Sha[ne's=
37  Viv:                                                [(°Yeah. °)
38  Nan:    °friend, [yeah
39  Sha:             [Oh that's good then. That's my friend
```

Vivian starts out by presenting calling friends as a project she and Shane will do together ('Wir' for 'We're', lines 1 and 3). After Shane has exhibited his orientation to the calling as teasing ('En then hang up. They go, "who was that?"', lines 12 and 14), Vivian re-launches the project as her own ('I', line 16). Nancy treats the beginning of Vivian's turn ('One guy thet I wanna cawl he usually comes out yihknow', lines 16 and 18) as unproblematic, offering a continuer ('Mmhm', line 19). On the other hand, Shane emphatically signals trouble with Vivian's utterance by halting the progress of action (lines 25–9), using a marked repetition to initiate repair (line 29) and explicitly marking the inserted sequence as a repair by asking 'what is this?' (lines 29 and 33). Although Shane's complaint/repair is not serious (evidenced by his laugh tokens and the exaggerated amplitude of his intervention), neither is it senseless. Vivian understands the problem perfectly well and is able to correct it simply, by saying 'No, we call' (lines 31–2). Shane's problem is that Vivian was going to call 'One guy', with strong emphasis on 'guy' (line 29). There are two problems for Shane: (1) the apparent exclusivity of Vivian's relationship with 'this guy' and (2) the sexual nature of the relationship implicated by the combination of this exclusivity and the gender categorization of 'this guy'.

Vivian's references to 'this guy' (line 13) and 'one guy' (line 16) are not designed to imply a romantic or sexual relationship, but are designed simply for non-recognitional reference. The machinery of sequence organization and person reference (system relevance) work to keep gender categorizations available on the surface of conversation. It is precisely in 'doing nothing special' that Vivian includes gender categorization in her references, but this makes her vulnerable to Shane's exploitation of gender as an inference-rich category (action relevance). Shane is making something of nothing, and he knows it. However, it is significant that the nothing he has made something of is the normative presence of gender categorization in non-recognitional reference. This illustrates how although gender categorization may not be action relevant in many cases of person reference, the system relevance that leads to its omnipresence paradoxically contributes to its omnirelevance as a social (rather than simply grammatical) category in talk.

Conclusion: The omnirelevance of gender

As Stokoe and Smithson (2002:79) point out, it is easiest to see that speakers are 'oriented to' gender when it is 'procedurally relevant for speakers, as evidenced through discursive phenomen[a] such as repair, disclaimers and "troubling" orientations to such categories'. However, gender categorizations are also present and 'procedurally relevant' in conversation when speakers do not orient to them as problematic. Specifically, because gender categorization is system relevant, it is normatively included in non-recognitional person reference – even when gender is not action relevant – and this inclusion is not treated as problematic by speakers or hearers. 'Unproblematic' gender categorizations are a resource to keep things running smoothly (see Kitzinger, 2005a; 2005b); gender categorizations in initial person references are a resource for recipient understanding and production of subsequent references, which are usually done with gendered pronouns. The exclusion of gender categorization is also procedurally consequential, as it signals special circumstances or trouble – the speaker may be hiding or lacking information about the person referred to. The normative inclusion of gender categorization as a minimum basic form of non-recognitional reference makes gender an omnipresent category of persons in talk. Through gender's action relevance – or usefulness in conveying information as an inference-rich category – this omnipresence is translated into omnirelevance.

The significance of gender categorization goes quite a bit further than conversation, however, because 'the "doing" of gender is embedded in the "doing" of categorization' (Stokoe, 2004: 117). If we want to be able to talk about a person, we need to know their gender. This has the consequence that we must constantly notice people's genders as we monitor our experiences for tellability (Sacks, 1992: 773–83). Genders are socially constructed in the process of interaction and are not inherent in persons (J. Butler, 1990a; Garfinkel, 1967; West & Zimmerman, 1987). Therefore, it is more accurate to say that we *attribute* gender to the people we encounter, rather than 'noticing' or 'knowing' their genders. Kessler and McKenna (1978) describe gender attribution as an interactive process, with work being done by both perceivers and producers of gender performance. If we need to gender categorize people in order to talk about them and we need to attribute gender in order to gender categorize, we also need other people to perform recognizable-attributable gender constantly. More specifically, we require them to perform a gender that is recognizable-attributable within the binary gender system corresponding to the available pronouns. In turn, others require coherent binary gender performances from us so that they can do gender attribution and gender categorization. As West and Zimmerman (1987: 145) put it, 'Insofar as sex [gender] category is used as a fundamental criterion for differentiation, doing gender is unavoidable.'

The ongoing practices of doing gender, doing gender attribution and doing gender categorization 'sustain the illusion that gender is more a natural category than an ongoing accomplishment within social interaction' (Stringer & Hopper, 1998: 220). And there is a moral imperative to subscribe to this illusion: an inability or refusal to perform and/or recognize coherent binary gender is 'tantamount to calling ourselves into question as competent members of society' (West & Fenstermaker, 1995: 20). The iterative practices of (re)marking gender on the body and in conversation maintain the omnirelevance of gender.

Sustaining the social institution of gender in turn enables the maintenance of sexism, heterosexism and other 'gender-related oppressions' (Nagle, 1995: 305). The small but recurrent character of gender categorization practices in conversation is one systematic source of the robustness of gender as a social institution and its omnirelevance in social life.

Appendix

This excerpt follows Alex's description of being taught to dance salsa by a 'fine' Colombian woman he met in a bar.

Extract A Hanging out (00:55:46)

```
1   Gav:   Salsa's probly not easy to do u:h
2   Ale:   [Na:w it's no:t          ]
3   Tyr:   [No it's not easy at all] it's real hard
4          [uhuk-     ]                    [HKKKK ] ((cough))
5   Ale:   [(Ehyushuo)] get drunk enou[gh     and] you have someone ho-
6          >eh- some hot chick teaching you it's prett(h)y
7          e(h)as(h)y
```

Alex appears to have been headed for the reference 'someone hot' in line 5, before switching to 'some hot chick' (line 6). The lack of gender categorization in the reference 'someone hot' could be accounted for by its prospective nature – gender would not be missing if it wasn't there. However, since the gender(s) of one's chosen dance partners is treated as an index of sexual orientation, the (preferred) gender of future dance partners can be specified in advance. By adding a gender categorization, Alex limits his prospective dance partners to 'hot chicks', rather than 'someone hot', thereby announcing his heterosexuality.

Part II

Gender, repair and recipient design

5   'Girl – woman – sorry!': On the repair and non-repair of consecutive gender categories

Elizabeth Stokoe

Introduction

This chapter examines how speakers make and repair consecutive references to third parties using the gender categories 'girl', 'woman' and 'lady', within the context of debates about when and how gender is relevant in talk. The chapter starts with a brief summary of language and gender research, before moving on to explain the practices of 'repair' and 'person reference' in conversation analysis. The analysis focuses on instances of 'same-turn' or 'self-initiated self-repair' (Schegloff, 1979; Schegloff *et al.*, 1977), in which a speaker marks some aspect of their ongoing talk as problematic and repairs it within the same turn (e.g., 'that girl over – that *woman* over there'). This is in contrast to other types of repair in which recipients initiate and produce repair. Four analytic sections focus on a particular format of 'XY' repairs, in which X is a first gender category and Y is another. The first section examines canonical XY repairs; the second focuses on cases in which the repair segment contains a marked orientation to the repairable. The third section examines cases in which 'or' is a feature of the repair segment. The final section focuses on instances of consecutive alternative reference where no features of repair are present. Both the third and fourth sections therefore consider cases of probable non-repair, or 'doing' non-repair. Overall, the chapter considers how different formats for producing consecutive alternate gender categories display speakers' 'commitment' to one category or the other, and their relevance for evidencing speakers' 'orientation to gender'.

Language, gender and conversation analysis

Since its inception as a field of study, gender and language research can be grouped loosely into three areas. First, studies of sex differences in conversational style, pioneered by Robin Lakoff (1973), continue to be reported (e.g.,

I would like to thank Derek Edwards, Celia Kitzinger and Susan Speer for their very thorough feedback on various drafts of this chapter, as well as members of the Loughborough CA Day group for their helpful comments when I presented some of these extracts at a data session. All errors are, of course, my own.

Brooks & Marianne, 2004; Drescher, 2006) despite sustained criticism about methodological flaws, the reification of gender binaries, gender essentialism and so on (see Stokoe, 2000). Second, rejecting 'sex difference' approaches, researchers have investigated the construction or 'doing' of gender identities in everyday, institutional and interview contexts, focusing on 'the process of gendering, the ongoing accomplishment of gender, as well as the dynamism and fluidity of the process' (Holmes, 2007: 54–5). Third, and in contrast, conversation analysts study gender and language not by making claims about sex differences or how, say, women 'perform' femininity, but by showing how a particular (gender) category is relevant to a stretch of interaction, and how it is linked to specific actions by the participants themselves.

For example, Stringer and Hopper (1998: 213) analysed repair sequences initiated by speakers' use of the generic 'he' when referring to 'sex-unspecified incumbents of traditionally male social categories'. Relatedly, Hopper and LeBaron (1998) described a stepwise process through which 'gender creeps into talk', that is, how gender gets 'noticed' and becomes focal, rather than peripheral, in talk. So there may be 'peripheral gendered activity', a 'gendered noticing' followed by the 'extending of gender's relevance' (p. 72). In the following example from their paper, Hopper and LeBaron argue that Jill's announcement contains a possible 'implicit indexing of gender' (1998: 69).

Extract 1 Hopper and LeBaron (1998: 69)

```
1   Jill:  I've signed up for one of those informal classes about
2          car maintenance and repair.
3   Pip:   That's a good idea. A lot of women can really learn a
4          lot from these classes
5          ((short pause))
6   Pip:   Well, I guess there's a lot of guys who can learn from
7          'em too.
```

Pip 'notices' gender in her response to Jill's announcement, which 'pragmatically presupposes the particular relevance to women of this kind of class' (p. 69). After a pause, Pip reformulates her response, deleting the stereotypical notion that only women need car maintenance classes.

For conversation analysts, then, evidence of gender relevance comes from, say, sequences of interaction in which gender categories and terms of reference are repaired, reformulated, or topicalized in some way that displays an orientation to the gender of the category or term of reference as the repairable. However, this does not mean that using a gendered reference such as 'man', 'woman', 'he' or 'she' is necessarily evidence that gender is a relevant participants' concern. As Kitzinger (2007b: 46) explains,

participants' deployment of sex category person terms ('man', 'lady', 'chick', etc.) is neither sufficient nor necessary to establish the relevance of gender to participants in talk-in-interaction. It is not sufficient, since … terms like 'woman' may be used without any specific orientation to gender *per se*, and in the service of other interactional goals entirely.

This chapter makes a further contribution to this ongoing debate, focusing on conversational practices that provide, intuitively at least, evidence of speaker orientation to gender: repairing one gender category with another.

Conversation, repair and alternate person reference

In their pioneering work on repair, Schegloff *et al*. (1977) make various observations about the particular type dealt with in this chapter: self-initiated self-repair. Consider the following example.

Extract 2 Schegloff *et al*. (1977: 366)

```
1   N:   But c'd we- c'd I stay u:p?
2             (0.2)
3   N:   once we get // ho:me,
```

Here, repair is *initiated* with the cut-off on 'we-'. This follows the *trouble source* or *repairable* item in the preceding talk ('we'). Speakers commonly repeat a bit of the talk prior to the repairable in order to *frame* the repair (Schegloff, 1979). So the repeated word 'c'd' pre-frames the *repair solution*, which is the word 'I', which in turn 'replaces' the trouble source. Repair initiation can occur within the same turn as the trouble source, as in the example above, within that turn's 'transition space', in 'third position', or later. And repairs can be initiated by within-word or within-sound cut-offs, sound stretches, non-lexical 'speech perturbations' and 'uhs'.

   The focus of the current chapter is less on further specifying the technicalities of repair segments than on the actual *content* of trouble sources and their repairs, and the interactional work they do. Relevant to this focus is Jefferson's (1996: 18) analysis of the 'poetics' of everyday talk and, in particular, a group of repairs that she calls 'category-formed errors':

in which you have objects that very strongly belong together; sometimes as contrasts, sometimes as co-members, very often as pairs. Up–down, right–left, young–old, husband–wife. What seems to happen is that a gross selection-mechanism delivers up a category, but not the specific *member* of that category, and it's sort of a matter of pot luck whether the correct one gets said. It's like the whole package gets dropped down, and it's up to … who knows what? your taste buds? to decide which word is going to come out.

Here is an example from Jefferson's work.

Extract 3 (GH:FN) (Jefferson, 1996: 10)

Larry: Hi. I'm Carol's sister- uh brother.

Jefferson argues that some repairs result from categorial 'errors' in which speakers select the 'wrong' category from a collection. Those 'wrong' categories are strongly associated with the 'correct' category that the speaker was presumably heading for. Here, Larry produces 'sister', cuts off, produces a further repair initiator 'uh' followed immediately by the repair solution ('brother').

Also relevant to the current chapter are studies of 'person reference' (Enfield & Stivers, 2007; Lerner & Kitzinger, 2007a; Sacks & Schegloff, 1979; Schegloff, 1996c; see also Jackson, this volume; Klein, this volume). Given that on any given occasion, there are indefinitely extendible ways to refer to a person (e.g., 'this girl', 'Karen', 'my neighbour', 'the nurse', 'Mrs Smith', etc.), reference selection and its conversational function are of immediate analytic interest. A key question is how speakers produce references 'so as to accomplish, on the one hand, that nothing but referring is being done, and/or on the other hand that something else in addition to referring is being done by the talk practice which has been employed' (Schegloff, 1996c: 439).

A speaker's reference selection may be accounted for by the principle of *recipient design*. There are preferences for using terms with which recipients can identify the person being discussed ('recognitionals'), and for using one rather than multiple terms ('minimization'). Relevant to the notion of 'minimization' is the 'economy rule' in Sacks's (1992) work on 'membership categorization': a single category term from any membership categorization device can do adequate reference. If more than one reference occurs then the members' – and hence analysts' – interest is in why one was not adequate and what work is being done by the second. Both names (e.g., 'Susan') and descriptions ('the woman from Manchester University') are potentially 'recognitionals', depending on the recipient. However, there is an additional *preference* for using names rather than descriptive recognitionals, as the following repair sequence demonstrates:

Extract 4 Trip to Syracuse, 1:10–11 (Schegloff, 1996c: 463)
```
10    Charlie:   hhhe:h .hhhh I wuz uh:m: (.) .hh I wen' ah:- (0.3)
11               I spoke teh the gi:r- I spoke tih Karen.
```

In Charlie's turn, the descriptive recognitional ('the girl') is 'upgraded': it is 'cut off and replaced by a first name recognitional' ('Karen') (Schegloff, 1996c: 463). But while Jefferson's 'category-formed' examples are easily understandable as 'errors', and Schegloff's example demonstrates that recipient design may be crucial to the way a speaker refers to an absent third party, the data presented in the current chapter are different from these cases. Consider the following three examples (b and c are invented):

(a) 'I spoke teh the gi:r- I spoke tih Karen ...'
(b) 'I spoke teh the gi:r- I spoke tih the boy who ...'
(c) 'I spoke teh the gi:r- I spoke tih the woman who ...'

Each example contains consecutive alternative references to an absent third party. However, each is different in terms of the 'referential' adequacy of the first category 'girl', and the work done by the replacement repair. They are also potentially different in terms of 'gender relevance'. By 'referential' adequacy, I mean that a category is a possibly 'correct' reference and not a 'category-formed error' like 'sister/brother'. I do not mean to imply that categories are objectively 'correct' outside their interactional context – the very fact of the repair means that the speaker treats the first category as in some way inapposite. So, in (a), although 'the girl' is not an 'error', in that it could be a referentially adequate reference in another context, repairing 'the girl' with 'Karen' demonstrates the preference for using names rather than descriptive recognitionals; for using unique identifiers generally; and for the minimization rule. In (b), 'the girl' in 'the girl/the boy' is a referentially *inadequate* 'category-formed' error which, if the speaker did not correct, might be made accountable by the recipient via other-initiated repair (see Klein, this volume; see also Speer, 2005b, for an analysis of gender attribution in which 'the girl' and 'the boy' are *both* potentially referentially adequate).

In (c), 'the girl/the woman', 'the girl' is not a category-formed error, and is replaced not with an alternative type of person reference but with an alternative category from the collection used to refer to 'women' ('girls', 'ladies', 'females', 'lasses', etc.). It is routine in both British and American English to use 'girl' to refer to adult 'women', although etymologically 'girl' connotes youth. Despite feminist critiques of, and ubiquitous public policy statements about, the use of sexist language (e.g., in guidelines for public writing), including using 'girls', not 'women', to refer to adult females, the term 'girl' is used mundanely in public and private discourse. So, for example, the phrase 'Girls' Night Out' refers to adult women, not female children; likewise 'Lambrini Girls' refers to adult women consumers of an alcoholic drink (Benwell & Stokoe, 2010). However, I do not want to argue that the category 'girl' is intrinsically 'sexist' outside of its context of use. In (c), given that 'the girl' is a plausible reference term and the repair is not fixing a 'category-formed' error (as in (b)) or a preference for types of person reference (as in (a)), what is left to account for is what, interactionally, motivates the repair.

Both (a) and (b) provide evidence of 'gender relevance' in a grammatical sense, given that the English language provides for the omnirelevant categorization of people as male or female. However, in (c), 'the girl/the woman', the repair attends to a potentially wide range of interactional contingencies, including fixing the category-bound resonances each carries, the action being done in the turn containing the reference, the adequacy of the reference for characterizing the object of the description, and the speaker-identity issues that may be invoked by using particular forms of gender categories (e.g., being a 'gender aware' speaker). It is these issues, and this third type of repair, that are the topic of the current chapter.

Analysis

The data for this chapter come from a variety of mostly British sources, including ordinary conversation, university tutorials, speed-dating, neighbour mediation sessions, police–suspect interviews,[1] online blogs, and scripted dialogue. I collected all instances of consecutive gender reference, done as possible self-initiated self-repair (SISR). The extracts presented come from a large collection of consecutive references involving numerous gender categories (e.g., 'man', 'bloke', 'wife'), from which I have selected the 'girl/woman/lady' cases to manage the chapter's length and focus. SISRs are particularly interesting with regard to whether, and how, they are evidence that speakers are 'oriented to gender'. While 'other-initiated' repairs necessarily involve more than one speaker, making the repair segment and its topic occupy at least two turns, in SISR the repair segment is contained within one turn at talk. Given that basic 'referential' work is accomplished with the first category, and given that the *recipients* do not (at least in my extracts) initiate the occurrence of a second or topicalize the SISR, the repairs are done by speakers for the production of their turn. Yet these repairs are still presumably recipient-designed in some way: this is a basic issue for the analysis.

The first analytic section examines canonical 'XY' formatted repairs; the second analyses instances where the repair segment is marked; the third examines cases in which 'or' is inserted between X and Y categories; and the final section deals with cases of 'non-repair', but ones that nevertheless include consecutive alternative references.

XY-formatted repairs

In 'XY' cases, repair is initiated by within- or end-of-word cut-offs acting on some already-produced part of the turn. The repair solution occurs immediately or almost immediately after repair initiation. The extracts are instances of 'consecutive reference to the same objects', which Jefferson (1987: 90) discusses in her work on 'exposed' and 'embedded' correction. Jefferson lists various procedures by which speakers may produce consecutive references (e.g., using a pro-term as a subsequent replacement reference, or repeating the initially introduced term). The procedure most like this chapter's phenomenon is that in which 'an item is introduced and a next speaker uses an alternate from the

---

[1] The police and mediation data were collected as part of ESRC grant number RES-148-25-0010, 'Identities in neighbour discourse: Community, conflict and exclusion', held by Elizabeth Stokoe and Derek Edwards.

same syntactic class' (p. 92), although I focus on repair rather than correction.[2] Here is an example of embedded correction in Jefferson's paper.

Extract 5 Jefferson (1987: 92–3) GTS:II:60:ST

Ken: Well- if you're gonna <u>race</u>, the police have said this to
        us.
Roger: <u>That</u> makes it even <u>bet</u>ter. The <u>chall</u>enge of running
        from the <u>cops</u>!
Ken: The cops say if you wanna race, uh go out at four or five
        in the morning on the freeway ...

In his second turn, Ken uses the term 'cops' used by Roger, rather than his own initial term ('police'). Jefferson suggests that Roger's use of an alternative item, rather than a pro-term (e.g., 'they') or repeat, is an 'embedded' form of correction; that is, there is a replacement but it does not become the business of the utterances or get accounted for.

In contrast to consecutive references that are *corrected across* different speakers' turns, the following extracts focus on consecutive references *repaired within* one speaker's turn. Extract 6 comes from a telephone call to a council antisocial behaviour helpline, in which the caller is describing a contrast between one neighbour and another. Extract 7 comes from a marriage-counselling interview with a couple, 'Connie and Jimmy' (Edwards, 1998). The couple separated when Jimmy had an alleged affair, leaving Connie with the children. Jimmy has said his affair had nothing to do with their separation; Connie 'can't accept' this.

Extract 6 AC-8

1   C: .hh y'see 'e <u>doe</u>sn't- 'e's not like hh (0.2) that-
2   the- thē- thē- <u>Eri</u>ca.
3   (0.2)
4   C: → Uh- the wo- lady [down]stairs: .hhh (one door that-)=
5   A: [Mmm.]
6   C: =.hh 'e- 'e's: it's <u>be</u>cause I won't speak to him.

Extract 7 DE-JF:C2:S1:p.2

1   (1.3)
2   J: U::m (1.0) it's NOt right to sa:y that- (0.6)
3   I didn't leave °↓Connie for another woman.°
4   (0.6)
5   J: But- (0.6) I was liv- livin' away for: (1.0) 'bout
6   three- (0.2) <u>three</u> weeks: (.) four weeks three
7   weeks, (0.3) *whatever,* (0.9) when I moved in:
8   →   (.) <u>with</u> a wo- (0.2) <u>gi</u>:rl. which I <u>did</u> have (1.2)

---

9   a: bit of a <u>fl</u>ing with: (0.4) when Connie was on
10   holiday last (April.)
11   (1.6)

In both extracts, the speaker replaces one gender category, halting its production with a cut-off that initiates the repair, with a co-class member from the collection of terms used to refer to 'females'. In Extract 6, the trouble source 'woman' is replaced with the repair solution 'lady'. There is no 'framing' present: the caller does not repeat 'a' to form the phrase 'a lady'. Similarly, in Extract 7, Jimmy cuts off on 'wo-[man]', the trouble source, producing the repair solution 'girl' with no framing. There is a 0.2-second delay before the repair solution is provided, making the trouble more visible than in Extract 6.

In Extract 6, the target repair itself replaces an earlier reference: the caller is replacing the name '<u>E</u>rica' with another locally initial form, the descriptive recognitional 'the wo- lady'. The multiple repair initiators ('that- the- the̅- the̅-') that precede '<u>E</u>rica' at lines 1–2 indicate that C had started to produce a descriptive recognitional, and was having trouble selecting the appropriate reference. Although names are preferred over descriptive recognitionals *where possible*, in this instance we might assume that the call-taker does not know C's neighbour by name. In Extract 7, Jimmy has denied leaving '°↓Connie for another woman.°'. The reference 'another woman', rather than a named person, generalizes Jimmy's denial via a 'recognizable cultural idiom for [such an] activity' (Edwards, 1998: 26). In the target line 8, Jimmy says that he moved in '<u>w</u>ith a wo- (0.2) gi:rl.', sticking to descriptive recognitionals rather than names. He therefore avoids naming the person he had a 'bit of a <u>fl</u>ing with:', creating some relational distance between Jimmy and the woman now as he talks about her in the co-presence of his wife.

In both extracts, the first, trouble-producing reference is the gender category 'wo[man]'. Their replacements are not alternate *types of person reference*, but alternate *gender categories*: 'lady' and 'girl'. Given that in both instances the first reference 'woman' was neither a category-formed error, nor 'referentially' inadequate in any objective sense (indeed, Jimmy used 'woman' five lines earlier in Extract 7), the question remains as to why 'woman' is a trouble source. There are several provisional, rather than definitive, answers. One lies in Sacks's (1992) notion of membership categorization and the 'inference-rich' properties of categories. Sacks wrote that categories are 'store houses' and 'filing systems' for the common sense knowledge that members have about what people are like, their category-bound activities, features, characteristics and so on. The categories 'lady', 'girl' and 'woman' have overlapping but different resonances rooted in their differing etymologies: 'woman' connotes 'default' reference to an adult female; 'lady' connotes older age, status, grace; 'girl' connotes female child, youth, unmarried and so on. Any person labelled as, say, a 'lady', is taken to be a representative of that category, someone who has *those* characteristics and features. Thus speakers can infer different things about the person being referred to, via their category selection. Such inferences are particularly tangible when categories are repaired because the fact *that* alternatives are possible is made salient. In both extracts, the word 'woman' is in some way *functionally inadequate* for the work the speakers are designing their category selections to do.

In Extract 6, the caller's repair from 'wo[man]' to 'lady' specifies which aspects of being 'female' are to be understood about her neighbour: calling her a 'lady' implies features such as maturity, status and respectability, in contrast to the caller's problematic male neighbour. Thus the switch from 'woman' to 'lady' in this context sharpens the contrast between the caller's problematic and unproblematic neighbours. In Extract 7, it is useful to know that earlier in the session, Jimmy's wife Connie stated that she believed 'that this girl was here all alo:ng' and is the cause of her marital problems. Edwards (1998: 25–6) observes that

whereas Connie might well have said 'this woman', the expression 'this girl' serves to downgrade her status, if not her threat, as an unattached, unmarried, available, possibly young, female. I do not want to make too much of those connotations ... nor hinge an analysis on a single word: it is not possible to nail down precise meanings of that kind. Indeed, that is part of the functionality of such fuzzy categories, that they can invoke various indexical possibilities without making explicit claims that might be easier to rebut ... The category [Jimmy] uses switches from the denied and generalized one ('another woman'), to the particular person with whom he admits he 'moved in'. Aligning himself with Connie's description, 'girl', enables Jimmy to make his own use of any downgrading of her status that the switch allows ... So Jimmy's adoption of the term *girl* manages to align with Connie's, while helping to downgrade the status of his relationship with the 'girl,' and counter Connie's claim that something more serious, long-term, and marriage-threatening had been going on 'all along'.

The kinds of repairs we are encountering deal with what Edwards (2005; 2007) calls the 'speaker indexical' nature of interaction, and how speakers manage both the 'object side' and 'subject side' of the actions (complaints, justifications, affiliations) their talk is designed to accomplish. Drawing on Sacks's (1992) observations about the 'speaker-indexical properties of compliments', Edwards (2005: 6) argues that talk of all kinds is 'available for evaluative inferences about the speaker'. In Extract 6, C's repair 'wo- lady' manages the 'object side' of her account, constructing the 'object' of her talk – her neighbour – as a particular type of older, respectable woman. But the repair also attends to the 'subject side' of C's description: a recipient-designed method for telling the antisocial behaviour officer something of the kind of person C is. In other words, C's repair is 'indexical' or self-presentational, relevantly to the current interactional context, in which C is complaining about a neighbour, but does not want to present herself as someone who *regularly* falls out with her neighbours – she respects and gets on with at least one of them!

The other two extracts in this section are also instances of consecutive, repaired references, but their design is different from Extracts 6 and 7. Extract 8 comes from a 'speed-date', organized by a dating company, in which equal numbers of men and women each spend approximately five minutes talking to each other before the man moves on to a next partner. Here, the woman (F) has just agreed to her five-minute conversation being recorded, and is talking to her current interlocutor (M) about the researcher who has set up the recording equipment.

Extract 8 SD-28

```
1  F:  →  Just igno:re- this (.) lād[y]- this gi:rl who's doing um::
2              (0.4)
3  M:     I know, don' worry.
4              (0.3)
5  F:     Sociology degr*ee:,*
```

F is telling M to ignore the researcher setting up the equipment. She initially formulates the researcher as 'this lād[y]-', but cuts off in favour of an alternative gender category, 'gi:rl'. Possible trouble with the category selection is indicated even earlier than the cut-off in the micropause after 'this'. In contrast to Extracts 6 and 7, the repair solution 'gi:rl' contains pre-framing – the repeated word 'this'.

Given that F's repair is not topicalized by M (e.g., with a repair initiator; 'don' worry' is about the research recording), the question remains as to the function of the repair 'this lād- this gi:rl'. The term 'lady' is not 'referentially' inadequate: 'this lady who's doing um Sociology degr*ee:,*' could do the job of referring. There is no notion that a name, rather than a descriptive recognitional is preferred. But its repair indicates its inadequacy, for which there are various possible accounts. Both 'girl' and 'lady' belong to the same collection of categories as 'woman' in Extracts 6 and 7. By repairing one with another, F displays an understanding of the 'inference-rich' properties of categories: whatever characteristics resonate with the category 'lady' are a source of trouble for F, who selects 'girl' as an alternative. F's trouble may be to do with the age-differential inferences of the categories. Within the 'stage-of-life' membership categorization device, 'girl' is younger than 'lady'. F may have used a reference that is 'too old' for the researcher (who is a postgraduate student, and 10–15 years younger than F) relative to F, in this context. The repair may be designed *for* the researcher, as a possibly overhearing recipient. Furthermore, in the context of reassuring M about having their talk recorded, F's switch from 'lady' to 'girl' may be status-oriented, positioning the researcher as a 'harmless student'. Even more speculatively, a switch from 'lady' to 'girl' may formulate the researcher as too young for the current speed-dating environment, and not a potential date for M!

Finally, Extract 9 comes from a neighbour-dispute mediation interview, in which a mediator (M) is talking to a client (C). C is the subject of a complaint from her neighbours, for making excessive noise. C has said that it is her neighbours, not her, who are noisy and that although they were friendly when she first moved in they no longer talk to her. Here, C is explaining possible reasons why her neighbours are no longer friendly.

Extract 9 DM-C01-P2

```
1  C:    We:ll, (1.3) It's hard to explain about the
2        girl at the- the: LA:dy at the end because she
3        doesn't talk to anybody.
4  M:    Ri::ght.
```

C refers to her neighbour as 'the girl at the-' (lines 1–2). We can see from the subsequent repair she was headed towards 'the girl at the end [of the row of houses where C lives]'. However, C cuts off on 'the-', not to produce a different reference *form* (e.g., 'my neighbour', 'Mrs Edge') but to formulate a different descriptive recognitional by replacing 'girl' with 'lady' (in contrast to the previous extract, in which 'lady' was replaced with 'girl'). In contrast to Extract 8, the repair contains both pre- ('the') and post-framing ('at the'). Although C's replacement runs in the opposite direction from F's in Extract 8 ('girl → lady' versus 'lady → girl'), it may also be oriented to selecting a more age-appropriate category, used to separate C and her neighbour in terms of their relative ages. The switch also possibly signals C's respect for the (older) neighbour and their formal relationship (Stokoe, 2003). The repair manages the 'object side' of C's account, her neighbour, invoking the category's resonant features. On the 'subject side', the repair communicates implicitly that C is respectful of her neighbour, in the context of defending herself against a complaint.

Each of the four extracts considered so far contains a repair from one gender category to another (woman/lady; woman/girl; lady/girl; girl/lady). Comparison of the extracts leads to four preliminary observations. First, the differing content and direction of the repairs provides basic evidence for Edwards's (1998) argument that categories do not have absolute meanings, making them objectively 'accurate' or 'errors'. Rather, the same category can do different inferential work, depending on its local context; it can be a trouble source in one turn and the repair solution in another. Second, in none of the extracts do recipients topicalize the repair. As in SISR generally, the repairs are not oriented to as the main business of the utterance. Indeed, it is rare for recipients to topicalize self-initiated repairs, although here is an instance from a speed-date, in which F has just asked M why he is living in the place he does; he answered that he 'followed a woman' there. F's category-formed error is topicalized by M at line 2.

Extract 10 SD-5

```
1  F:  →  I: followed a woma- a ma:n.=um [not a woman.
2  M:                                    [Yeh: £you followed
3          a woman as well.£
4  F:      £I f(h)ollo(h)wed£ a m(h)a:n to Newtown.
```

Third, in Extracts 7, 8 and 9, the repair solution is delivered with noticeable pitch shift relative to the trouble source; that is, it is 'done more "emphatically" than the repairable' (Plug, 2006: 12). This leads us to a final observation that we explore throughout the chapter, to do with the level of exposure, embeddedness or markedness of the repair. The issue is something like this: how troubling was the repairable, and how committed are speakers to their repair solution? How much do the speakers want recipients to 'ignore' their 'mistaken' first category selection? There are a number of possibilities. The speaker may design the repair segment such that they display no marked preference for one category over another. They may mark their error and account for their use of the repairable category. They may produce the repair solution with an immediacy that implies a crossing out of the first category and commitment to the second. The inclusion of pre- and/or post-framing may be an important feature of these alternative designs. The more framing items that are included in the repair segment, the more space is taken up in the turn by the repair, and hence the more marked it becomes. These possibilities have implications for claims about participants' orientations to gender, which are explored in subsequent sections.

Marked XY repairs

Jefferson (1987) shows how in other-initiated repair the business of correcting may take over from whatever else had been going on in the sequence: this is 'exposed' correction. In our examples of SISR, although *speakers* may temporarily suspend their turn's progress towards completing its original action, *recipients* do not expose or mark repairs (cf. Extract 10) but respond to the primary action of the turn.

The following extracts all contain some 'exposure' of the trouble source and its repair. Extract 11 comes from a university tutorial in which trainee teachers have been discussing strategies for teaching children to write. However, they have shifted off this topic and Sam is talking about *a cappella* singing (see Stokoe, 2006; 2008a, for other discussions of this extract).

Extract 11 UT-25

```
1            (0.5)
2  S:     .hhh N:o it's where you all start singin.=we used
3          to do that in De:von.
4            (0.5)
```

a)

Sam
produces
'f̲:our
gi̲:rls'

5   S: →   Brilliant (l-) but I saw f̲:our gi̲rls, (0.4)

b)

Sam looks
away from
other
students on
'at um::'

6   →   at um::
7   (0.2)

c)

Sam rolls
his eyes
up on
'four
wo̲:men'

8   S: four wo̲:men (0.7) at um:: (1.0) >Por'obello Road
9   market.<

```
10                (0.7)
11   S:      They were incre::(h)dible.
12                (1.1)
```

d)

Sam picks up his papers and gets up from his chair on '<u>S</u>::tunning'.

```
13   S:      <u>S</u>::tunning.
```

Sam starts to formulate the singers as '<u>f</u>:our <u>gi</u>:rls,' (line 5). This is followed by a 0.4-second pause before he continues with the location part of his description 'at um::' (line 6). Sam then stops and reformulates '<u>f</u>:our <u>gi</u>:rls,' as 'four w<u>o</u>:men'. So here, the trouble source is '<u>gi</u>:rls', the repair solution is 'w<u>o</u>:men', and the repair is both pre-framed ('four' is repeated) and post-framed ('at um' is repeated when he completes his turn).

The video-recording permits examination of Sam's gaze and embodied conduct, which works in aggregate with the talk to project trouble, orient to its source, and repair it. So, on '<u>f</u>:our <u>gi</u>:rls', Sam's gaze is directed towards his interlocutors (line 5). However, during the 0.4-second pause he begins to look away from his recipients, and is looking to his right as he says 'at um::' (line 6). As he produces the repair 'four w<u>o</u>:men' (line 8), his eyes swivel upwards exaggeratedly, explicitly marking his use of the repairable item '<u>gi</u>:rls'. Sam's eye-roll indirectly *assesses* his category selection (a gloss might be 'oops, I said "girls" when I should have said "women"'). But the other participants topicalize neither Sam's repair – note the 0.7- and 1.0-second pauses in and following the repair segment – nor the 'Por'obello Road' singers – note the gaps at lines 10 and 12.

Sam's switch from 'girls' to 'women' is a recipient-designed management of the 'subject side' of his description. By orienting to, repairing and upgrading his formulation of the singers from 'girls' to 'women', Sam pre-empts possible objections to his use of 'girls' in the context of this particular group and its gender composition; his repair therefore has something of an *affiliative* function and deals with 'subject-side' concerns to do with being a 'gender-aware' speaker.

Extract 12 comes from a police interrogation. The suspect (S) has been arrested on suspicion of criminal damage to a neighbour's door. Here, the police officer (P) is asking S about his alleged confession to the door's owner.

Extract 12 PN-19

```
1   P:                    [Right- YE:ah.=so] that comment's: wrong
2       →    then:. that you didn't– (0.2) y'didn't admit. to this
3       →    girl then. (.) °that-° this woman >sorry< that uh::
4            you punched 'er door.
5                    (0.3)
6   S:    Well I can't (0.3) remember tha:t no.
```

P's repair is initiated at line 3 by a cut off on '°that-°'; he replaces the trouble source 'girl' with the solution 'woman' which is both pre- ('this') and post-framed ('that'). In contrast to previous extracts, P inserts an apology ('>sorry<') before producing the post-framing that tells recipients the turn is back on track.

P's 'sorry' is an 'index of an offence' (Robinson, 2004); in this case, regarding his selection of the appropriate reference term for an aggrieved party. P is neither fixing a category-formed error, nor making his reference consistent with S's: S has used 'girl' but *not* 'woman' during the interview. P's 'offence' may be the production of an insufficiently neutral descriptor. As mentioned earlier, although no category is value-free, in this context 'girl' carries potential status-downgraded inferences relative to 'woman', making 'woman' the 'default' or unmarked term (i.e., 'men and women' is unmarked, 'men and girls' marks 'girls'). As such, like Sam's repair in Extract 11, the repair functions on the 'subject side' to maintain P's 'neutrality' and identity as a 'gender-aware speaker'. The repair and apology may also be oriented to future overhearing audiences such as lawyers, judges and juries in court.

As Robinson (2004) has demonstrated, apology tokens can occur at various sequential positions, including those which make apologizing the primary action of the turn. In contrast, the main action of P's turn remains the *questioning* of S, and S answers P's question in his next turn. Moreover, P's apology, with its speeded-up delivery and placement prior to post-framing, is designed not to be responded to. The repair is marked by P, but not by S. This is in contrast to a number of 'post self-repair apologies' reported in Robinson (2005), in which the repairs-plus-apology are the focus of the talk. However, Robinson's examples all contain *referentially inadequate* first references, in which the speakers make a 'factual' error of some kind.

Extract 13 provides a dramatic – literally – example of marked XY repair. It comes from an episode of the American television comedy *Friends*. Two of the characters, Ross and Phoebe, are discussing recent events in which Ross, already twice married and divorced, married another character, Rachel, while drunk in Las Vegas. Rachel wants to get the marriage annulled, and Ross has told her that he has done so. However, he admits to Phoebe that he has not organized the annulment and is telling her why.

Extract 13 *Friends* Season 6, Episode 2: 'The One Where Ross Hugs Rachel' (Bright/Kauffman/Crane Productions and Warner Bros. Television)

```
1   R:      ↑All I know is: I- I ↑can't have another (.) failed
2           ma:rriage.
```

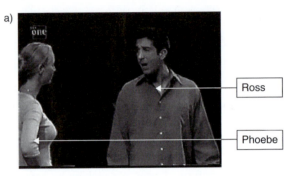

```
3   P:  →   ↑So: okay what.=you're gonna be ↑ma:rried ↑to a ↑girl who
4           ↑doesn' even know: ↑about ↑it?
5                        (0.2)
6   P:  →   ↓O:h. WO:man.SO:rry.
```

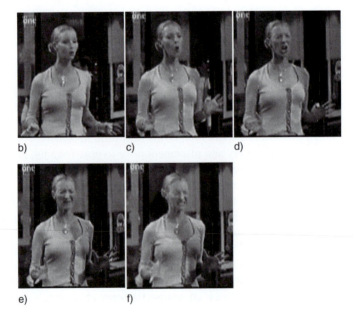

7	P:	[((continues with facial grimaces and hand gestures))
8	A:	[HEH HEH HEH HEH HEH HEH HEH heh heh
9	R:	<u>We</u>ll: okay so:: I don't have it all worked out
10		quite yet.

This is, of course, a scripted rather than natural conversation. Nevertheless, one can assume scriptwriters construct dialogue using their members' knowledge of how conversation works, such that play scripts 'can be taken seriously as objects of conversation analysis' (McHoul, 1987: 83; Stokoe, 2008b). The repair in Phoebe's turn 'girl…<u>wo</u>:man. <u>so</u>:rry.' shares several features with other extracts, including the same trouble source and repair solution categories, and the same likely 'subject-side' function of fixing a 'marked' gender category (Phoebe's character is arguably the most 'feminist' in the programme; this bit of scripting gets its humour from her use of a 'sexist' formulation).

Like Extract 13, Phoebe's apology is oriented to her word selection, done somewhat parenthetically to the overall action of the turn and in a new TCU. Notice Phoebe's embodied production of the repair, an exaggerated parody of the eye-roll that accompanied Sam's repair from 'girls' to 'women' in Extract 11. Phoebe's facial expressions and arm movements work in aggregate to 'notice' that there was trouble in her preceding talk (line 3, '↓O:h.'), produce the repair with a marked increase in volume and pitch movement ('<u>WO</u>:man'), and deliver the apology with a lengthy grimace ('<u>SO</u>:rry').

Here are four further marked XY repairs, containing the same categories, taken from internet 'blog' data dealing with a variety of different topics.

Extract 14 www.anothermonkey.blogspot.com
There's definitely a girlish quality about it, in the way that the
Lifetime channel or a Lisa Loeb video have a girlish feel to
them. Which is not surprising, given that Jen is, in fact,
a girl. Woman. Sorry. Woman.

Extract 15 www.doeuv.com
Is this a joke? Sorry if not, but this same post, almost exactly, was
posted in alt.autos.toyota about a week ago by **a girl (woman?**
Sorry …). You can see the responses there, since all the guys in the
group (yours truly included) were tripping over themselves to answer
her post!

Extract 16 http://profile.myspace.com
But about me: I'm married to a fantastic **girl (woman, sorry)**, we have
the world's cutest dog, and I doubt I'll ever have a clue what the word
'career' means.

Extract 17 http://tropa23.blogspot.com/2007/06/she-did-it-again.html
My ma is trying to set me up with this **girl/woman sorry** named Aileen.

Writing about the relative value of interactional versus linguistic analysis of repair, Schegloff (1979: 263) argues that in linguistics 'much of the available analysis is for written sentences or for "might-as-well-be-written" sentences'. However, these extracts demonstrate the elision of spoken and written discourse. What is particularly interesting about these repairs is the fact *that* they are written. Why purposefully mark a repair when the 'error' could be deleted and the 'correct' version published? The answer lies once more in understanding the subject-side, 'speaker-indexical' organization of description (Edwards, 2007). The repairs are not done to be 'accurate' about the age (or whatever else) of the person being described. The writers are *doing* 'doing repair' ironically, with regard to their use of 'neutral' or 'non-sexist' gender categories.

In all extracts in this section, the speaker (or writer) marked their repairs via eye-rolls, gestures, prosodic features and/or apology tokens. These procedures, when accompanying 'girl/woman' repairs, provide evidence of participants' orientation to *gender* in ways that Extracts 6–9 did not. The speakers and writers demonstrate, by exposing the repair, their (albeit ironic) commitment to the repair solution, deleting 'from the record' the repairable category.

The next section examines XY repairs that include the word 'or'. As we will see, some cases are possibly not repairs at all, are ambiguous, or are 'low-commitment' cases in which speakers do not demonstrate commitment to the trouble source or to the repair solution.

X 'or' Y formatted repairs and non-repairs

In Extract 18, a suspect (S) has been arrested on suspicion of criminal damage and threats to kill two of his neighbours. S has told the police officer about long-term noise problems from his neighbours, who kept his daughters awake on the night in question. S says that he shouted to his neighbours to be quiet, and banged on his ceiling (their floor) with a pickaxe handle. Five minutes later S reports that he heard banging on his front door. This extract illustrates the point made earlier that 'girl' may be used routinely to refer to adult women: the discussion is about a homeowner who is presumably an adult.

Extract 18 PN-22

```
1                    (0.3)
2   S:      W'll- (0.7) .hhh an' I come out.
3                    (1.5)
4   S:  →  Then the woman (0.4) or the girl that lives there:
5           is coming chargin' down the stairs.=goin' come on
6           then if that's what you wanna do: we'll get it on.
```

7   (0.6)
8   S: I was like well: fhuck off. Hh
9   (1.4)

S is narrating one of his neighbours' actions, describing her as 'the woman'. The TCU continues after a 0.4-second pause with 'or the girl' (line 4). There are two ways of reading this turn. First, it is possible to hear 'or the girl' as a repair segment *inserted* into the turn, without which it would have run off as 'the woman that lives there'. In this case, the pause is a candidate repair initiator (see Schegloff, 1979: 273), 'the' is the candidate pre-framing and 'girl' is a candidate repair solution. However, the inclusion of 'or' gives a different quality to the turn. A second reading is therefore that 'or' functions to *cancel the second category ('girl') as a repair* and install it as an *alternative to*, rather than replacement for and cancellation of, the first category ('woman').

When compared to Extract 7, which contains the same consecutive categories ('a wo- (0.2) gi:rl.'), we can see how the different structure provides for a different function. The repair in Extract 7 had an affiliative function. In Extract 18, the use of 'or' provides for an *epistemic* function regarding the speaker's knowledge of the 'correct' category for referring. The suspect is describing a dispute, in mitigation of his alleged criminal activities. The use of alternative categories, produced *as* alternatives with 'or', creates an epistemic or relational distance between the suspect and the aggrieved at a time when the suspect's motive for his actions are at stake. To illustrate this more clearly, consider these extracts, also from suspects' talk in police interrogations: 'his:: (0.2) wife or his girlfriend's looked out the window', 'with him an' his girlfriend, or wife:,'. In both cases, using a single reference would imply that the suspect *knew* the relationship status of the people being described. In matters of criminal dispute, not knowing the aggrieved party, and having no 'history' with or relationship to them, removes one possible motive for the dispute and gives the suspect room to direct blame for it away from himself or herself. Selecting alternative categories using 'or' implies a lack of precise knowledge, and therefore a lack of relationship with the aggrieved; it does 'subject-side' work for the suspect as a careful witness who does not claim more than he knows, and it also implies that the gender category is not the most important thing in the overall narrative. S does not know his neighbours beyond the noise they make; he is not invested in knowing about them; his dispute is their fault, not his. In Extract 18, then, given that 'girl' is *not replacing or repairing* 'woman', we are left with the notion that the person on the stairs was describable with *either* category.

The next extract comes from the Holt corpus of British telephone conversations, from a conversation between two friends, Joyce and Lesley. Here, they are talking about Nancy, who called Joyce that morning, apparently to rescind an offer of help.

Extract 19 Holt Oct 88:1:8:8[3]

```
1    J:                                    [Well I]really wz]↓cross:.
2             (0.7)
3    L:     ihYe[s:
4    J:         [I mean[a-
5    L:                [She ↑'asn' given you much (0.4)
6             n[otice.  hh]
7    J:        [Well ex↓a]ctly,
8             (0.3)
9    J: →   .hh she said I've got this Australian: girl e-who's
10           wintering in Galhampton 'nd: .hhh *or* Australian: woman.
11           or some[thing,
12   L:            [Au pairing I expect hh
13                 (1.4)
```

Joyce is '↓cross:.' with Nancy. Lesley affiliates with her friend (line 3) and supplies the reason for Joyce's annoyance (lines 5–6) which Joyce ratifies – 'Well ex↓actly' – before launching into a spate of reported speech about what Nancy said on the phone: 'she said I've got this Australian: girl e-who's wintering in Galhampton 'nd:'. Joyce is continuing with her turn ('[a]nd') before she takes an in-breath, which is a candidate repair initiator if the trouble source is 'girl', its solution is 'woman', and 'Australian:' is its pre-framing. Her turn also contains an 'or' (line 10), and the generalizer 'or something' (line 11).

As in Extract 18, the use of consecutive alternative references has an *epistemic* function. Joyce is quoting Nancy rather than formulating her own talk: the repair is fixing her report of what Nancy 'actually' said. The addition of 'or something' suggests that the precise gender category used is not important – the gist of what Nancy said has been communicated to Lesley, who seems oriented to this latter interpretation, as she does not pick up on the replacement of the gender category but instead provides an account for why Nancy might have an Australian female living near her at all ('Au pairing I expect'). As 'au pairs' are normatively young single women, maybe teenage but old enough to look after children, do housework and live away from home in another country, they are unlikely to be under 14 or over 30, or married, or with their own children. However, Joyce and Lesley are middle-aged women with families. Lesley's suggestion that the person being discussed is an au pair is an *uptake* from what Joyce has just said. As such, it is a possible orientation to, and indeed a proof procedure for, Lesley's hearing Joyce as referring to a female in her late teens or early 20s, and *therefore* unsure which to call her, out of 'girl' or 'woman'.

---

[3] Part-retranscribed from the original.

So the notion of whether to call this person a 'girl' or 'woman' may be a function of, and may index, not only what Joyce does or does not know about her, but also Joyce's own relative age with regard to her, and her indeterminate status, for Joyce and maybe Lesley, as 'girl' or 'woman'.

As with Extract 18, using 'or' retains the ostensible trouble source ('Australian girl') as a viable description, cancelling the second description ('Australian woman') as a repair and establishing it as an alternative, with further unspoken alternatives also possible. 'Or something' further implies a lack of commitment to the ostensible 'repair solution', because both descriptions, and perhaps others, remain viable.

Extract 20 comes from a radio discussion, in which the speaker, a Member of the European Parliament, is discussing gender discrimination in the workplace.

Extract 20 BBC Radio 4 *Woman's Hour* 12.11.07

```
1   MEP:   .hhh uh an' think it's (.) te:rrible that uh young
2          ladies are .hh or young women are discri:minated
3          against in this wa:y.
```

As a possible repair, the initiator is the brief in-breath ('.hh'), the trouble source is 'ladies', the repair solution is 'women', and it is both pre-framed ('young') and post-framed ('are'). What motivates it as a possible repair is the 'subject-side' concern about being a 'gender-aware' speaker. As a possible 'non-repair', the insertion of 'or' leaves both categories viable as descriptive terms. However, the inclusion of post-framing ('are'), indicating that the MEP was already progressing with his turn 'young ladies are …' before stopping, leaves lingering somewhat the problematic use of 'ladies' in a way that an absence of post-framing 'young ladies or young women' might not. Indeed, formulating the phrase with no framing at all ('young ladies or women') would shore up its 'list-of-alternatives' rather than 'repair' quality (e.g., 'do you want brown or white rice?').

This ambiguity – whether a turn contains a repair or list of alternatives – rather than being a problem for analysis, is a crucial members' resource for doing accountable description. In Extract 20, it is hard (at least for me, as a feminist!) not to hear the MEP (a middle-aged man speaking with 'received pronunciation') correcting his use, in this context, of the sexist, paternalistic phrase 'young ladies' with the term 'women' (which is used consistently by the host and other guest). In that sense, his 'repair' has both a 'subject-side' function *and* an affiliative function, in a context in which gender discrimination is the topic at hand, being discussed on the British radio programme *Woman's Hour*. However, the use of 'or' makes fuzzy the issue of whether he is repairing categories or listing alternatives, and that ambiguity makes him less readily accountable for either.

The two final extracts in this section do not contain 'girl/woman/lady' categories, but they allow us to see the work done by 'or' to make a turn ambiguous with regard to whether repair has been done, and, if so, what is being repaired, and what the function of any repair is. Extract 21 comes from a dinner-time conversation between two parents and their daughter. Cindy and Mom have been telling Dad about a school trip in which there was some confusion over a miscalculated bill. Extract 22 comes from a radio show, in which the host, Jonathan Ross (R), is talking to a comedian, Michael McIntyre (M). They are discussing reviews of McIntyre's recent show, all of which were good except one.

Extract 21 Stew dinner: 12[4]

```
1  D:     £Somebody hit a wrong button or some[thin'?,£
2  M:                                       [.hhh Well
3         what they d:id is they showed you where- th'waiter,
4    →    an' w- (.) or waitress *goes.*
5  D:     Mm h[m:,
6  M:         [An' pu- punches in your order. [ … ]
```

Extract 22 BBC Radio 2 *Jonathan Ross* 15.9.07

```
1   R:    [So you got] good reviews apart from the one
2         (.) [↓bad *reviewer.*]
3   M:    [ Ye:ah.        ] yeh they li:ed.
4         (.)
5   ?:    Mhm [heh
6   M:        [What- what were they ↑on about. [    three   ]=
7   R:                                         [What- what-]
8   M:    =£sta:rs?£
9   R:    ↑Obviously we're mostly interested in the ba:d
10   →    review.=what did ba:d review- what did 'e find or she
11   →    find fault with in your performance.
12  M:    We:ll I think it's- so- I jus'- I well- it's-
13        (0.2) .h ↑↑heh £↑↑let's ↑↑not ↑↑focus ↑↑on a
14        b(h)a:d [one£
```

In Extract 21, it is tempting to see Mom's addition of 'waitress' as a repair dealing with the gendered assumption that waiting staff are generically male, or that generic 'persons-in-stories' are male (which was my initial reason for collecting this extract). However, the word 'and' is the trouble source in this turn, not the gendered suffixes of the person references. The repair initiator is the cut-off on 'w-', and the repair solution is 'or', post-framed with the 'w' of 'waitress'. Mom is aiming for the *phrase* 'waiter *or* waitress', not 'waiter *and*

---

[4] Retranscribed from the original.

waitress': the repair fixes the action being done, which is listing alternatives, not 'doing a repair'!

In Extract 22, the target lines are 10–11, in which Ross is asking the question, 'what did 'e find or <u>she</u> find fault with ...'. There is no clear repair initiation here; no cut-off or pause. As a possible repair, the trouble source is '[h]e', the repair solution is 'she', and it is post-framed with the word 'find'. As a repair, it does 'subject-side' work to present Ross as a 'gender-aware' speaker. As a non-repair, the lack of repair initiation and use of 'or' gives a 'list-of-alternatives', epistemic quality to the turn: Ross does not know the gender of the reviewer. However, the inclusion of post-framing indicates that Ross was already continuing with his turn past the problematic category. As we saw in Extract 20, this leaves lingering the assumption that the reviewer was male. That is, the 'list-of-alternatives' possibility is somewhat weakened by the inclusion of post-framing. Saying 'what did he or she find ...' without post-framing would be a gender-inclusive method for referring to a single unknown reviewer, replacing the locally initial reference 'reviewer' (line 2) with locally subsequent pro-terms. This is in contrast to using 'they', which McIntyre does at lines 3 and 6 (and which is a common practice as a gender-neutral pronoun in cases of singular reference), or the more problematic 'generic he'.

To sum up, the inclusion of 'or' between X and Y categories, even where repair segment features are present, gives a 'list-of-alternatives' quality to the turn, thus somewhat diminishing its hearability as 'repair'. 'Or' frames both categories uttered as viable descriptions, where the speaker has no commitment to one or the other. The 'X or Y' format attends to matters of practical epistemology, such as being heard to do accurate, non-invested description, or being a careful witness. Alternative references may be produced in ways that imply neither category is important for the ongoing action of the turn, as long as recipients understand who is being referred to. So in contrast to marked XY repairs, the insertion of 'or' downgrades the speaker's commitment to either category. The production of 'X or Y' works against the status of Y as replacing or repairing X, keeping X alive for inferences about whoever is being described, and for the business done by the describing. But in some cases, it can imply a person of a *specific* rather than very open age and status, as being young adult or late teen, given that both categories are provided as still-viable descriptions (e.g., 'girl/woman/something' is more restricted in age range than just 'woman').

The final section focuses on a collection of consecutive alternative references in which features of repair, if present, are ambiguous.

XY non-repairs: Intensifying, cumulating, specifying

Extract 23 comes from a police interview in which the suspect (S) has been arrested on suspicion of stealing a credit card. The police officer (P) has pursued a line of questioning about the involvement of S's partner in the alleged crime, which S has denied, stating that she has never been in trouble. We join the interaction just after S has said that he wants a quiet, crime-free life with his partner.

Extract 23 PN-94a

```
1    P:      So you'd sa:y you'd landed on y'feet then.
2                    (0.3)
3    S:      .HHHHH::oh fuckin' 'e:ll.
4                    (0.5)
5    S:  →  ↑↑She's a ↑fuckin' ↑fantastic wo:man.
6                    (0.2)
7    S:  →  ↑She's: (.) a wo:man.
8                    (0.2)
9    S:  →  A la:dy.
10                   (0.2)
11   S:  →  Not a- (0.2) some girl on the stre:e'.
12                   (0.5)
13   S:      Righ',=what I'm sayin' is: wha- ye:ah, .hh she
14           KEeps me outta tro:uble.
15                   (0.2)
```

P formulates S's description of his current life with his girlfriend (line 1), which S responds to with a set of assessments of his girlfriend prefaced by '.HHHHH::oh fuckin' 'e:ll.' (line 3). S's first assessment is '↑fuckin' ↑fantastic wo:man.' (line 5), done as one complete TCU. After a short gap he produces another '↑She's: (.) a wo:man.'. Note that this TCU is a partial repetition of the first, but with '↑fuckin' ↑fantastic' deleted from it. Whereas '↑fuckin' ↑fantastic wo:man.' does not specify a particular characteristic, the truncated repeat '↑She's: (.) a wo:man.' (line 7) isolates and emphasizes 'wo:man.', signalling that she represents some kind of archetype or essence of the category.

After another short gap, S produces another assessment-implicative categorization of his girlfriend, 'A la:dy.' (line 9), which further specifies which qualities of 'woman' are relevant (e.g., refined, genteel, polite), all of which works to characterize her as someone *dispositionally* uninvolved in criminal activity. Indeed this characterization is provided explicitly by the subsequent contrast 'Not a- (0.2) some girl on the stre:e'.' (line 11). S does not say what his girlfriend is not ('not a-' – candidates are any number of derogatory terms such as 'tart', 'scrubber', 'slag', etc.), instead producing the repair 'some girl'. S therefore constructs a contrast between possible ways of describing his partner as a 'girl', 'lady' or 'woman', which displays his understanding *that* different categories carry different characterological resonances.

In terms of describing S's turns as *repair*, each successive turn is produced as 'complete', rather than cut off, so there is no clear repair initiation between assessments. Although pauses between turns may be indicative of transition space repairs, each assessment *specifies*, *intensifies* or *builds cumulatively on* the prior one, and they all work to produce a contrast to the alternative categorization of S's girlfriend as 'some girl on the stre:e'. Each successive assessment 'fixes' the content of the previous one, through due to their functional inadequacy for convincing P that S's girlfriend is not the type to be involved in criminal activities.

The final extract of the chapter comes from Edwards's (1998) marriage guidance counselling data. This time, we hear from Connie, who is describing what happens on a 'girls' night out' – in contrast to Jimmy's jealous concerns about what she is like when she is out 'with a load of ↑people.' (p. 28).

Extract 24 DE-JF:C2:S2: (Edwards, 1998: 29, line numbers altered)
```
1   Con:  →   [ … ] when I go out with the gir:ls, it's a:ll married
2         →   women talking about our ki:ds or somebody rin:gs (.)
3             .hh they have a pro:blem, y'know (.) "d'you fancy go-"
4             (.) that's uh- (.) the gir:ls night out
```

Again, of interest are the consecutive references 'the gir:ls' and 'married women' in Connie's description of what happens on a 'girls' night out'. As Edwards points out, the reformulation from 'girls' to 'married women' (lines 1–2) works to construct the category 'go out' as a non-sexualized event involving, in Connie's words, the category-bound activities of 'talking about our kids' (line 2) and discussing each other's problems. As two different ways of describing the people she goes out with, 'married women' is a useful reformulation of 'girls' in this context. But it is not a repair: as in Extract 23, the categories work in tandem, cumulatively, and in a recipient-designed way to construct a version of events aligned to specific interactional goals. For Connie, her descriptions and accounts manage 'subject-side' concerns to present herself as the innocent party in her marital dispute.

Concluding remarks

This chapter has investigated the way speakers select, formulate and repair consecutive alternative gendered categorial references to absent third parties. The repairs did not accomplish 'category-formed' correction (e.g., replacing 'sister' with 'brother') in cases where speakers were evidently heading for one category but began to utter its 'partner'. They were not person reference repairs (e.g., replacing a description with a name), and they were not done to disambiguate the first reference. In all cases, the first reference did the work of referring in a way that caused no apparent problems of recognition or understanding for the recipient. Although self-initiated self-repairs interrupted the progress of the turn in which they occurred, they did not interrupt the overall progressivity of the action being accomplished by it, and recipients did not orient to or further topicalize any of the repairs examined (with the exception of Extract 10). So, when the first categories uttered do the job of referring, but get repaired anyway, speakers fix the *functional inadequacy* of the first reference for the overall project of their turn: for 'object-side' description, for 'subject-side' implications for the speaker (including being a 'gender-aware' speaker), and for getting some bit of interactional business – affiliation, assessment, counter-complaint – accomplished.

In all cases of consecutive alternate reference, whether they were formatted as repairs or not, participants nevertheless demonstrated their understanding *that* there are different ways of referring to women and *that* different categories carry different resonances and implications. And *that* speakers replaced one category with another, without saying why or specifying them, displayed a mundane *participants'* orientation to Sacks's (1992) notion that people do inferential work with the categories they use. It is clear from these cases, and other studies of repair and person reference (e.g., Lerner & Kitzinger, 2007a), that word selection *matters* to people, even when a first term is referentially adequate and the replacement is its near synonym. Of course, this applies to all categories, not just gender categories (Edwards, 1991). So what can we say about the relevance of gender in the cases examined, particularly in the light of debates about what counts as an 'orientation' to gender?

In the first section of 'XY'-formatted 'standard' repairs, none of the cases displayed 'subject-side' concerns of being a 'gender-aware' speaker in the 'feminist' sense. Rather, the alternatives selected were to do with 'object-side' age-awareness, affiliation with co-participants, and 'subject-side' concerns to do with being a respectful person. In contrast, many of the marked repairs, all containing 'girl/woman' categories in that order, managed 'subject-side' concerns of being a gender-aware speaker, albeit in an ironic way in some instances. In the final section, which examined non-repairs, the alternative references did cumulative work in tandem with each other, and in contrast to each other, specifying and fixing the category-bound resonances of one with the next.

In the third section, it emerged that the inclusion of 'or' between categories weakened a turn's hearability as a repair, giving it a 'list-of-alternatives' quality instead. However, the inclusion of candidate repair features, particularly post-framing, weakened a turn's 'list-of-alternatives' quality, pushing it back towards its hearability as a repair. At the 'list-of-alternatives' end of this continuum, 'X or Y' formulations had an epistemic function, to do with the speaker's displayed knowledge of the person/s being described. In cases where a second category is *not replacing or repairing* the first, we are left with the notion that the person/s referred to are describable with *either* category uttered. This, in turn, implies a lack of commitment to the ostensible 'repair solution', because both descriptions remain viable. This is in contrast to XY-formatted repairs, and marked repairs, in which speakers, by producing immediate repair solutions or including an apology token, demonstrate commitment to the second category being the one to remain 'on the record'. At the 'repair' end of the continuum, the inclusion of post-framing leaves lingering a speaker's lack of 'gender awareness' (e.g., '... young ladies **are** .hh or young w̲omen **are** ...', in Extract 20) implied by the use of the problematic first category.

Overall, then, it appears that gender-category repairs may or may not be 'oriented to gender' in the feminist, political sense that this interest in conversation stems from. Being a 'gender-aware speaker' is analytically capturable in some instances, depending on the format of the repair, and the speaker's own identity. Other cases remain ambiguous, perhaps designedly so, because language, as a system of meaning-making, provides for speakers to imply, infer, deny and be held to account for the actions they do in turns of talk designed to accomplish them.

6

Gender, routinization and recipient design

Sue Wilkinson

Introduction

In organizational contexts – such as medical consultations, emergency calls or health-visitor interactions – each service provider interacts, over time, with successive individual clients in order to achieve a set of identical institutional tasks. Although for each client their case is unique and personal, from the organizational perspective most clients are 'routine cases', and 'all agencies have procedures for the routine management of multiple cases, for "process-ing" cases by assigning them to routine categories and so on' (Drew & Heritage, 1992a: 51). Even (or perhaps especially) in situations that are very traumatic for the individual client concerned, service providers use routine interactional pro-cedures to accomplish their institutional goals, such that analysts working with institutional talk are likely to find 'a "density" or concentration of repeatedly deployed particular conversational machinery' (Zimmerman, 1992b: 459–60) in these interactions. Analysis of calls for emergency assistance, for example, shows common 'interrogative-insertion' sequences, designed to elicit repair on or verification of a prior turn (Zimmerman, 1992b); and medical encounters in which doctors tell parents that their children have developmental disabilities commonly show a routinized 'perspective display series', designed to elicit from the parent their view of the child's disability in the hope that the med-ical diagnosis can be done as an agreement with the parents' views (Maynard, 1992). Across multiple different interactions, then, the same protocol is fol-lowed, the same kinds of questions asked, the same advice proffered, the same 'conversational machinery' employed.

These observations about the routinization of organizational interactions co-exist with an emphasis on 'recipient design' as a key principle of conversation analysis. 'Recipient design' refers to the 'multitude of respects in which the talk by a party in a conversation is constructed or designed in ways which display an orientation and sensitivity to the particular other(s) who are the coparticipants' (Sacks *et al.*, 1974: 727). Put simply, speakers say different things, in different words, implementing different actions, depending on who they take their recipient(s) to be. A classic study by C. Goodwin (1979) shows how a speaker redesigns an utterance, mid-course, when he finds his intended recipient otherwise engaged, so redirecting his talk to another. The design of talk with attentiveness to the particularities of the recipient is pervasive across talk-in-interaction and operates at a variety of levels.

One feature of recipient design is lexical choice, such that references to persons or to places are made 'with an eye to who the recipient is and what the recipient knows about the reference' (Schegloff, 1996c: 459). Specialist terminology may be selected (or avoided) depending on the speaker's understanding of who the recipient is (as when a birth professional uses the word 'doula' unproblematically when addressing a midwife, but avoids it, or try-marks[1] it as potentially troublesome, in talking with a non-professional; Kitzinger & Mandelbaum, 2007). Another feature of recipient design is topic selection: 'The things one talks about with another are selected and configured for who that other is – either individually or categorically' (Schegloff, 2007e: 89), so that speakers select some topics with some co-interactants and avoid them with others. Recipient design is also made manifest through the way in which questions are designed with reference to the 'thick particulars' of any given interactional moment. For example, in the context of medical history-taking, a physician who regularly asks the question 'What kind of contraception do you use?' (embodying the presuppositions that the patient both needs and uses contraception) might modify that question to ask 'Are you using any contraception? Is that necessary for you?' when faced with a patient he knows to be around 50 years old, who is divorced and who has previously been sterilized (Boyd & Heritage, 2006). Even rather 'formulaic' turns, such as the 'how-are-yous' that regularly open interactions, can be imbued with a speaker's awareness of a recipient's special claims to concern about their wellbeing (Schegloff, 2007a: 199). In a multitude of yet-to-be-explored ways, 'interactants particularise their contributions so as to exhibit attention to the "this-one-here-and-for-now-for-us-at-this-point-in-it" character of the interaction' (Schegloff, 1972: 115), even when their talk 'fosters the impression that it is "ritual" or even "merely ritual"; that it is "virtually automatic" or "(pre)scripted"; that it is "routine"' (Schegloff, 1986: 112).

In his work on calls to a suicide prevention line, Sacks (1992, II: 384–90) began to sketch out both the routinized and the recipient-designed features of helpline interaction. In an extended analysis of a single call, he describes the early part of the call-taker's interaction with the caller as building 'a relatively pre-cast conversation' (p. 389) in which the call-taker is 'making a routine for himself' (though here the routine is constituted by repetition *within* a single

---

[1] This is a technical term, used to indicate that the speaker produces the word in a way designed to seek confirmation from the recipient that she knows and understands it – typically, with upward intonation.

call, rather than *across* calls, as in my analysis). According to Sacks's single call analysis, the caller responds to the call-taker's routine (constituted in part by his thrice-repeated advice that she should attend a psychiatric clinic) by, in effect, accusing him of sounding bored and of not listening to her properly (pp. 387–8). The call-taker then remedies his talk, so that she can see that he *has* been listening to her, by 'trying to design whatever he's going to say by reference to what she's telling him' (p. 389). Building into a turn that offers a problem solution some evidence that the turn is responsive to the specifics of the problem presentation may make the proffered solution more acceptable to its recipient – even if, in fact, the solution is prefabricated and has been routinely offered to many previous callers:

It appears that if in offering a solution you can show that it's a solution devised for just this person, then they will routinely feel happier with it than they will if you deliver it as soon as they say 'hello', though you could perfectly well do that. (Sacks, 1992, II: 390)

In other words, Sacks suggests that people prefer to be offered information and advice apparently tailored to them as individuals, and that service providers may be sensitive to this even in the course of providing routinized advice.[2]

This chapter analyses one particular piece of prefabricated talk repeatedly used by a single call-taker across a series of calls to a helpline. It shows how, despite being produced in multiple very similar iterations, this prefabricated talk is none the less recipient-designed and packaged in a way that displays sensitivity to callers as individuals or as category members, thereby manifesting some basic principles of recipient design. As I will also show, a key feature of recipient design that informs the call-taker's selection (or not) of this prefabricated talk is the perceived gender of her recipient.

The Data

The data set from which the analysis presented in this chapter is drawn consists of (so far) 190 calls made to 4 different volunteer call-takers working on the national telephone helpline of the Fibromyalgia Association UK (FMA (UK)) during 2007. The helpline volunteers all have personal experience of fibromyalgia.

Fibromyalgia (sometimes abbreviated to 'fibro') is a 'chronic, painful musculoskeletal disorder of unknown aetiology' (Fransen & Russell, 1996: 7). It is characterized by widespread and persistent pain in the muscles and surrounding structures, typically accompanied by a host of other diverse symptoms, most notably fatigue and sleep disturbances. The disorder typically takes some

---

[2] See Sanden *et al.* (2001) for an example of this in relation to oncology consultations.

time to diagnose, with formal diagnosis most commonly made by a rheumatologist. It is diagnosed about seven times more often in women than in men
(Pellegrino, 1997: 7).

Well over half of the calls in my data set are requests for information about
fibromyalgia from newly diagnosed callers. The call-taker's standard response
is first to tell the caller how to obtain the FMA (UK) information pack (which
involves sending an A5 stamped, addressed envelope to the organization's office
in Stourbridge), and then to offer to answer any questions they might have there
and then. Common questions raised by callers (also commonly covered in self-
help books, e.g., Chaitow, 1998; Ediger, 1993) are: the relationship between
fibromyalgia and other conditions (e.g., rheumatism, myalgic encephalomy-
elitis (ME), menopause); whether particular problems are fibromyalgia symptoms or might have other causes; how best to manage pain; the value of various
prescribed medications and 'alternative' remedies; and eligibility for disability
benefits (though there is also a separate disability benefits inquiry line). Most of
these issues are covered in a 'question-and-answer' format in the organization's
Telephone Helpline Prompt Sheets, with which all call-takers are supplied.

Consistent with findings from other research on institutional interaction (e.g.,
Drew & Heritage, 1992b), the FMA (UK) helpline call-takers tend – because
they are dealing repeatedly with the same concerns – to develop rather formulaic responses across at least parts of their interactions. It is also readily apparent from listening to the data that, despite the generic guidance provided in the
organization's *Prompt Sheets*, some of these formulaic responses are nowhere
represented in the organization's literature, differ substantially from call-taker
to call-taker, and constitute distinctive 'signature' formulations: little bits of
prefabricated talk that they use repeatedly in providing information and advice.
In this chapter I focus on just one of these signature formulations employed by
a single call-taker (none of the other three call-takers says anything remotely
similar) on twelve separate occasions in the first fifty calls she recorded (with
forty-six people, since three called twice each and one called three times).

Extract 1 shows a call from the beginning of the recording. The focus of this
chapter is on (what I will show is) the prefabricated bit of talk at lines 109–17,
highlighted in **bold**.

Extract 1 Penny[3] (SW:FM:A013)

```
01   Clt:   Ri:ght. How can I he:lph[h.  ]
02   Pen:                      [Uh]:m (.) I've-
03          I've been having loads of problems since
```

---

[3] Audio files for some of the data extracts in this chapter can be accessed from my university web-
page (www.lboro.ac.uk/departments/ss/staff/wilkinson.html). All names of persons and places
are pseudonyms. The call-taker is denoted as 'Clt' and callers are pseudonymized as Penny
('Pen'), Lettie ('Let'), Karen ('Kar') and so on.

04   Janua:ry
//   ((22 lines omitted[4] in which Penny describes
             her problems which include sarcoidosis and symptoms
             of Bornholm's disease))
27   Pen: [.h]h An:d I've
28   been (.) waiting since January an' I finally
29   came up wi:th uhm (.) diagnosis today after
30   (.) thankfully everything else had proved
31   negati:v[e.]
32   Clt: [Ye]a:[h]
33   Pen: [.h] But I am finding it
34   quite disa:bling.
35   Clt: .hhh You (.) probably ar:e at the moment.
36   .hh uh:m (.) it's- ((coughs)) how much
37   d'you know abou:t it.
38   Pen: O-only just the leaflet that I-I was
39   given at the hospital toda:[y.]
40   Clt: [.hh] Oka:y.
41   Let's start from the beginning again then
42   shall we¿ [.hhh] We'll break the na:me dow:n.
43   Pen: [Mm hm]
44   (.)
45   Clt: Uhm fibromyalgia is obviously (.) Latin name.
46   Pen: [Yes]
47   Clt: [>Being a] medical name.< .hhh Fibro is fibre.
48   Pen: [Yes]
49   Clt: [My] is muscle. Algia is pain.
50   Pen: [mm hm]
51   Clt: [.hhh] Basically the fibres or tendons or
52   ligaments >whatever you'd like to call 'em<
53   .hhh u:h that attach your muscles to your
54   bones are permanently infla:me[d.]
//   ((22 lines omitted describing pain and ways
             of dealing with it))
77   Clt: .hh Uh:m other parts of the body are
78   affec:ted obviously: uh:m (0.2) .hh
79   sometimes it's one bit someti(h)mes it's
80   an(h)other bit .hh but I mean there's
81   about (0.8) thirty odd (0.2) clinical
82   symptoms. [of fi]bro. Rangin' from: .hhh=
83   Pen: [mmm]
84   Clt: =blurred vis:ion: (.) uh:[:m]
85   Pen: [Oh] ri:ght.

---

[4] The omitted lines are given in the appendix to this chapter.

86		(>Cause I was-<) cause I was going to
87		go and get my eye:s tes:ted agai:n.
88		Cause my eyes have been-
//		((12 lines omitted on Penny's eye problems))
101	Clt:	Well ma̲ke su̲re you tell your optician
102		you've been diagnosed with fibromyalgia.
103	Pen:	Mm hm
104	Clt:	Okay? Uh:m we go from the:re to sort of
105		uh:m .hh muscle spa:sms breathing
106		proble[:ms] .hh uh::m restless le::gs=
107	Pen:	[Yes]
108	Clt:	=.hh (.) swollen feelings in the tissues
109		an' **a cla̲s̲s̲ic example the̲re for a lo:t of**
110		**women with fibromyalgia is before you**
111		**develop°ed° the disease .hh the first thing**
112		**you did when you got 'ome was kick your**
113		**shoes off [.hh] after you develop the=**
114	Pen:	[Yes]
115	Clt:	**=disease the first thing you do is take**
116		**your bra̲ off cause it don't matter what**
117		**size it is it feels too sma:[ll.]**
118	Pen:	[Mm] huh
119		huh huh[hh]
120	Clt:	[£Uh]:m£ (.) y-you know it
121		rea:lly i:s there are ju-u-m- ve̲ry
122		dive̲rse symptoms.

As is typical of many of the calls in the corpus, here an initial offer of help is followed by the caller's account of having been recently diagnosed with fibromyalgia. Either assuming (or, in this case, after having established) that the caller knows relatively little about the condition ('O-only just the le̲aflet that I-I was given at the ho̲spital today', lines 38–9), the call-taker conveys information about fibromyalgia – in this case adumbrating a long information-conveying turn with the pre-pre[5] ('Let's start from the beginning again then shall we¿', lines 41–2). Although this 'mini-lecture' on fibromyalgia is clearly recipient-designed to the extent that it is being delivered to someone who has been diagnosed with the disorder just that day, and who has called the helpline and might therefore be expected to want to know about fibromyalgia, it also – as we will see – includes many prefabricated elements. The analytic focus here is the call-taker's description of 'a classic example' of one of the symptoms of fibromyalgia ('swollen feelings in [soft] tissues') as displayed in Extract 1, lines 109–17.

[5] This is a technical term, referring to material that is 'preliminary' to some other 'preliminary' material (hence 'pre-pre'). It often involves the naming of an action that is to follow.

It is prefabricated in the sense that she uses virtually the same words in eleven of the other forty-nine calls. Here it is in two more of its iterations:

Extract 2 Lettie (expanded version appears as Extract 9) (SW:FM:A024)

```
17   Clt:                      [A-   .hhh] a classic example=
18   Let:                      [ Mm hm ]
19   Clt:    =for a woman i:s before you developed fibro:
20           .hh the first thing you did when you got
21           'ome was take your shoes o:[ff. Aft]er you=
22   Let:                               [ Ye::s ]
23   Clt:    =develop fibro the first thing you do is
24           take your bra off [cause] it don't matter=
25   Let:                      [Yeah]
26   Clt:    =what si:ze it is it feels too sma:l[l.]
```

Extract 3 Karen (SW:FM:A038)

```
01   Clt:    A classic example for a- a woman with fibromyalgia
02           is .hh before you developed it the first thing
03           you did when you got 'ome was kick your shoes
04           o:[ff.   .hh] After you develop it the first=
05   Kar:      [ °Yeah° ]
06   Clt:    =thing you do is take your bra off cau[se   it] don't=
07   Kar:                                          [Yeah ]
08   Clt:    =matter what size it is it feels £too small£ after
09           about half an ho:ur.
```

These extracts, involving the same call-taker in interaction with three different women across a five-week period, are unlike the single case analysed in Sacks (1992, II: 384–90) in which the call-taker says 'the same thing' (p. 387) three times to the *same* recipient. In Extracts 1, 2 and 3, the call-taker says (what for now I will gloss as) the same thing to each of three *different* recipients, each of whom is hearing it for the first time, and none of whom displays any suspicion that this formulation is not recipient-designed for her in particular. Rather, it is 'routine' in the sense that the call-taker has it available as a prefabricated package that she delivers in pretty much the same way each time. It constitutes, for the call-taker, a small part of the routine talk in her helpline calls.

Routinization

What I mean in claiming that the call-taker is saying 'the same thing' and does so 'in pretty much the same way' can be illustrated with reference to the three data extracts above, which typify the collection overall in the following respects:

- The signature formulation begins (in ten of the twelve iterations) with the same words 'a classic example' (Extract 1, line 109; Extract 2, line 17; Extract 3, line 1).
- It is followed (in eleven of the twelve iterations) by the words 'for a woman' (Extract 2, line 19; Extract 3, line 1) or some minor variation on it (Extract 1, lines 109–10).
- The formulation is (in all twelve iterations) designed as a 'before and after' contrast, in which the first turn constructional unit (TCU) ('before you developed fibro …') strongly projects some subsequent TCU with an 'after you developed fibro …' format. The first ('before') TCU projects a second ('after') TCU from the same speaker: it holds the turn and does not make it relevant for the recipient to speak – with other than a minimal receipt (e.g., 'yes') – until the 'after' component of the turn is complete (in fact it is extremely rare for recipients to come in with other than a minimal receipt of the first TCU: there are no examples here). Minimal receipts follow the 'before' component in Extract 1 ('Yes', line 114), Extract 2 ('Yes', line 22), Extract 3 ('Yeah', line 5), Extract 5 ('Mm', line 15), Extract 8 ('Yes', line16) and Extract 9 ('Yes', line 22); there is no response to the first TCU in Extracts 4 and 6.
- In all twelve iterations, the 'before' component proposes as a known-in-common ordinary observation that the first thing a (non-fibromyalgic) woman does on returning home is to 'take' (Extract 2, line 21), or more commonly 'kick', her shoes off (Extract 1, lines 112–13; Extract 3, lines 3–4) – presumably due to the discomfort of high heels or pinched toes associated with formal or fashionable footwear for women (though this is treated as sufficiently known-in-common not to need specifying). In addition to its literal meaning, the phrase 'kick off your shoes' has the idiomatic or metaphorical meaning 'to relax' (it features in this sense in a number of popular songs by artists ranging from Elvis Presley to Don McLean), and this commonplace usage contributes to hearing the action to which it refers as an ordinary piece of behaviour not requiring special explanation.
- In all twelve iterations, this 'before' component is contrasted with an 'after' component proposing that the first thing a woman who has developed fibromyalgia does is 'take your bra off' (Extract 1, lines 115–16; Extract 2, line 24; Extract 3, line 6). The 'before and after' contrast treats bra removal as an action specifically 'alternative' to the ordinary behaviour of removing shoes – and unlike the removal of shoes (which is not accounted for), the removal of a bra is *always* accounted for – and in virtually identical words each time ('cause it don't matter what size it is it feels too small'; Extract 1, lines 116–17; Extract 2, lines 24 and 26; Extract 3, lines 6 and 8–9). The contrast and the asymmetrical accounting (in all twelve cases) work together to constitute as *out of the ordinary* (for women in general) the swollen feelings

in breast tissue that lead some women to want to remove their bras, thereby rendering it a 'symptom' (of fibromyalgia). The comparison also serves to normalize painful breasts for women with fibromyalgia, by producing it as a 'normal' (or, in the call-taker's words, a 'classic') symptom of fibromyalgia – as common a problem for women with fibromyalgia as painful feet are for women more generally.

- In all twelve iterations, the signature formulation addresses the recipient as a member of a categorical 'you' (where 'she' or 'they' are the grammatically 'correct' possible alternatives, given the unfolding TCU). This 'you' is hearable in context as 'women with fibromyalgia' (Extract 1, line 110) – including the speaker herself.

Responses to the signature formulation vary depending on the extent to which recipients elect to display it as being consonant with their own experience. There are broadly three types of response: a minimal receipt – e.g., 'Yeah.' (Extract 8, line 22); an endorsement – e.g., 'Yeah. I do that' (Extract 5, line 20); or a rejection – e.g., 'Well that never happened to me::.' (SW:FM:A008). As noted above, other-than-minimal responses between the 'before' and 'after' components of the signature formulation are rare – these almost always occur at the possible completion of the second, strongly projected, TCU.

Finally (as I will show in Extracts 4–6 below), this signature formulation is very often preceded by information giving that is also formulated in very similar ways across many (though as we will see, not all) the calls. In Extract 4 below the signature formulation is delivered in the routine way we have already identified: with the words 'a classic example' (line 6); followed by 'for women' (line 6); followed by the 'before and after' contrast (lines 6–10), constructed exactly as in Extracts 1–3. Here, though, as in many of the conversations (compare Extract 1, lines 80–4 and 104–8), it is preceded by some informing about symptomatology, of which the 'before and after' formulation is presented as an 'example'.

Extract 4 Yvonne (SW:FM:A044)

```
01   Clt:   ... there's abou:t (.) thirty different clinical
02          symptoms to fibro ranging fro:m .hh blurred vision
03          to heart palpitations irritable bowel syndro:[me]
04   Yvo:                                            [Ye]s
05   Clt:   .hhh Swollen feelings in your soft tissues I mean
06          a classic example for women is before you developed
07          i:t .hh the first thing you did was kick your shoe:s
08          off. .hh After you developed it the first thing you
09          did when you got 'ome is take your bra off cause it
10          dun't matter what size it is it feels too sma:ll
11          after about 'alf hour.
```

Half of the iterations of the signature formulation are prefaced by some version of a claim about the number of fibromyalgia symptoms (as in Extract 4, lines 1–2; Extract 1, lines 81–2). Although there is some variability across the calls in the estimated number of 'clinical symptoms', the number is always presented as approximate: 'about thirty' (Extracts 4 and 5 below), 'about thirty odd' (Extract 1) in other data, 'about thirty to forty'; 'about forty' (Extract 6 below); and, in one case, 'a lot of fu::nny little symptoms'. The claim about the number of symptoms associated with fibromyalgia is generally followed (as in Extract 4, line 2; Extract 1, line 82) by the list-launcher 'ranging from' (thereby projecting that the speaker will produce at least two such symptoms) and then by a list of between two (in one call) and five (in two calls) symptoms. The symptoms cited (in order of frequency of mention) are: swollen feelings in (soft) tissues (six calls); blurred vision (six calls); heart palpitations (four calls); breathing problems (three calls); hearing disturbances (three calls); muscle spasms (two calls); and irritable bowel syndrome and restless legs (one call each).[6] When this list precedes the signature formulation, 'swollen feelings in (soft) tissues' is always the *last* item listed (as in Extract 4, line 5; Extract 1, line 112), thereby enabling it to be topicalized by the signature formulation which follows[7] (as in Extract 4, lines 6–11; Extract 1, lines 109–17).

In this section, then, we have seen how a piece of talk is produced in (what is analysably) a routinized and formulaic way over a number of iterations. Across a series of calls, this call-taker apparently deploys the same 'conversational machinery' with her co-interactants, such that her talk seems very *little* designed for this particular recipient on this particular occasion in this particular interaction. What makes her talk seem routinized or pre-fabricated, and not recipient-designed, is that she is saying 'the same thing' to multiple callers to the helpline, without regard to their differences.

Recipient Design

I want to show that, despite the fact that the call-taker produces effectively the 'same' piece of information across twelve of her first fifty recorded calls, she is none the less recipient-designing her talk: (1) by selecting designated recipients for her prefabricated talk, and (2) by variations introduced into this talk

---

[6] This list of symptoms shows some overlap with the *FMA (UK) Telephone Helpline Prompt Sheets'* description of fibromyalgia symptoms – which does *not*, however, include 'swollen feelings in (soft) tissues'. Some self-help books do include this symptom (e.g., Fransen & Russell, 1996: 13).

[7] The prefatory material (the claim about the number of symptoms; the list-launcher 'ranging from' and the list of indicative symptoms) is clearly itself routinized, but I am treating it here as a 'bridge' between the prior talk and the signature formulation (rather than as a routine in its own right, or as part of the signature formulation).

specifically for particular recipients on particular occasions of use. In this section I will show, first, how the call-taker produces her prefabricated signature formulation with an orientation to 'who the recipient is' (Schegloff, 1996c: 459), including their need to know the information, their not already knowing it, and their gender. I will then show how she introduces variations into both the prefatory material and the signature formulation in order to tailor these elements of the talk to particular recipients on particular occasions in particular interactions.

Selecting designated recipients for prefabricated talk

Conversation analysts have usually seen recipient design at work when speakers select what they say so as to make it fitted to the particular recipient they are addressing, as in the example given earlier in which a standard question about contraceptive use is redesigned for a possibly post-menopausal, single or infertile recipient (Boyd & Heritage, 2006). Here, however, I want to suggest that recipient design can also be analytically visible when speakers say 'the same thing' to multiple different recipients, if there are other potential recipients to whom they do *not* say it. In other words, recipient design can involve selecting only designated recipients for prefabricated talk as well as designing talk specifically for particular recipients.

The call-taker's signature formulation is designed for recipients who are: (1) newly diagnosed fibromyalgia sufferers and therefore need to know about its symptoms and how to deal with them; (2) people to whom it is news (i.e., not people to whom she has already delivered it); and (3) people of the appropriate gender to be addressed as if they might wear a bra, i.e., female. I will (briefly) consider her selection of each type of designated recipient in turn.

Designed for the recipient who needs to know
(i.e., fibromyalgia sufferers)

Many of the callers in the first fifty calls are not themselves fibromyalgia sufferers: some are the carers or relatives of people with fibromyalgia and one is calling in a professional capacity as a pharmacist. A quarter of the callers suspect they may have fibromyalgia but have not been formally diagnosed: these are overwhelmingly short calls in which the call-taker simply recommends seeking a referral to a rheumatologist and suggests calling again if a diagnosis of fibromyalgia is made. In none of these calls does the call-taker produce her signature formulation.

There are some calls with fibromyalgia sufferers in which the signature formulation is *not* produced: three are calls from long-term sufferers with narrowly focused interests in how to apply for disability benefits; three are from newly diagnosed individuals, who, after being told about the availability of the information pack, decline the call-taker's offer to ask her questions about the condition (e.g., 'No, I'll wait for the pack') and move into pre-closing.[8] Others sound like repeat calls (although the earlier calls were not recorded), raising the suspicion that the signature formulation may have been produced in the earlier calls.

In sum, then, it seems that the call-taker produces her signature formulation *only* to recipients who are formally diagnosed (by a rheumatologist) as fibromyalgia sufferers. Since conversation is co-constructed, she is not *always* able to do so (sometimes such potential recipients have other compelling agendas or move to close the conversation before she has the opportunity to produce it), but the evidence suggests that she selects formally diagnosed – typically, newly diagnosed – fibromyalgia sufferers as the designated recipients of her prefabricated talk.

Designed for the recipient who does not already know

The call-taker does *not* produce her signature formulation in conversations with repeat callers to whom she has already delivered it in a previous call. This is one way in which her 'memory' of the previous conversation is made manifest (compare R. Shaw & Kitzinger, 2007). It is also evidence that the call-taker is recipient-designing her talk for these recipients in particular, to avoid telling them something she should assume that they already know (Schegloff, 2007a: 51) – and here she should assume they already know it since she has already told them. As evidence that this is a feature of recipient design (and not simply, for example, that she never produces the signature formulation in conversation with repeat callers), note that she *does* on one occasion produce her signature formulation for someone calling for a third time, thereby making manifest (correctly) her memory that she had not so done in either of their two previous conversations and treating the caller as an appropriate recipient for this piece of prefabricated talk.

Designed for the gender-appropriate recipient

The call-taker produces her signature formulation in talking with twelve of the forty female callers, but none of the six males. The strong implication (though the numbers are small) is that in selecting (or not selecting) her signature formulation, she displays an orientation to the gender of her recipient as either being, or not being, the 'correct' gender to wear a bra.

---

[8] This is a technical term, referring to the phase of an interaction that precedes its possible closure.

In a discussion about how gender may be oriented to in interaction without being explicitly named, Kitzinger (2002) suggested, on the basis of an unrecorded field observation, that the visual cues of embodied gender can have consequences for question design. Encountering what appeared to be a man and a woman in a hotel dining room, hotel staff routinely asked only 'Smoking or non-smoking?', then showed them to a table for two; encountering what appeared to be two women, an additional question was asked ('How many people?'), thereby, Kitzinger suggests, displaying an orientation to the female gender of her recipients and (in a display of heteronormativity) entertaining the possibility of two tardy male partners. My recorded data suggest an orientation to gender based on auditory cues.

Of course there are sometimes other cues to gender (e.g., mentions of pregnancies or of a 'husband' or 'wife'; quoted speech in which the speaker self-references as 'she' or 'he'). However, in seven of the twelve interactions analysed here, the call-taker launches her signature formulation within the first six minutes of the beginning of the recording (in two she produces it in less than a minute), and in six of these seven interactions there is no recorded evidence of gender other than the caller's voice quality. As Schegloff (1999) observes, when unknown interactants speak to each other on the telephone – especially when, as here, they do not exchange names – their understanding of the gender of the person with whom they are interacting relies on the largely (though not entirely) distinctive pitch ranges of men's and women's voices. People *do* regularly make gender ascriptions from the sound of a co-participant's voice, and the ominipresence of that sound in all oral communication means that gender may be at any time relevant to the participants because 'the conversation is bathed in its acoustic waves and the relevance they impart' (Schegloff, 1999: 566). However, as Schegloff also says, 'not everything that is physically present is on that account treated as relevant by the parties' (p. 566) (see also Kitzinger, 2007b). The physical presence of a voice that 'sounds female' is here *treated as relevant* by the call-taker when she launches a signature formulation that targets women only. Whether she names the gender category (as she usually does: see Extracts 1–4 above and 6, 8 and 9 below) or not, the production of her signature formulation constitutes a mundane example of orientation to gender in so far as it treats the recipient as a member of the category of persons who might wear (and therefore need to remove) a bra – persons normally taken for granted as female. The prefabricated talk is, in this sense, recipient-designed in that it treats the recipient as a member of the category 'woman' and is designed for a member of just such a category.

In sum, evidence that the prefabricated talk is designed for these potential recipients is that, while regularly producing it in conversation with first-time female callers diagnosed with fibromyalgia, the call-taker does *not* produce it in conversation with other callers (i.e., those *not* diagnosed with fibromyalgia, those she has already informed about this 'classic symptom', or men). The selection of only some callers as recipients suggests that recipient design is operating even here in the production of a very routinized prefabricated piece of talk, in so far as callers are assessed for their suitability as recipients of it.

Recipient-designed variations in prefabricated talk

In addition to selecting only designated recipients for her prefabricated talk, the call-taker also designs her talk specifically for particular recipients. In this section, I will give some examples of how she modifies her prefabricated talk to fit particular recipients on particular occasions in particular interactions. Precisely because of the repetitiveness of the signature formulation and its prefatory material across calls, recipient-designed variations are readily identifiable. I will focus, first, on variations in the prefatory material, and then on variations in the signature formulation itself.

Variations in the prefatory material

In Extract 5 below, the call-taker introduces a variation into what is otherwise a very familiar routine (to her, and to us as analysts). Following the claim about the number of different symptoms (lines 6–7), she produces something clearly designed for just this recipient, who has spent the first four minutes of the call complaining about the severity of her pain and the disruption of her sleep pattern (both problems summarized in lines 1–4). After making her routine 'about thirty symptoms' claim, the call-taker recipient-designs her talk by specifically including these two particular symptoms, while also indicating that they have already been topicalized (lines 7–8, in bold).

Extract 5 Winnie (SW:FM:AO40)

```
01   Win:   I never get a good night's sleep an' if
02          the pai:n doesn't wake me up the:n uh
03          reaction to t' tablets medication
04          wi[ll (              )]
05   Clt:      [Yeah. That is anoth]er thi:ng. Th-there's
06          about (.) .h thi:rty different (.) clinical
07          symptom:s to fibromyalgia apar:t from the
08          pai:n and the sleep. .hh uhm ranging fro:m
09          .hh palpitations blurred vision hearing
10          disturbances .hh swollen feelings in your
11          soft tissues .hh I mean a classic example
12          for women with fibro is .hh before you
13          developed it the first thing you did when
14          you got 'ome was kick your shoe:s o:f[f.    .hh]
15   Win:                                          [ Mmm ]
16   Clt:   After you developed it the first thing you
```

```
17          do is take your bra off cause it doesn't
18          matter what size it is it feels too
19          sma:l[l.   .hhh    ]
20   Win:      [ Yeah. I do] that.
```

As I indicated earlier, there is some variability in the call-taker's list of symptoms of fibromyalgia, and the evidence suggests that the symptoms she selects may be part of the recipient design of this turn. For example, in Extract 1, 'muscle spasms' and 'breathing problems' (lines 105–6) are selected as part of the call-taker's list of symptoms for a caller who has said previously (data shown in appendix to this chapter) that she had been (probably wrongly) diagnosed with Bornholm's disease before receiving her fibromyalgia diagnosis. Bornholm's is a viral infection that causes spasms in the muscles of the chest wall (the caller referred to them as 'intercau:stal muscles') and pain when breathing ('I couldn't breathe prop'ly'). This same caller has also reported having had sarcoidosis, the symptoms of which (probably known to this call-taker, who is a retired nurse) include coughing, wheezing and shortness of breath.

In Extract 6 below, we see another – more analytically complex – variation. The call-taker's claim about the number of different symptoms of fibromyalgia (lines 84–5), is followed by a list-launcher ('ranging from', line 86) and a list of symptoms (lines 87–8 and 90), ending with 'swollen feelings in your soft tissues' (lines 90 and 92). But then, instead of moving directly into her signature formulation, she produces something clearly designed for just this recipient (lines 92–3) – though the action that it performs will take a little more unpicking than with the previous extract.

As Extract 6 opens (around eleven minutes into the call), the caller, Geri, is asking whether her experience of fluctuating body temperature might be one of the symptoms of her fibromyalgia. It so happens that this is *not* normally associated with fibromyalgia, and the call-taker avoids giving a direct answer by moving instead into her routine, with the variant material ('which is where this chappie obviously got that fro:m.', lines 92–3, in bold) interposed between the last symptom listed and the usual 'classic example' of it.

Extract 6 Geri (SW:FM:A050)
```
81   Ger:   An-an- an' do you- #uh# is it- .hh i-is:
82          to be very cold and the:n to become very
83          ho:t (.) °something that mi:gh[t°   ]
84   Clt:                        [Th]ere's
85          about forty different clinical symptoms
86          to fibromyalgia love .hh ranging fro:m
87          .hhhh blurred vi:sion: hea:ring
88          disturbance:[:s   uh: ] heart palpitation:s
89   Ger:          [ Mmm ]
```

```
90   Clt:   [.hh] swo̲llen feelings in your so̲ft=
91   Ger:   [Mmm]
92   Clt:   =tissues which is where this chappie
93          obviously got that fro:m. [.hh] uh:m=
94   Ger:                              [Yes]
95   Clt:   =a classic example .h for wome:n .hh i:s
96          before you developed fibro th- probably the
97          first thing you did when you got ho̲me
98          was kick your shoe:s off. .hh A̲fter
99          you developed fibro u̲sually the first
100         thing you('d) do is take your bra̲ off cause
101         it doesn't matter wha̲t size it i:s it
102         feels too sma̲ll after about half an hou:r
```

One way in which a speaker can display an 'orientation and sensitivity' (Sacks *et al.*, 1974: 727) to a co-conversationalist as an individual is by re-referencing something in their recipient's prior talk, thereby displaying evidence of having been listening. 'This chappie' is recipient-designed for this recipient as a subsequent reference to a person she referred to around a minute and a half earlier as 'the consultant I spoke to': here is a segment of that earlier conversation, with the initial reference on line 42, taken from the conversation prior to Extract 6.

Extract 7 Geri (SW:FM:A050)

```
01   Ger:   None of these uh:m (.) dru̲gs there's
02          something that's bee:n .hh licensed fo:r
03          fo:r (.) I think for rheumatoid arthri̲tis
04          none of tho̲se affe:ct uh:m have any uh:m
05          (0.2) [great] help rea:lly.
06   Clt:         [.hhh ]
07   Clt:   Well no̲:: because it's no:t rheumatoid
08          arthritis bas(h)[ica(h)]lly.
09   Ger:                   [ No. ]
10   Ger:   No̲::. .hh I was to:ld it's like
11          rheumatism of the so̲ft tissue. Is that (.)
12          uh:m [(              )]
13   Clt:        [.hh Well it's not] rea:lly a rheuma̲tic
14          disea:se. [to be ho̲nest] with you. .hh They=
15   Ger:             [ Oh really¿ ]
16   Clt:   =use:d to thi̲nk it wa:s ((continues))
//          ((about 30 seconds omitted on the history of the
            fibromyalgia diagnosis))
40   Ger:   .hh But when I had my las:t uh:m appointment
41          at uh:m .hh Ci̲ty uh::m (.) rheuma: rheumatic
42          hospital .hh the consultant I spoke to
43          descri:bed it as rheumatism of the soft
```

```
44          tissues so: [(        it's not very helpful)]
45   Clt:                [.hh Well actually it- it's got ]
46   Clt:   nothing to do: with tha:t.=
47   Ger:   =It's not [very helpful then is it.]
```

There is a tussle here between the caller's view (citing her consultant as its source) that fibromyalgia is (or is like) 'rheumatism of the soft tissues' (lines 10–11 and 43–4) and the call-taker's view that it is 'not really a rheumatic disease' (lines 13–14) and has 'got nothing to do with [rheumatism]' (lines 45–6).[9] As we have already seen (in Extract 6), about a minute and a half later (after some discussion of the effects of the weather on fibromyalgia symptoms; data not shown), the call-taker re-references 'the consultant I spoke to' (Extract 7, line 42) as 'this chappie' (Extract 6, line 92). However, 'this chappie' is doing much more than a subsequent reference to someone mentioned earlier: it is also, by virtue of downgrading the 'consultant' to a 'chappie', stripping him of his professional qualifications, and is thereby hearably dismissive of, or hostile to, the person concerned (Stockill, 2007).[10] The variation introduced into this routine turn (with 'which is where this chappie obviously got that from', lines 92–3) offers an account for the consultant's erroneous characterization of fibromyalgia by acknowledging that one of the symptoms of fibromyalgia is similar to that of rheumatism – and by so doing displays and reinforces the call-taker's continued position that fibromyalgia is *not* a rheumatic disease.[11] The variation is recipient-designed, then, for this recipient in particular, not just to show an 'orientation and sensitivity' (Sacks *et al.*, 1974: 727) to her as an individual – although it also does this – but to insist on the speaker's own view of the nature of fibromyalgia in contradistinction to that of her recipient. Downgrading the consultant from a professional to a man in the street (a 'chappie'), and accounting for his (mis)characterization of fibromyalgia as a type of rheumatism, serve

---

[9] The nature of fibromyalgia is contested. According to call-takers, FMA (UK) does not support the view that it is either a form of rheumatism (as reportedly advanced by this consultant) or a form of arthritis (as advanced, apparently, by Arthritis Care).

[10] Through her use of the linguistically masculine 'chappie', the call-taker manifests an assumption that the consultant rheumatologist is male, although no indication of this person's gender is available in Geri's talk.

[11] There are a couple of other non-routine elements of this turn. One is the call-taker's use of the endearment term 'love' (line 86). According to Lerner (2003), TCU-terminal endearments and personal names used (as here) when recipiency is already established can be understood to 'personalize' the interaction: they 'underline the very act of speaking expressly to the already addressed recipient' and can 'underscore personal concern for a problem' (Lerner, 2003: 185). In other words, in the very act of answering a non-standard inquiry with a prefabricated routine response, the call-taker uses a device (the endearment term) that claims she is 'speaking expressly' to her caller as an individual. Another non-routine element is the self-initiated repair to insert 'probably' (line 96) and the inclusion of 'usually:' (line 99), both of which mitigate the call-taker's claim to know about Geri's behaviour before or after she developed fibromyalgia. The strength of this claim is softened in other iterations by limiting it to 'a lot of women' (Extract 1, lines 109–10) or 'most women' (SW:FM:A023).

to undermine his authority as a source of information about the disorder; and to reinstate her own position – that fibromyalgia and rheumatism are unrelated.

Another variation (which occurs twice in the collection) is for the call-taker to preface her signature formulation by the phrase 'I always say', thereby specifically marking it as prefabricated. This preface replaces the list of symptoms that more commonly prefigures the signature formulation, and on both occasions it is recipient-designed for callers reporting swelling (or feelings of swelling). In Extract 8 below, the caller is asking a question that attempts to reconcile what she has read about the illness (that the pain is *not* caused by swelling) with her own experience (of a swollen ankle).

Extract 8 Martha (SW:FM:A027)

```
01  Mar:   Now they sa:y- I've read the book- uh
02          the magazines an' that an' they say that
03          it's not due to swell:ings (.) uh:m but
04          I have got- (.) a swoll:en ankle
05          someti:mes round the bo:ne.
06  Clt:   Yea:h.
07  Mar:   .hh Uh:[m    ]
08  Clt:           [You] do ge:t swollen feelings in
09          your soft tissues. [ .hh uh]:m (.) I always=
10  Mar:                       [ Mmm ]
11  Clt:   =say a classic example for a woman with
12          fibro before you developed [i:t .hh ] the=
13  Mar:                               [ Yeah ]
14  Clt:   =first thing you did when you got home was
15          kicked your shoes off. [.hh (In fa]ct) now=
16  Mar:                           [ Yes-    ]
17  Clt:   =you've developed i:t [ (0.2) ] (0.2) the first=
18  Mar:                         [Yeah ]
19  Clt:   =thing you do when you get home is take your
20          bra off cause it doesn't matter what size
21  Clt:   it is it feels too sma:ll.
22  Mar:   Yeah.
23  Clt:   You know i-i- it's a classic (.) symptoms
24          of-of- [(0.2) swo:]llen fee:lings in=
25  Mar:          [ Oh is it¿ ]
26  Clt:   =[    your tissues.          ]
```

The 'I always say' preface (on lines 9 and 11, in bold) normalizes this particular recipient's symptoms as typical of the disorder. It also builds a contrast between what 'they say' (lines 1 and 2) and what 'I always say' (lines 9 and 11), where 'always' works to treat the call-taker's opinion as already established and held independently of the report she is being given. She is speaking here as an authoritative expert, able to confirm or to disconfirm whatever the caller has read in magazines with her own independent and well-established knowledge. Ironically, then, one way in which the signature formulation can be recipient-designed is by the call-taker's claim (in the prefatory material) that it is *not* recipient-designed for this particular recipient on this particular occasion, but is something she has said many times before.

Variations in the prefatory material, then, may be recipient-designed to display 'listening' to the caller's problem presentation by re-referencing previously mentioned symptoms or concerns. Such variations may also be designed to perform particular (additional) actions, such as insisting on a particular viewpoint in the face of challenge (Extract 6) or normalizing a caller's symptoms (Extract 8). I turn now to variations in the signature formulation itself.

Variations in the signature formulation

As the data shown above illustrate, the signature formulation is remarkably formulaic. However, it is not produced in *exactly* the same way on each occasion. One striking locus of difference is in the call-taker's variable use of 'don't' or 'doesn't' in the phrase 'it doesn't/don't matter what size it is'.

In seven of the twelve interactions, including Extracts 1–4, the call-taker says 'it **don't** matter what size it is' (Extract 1, lines 116–17; Extract 2, line 6; Extract 3, lines 6 and 8; Extract 4, lines 9–10; Extract 9, lines 24 and 26) – using 'don't' (the pronunciation of which has been rendered as either 'don't' or 'dun't') in a phrase where 'doesn't' would adhere to standard English grammar for third person singular with a present tense simple negative verb (i.e., 'it doesn't matter what size it is'). In these extracts, she also always drops the aspirated 'h' at the beginning of the word 'home' (rendered in the transcript as ''ome': Extract 1, line 112; Extract 2, line 21; Extract 3, line 3; Extract 4, line 9; Extract 9, line 21). These two features of grammar and pronunciation combine to create a distinctively informal 'style' or 'register' of conversation.

By contrast, in five of the twelve interactions, including Extracts 5, 6 and 8, she produces this same phrase using the more formally correct grammatical version, 'doesn't' ('it **doesn't** matter what size it is'; Extract 5, line 17; Extract 6, line 101; Extract 8, line 20), and in two of these she also produces an aspirated 'h' at the beginning of 'home' (Extract 6, line 97; Extract 8, lines 14 and 19).

Gail Jefferson (2004a: 21) has drawn attention to variations in grammar and pronunciation across the utterances of a single speaker, citing findings that the same speaker pronounces the same word sometimes with a trilled and sometimes with an untrilled or 'hard' 'r'; or varies between the use of 'this' and 'dis'; or shifts from 'kiln' to 'kil'. She suggests that these variations may be systematic and have interactional import: 'Not only do people produce words in one way or another, but they produce them in the course of interaction. And when people interact, they do so at a range of levels, including that of pronunciation' (Jefferson, 1983: 11).

My analysis here is speculative and intended to encourage more research in this area, but I suggest that the call-taker's selection of the grammatically formal 'doesn't' (and aspirated pronunciation of 'home') contributes to the action of talking as an authoritative 'expert' about fibromyalgia, whereas her use of the less formal 'don't' (and non-aspirated ''ome') contributes to the action of talking as a co-sufferer. For example, in the data shown earlier in this chapter there are only two instances in which she uses 'doesn't' and aspirates the word 'home', and in both she is challenging some other source of expertise about fibromyalgia cited by her co-conversationalist. In Extract 8, the turn in which the 'formal register' is used is focally preoccupied with providing counter-evidence to the claim (from magazines the caller has read) that swelling is not involved in the pain of fibromyalgia. In Extract 6, the turn in which the 'formal register' is used is ostensibly simply an informing about the symptoms of fibromyagia, but (as I have shown) is also focally concerned with accounting for – and thereby dismissing as erroneous – the opinion of the 'consultant'/'chappie' who is reported to have described fibromyalgia as 'rheumatism of the soft tissues'. In setting herself up as a competing authority on fibromyalgia, and in challenging the claims of other purported experts, she is using the formal register associated with power and authority in British speech.[12]

The call-taker employs a more informal speech style as part of bringing off talking as a 'co-sufferer' of fibromyalgia. Here, for example, is the interaction that precedes and leads into the data already quoted as Extract 2 (in which the signature formulation uses 'don't' and ''ome'). It opens as the caller asks the call-taker how long she has suffered from fibromyalgia.

Extract 9 Lettie (Extract 2 expanded) (SW:FMA024)

```
01   Let:   <How long have you ha:d it.
02   Clt:   Fifteen yea:rs.
03   Let:   Have you rea:lly.
04   Clt:   Yeah.
05   Let:   An' whereabouts have you: mainly got it.
06          Is it everywhere or:[:    ]
07   Clt:                      [My-] my co:re (.) i:s
08          i:n my: (.) breastbo:ne neck shoulders arms
09          and spi:[ne.  ]
10   Let:           [Ye:s] ye::s
11   Clt:   Uh:m (0.2) that's usually there all the
12          time to a greater or lesser degree[:.   ]
13   Let:                                      [Yes]
14   Clt:   Uh:m .hh other times it's your le:gs your
```

---

[12] I have not been able to detect any systematic relationship between the style of speech used by the caller and the style of speech adopted by the call-taker.

```
15          fee[:t your han:]ds. [ An' I'll     ] give you=
16   Let:        [ Okay: yes.]    [<How often-]
17   Clt:   =a little ti:p. [A-  .hhh] a classic example=
18   Let:               [ Mm hm ]
19   Clt:   =for a woman i:s before you developed fibro:
20          .hh the first thing you did when you got
21   Clt:   'ome was take your shoes o:[ff. Aft]er you=
22   Let:                        [ Ye::s ]
23   Clt:   =develop fibro the first thing you do is
24          take your bra off [cause] it don't matter=
25   Let:                     [Yeah]
26   Clt:   =what si:ze it is it feels too sma:l[l.  ]
27   Let:                            [Ye]ah.
28          Yeah.
29   Clt:   .hh It is a bi:g problem with us:.
```

In talking as another woman with fibromyalgia about her personal experience, and offering 'a little tip' (line 17) from one sufferer to another ('us' (fibro sufferers), line 29), she uses the 'informal register' associated with talk between equals.

Variations in the signature formulation, then, may be recipient-designed to display an orientation to 'who the recipient is' (Schegloff, 1996c) in relation to the call-taker. Here I have shown – albeit speculatively – that grammar and pronunciation may contribute to the action of talking as an 'expert' on fibromyalgia, or talking as a 'co-sufferer'. In sum, variations in both the prefatory material and the signature formulation provide compelling evidence that even (what appears to be) highly routinized talk none the less manifests a considerable degree of recipient design.

In this section, then, we have seen how an apparently prefabricated piece of talk that is produced in (what is analysably) a routinized and formulaic way over a number of iterations is none the less also analysably recipient-designed for particular recipients on particular interactional occasions. One type of evidence for this is that the call-taker apparently designates only some callers (first-time female callers diagnosed with fibromyalgia) as appropriate recipients for her signature routine; and she does not deliver it to callers not so designated. Another type of evidence is provided by specifiable, systematic variations in both the prefatory material and the prefabricated signature routine. These include the incorporation of additional or different elements into the prefatory material, and variations in the grammar and pronunciation of certain words within the signature routine. For the analyst, who can track such variations across different calls, they are analysable as displaying an 'orientation and sensitivity' (Sacks *et al.*, 1974: 727) to callers as individuals or as category members, thereby manifesting the basic principles of recipient design, and beginning to specify some of the practices through which it may be accomplished.

Conclusion

In this chapter, I have examined how one particular piece of prefabricated talk is produced in multiple very similar iterations across a series of helpline calls. Building on Sacks's early observations suggesting that although (parts of) help-line interactions may be 'relatively pre-cast', call-takers none the less attempt to offer a problem solution that appears 'devised for just this person' (Sacks, 1992, II: 389–90), I have further shown that even such a routinized and formulaic bit of talk may be recipient-designed in ways that are attentive to the particularities of a conversational co-participant. The prefabricated talk may be produced only for designated recipients; and it may be modified, in specified (and further spe-cifiable) ways, for particular recipients on particular occasions.

I have addressed the issue of how gender may be oriented to in interaction, particularly when not explicitly named (see Cameron, 2005b; Kitzinger, 2002; 2008a; Speer, 2002b; Stokoe & Smithson, 2001; Weatherall, 2000; and the introduction to this volume for further discussion of this issue). I have shown how this call-taker displays an orientation to gender through selecting, as desig-nated recipients of her signature formulation, only those callers she takes to be women. Analytically, this orientation to gender is identifiable on comparative grounds. However, whereas comparative 'sex differences' research (includ-ing some by conversation analysts, e.g., Jefferson, 2004b) typically starts with the (analytically defined) categories 'male' and 'female' and looks for differ-ences and similarities across interactions with participants so categorized, this research began by noticing a practice in talk (the signature formulation) and then observed that its production was attentive to the presumed gender of the participants. Gender is thus endogenous to the interaction rather than imposed upon it by the analyst. Moreover, it is (partly) through the call-taker's provision of this gender-specific advice and information that these callers are constituted *as* women. The key challenge for comparative work of this type is to specify exactly *how* an orientation to gender (or some other category set) is consequen-tial for the content and course of the interaction.

Finally, the analysis presented here contributes to our understanding of some of the formal features through which recipient design of routinized material can be achieved. Although grounded in the practices of a single call-taker on this particular helpline, it is likely to be applicable across a range of settings in which routinized information is conveyed, or routinized actions performed, on multiple occasions with multiple clients by a single service provider. It is inevitable that service providers will continue to use routine interactional procedures to accom-plish their institutional goals; however, the analysis presented here demonstrates that such routinization is not incompatible with displaying a considerable degree of sensitivity to the needs and concerns of individual clients. Service providers – as human interactants – are also experts in recipient design.

Appendix

The lines omitted from Extract 1 are as follows:

```
05  Clt:   Yeahh.
06  Pen:   Uh:m (.) preceding that last year I was
07         quite ill with sarcoido:sis
08  Clt:   Yea[h ]
09  Pen:       [.h] An' then I go:t somethink else
10         called Bromholm's disea:se .hh[h   ]
11  Clt:                                [Wh]at the
12         devil's tha:[t.   ]
13  Pen:              [Uh]:m it's to do with thu:h
14         .hh well I mean >I'm not even too sure<
15         if that wa:s it .hh but it- cause this all
16         started round about the same ti:me but
17         he thought- thuh consultant thought it
18         was thee .h (.) intercau:stal muscles
19         [because (like) I] could[n't ] breathe=
20  Clt:   [O:h yeah-yeah ]      [yep]
21  Pen:   =prop'ly.
22  Clt:   Yea[h ]
23  Pen:      [.h] An' the:n (0.4) <cause I was under
24         a lung specialist who then r: referred me
25         to the rheumatologis:[t   ]
26  Clt:                        [M]m h[m ]
```

7

O
th
ta
g

136   Alexa Hepburn and Jonathan Potter

they indirectly build a course of action (that has already b
able for, and desired by, the recipient. At the end of the
the implications of these moves for research into ge

Some preliminaries

For those unfamiliar with tag questions
has two parts. The first is a statement (
assessment, or an imperative); for e
tive component can then underg
interrogative clause or 'tag',
have positive or negative '
reversed from declarativ
'you haven't been aw
forms we can note
the speaker's sta
has not been a
confirmatio
This
abstra
tag

Holmes, 1995; Speer, 20..

This chapter will bracket off the wide-rang...
tags do or do not mark a gender difference, or whether the grammatical p...
underlies some psychological state such as a lack of confidence or assertiveness.
Nevertheless, to help us engage with the sociolinguistic literature we will work
with a selection of tag questions produced by female speakers addressing male
recipients. These will be taken from a varied set of contexts: a child protection
helpline, mundane talk and a television programme where house buyers are
helped in their search. Our broader aim, however, will be quite discrete. We
will attempt to show the operation of one practice through which tag questions
are systematically exploited to press subtly and rather indirectly for a course
of action that has already been resisted. Our analysis will move away from the
picture of psychological states such as 'confidence' and 'assertiveness' lying
behind and driving interaction – a picture common to both Lakoff and many of
her sociolinguistic critics – and focus instead on the way psychological states are
sequentially and publicly invoked as parts of practices. Indeed, we will suggest
that tag questions can be somewhat *invasive*, in the sense that they reconstruct
the recipient's psychological states, and somewhat *coercive*, in the sense that

een resisted) as desir-
chapter we will explore
nder and interaction.

in grammatical terms a tag question
.g., a declarative such as a description or
xample, 'you've been away'. The declara-
o inversion with the addition of the attached
.g., 'you have' to 'have you?' Statements may
olarity' (have/haven't) and most commonly this is
e to tag – e.g., 'you've been away, haven't you?' or
y, have you?' In comparing these positive and negative
the outset that the declarative component seems to display
ce towards or understanding of the recipient (she or he has or
way) and the interrogative elicits some kind of agreement and/or
n from the recipient, for whatever reason.
asic grammatical structure leads us to see tag questions in a more
t way, giving rise to Lakoff's (1975: 15–16) original understanding of
questions:

A tag, in its usage as well as its syntactic shape (in English) is midway between an outright statement and a yes-no question: it is less assertive than the former, but more confident than the latter.

And:

A tag question, being intermediate between [asking a question and making a statement], is used when the speaker is stating a claim, but lacks full confidence in the truth of that claim.

The figuration that is central to Lakoff's account of tag questions treats their use as a straightforward function of both the speaker's and the addressee's internal states and dispositions. Speakers of tag questions have more *confidence* than would be shown by other forms of question,[1] but are not as *assertive* as would be shown by an assertion – language is both *driven by* such psychological states and objects, and *expressive of* those things. Although subsequent researchers have disagreed with Lakoff's specific claims, they have often approached interaction with a similar picture of language use: women are treated as speaking the way that they do because of some psychological presence or absence of assertiveness (but see Speer, 2005a, for a critique of this).

---

[1] And note that they are often treated as 'yes/no questions' or interrogatives (Raymond, 2003).

However, in this chapter we want to start with the assumption that 'tag' and 'question', like many other grammatically defined phenomena, are theoretically and analytically presumptive items suggesting things about placement and action that are yet to be specified fully. The grammatical categories may or may not map on to the kind of study of action and interaction we engage in here. Our aim is to build on conversation analytic work (e.g., Heritage, 2002a; Heritage & Raymond, 2005; Sacks *et al.*, 1974) that approaches tag questions as situated and locally managed objects.

The tensions between our own and the sociolinguistic approaches suggest some important questions: how can things like 'gender' or 'psychological states' enter into an analysis of tag questions? Are they to be imputed by the researcher? Do they provide a plausible gloss for explaining conversational regularities of different kinds, including the regular (but, now, controversially irregular) difference in tag counts between women and men? Rather than speculate more on this, we will turn to some data: we have chosen one example from our corpus of calls to a child protection helpline, one example from a telephone call between a heterosexual couple, and one example from a well known (in the UK) television programme. We have chosen a collection entirely composed of tags where women address men. This is not because we see gender as necessarily relevant in these examples; rather we seek to engage with the thinking that gender can be explored through grammatically defined categories, and to rethink the inferred relationship between individuals and interaction. We begin with a discussion of some related work on tag questions.

Designing the recipient

For several years we have worked with the UK National Society for the Prevention of Cruelty to Children (NSPCC) to try to understand more fully what happens on their child protection helpline. Child protection officers (CPOs) take calls, and callers (both adults and children) are often reporting disturbing events or worries about themselves, friends, relatives or neighbours.[2]

In a development of the programme of work on interaction in the child protection helpline (Hepburn & Potter, 2010) we have noted that tag questions are commonly produced by CPOs in sequences where advice is being offered and the caller is resisting that advice. In this environment they share a number of common features, and also some striking similarities with examples in our

---

[2] Although the helpline can provide counselling, information and advice, its central role is to field reports of abuse that may require action. When serious abuse is suspected the NSPCC is legally mandated to pass the report on to police or the relevant social services department. A range of features of the helpline interaction have been studied in our previous work (Hepburn, 2005; Hepburn & Potter, 2007; Hepburn & Wiggins, 2005; 2007; Potter & Hepburn, 2003; 2011).

corpus of calls devoted to the study of crying[3]: the declarative is often idiomatically reformulated advice that the caller has already resisted; it is also often phrased as a B-event statement, which means it is a statement that includes descriptions of people or events that the recipient has primary access to or knowledge about, in the service of promoting some future course of action related to the caller; and more is often added after the tag has been issued. These types of tag questions are not common elsewhere in our corpus, and relatively rare in the everyday conversation corpora that we have searched.

Let us consider an example. In the following call, the caller is phoning about his daughter, whom he has occasional custody of. The caller voices the suspicion that his daughter has been getting fleabites at her mother's house and he wants the NSPCC to check it out. The (female) CPO has already advised the caller to ask the mother directly, but the caller suggests that an acrimonious split prevents him from doing that. The following sequence ensues:

Extract 1 Daughter and fleas

```
 1   CPO:      Y:ep. Yep. Okay, .h have ↑you got↑ parental
 2             responsibili↓ty for your daughter.↓=
 3   Caller:   =Only when I have her.<O[r  ] er:m (0.4)
 4   CPO:                            [tk]
 5   CPO:      Right. So you haven't l:i- e- you're an unmarried
 6             couple are you:?
 7                        (.)
 8   Caller:   No ah wus ma- married so I [have]
 9   CPO:                                 [You ] were
10             ma[rrie:d ru- at the time of her birth]
11   Caller:     [Yeah (I was married) (        )]
12   CPO:      S[o ye have] got parental responsibility <.h[h that]=
13   Caller:    [ Yeah. ]                                 [Yeah.]
14   CPO:      =means <↑you have↑> actually got the right to take
15             her to: e- a gee: pee: >or something °sh- s-°< or
16             to actually .hh (0.3) tch uh:m: <be involved> in
17             aspects of her life.<I me[an what] I would suggest=
18   Caller:                            [Ri:ght  ]
19   CPO:      =.hh would be that ee- u- however: (.) difficult the
20             situation i:s:,=
21   Caller:   =Yep=
22   CPO:      =.h uh:m: I think >you know I mean< your <child's health>
23      →      hass to come f[ir:s ]t. Doesn' i:t.=.hh M'n there=
24   Caller:                 [Yep]
25   CPO:      =can be many reas[:ons   why  ]
26   Caller:                    [Mean I've ta]:ken 'er to the doctor's
27             b[efor]e:, an they've basically said she=
```

[3] Hepburn (2004); Hepburn and Potter (2007); Hepburn and Potter (2010).

```
28   CPO:              [Mm ]
29   Caller:   =needs to go to 'er own gee pe[e. ]
30   CPO:                           [Y ]ep.=
31   Caller:   =.hh And I don' know what 'er own gee pee i[ :s. ]
32   CPO:                                              [ Yu]p.
33                      (.)
34   CPO:    Yup.
```

Following some resistance to the CPO's prior advice, which suggested that the caller needs to sort out his own problem and contact his daughter's mother (receipted by 'Y:ep. Yep. Okay', line 1), the CPO seeks information about the caller's legal rights as a parent (lines 1–2). This being established by line 12, it is then suggested that the caller could 'actually' be '<involved> in aspects of her life' (lines 16–17) or that he could take his daughter to a doctor (GP). The caller responds (line 18), and there is evidence (his turn at line 26 returns to the issue of the GP) that he might have taken a more extended turn here if he had been given the chance. The CPO, however, rushes through into our target turn, a compound turn constructional unit (TCU), prefaced with 'I me[an what] I would suggest .hh would be' (lines 17 and 19). Note the way the CPO's formulation is scripted (Edwards, 1994; 1997) – it is the advice that the CPO *would* normatively deliver. Scripting may be a useful device in advice giving (especially where there is resistance) as it avoids a stark *ad hominem* suggestion (e.g., 'what you ought to do is ...'), and presents the advice as generic. The CPO continues with a further preface to her actual advice 'however: (.) difficult the situation i:s:,' (lines 19–20), which is hearable as heading off the future resistance that is projectable by the CPO, given the caller's stated inability to talk to the child's mother. It may also allow the caller to project that further unwanted advice of a similar kind is in the offing.

The declarative element of the tag question has idiomatic qualities, which is typical of a number of our examples in advice-resistance sequences, and of responses to crying as we noted earlier. In this environment the value may be in the difficulty of countering idiomatics (Edwards & Potter, 1992; Kitzinger, 2000b) – it would be difficult to disagree with the statement 'your <child's health> hass to come f[ir:s]t' (lines 22–3). This TCU comes to a close, and the interrogative is added as an increment. Typically in our corpus of these tag questions, the declarative is also formulated as a 'B-event statement'. Other analyses (Labov & Fanshell, 1977; Pomerantz, 1980) have suggested that B-event statements make a response relevant even without the interrogative.[4] It therefore seems plausible that the declarative on its own would have made

---

[4] We are cautiously applying this finding to our institutional talk, where being offered advice or professional judgements on crucial features of your own life can be part of the business of the call. This may transform the kind of action a B-event statement is heard to be performing.

some kind of uptake relevant from the caller, even without the tag question. The declarative also contains a stretched emphasis on 'child's health', which, combined with the idiomatic quality of the formulation, may allow the caller to project the completion of the TCU and arrive in overlap (line 24).

It seems plausible that the CPO may have already heard the caller's agreement before she issues the tag component of this turn, given there is a normal transition with a 'beat of silence' (i.e., the interrogative is not latched straight on to the candidate TCU). So why would the CPO, in issuing the interrogative component, (continue to) produce the caller as in a position to confirm the contents of a declarative that he has already confirmed? Note that the caller does not respond in a type-conforming (yes/no; cf. Raymond, 2003) way to the interrogative 'tag' ending. Note also that the orthodox Lakoffian position on this would be that the CPO has weakened her turn by adding the tag ending, which reflects her lack of confidence in what she has just asserted. And indeed there are other reasons, more empirically grounded in interaction, which might lead us to think of tag questions as 'weakened' interrogative forms that make a response less relevant[5] (e.g., Heritage, 2002a; Heritage & Raymond, 2005). Before entertaining this possibility, however, we will explore some interactional features related to the responsiveness of this turn.

First, 'your <child's health> hass to come f[ir:s]t' (lines 22–3) is hearable as another attempt to persuade the caller to bury his difference with his ex-wife and put his daughter's health 'first'. The advice that it packages has *already* been resisted earlier in the call (and the same advice is re-offered more explicitly later in the call), and the CPO takes great care to preface this utterance in a way that heads off any further resistance. The idiomatic formulation and the fact that this is a piece of advice coming from a child protection expert also make resistance difficult.

Second, although the interrogative ending is added on as an increment, it is in turn-medial position[6] – the CPO rushes through into her next TCU with

---

[5] At least where they occur sequentially in second position. Simply put, an utterance in first position is an initiating action, whereas in second position it tends to be a responsive action. As Schegloff (2007a) shows, this can get more interesting and complex through various expansions to the basic form (and see Heritage & Raymond, 2005, for some interesting insights into some of the implications of doing a tag question in first or second position).

[6] Initial analysis suggests that there are different types of turn-medial tag question. Some, like this one, occur at transition-relevant places (TRPs) (which can carry on with the addition of something incremental, or a whole new TCU), and a smaller number project more to come post-tag (e.g., 'An' it's js terrible isn't it how the months go by'n it's been so cold ...'; Hepburn, 2007). Note that the former tend to get a response in overlap, while in the latter responses occur at TRPs (here occurring after 'months go by'n ...'), although responses to the specific component targeted by the tag may sometimes not appear at all, suggesting that they simply mark the prior (e.g., 'it's terrible') as something the recipient does not need to be told, let alone respond to. These examples await a larger corpus and further analysis.

a hearable in-breath, projecting more to come[7] at a transition-relevant place (TRP). A TRP, broadly speaking, refers to a place where the speaker seems to have finished and the recipient could have taken a turn (see Sacks *et al.*, 1974). The addition of further talk after the tag ending fills the transition space where there would have been a stronger requirement for some kind of uptake from the recipient. To move beyond that requirement and treat the caller's earlier agreement (which, given what comes next, is almost certainly a *pro forma* agreement prefacing further resistance) as sufficient leaves intact the 'recipient-designing' role of the tag question – to assume the declarative is known or accepted by the recipient. What the CPO is doing here is hardly 'weak'. In the face of the caller's advice resistance he is constructed by the declarative + tag as *already knowing* what he has been resisting.[8]

Let us try to lay this out more schematically as a conversational practice that seems prevalent across a number of our advice-resistance sequences.

1   The declarative rephrases the recipient's action-relevant version of himself or herself. In this case the CPO rephrases the caller's extended resistance to conversing with the child's mother with 'your child's health has to come first'.
2   This rephrasing makes relevant a competing course of action for the recipient (in this case, talking to the child's mother).
3   The interrogative (tag) that follows the declarative treats the caller as already knowing (in the sense that he is treated as being in a position to confirm) the rephrased version. The recipient has been designed as already knowing that this is the appropriate course of action, despite having shown considerable resistance to putting his daughter's health above his personal differences with her mother up to this point.
4   Further practices dampen the recipient's response requirement:
     (a)   continuing past the TRP for the tag question, and
     (b)   employing a broadly idiomatic formulation.

These features are interestingly similar across a number of our NSPCC examples, both in the advice-resistance corpus itself and in a corpus of calls where crying is present. In the latter, Hepburn and Potter (2010) have found that the use of B-event and idiomatically formulated declaratives, and the tendency to continue beyond the point where a recipient's uptake is immediately relevant,

---

[7]   Albeit in a non-vocal way that may leave room for the recipient to offer a (preferred) response without requiring overlapping talk.
[8]   Unfortunately for the CPO, her earlier advice in this turn is something that the caller is able to resist – he has already tried taking his daughter to his own GP, as he points out with his invasion of the CPO's ongoing turn (line 26). The CPO's repetition of 'Yep' and 'Yup' (lines 30, 32 and 34) is interesting here (as is the caller's repetition of it, lines 21 and 24). It may be that as a hearably clipped version of 'yes' it is a form of agreement that displays the redundancy or 'already known' nature of the thing it is designed to agree with.

have been shown to be prevalent across a range of CPOs who are responding to caller upset. As such this finding may relate to some specific institutional (and possibly peculiarly British[9]) practices that are live for the callers and CPOs.

For the callers, they are reporting abuse, which brings with it specific concerns; for CPOs, they are assessing both the seriousness of reported situations, and whether further support services will be needed, plus advising, soothing, and offering judgements on various situations that callers may not particularly like.

Our first example has come from a rather specific institutional environment where the female CPO has been in a position of some authority over the male caller – this might be argued as a defence both of tag questions as 'weak moves' (they soften the authority of the speaker) and of women as using more tags to downgrade their authority. We have started to show how making this type of claim, which relies on abstracted notions of gender and grammar, can ride roughshod over the specific interactional business being done, but it will nevertheless be interesting to explore whether tag questions can operate in more everyday situations in these ways.

Tags in everyday conversation

Out of 158 British everyday telephone calls in a corpus we have worked with we found 190 tag questions. None resembles the tag questions in our NSPCC collections, i.e., none possesses the four broad features we have identified – turn medial, with an idiomatically constructed, B-event declarative, in pursuit of alignment in the face of resistance. So far sixty-seven of our mundane corpora are cross gender (42 per cent) – forty-one of these are female to male (61 per cent), twenty-six male to female (39 per cent).[10] At first glance, this seems to be in line with Lakoff's earlier observation and to run counter to some subsequent quantitative claims. However, as our analyses have started to show, this kind of gross categorization misses much that is important about the operation of tag questions in different environments. Let us return to considering tags in their specific sequences.

The following example comes as close as we could get to the examples we have worked with so far – it is a female-to-male tag question that seeks

---

[9] Schegloff, personal communication.
[10] To offer yet grosser categorization, thirty-five are turn-medial tags; none has all four features found in the NSPCC corpus; however, eight are both B-events and turn-medial tags. Of these only two are female to male; nine find themselves in competitive overlap (five of these are abandoned). And in a further six (not included in the thirty-five) the speaker continues after waiting for uptake. We are uncomfortable about reading too much into these kinds of counts, and the categories (especially 'male/female') that go into producing them. The example we use here is not turn medial, but has been chosen as it is a female-to-male tag doing persuasive work in the face of resistance.

alignment in the face of some resistance. Skip is phoning his wife Lesley from work to find out what has been happening about the burglary they had in their house the night before. The call so far has been devoted to this topic, but Lesley now launches a new topic, related to the arrangements for picking up their student daughter Katherine for the Christmas holidays. Lesley cannot drive, so these plans have implications for Skip.

Extract 2 Field:X(C)2:1:6:14–15

```
 1 Les:    Oh Katherine rang 'n she'd like t'come home Monday 'n I
 2         said well Monday evening's no good f'r us cz of getting
 3         Granny Fee- Ande:rs,
 4                    (0.4)
 5 Ski:    Ye:s.
 6                    (0.3)
 7 Les:    An' so she said well: (.) do you think, if she came
 8         home Mondee cz Brad'll help her with her ca:se
 9                    (.)
10 Ski:    (          )
11 Les:    Uh:m you could pick 'er up fr'm Glast'nbury.
12                    (1.0)
13 Ski:    (                   [    )
14 Les:                        [I can't hear you,
15                    (.)
16 Ski:    On Mondee as we:ll,
17                    (0.8)
18 Les:    .t[ee- ee-] eYes well ↑I thought Glast'nbury'd be a lot=
19 Ski:      [eh:::: ]
20 Les:    =easier for you th'n going to Bristo:l,
21                    (0.4)
22 Ski:    We:ll yes, (0.3) it's jus(.)t that if I've got to go to
23         Yeo: vil an' then back[to (    )
24 Les:                          [We: may not. We er may only haf't'
25         go t'↓Sparkford,
26                    (0.6)
27 Ski:    [Yes
28 Les: →  [An' you're coming home early that night anyway
29       → ar[en't you. ]
30 Ski:      [Y e s ↓a]m.
31                    (0.9)
32 Ski:    Yeah that's ri:ght
33 Les:    An' it ↑dzn' matter what time you pick 'er up fr'm
34         Glastonbury,
35 Ski:    No:, no.
36                    (0.8)
37 Ski:    ↑Oka:y,
38                    (.)
```

```
39   Les:   ↑Oka↑:y?
40              (0.4)
41   Ski:   Yah.
42   Les:   .hhh Well(g) (0.2) jus' give me a ring later 'n see-
43          see if I'm still in the land a' the living will you,
```

Lesley reports Katherine's request to be picked up on Monday, and reports her own initial response to this (line 2) – 'Monday evening's no good' because it would be the same day that 'Granny Anders' needed to be picked up. Skip produces a delayed continuer (line 5), hearing that there may be more to come on this topic, but displaying a lack of enthusiastic commitment. Lesley then reports Katherine's response – that she wants to travel down with Brad, who can help her with her case, and that this will mean a shorter journey to Glastonbury for Skip.

Interference in the call prevents Skip's initial response from being hearable even by Lesley, but his turn at line 16, 'On Mondee as we:ll', is at least hearable as a reiteration that he will have two people to pick up on Monday. The delayed uptake, the repair format and the emphasis on 'Mondee' and 'well' makes this turn hearable as a (preface to) refusal. Lesley certainly hears it as trouble – her delayed and 'well'-prefaced response provides a justification – that Glastonbury is a shorter journey for Skip than Bristol would have been,[11] and is therefore a preferable arrangement. Her '↑I thought ...', with heavy emphasis on 'I', reveals this as something that Lesley is committed to – she no longer presents these arrangements as solely Katherine's request.

Skip's similarly delayed and 'well'-prefaced response to this also contains a *pro forma* agreement, followed by his own counter: he already has a trip to Yeovil on that day, and he begins listing the implications of this – 'I've got to go to Yeo:vil an' then back to'. His subsequent list is inaudible due to Lesley's turn incursion providing a counter to Skip – 'We: may not.' Skip's collection of Granny Anders may only involve a trip to Sparkford, which is closer than Yeovil.[12] Note again a change in person reference, from Skip's 'I've got to go' to Lesley's 'we may not', producing the responsibility for picking up Granny and Katherine, and thereby perhaps the decision-making power about when to do so, as something that both share.

After some delay Lesley continues with our target turn (line 28) – 'An' you're coming home early that night anyway'. This has a number of features to note, some of which are familiar from our earlier examples. First it tells Skip something about himself that he plainly knows already – a B-event. The 'anyway' produces this particular bit of information (that Skip will have more time

---

[11] Glastonbury is about 12 miles away, Bristol about three times further.
[12] Yeovil is about 12 miles away, Sparkford only about 3.

than normal) as independent of all the prior reasons why it will be OK to pick
up two people in one night.

Conforming to the normative response requirement (in everyday talk at least)
of items loosely termed B-event statements, Skip confirms this in overlap with
Lesley's interrogative 'aren't you'. Her addition of this adds to the sense of
the declarative as something that Skip has rights to know about, and it prefers
a yes response. Unlike our previous example, where the CPO rushed into her
next TCU after issuing the interrogative, Lesley waits for a further response
from Skip (line 32), before continuing with a further persuasive formulation
'An' it ↑dẓn' matter what time you pick 'er up fr'm Glạstonbury' (lines 33–4).
Once again, Lesley does not treat Skip's mere agreement with this (line 35) as
sufficient, and waits for him to assent to the plan more definitively (line 37),
which she checks by instigating a further post-expansion sequence (Schegloff,
2007a) (line 39).

The tag-formatted turn in this extract has some similarities to our NSPCC
examples, in that it rephrases the recipient's action-relevant version of himself
(as unable to pick up two people in one night), making relevant a competing course of action for the recipient. The interrogative (tag) that follows the
declarative treats the recipient (Skip) as already knowing (in the sense that he
is treated as being in a position to confirm) the rephrased version, which in
this case acts as further inducement to comply with Lesley's proposed course
of action.

However, in contrast to our previous examples from advice-resistance
sequences and crying uptake, rather than running on with further information and softening the requirement for a response, Lesley stops and waits for
Skip to confirm her tag question. It seems that, unlike the previous examples, eliciting explicit acceptance is the business of this sequence, so Lesley
does not suppress the preference for a yes response that her tag question has
made relevant by rushing past it, but waits until a positive response appears
from Skip. Broadly, Skip is being manoeuvred into giving the lift in a manner that formulates his business (his comings and goings and availability)
and leaves him little space for refusal without contradicting Lesley outright.
There is no evidence here of the tag as something diagnostic of Lesley's lack
of confidence.

Although we have focused on female-to-male tags, there is no indication
from these examples that gender is relevant to their role. Our point is that
the tag question can be exploited as part of this practice; it is not intrinsically 'weak' or 'strong', and it does not index a psychological state of 'weak
agreement' or 'strong agreement'. Rather, it is a functional building block in
this particular practice – it may be used differently in other practices. Making
the general correlation between the grammatical form and the social category
misses this level of granularity.

Tags on location

Our final example is taken from a UK television programme called *Location, Location, Location*, which features people looking for a house to buy, often with limited funds and boundless ambition. They are helped ('helped') in this by two presenters, Kirsty and Phil, who are not a couple, but who make gender relevant in a range of ways with each other and the prospective buyers in their on-screen interaction. In this episode, Hazel and Bill are a heterosexual couple who are shown as having very different ambitions in their search for a house. Hazel says she wants somewhere to move straight into; Bill repeatedly claims to want something he can add value to by doing improvements in his spare time. Disagreements arise at various points. The extract that follows comes as the four people emerge from the front door onto the pavement following their final viewing.

Extract 3 *Location, Location, Location* (Channel 4)

```
 1   Hazel:  →   It's everything we've ever wanted.=isn'it.
 2                    (0.2)
 3   Hazel:      Everything's n:ew an [nice an] clea::n an .hh lovely:.=
 4   Bill:                         [.h h h  ]
 5   Hazel:      ='n I [wan:]t it.
 6   Phil:            [Bill?]
 7                    (.)
 8   Bill:       Thi- °i-° there's not a lot you can add to it bu:t
 9               (1.2) i's great anyway I love- (.) I love that-
10               everyth- par:t've [it
11   Hazel:  →                    [I think you'll get o:ver it though
12           →   won't you.=
13   Bill:       =Yeah.
14                    (.)
15   Bill:       Th[e  shed-]
16   Kirsty:       [H H h i] h [h h u h    h huh    h h a h    h a h ]=
17   Phil:                     [I don't [think you're gonna give 'im]=
18   Hazel:                             [a h H A H H A ↑HA ↑HAH ]=
19   Phil:       =[a MO:MENT'S CHOI:CE:! ] [Hh ]
20   Kirsty:     =[hih ha hah hah ha .h       ] [ i.h ]   h  ]
21   Hazel:      =[ahah hah ha hah .hh        ] [h h        ]
22   Bill:                                      [hihyeahh]
23   Phil:   →   [.H[hughh I thi(h)nk you'll geddover it W:ON:'T you:,!]
24   Hazel:      [ee[ huh huh huh ha hah hah hah ↑hah ↑hah      ]=
25   Kirsty:        [.H h h ↑↑I: ↑↑thi::::- huh hhuh huh hhuh huh    ]=
26   Hazel:      =[hah ha ↑hah ↑hah]
27   Kirsty:     =[huhh huh huh      ] .hhh
28   Phil:       Buddid is importan' in- in en- an:y house search…
```

We will take the three tag questions in this extract in turn.

'It's everything we've ever wanted.=isn'it.'

We cannot make too much of this first example, as there has been some editing prior to this sequence, but we can note some important features of the turn design. The declarative element, which is in response to Phil but also addresses Hazel's husband, Bill, is built from two extreme case formulations (Pomerantz, 1986) – 'it's *everything* we've *ever* wanted'. This leaves no room for doubt about Hazel's investment (Edwards, 2000) in this house. Moreover, 'everything we've ever wanted' is an idiomatic construction – it does not offer descriptions at a level of granularity that Bill can easily counter. Hazel's choice of person reference in her assessment builds it as something shared with Bill – 'it's everything *we've* ever wanted'. She constructs her husband's desires as shared, despite the fact that this is hearably out of line with Bill's previous claims, at least as presented by the programme makers.[13] She then latches the tag question 'isn't it' directly onto the assessment, which not only treats Bill as in a position to confirm the assessment but also as *sharing* the assessment.

Our sense is that there is a brief edit at this point. How brief is not clear – the camera moves to close-up. This means that we have to be cautious in discussing Bill's absent turn as responsive to (or relevantly absent as a response to) Hazel's declarative + tag. Nevertheless, Hazel's utterance in lines 3–5 makes sense if Bill has indeed not responded to the tag question (and 0.2 seconds is already, before any edit has taken place, a hearable delay before responding to a strongly positive assessment; Pomerantz, 1984a). Hazel provides further extrematized assessments of the house: *(everything's) new, nice, clean, lovely.* This is closed with an upshot that is directly related to the future purchase: *'and I want it'.* Note the upshot is *I* want it – this marks out a difference from the tag-formatted construction in line 1 which jointly characterizes her and Bill's wants up until this time. In line 5 Hazel is not speaking on behalf of Bill's *current* response to the house. Nevertheless, in characterizing his previous desires so strongly and assessing the house so positively it leaves Bill in a position where to disagree will involve some work. There is a lot of interactional 'push' in Hazel's construction; Bill will need some serious 'push-back' to counter it.

As television presenters, Phil and Kirsty often explore tensions between the buyers and highlight a range of issues for the audience. This helps to construct the interest, entertainment and intelligibility of what is going on. In this case, note Bill's audible in-breath at line 4 – his first contribution (that we see anyway)

---

[13] Of course, it is also in some sense addressed to a potentially complicated mixture of hosts, film crew and television audience.

that may be relevant to Hazel's assessments. It could signal his attempt to offer a different view, more in line with his earlier arguments in favour of purchasing an old house that gives them an opportunity to add value. Phil encourages him to contribute at line 6 (perhaps picking up from what might have been the start of a turn at line 4). Bill is left with the choice of agreeing with the assessment (somewhat in contrast to his earlier expressed view) or developing some kind of disagreement. The difficulty here can be seen from the hitches at the start of Bill's turn at line 8, which then starts with a disagreement 'there's not a lot you can add to it' before developing an agreement.

Bill struggles with the agreement. Note the 1.2-second pause after the 'but' (line 9) – he has grammatically marked that more is to come in the turn with the 'but'; yet he is struggling to provide it. He does a strong positive 'i's great', but then is in more trouble as he starts to provide a warrant for the assessment that it is 'great'. His trouble is that in spelling out what is great about the house he may go against precisely what he has previously highlighted as his most important criterion (scope for development – i.e., specifically *not* 'new' and 'clean'). He has three runs at this. The first cuts off on 'love' and the second cuts off on 'that', and then he cuts off again before the end of 'everything'. The problem here is that in trying and failing to do a smooth positive assessment (he is hearably settling on 'I love every part of it') he displays trouble with the house and the purchase. Bill's troubled assessment (lines 8–10) is the environment for Hazel's second tag question.

'I think you'll get over it though won't you'

Here (lines 11–12) Hazel produces Bill as going to 'get over' something, presumably any disappointment indexed by his trouble in producing an assessment, and his initial non-aligning response 'there's not a lot you can add to it' (line 8). As with Hazel's previous tag, and our first two examples, the form of 'you'll get over it' is broadly idiomatic (with all the robustness that brings with it).[14] Note that the 'though' marks the declarative as contrastive to what came before, invalidating somewhat the positively assessing (though troubled) elements of Bill's turn. The tag, 'won't you', treats Bill as being in a position to confirm the claim that he will 'get over it' and projects agreement. Bill is built as both going to 'get over it' and knowing that he will 'get over it', and as someone who will, roughly, come to be pleased that they are buying this house.

---

[14] We have found that demonstrating that a phrase is idiomatic is not straightforward, beyond the sense of its being familiar. A Google search for the string reveals more than a million hits and included at least two films, songs and a variety of emblematic quotations. The phrase finder lists it as far back as 1839, but in wide use in the US from the early 1990s. For example, it appears in the US gay community slogan, 'We're here and we're queer – get over it.'

As we have seen in our previous examples, offering a description of another person's inner states (a prototypical B-event) is often a delicate matter to be managed with some care. However, in this case, Bill is treated as *already knowing* that he has this trajectory of change, a coercive and invasive move that reworks what might be thought to be Bill's business through rebuilding his desires.

'I thi(h)nk you'll geddover it W:ON:'T you:,'

What comes after the second tag is particularly interesting for how we can understand the working of the talk up to now and, importantly, how the participants themselves understand it. Bill delivers the projected and preferred agreement (line 13) after the tag question. He thereby ratifies the reconstructed version of himself. However, after a micro-pause he starts with 'the shed-' (line 15). This may be the stranded start of a new turn. Alternatively, it may be a delayed element of his previous turn. The shed has been a feature of the house that Bill has already assessed positively (as somewhere where he can practisce his DJ skills). It is possible that 'the shed' was something that Bill was working towards in his troubled turn – 'it is hard to add value, but... *it has this great shed*' (lines 8–10). Bill then drops out of the turn as Kirsty, who has been monitoring and smiling up to now, starts to laugh loudly, and her laughter continues through the rest of the extract. In terms of timing, Kirsty's laughter starts shortly after Bill's agreement with the tag question. Phil picks up on this and provides his own commentary on the business done by Hazel's turn, followed by an exaggerated repeat. The commentary constructs Hazel as restricting Bill's choice – 'I don't [think you're gonna give 'im a MO:MENT'S CHOI:CE:!' (lines 17 and 19). Most interesting for us is what Phil does next (after further laughter): he repeats Hazel's tag question 'I thi(h)nk you'll geddover it W:ON:'T you:,!' (line 23), dispensing with the word 'though' and adding a laughter particle into 'think'. His repeat hugely exaggerates the emphasis on the tag element, 'won't you' – the words are stretched and delivered with increased volume. At the same time his repeat is accompanied by an exaggerated pointing gesture that starts at the same time as 'I think' and ends on the 'won't you' with an elaborated stabbing with the finger alongside his whole body leaning forward. This gesture is directed at Bill. Kirsty looks at Phil and laughs throughout; Hazel looks at Bill and also laughs.

The interest for us is the way the laughter, commentary and gestures reveal a participant's understanding of the potentially coercive use of tag questions. This offers a kind of vernacular confirmation of our more technical analysis. Phil's gesture and repeat precisely pick out the tag question and act out its force. Note the way that Phil picks out 'won't' as a key item as he reanimates

the tag construction. It is theatrically delivered by Phil as the word with the most interactional 'push'.

Summary, thoughts and problems

Our goal in this chapter has been to show across some diverse examples how tag questions ('declarative + tag' constructions) can operate in a way that is both *coercive* (attempting to alter, or place constraints on, the recipient's conduct) and *invasive* (attempting to re/construct the recipient's desires, beliefs, knowledge or other 'psychological' matters). When in Extract 3 Phil re-enacts the tag, he theatrically brings alive precisely the coercive and invasive potential of tags. Our aim has not been to survey the distribution of such actions and their sociolinguistic coordination with gender. Rather it has been to reveal in detail one practice, taken from our NSPCC study of advice resistance, and applied to some everyday examples in which tag questions are employed by women talking to men.

In the broader gender-based collection of extracts we have found a repetition of the basic form found in our advice-resistance examples – to reiterate.

Some basic features of the practice are as follows:

1 The declarative rephrases the recipient's action-relevant version of himself or herself.
2 This rephrasing makes relevant a competing or alternative course of action for the recipient.

3   The interrogative (tag) that follows the declarative treats the recipient as *already knowing* the rephrased version.
4   Additional practices common in our institutional data may be added to dampen the recipient's response requirement further:
    (a) continuing past the TRP for the tag question, and
    (b) employing an idiomatic formulation.

The combination of (4a) and (4b) limits the conversational space for disagreement, and is prevalent in our advice-resistance and crying corpuses.

We must emphasize again that we are not claiming that tag questions are *always* used in this way. We hope to have developed a discussion of gender and tags that is different to previous research, and that suggests a way forward for those wishing to contribute further to these kinds of debate. Rather than considering the question of whether women do or do not use more tag questions, we have instead focused on the assumption that tag questions reflect a lack of 'confidence' or 'assertiveness'. Whereas some researchers have disputed Lakoff's claims from more traditional sociolinguistic perspectives, we have used a detailed analysis of our examples to highlight two sorts of problem with this.

The first sort of problem is with the idea that tag questions are a feature of powerless, ineffective or weak talk. It is not hard to see why tag questions should be viewed in this way, as they are conversational formats that treat the 'content' of what has been said in the declarative part of the tag as in need of confirmation by the recipient. We expect that there are indeed practices in which the current speaker uses tags to affirm or even subordinate to an existing position of the other. This is, no doubt, the kind of observation that stimulated Lakoff in the first place. Yet, as we have shown, tag questions can also be used very differently. In this case what we see is the declarative constructing, simultaneously, an element of the world and the speaker's stance towards it. The tag element treats these matters as shared by the recipient.

The second sort of problem is with the idea that tag questions are reflective of some underlying psychological state, which can then be mapped on to some pre-defined notion of gender – e.g., 'women are less assertive'. By providing a detailed specification of how tag questions can be coercive, we have shown how psychological matters, whether they can sensibly be seen to lie *behind* the talk or not, are certainly part of the *business* of talk. Whereas traditional sociolinguistic work on gender relies on the analysts' identification of gender as related to presumptive constructions of the inner life of interactants, we have sketched a picture that highlights the importance of taking seriously the specific interactional context in which a tag question is produced. In these examples the conflict about actions is managed, in part, through psychological constructions (or, more broadly, B-event statements) embedded within conversational sequences.

The challenge for sociolinguistic or other approaches that link forms of talk with social categories such as gender and inequality is to do so in a way that is sensitive to the specific conversational practices that we have started to show are operating. This is an interesting and fruitful challenge for gender researchers, in which sociolinguists, discursive psychologists and conversation analysts might come together to build a more sophisticated and sensitive picture of the way activity and gender may or may not be related.

Part III

Gender and action formation

8   On the role of reported, third party compliments in passing as a 'real' woman

Susan A. Speer

Introduction

My aim in this chapter is to examine the role of reported, third party compliments in transsexual patients passing[1] as 'real' men or women. This research forms part of a broader conversation analytic (henceforth CA) study examining the vocal and embodied production of gender identities in interactions between transsexual patients and psychiatrists in a large British National Health Service (henceforth NHS) gender identity clinic (Speer & Green, 2007; 2008). The gender identity clinic (henceforth GIC) is a distinctive institutional setting where individuals who identify as transsexual[2] and who (usually, but by no means always) desire male/female 'cross sex' hormones and 'gender confirmation' or 'sex change' surgery' (Press for Change, 2007: 2) attend for assessment by at least two psychiatrists. Gender clinic psychiatrists are renowned for acting as 'gatekeepers' to hormones and surgery (Speer & Parsons, 2006). They assess patients according to a pre-defined set of medical criteria, and aim to produce a 'differential diagnosis' (that is, to diagnose the type of gender identity disorder

The research reported here was funded by ESRC Award number RES-148–25-0029. Richard Green arranged access to the field site, coordinated data collection on site, and provided brief explanation on the clinical management of patients. I am indebted to John Heritage for his input during the early development of ideas presented here, and Celia Kitzinger, Elizabeth Stokoe and Clare Jackson for their comments on early drafts. I take full responsibility for the views presented, and any errors are my own.

[1] I use the concept of 'passing' in this chapter from within an ethnomethodological framework, to describe the activities that we all engage in as part of our everyday lives in order to be taken, or 'read', by others in a particular way (e.g., as a feminine woman or a masculine man; Speer & Green, 2007).

[2] Transsexualism is formally designated in the *Diagnostic and Statistical Manual of Mental Disorders* (American Psychiatric Association, 1994) as a 'gender identity disorder' (GID). Persons with GID are said to exhibit 'a strong and persistent cross-gender identification and a persistent discomfort with their sex or a sense of inappropriateness in the gender role of that sex' (Harry Benjamin International Gender Dysphoria Association, 2001: 4). Throughout this chapter I use the medical term 'transsexual', as opposed to the more political term 'transgender', to describe my research participants, because this research deals specifically with individuals who seek medical treatment to change their sex. The notion of transgender is often used in a political context by transgender activists in order to avoid medical categorization.

(GID) accurately and to determine that the patient is not suffering from some related or unrelated mental health problem). Although psychiatrists at the clinic in my data do not work with a standardized patient interview protocol, part of their concern when assessing patients is to examine their motivations for transitioning, and to judge whether or not they have a *realistic* view of themselves in their new role.[3] Likewise, patients' primary concern when undergoing psychiatric assessment at the clinic is to persuade psychiatrists that they meet the requisite diagnostic criteria and are appropriate candidates for treatment.

Officially, patients' physical appearance and success in passing in the preferred gender role are not a formal criterion in their assessment (Harry Benjamin International Gender Dysphoria Association, 2001). Indeed, as 'insiders', psychiatrists at the clinic already know whether patients were born male or female. In this sense, patients cannot possibly 'pass' with clinic psychiatrists in the same way they might with others outside the clinic environment who do not know about their 'transsexual' status. Despite this, there are numerous reports in the literature that gender professionals 'have judged transsexuals' authenticity on their ability to pass' *as* male/female (Lev, 2004: 264).

Certainly, I have found that it is not uncommon for psychiatrists (as well as patients) to comment on patients' physical appearance and overall ability to pass as men or women during their assessment sessions (Speer & Green, 2007). Clinicians have noted that 'clients often look for positive feedback on their presentation. They show off their bodily changes and boast about their new breasts or hair growth' (Lev, 2004: 263). Additionally, there is some evidence in my data that if patients do not attend their assessment session obviously dressed 'in role', the psychiatrists may treat this as an accountable matter. It is hardly surprising given this context that patients tend to believe that, in order to obtain their desired treatment, they must first persuade psychiatrists of the validity of their trans identity, by showing, through their talk, bodily comportment, appearance and embodied actions, that they can pass as men or women (May, 2002: 459).

In an effort to update the now classic ethnomethodological studies of passing and the social construction of sex by Garfinkel (1967) and Kessler and McKenna (1978), and provide a data-driven intervention into hitherto largely abstract, post-feminist debates about 'performativity' (J. Butler, 1990b; for an overview and critique of this work see Speer, 2005a), I set about identifying the range of techniques or practices that patients use to 'evidence' and 'objectify' their gender identity, and pass as trans men and women in their

---

[3] Although practices may vary cross-culturally (and between NHS and private treatment within the UK), these observations are based on prescriptions for practice set out in the internationally recognized Harry Benjamin International Gender Dysphoria Association's 'Standards of care for gender identity disorders' (Harry Benjamin International Gender Dysphoria Association, 2001), and on interviews with GIC psychiatrists.

interactions with clinic psychiatrists. The practice that forms the focus of this chapter is reporting the compliment of a third party. This involves patients reporting, through direct reported speech or summary (Clayman, 2007; Holt & Clift, 2007a), interactions they have had with others outside the clinic setting who have positively assessed their physical appearance or (arguably gendered) attributes. Examples of some third party attributions I explore in this chapter include 'she … said, "you look reallhy lovelyh"', 'the woman … said "you're about the most convincing one I've seen"' and 'other women say to me well I come across as a woman'.

The news I hope to bring in this chapter is that reported, third party compliments like these allow speakers objectively to 'evidence' (Pomerantz, 1984b: 608; Clift, 2006) positive (and, in the case of transsexual speakers, gender-relevant) features of their appearance, attributes or character (their identity), and hence get a positive assessment of who they are as a member 'on record', while avoiding the negative characterological inferences associated with overt self-praise or 'bragging'. The latter are actions that, as I will show below, tend to be subject to direct or indirect sanctions and efforts to detoxify the bragging, by recipients.

I suggest that reported third party compliments allow the speaker to avoid bragging, for two main reasons. First, the embedded character of the compliment creates epistemic distance between the speaker and the praise; that is, the speaker is not claiming rights to self-assess (Heritage & Raymond, 2005), but simply reporting what some, arguably more objective person (who *does* have epistemic rights to assess them) happened to say about them. Since the evaluation originated with, and derives from, the views of others, the speaker's accountability for the praise is lessened, and does not appear quite so invested or self-serving. Second, reporting the compliment of a third party is generally not the primary or *focal action* of the talk with which the speaker is currently engaged. Instead, reported, third party compliments are usually, in my data, embedded within narratives and deployed as *subsidiary* actions in the service of other, primary or focal tasks (for more on this see Kitzinger, 2008a: 200–3, and Speer & Green, 2007: 362). Crucially, speakers can use the phenomenon of reported third party compliments, as subsidiary actions, as *vehicles* through which to evidence their male or female status objectively. Through them they can *do gender* (or some other identity they value) in the interaction, and objectively evidence that they pass outside this setting as 'real' men or women, whilst engaging in *other* more focal actions not concerned with doing gender (Jackson, this volume; Kitzinger, 2007b; 2008a; Speer & Green, 2007: 362; Stockill & Kitzinger, 2007).

The fragile and contested nature of speakers' gender identities in the highly evaluative environment of the GIC makes the phenomenon of reported, third party compliments especially well suited for use by transsexual patients in this setting. Indeed, their use is clinically consequential in that, if patients are able to evidence how the gender identities they claim for themselves during their assessment sessions are externally validated by others outside this setting, then it makes sense that psychiatrists should also treat them as 'true transsexuals' (Newman, 2000: 400)[4] in the clinic. In this respect the phenomenon satisfies the needs of the compliment and the needs of the institution. For this reason, my primary concern in this chapter is to demonstrate how reported, third party compliments function in the talk of transsexual patients. The phenomenon I identify may be found most commonly in institutional settings where speakers' identities are contested (whether that contested element be their gender, competence, physical ability or something else). However, it is important to stress that the phenomenon is by no means *confined* to such settings. Indeed, part of my aim in this chapter, as I show in my analysis of the conversational extracts below, is to introduce the possibility that the phenomenon represents a practice that may have its 'home' in ordinary conversation, and hence a more generic function in evidencing positive features or attributes of the speakers' identity. Indeed, their descriptions are clinically consequential in that they have a direct bearing on whether or not the speakers will be deemed by psychiatrists to have an externally validated, realistic sense of themselves in their new role and hence on whether they will proceed to hormones and/or surgery. As with news interviewers, the formulations that trans patients choose are 'often conditioned by the pursuit of credibility' (Clayman & Heritage, 2002: 166).

I intend my analyses in this chapter to contribute to three broad bodies of literature. First, I contribute to linguistic and CA research on the vocal and embodied production of gender identities, with specific reference to the way in which gender identities may get 'done' or 'displayed' through the vehicle of subsidiary (rather than focal) actions (Kitzinger, 2008a: 200–3; Speer & Green, 2007). Second, I contribute to the broader CA literature on action formation; specifically, compliments and the epistemics of positive self-assessment, self-praise and 'bragging' (Golato, 2005; C. Goodwin & Goodwin, 1987; Heritage & Raymond, 2005; Pomerantz, 1978). Third, I contribute to the literature on the production of 'neutralism' in talk, particularly the use of self-repair to shift a speaker's footing and transfer epistemic responsibility for a positive self-assessment onto a third party (Clayman, 1992; Clayman & Heritage, 2002: 158–62; Goffman, 1981; Schegloff *et al.*, 1977).

Materials and procedures

The data in this chapter derive from three distinct corpora: The first consists of 194 recordings (made up of 156 audio-recordings and 38 video-recordings)

---

[4] It should be noted, however, that clinicians themselves no longer use 'true transsexual' as a diagnostic term.

of the ordinary, psychiatrist–patient consultation, collected by four different psychiatrists (three male, one female) between 2005 and 2006. The GIC is the largest in the world. Ninety-five per cent of all NHS referrals are dealt with here, and psychiatrists at the clinic see approximately 500 new patients each year. The patient sample represents patients at different stages of the assessment process, from initial intake interviews and sessions that monitor progress, to exit interviews where patients are signed off for surgery by a second psychiatrist, and post-surgery follow-ups.[5] Patients attend the clinic once every 3–6 months, and each recorded session lasts between 15 and 60 minutes. The sample comprises both male-to-female and female-to-male patients; however, the majority of patients who attend the clinic self-identify as pre-operative, male-to-female transsexuals.[6]

In order to gain a broader understanding of the concerns of transsexual patients attending the clinic, and their reflections on the assessment sessions they experienced, these data were supplemented with a second corpus of twenty-one recorded telephone interviews between myself and transsexual users of the clinic. Each interview lasted approximately one hour. Ethical approval for the collection of both sets of materials was granted by the NHS Central Office of Research Ethics Committees. Identifying details have been changed to protect participants' anonymity. The final set of data comprise a widely available corpus of audio- and video-recordings of ordinary conversations from the Sociology Department at the University of California at Los Angeles, which I supplemented with video-recordings from a variety of settings collected by my undergraduate students at the University of Manchester.

In an initial trawl of the three data sets I identified over twenty instances of the target phenomenon. There is insufficient space to consider the full range of examples in this chapter (but see Speer, forthcoming). For this reason, I have selected five illustrative cases for detailed analysis below. In order to give the reader a flavour of the generality of the phenomenon and issues described, I have chosen extracts from across the three data sets. The target phenomenon in each instance is marked in bold.

To contextualize the phenomenon in the CA literature, I begin by summarizing CA work on compliments and the epistemics of self-praise. I provide an analytic demonstration of 'bragging' and its consequences before moving on to a detailed examination of reported third party compliments in the three distinct settings represented by the data. In the last analytic section I provide

---

[5] Given the relative infrequency of patients' appointments, of the 194 sessions that were recorded, 12 were repeat visits. Thus the corpus contains recordings of 182 different patients.

[6] Although statistics on such matters are notoriously problematic, this reflects the much larger incidence of transsexualism amongst males in the population. Some of the latest figures from the Netherlands suggest transsexualism affects 1 in 11,900 males and 1 in 30,400 females (Harry Benjamin International Gender Dysphoria Association, 2001: 2).

evidence of participants' orientations to the norm against self-praise (and the interactional virtue of embedding self-praise within a third party attribution) by examining an instance in which a speaker repairs their talk, shifting their footing from a positive self-description to the reported compliment of a third party. I conclude by considering the implications of the analyses for CA studies of gender-relevant actions on the one hand, and action formation, compliments and the epistemics of positive self-assessment on the other.

Conversation analysis and the epistemics of self-praise

The concept of 'epistemics' is commonly used to describe speakers' management, regulation and sanctioning of their respective rights to know or assess a particular object, event, person or phenomenon (Heritage & Raymond, 2005; Raymond & Heritage, 2006). As Sacks (1984b: 424), observes, 'entitlement to experiences are [*sic*] differentially available'. Bound up with issues around 'face' (Lerner, 1996) and speaker identity, an examination of the way speakers 'index' and manage their differential epistemic rights and responsibilities in interaction can offer revealing insights into the interactional production and maintenance of social solidarity (Heritage & Raymond, 2005; Raymond & Heritage, 2006). To date, the majority of CA studies concerned with epistemics have focused on examining 'first' and 'second position' assessments of objects, events, persons or phenomena that are 'external' to the speaker (Heritage & Raymond, 2005; Raymond & Heritage, 2006). The epistemic management of *self-assessments* by interactants has received comparatively little attention. This is somewhat surprising given the pervasive centrality of notions of 'personality', 'self-concept', 'identity' and their various 'disorders' across the social sciences.

Saying positive things about oneself, one's appearance, character or attributes, is a tricky matter for reasons highlighted by both Sacks (1975) and Pomerantz (1978). In his seminal paper 'Everybody has to lie' Sacks (1975) makes an interesting observation concerning the epistemics of self-assessment. He says:

I intend to notice a difference between the way two different sorts of statements are dealt with. For the first, if, e.g., a little girl comes home and says to her mother, *Mama, I'm pretty* or *Mama, I'm smart*, the mother could say 'Who told you that?' For the second if someone says *I'm tired* or *I feel lousy*, etc., no such thing is asked. One is responsible for knowing some things on one's own behalf, in contrast to the situation in which one is treated as likely to be repeating what another has told him about himself. (1975: 72; emphasis in original; see also Pomerantz, 1980)

Here, Sacks seems to be suggesting that, for certain kinds of self-assessment, that is, *positive* self-assessments or compliments, there is an expectation by the recipient that such assessments must be second-hand, lodged or originating in the view of a third party. In Pomerantz's (1980) terminology, the little girl in Sacks's example is presenting something that should be a 'type 2 knowable' – that is, 'an assertion hearable as "repeated"' (1980: 188) – as a 'type 1 knowable', that is, one that '*subject-actors* have rights and obligations to know' (1980: 187; emphasis in original).

The issue that Sacks and Pomerantz highlight here points to the existence of, and speaker orientation towards, a norm which holds that we do not necessarily have the epistemic right or entitlement to compliment ourselves on our own behalf. Direct self-praise *by* speaker A *about* speaker A is problematic because the norm dictates that praise about speaker A should originate with, or derive from, speaker B. In Labov's (1972a: 254) terms, praise about speaker A should be delivered by speaker B as a B-event statement, that is, as something 'which B knows about but A does not'.

But why should self-complimenting actions be so problematic? Like complaints and numerous other actions, compliments involve speakers dealing with both the *object* of the action (that is, the thing being complimented) and its *subject*, that is, the complimenter (Edwards, 2005). Like all actions, compliments have 'speaker indexical' properties (2005:6). In other words, the speaker's management of the 'subjective side' of the action (2005:5) may make available 'evaluative inferences about the speaker' (2005: 6), for example that the speaker is objective and reporting the facts, or else invested, motivated or dispositionally prone to present themselves in a favourable light (in discursive psychological terms they have a 'stake' or 'interest' in the description; Potter, 1996:124ff). Speakers who compliment themselves run the risk of being seen as too invested in their own description, and hence as bragging. Indeed, in self-complimenting actions, the subject and object of the action are essentially one and the same. It follows that *others* can see and evaluate us more objectively than we are able to.

Pomerantz's (1978; see also Golato, 2005) work on compliment responses substantiates these claims. Pomerantz argues that recipients of compliments often disagree with and reject them. She suggests that the prevalence of disagreements and rejections of compliments by compliment recipients is the outcome of a 'system of constraints' which 'involves speakers' minimization of self-praise' (1978: 81). Pomerantz notes that this system of constraints governs 'how parties may credit or praise themselves. *Self-praise avoidance* names a system of constraints which is enforceable by self and/or other, in that order' (1978: 88; emphasis in original). Although it is not the primary focus of her paper, Pomerantz (1978: 88–92) outlines three ways in which constraints on self-praise are enforced by self and other:

(1) The recipient makes 'critical assessments of the self-praiser'.
(2) The speaker incorporates a disclaimer or qualification within the self-praise.
(3) Praise is initiated by one speaker *on behalf of* another present party.

A combination of the above is also possible.

An example of the enforcement of constraints against self-praise which supports Pomerantz's observations is presented in Extract 1, below (my data, not
Pomerantz's). Here three female university students have been asked to discuss 'achievements they are proud of' (in other words, they have been given
a licence by the researcher to engage in acts of self-praise).[7] They begin by
discussing their achievements in school. Rachel engages in two instances of
self-praise which I have highlighted in bold on the transcript.

Extract 1 (Speer Video: FG1F-b: 2.49/2.09mins)

```
 1  Rac:  Ye:ah, I did better at (1.2) Manor Cross- >like the
 2         college that I went to.< Than=
 3  Sar:  =Y[ea(h)h.
 4  Rac:     [when I did my >A levels< in the first place coz
 5         it was like (0.5) al:ways in school an' stuff it was a-
 6         .hh everyone was like getting 'A::y's' an:' if you got a
 7         'Bee' it was like oh my [gosh.
 8  Sar:                          [Pressure.
 9  Rac:  Ye:a[h definitely. .hhh An' then: when: we went to::
10  Sar:      [Yeah.
11  Rac:  (0.4) Manor Cross >all a' sudden it was like< ye:ah
12         top o' the class, am gonna ace this just cos
13         [(          th]ere.)
14  Sar:  [I kno:w, yeah,] [(>coz that's what it) was like,< ]=
15  Lou:                  [Ah  hah  h  a  h  hah  hah  ]=
16  Sar:  =[cos my: sc]hool was- like pos[her than (my-)
17  Lou:  =[.h h h h h]                 [Not being big head-
18            [ed or anything ( then / there )
19  Rac:       [No(h)t be(h)ing bi(h)g hea(h)ded or(h) an(h)ything
20         but I'm [just a wa:lking-Ay: student.    ]
21  Lou:          [I am the best. heh heh heh heh]
22  Rac:  .hhhhh Don't know what went wro[ng (when ah was like)]=
23  Lou:                                [.hh   hheh   heh  heh]
24  Rac:  =went to U:ni eh heh heh .hhhh Oh de:ar.
25  Sar:  Nah goin' to college was the best thing I ever did
26         li:[ke.
27  Rac:     [Ye:a[h.
```

---

[7] I am of the view that the licence the researcher gives the interactants to discuss their achievements does not make these data any the less 'conversational'. Indeed, it should make it less likely
that one will find examples of 'constraints against self-praise' in this extract than in extracts
where speakers have *not* been given a licence to praise themselves. Thus, while the set-up nature
of the data in this instance may have a bearing on the *frequency* with which speakers engage in
acts of self-praise or bragging, it seems to have little bearing on the precise way in which that
self-praise is sanctioned or detoxified. The research set-up is not procedurally consequential for
the phenomenon in this case (Speer, 2002c).

```
28   Sar:          [Loved it.
29          (1.0)
30   Rac:   I' wa' [well good.   ]
31   Sar:          [°Newcastle.°] (Mm hm,)
32   Rac:   AN:d it was like (1.0) minimum effo:rt to kinda (.) do
33          well.=I think it was >minimum effort to do well.=I
34          mean GCSE::s<⁸ we:re a piece a' piss.
35          (0.6) ((Sarah drops left arm from mug to chair in exasperated
36          fashion))
37   Rac:   They re:ally [were like, .hhh
38   Sar:               [((Sarah lowers head and stares pointedly at
39          Rachel))
40          (.)
41   Rac:   You were saying like you did hardly any revision.
42   Lou:   I know [(better to          )'coz] I were crap.
43   Rac:          [Night before revision.]
44          (0.6)
45   Rac:   An:' still came out wi' like (.) proper
46   Sar:   Yea:h.
47   Rac:   good grades an' then wen- went ta: college an' stuff,
```

The first instance of self-praise (lines 9 and 11–12) is delivered in the course of an experiential narrative that is designed to highlight how easy Rachel found college work. The second instance (lines 32–4 and 37) is 'and' prefaced and hence designed as an incremental expansion on and embellishment of her prior comments. Note that both instances of self-praise constitute the focal action with which Rachel is presently engaged. In other words, they are delivered directly by Rachel on her own behalf, 'for their own sake', that is, in order to evidence something positive about herself as speaker. Moreover, she delivers the praise as 'A-event' statements about matters which Rachel, but not the recipients, have primary knowledge and epistemic rights to notice and assess.

What is interesting for our present purposes is that although Sarah initially aligns with Rachel's self-praise (line 14), and initiates a 'second story' (Sacks, 1995) in which she affirms Rachel's experiences as like her own (lines 14 and 16), the recipients subsequently orient to Rachel's descriptions as problematic, and collectively sanction and work to detoxify that self-praise. They sanction Rachel in three ways. First, Louise laughs, clearly treating the initial instance of bragging as non-serious (line 15), and interrupts Sarah's narrative in order to disclaim any bragging on Rachel's behalf ('Not being big headed or anything (then/there)', lines 17–18). This orients to, at the same time as detoxifying, the possibility that Rachel's comments might be heard as self-serving, with negative implications for her identity (that she is 'big headed'). Second, while

---

⁸ GCSEs are a UK qualification taken by pupils at age 16.

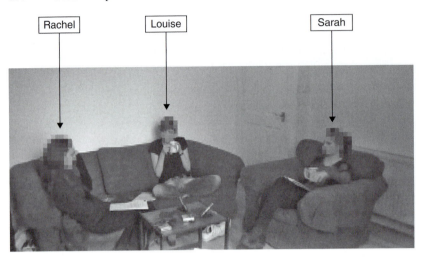

Figure 8.1

the first instance of self-praise is responded to by Sarah immediately and in an aligning fashion (line 14), after the second instance of self-praise, the recipients meet it initially with silence, withholding agreement or alignment (lines 35–6). In the absence of any uptake Rachel re-completes her assessment (line 37), opening up a further possible response slot. However, for the second time, this slot is not (vocally) filled (lines 38–40). Third, what we *do* get after the second instance of self-praise are embodied actions that exhibit exasperation by one of the recipients. On completion of Rachel's bragging there is a noticeable gap (line 35) during which Sarah drops her left arm down by the side of her chair. Immediately following this (lines 38–9), in overlap with Rachel's re-completion of her utterance (line 37), Sarah lowers her head and glares pointedly at Rachel (see Figures 8.1 and 8.2). In combination, these embodied actions represent Sarah's exasperation with Rachel.

Although it is not obvious whether Rachel or Louise can see what Sarah does here (it seems from their gaze direction that they do not), it is obvious that the camera will see, and indeed, Sarah's actions may well be designed for this 'overseeing' audience or participant.

There are three main reasons why Sarah may react in this way and why Rachel's bragging may be especially problematic at this point. First, Sarah has already had to work hard to get her own experiences heard in the just prior interaction (lines 14 and 16). Her talk is overlapped with laughter (line 15) and then cut off by Louise midway through her turn (line 16) as the others sanction and work to detoxify Rachel's bragging (lines 17–24). Sarah attempts

Figure 8.2

to resume her description of her experiences with a turn-initial 'Nah' (line 25) – something commonly deployed 'to mark a transition from non-serious to serious talk' (Schegloff, 2001b: 1948). Thus, just prior to Rachel's second instance of self-praise, Sarah appears preoccupied with getting the focus of the interaction away from Rachel, and on to her – something in which she appears to succeed. However, having reached an evidently sequence-closing agreement and alignment on the matter of Sarah's positive experiences of college (lines 27 and 30), instead of issuing a new sequence or topic, Rachel uses the (strongly emphasized) 'and' preface (line 32) to build her forthcoming assessment as a continuation of, and one that revisits, the prior talk, hence focusing the conversation, once more, on herself. Finally, Rachel brags for a second time, *after* her first instance of bragging has been (humorously) sanctioned by the recipients, and efforts have been made to detoxify it and (in Sarah's case) move the conversation away from her.

In response to her co-interactants' sanctions and efforts to detoxify the bragging, Rachel works to distance herself from the bragging and to re-establish the normative order of things. She does so first by backing away from the bragging, via humour. For example, after the recipients' humorous response to her first instance of bragging, Rachel repeats Sarah's disclaimer (line 19), before jokingly upgrading her original brag (line 20). In doing so she exhibits, in an exaggerated and self-mocking fashion, precisely the action she has just been sanctioned for, and, in the very same turn, disclaimed. This ironic upgrade is itself pre-empted by Louise (line 21), who completes Rachel's turn, in overlap, on her behalf. Second, Rachel engages in an act of self-deprecation – the interactional opposite of self-praise (Pomerantz, 1984a) – noting 'hhhhh Don't know what went wrong (when ah was like) went to U:ni eh heh heh .hhhh' (lines 22 and 24). Then, in the absence of any uptake at the possible completion of her turn construction unit (TCU) – the laughter essentially 'invites' recipients to come in here (line 24) (Jefferson, 1979) – Rachel closes the sequence by lamenting '<u>O</u>h de:ar' (line 24).

Third, Rachel designs her second instance of self-praise in a way that 'downgrades' its factual status, shifting from a global description of how easy GCSE are (lines 32–3) to a partial repeat prefaced with '<u>I</u> think' (lines 33–4; note the emphasis on the word '<u>I</u>'). It is in this way that Rachel manages what Edwards (2005) terms the 'subject side' of her description, explicitly orienting towards and emphasizing the subjective and potentially disputed nature of the assessment: as it is simply 'her' view, it is necessarily invested, and others in the room may not share the same experience, and hence may not agree or align with her (as, indeed, they subsequently do not!). Finally, in the absence of any alignment from her co-interactants, after the second instance of bragging, Rachel explicitly selects Louise as next speaker, initiating a new action sequence in which she attempts to recruit Louise's apparently parallel experiences (of finding the exams so easy she 'did hardly any rev<u>i</u>sion') to her cause, strongly encouraging her, through the design of her turn (citing something she was 'saying'), to align with her position (lines 41, 43, 45 and 47). Interestingly, although Louise's response (line 42) indicates that she aligns with Rachel's presuppositions about her behaviour, that she did 'hardly any revision', she does not align with Rachel's depiction of what may have caused this (i.e., that she too found GCSEs a 'piece a' piss'). On the contrary, Louise failed to revise, not because she found the exams easy, but rather because she was, according to her own assessment, 'crap' (line 42).

In sum, Extract 1 illustrates some of the ways in which the constraints on self-praise identified by Pomerantz (1978) are enforced. It shows that when self-praise is delivered directly *by* the speaker on their own behalf, and as the focal action with which a speaker is engaged, it tends not to go unnoticed or unsanctioned by recipients. As we have seen, participants engage in various attempts to detoxify the praise and re-establish the normative order of things. I want to argue that it is against this background of sanctions and efforts at detoxification, and the norm against self-praise that such actions orient towards and maintain, that reported third party compliments are so interactionally useful.

Reporting the compliment of a third party

During any particular action or description, speakers are sensitive to its possible receipt, and in particular to the possible inferences recipients may make about them. As I have noted previously, with self-praise in which the object and subject of the description are essentially the same, recipients may question the motives or character of the speaker (they may be deemed too subjective, biased or invested, for example) and thereby dispute the validity of the self-assessment (e.g., on the grounds that 'they would say that, wouldn't they').

Speakers deploy various strategies to manage and build their actions and descriptions so as not to appear self-serving or invested. As Edwards (2005) notes in relation to complaints, this management may involve 'objectifying' the action: 'the more a complaint can be built as a factual description of its object, the less available it is to be heard as stemming from the speaker's disposition to see, feel, or interpret things negatively' (2005: 6). Edwards cites 'verbatim quotations', 'independent corroboration by other victims and witnesses' and 'graphic narrative description' as some of the techniques speakers use to 'objectify' a complaint (2005: 6). In the remainder of this chapter, I demonstrate how reported, third party compliments, delivered by means of direct reported speech or summary (Clayman, 2007; Holt & Clift, 2007a), represent a similar means by which speakers can get 'on record' positive statements about themselves, their appearance, attributes or character (their identity), at the same time as objectifying (in this case making some 'other', third, party accountable for describing the object of the praise), thus enhancing the 'neutralism' of their claims (Clayman, 1992). By separating the subject of the compliment (the complimenter) from its object (the thing being complimented) the speaker may safely say what, in more direct forms of self-praise like those in Extract 1 above, is problematic or 'unsayable'.

Evidence from conversation

Consider, the following extract, which is taken from the same interaction that we observed in Extract 1. On this occasion, the young women are sharing their experiences of working part time. Rachel, once again, is the person whose actions I want to focus on.

Extract 2 Speer Video FG1F-b: 09.57/9.54 mins

```
1    Sar:  The other thing I do in the Summer is uhm:: work in the
2          psychiatric hospital but just on the coffee- bit, like
3          .hh the patients come in an' they love it, an' it's like
4          '↑hiya can I have a coffee' >and stuff like that< and you
5          ju[st chat to them an' it's canny.]
6    Rac:  [S-  I  love it-, I  love it like] with the regulars an'
7          [stuff (                )]
8    Sar:  [They'll draw you pi]ctures an' stuff.
9          (0.8)
10   Rac:  Ye:ah, it's well good, like all the r[egulars in the      ]=
11   ?:                                          [hmh hmh hmh heh]
12   Rac:  =sho:p.
```

```
13            (0.6)
14   Rac:    It's- it's a:ce.
15            (0.6)
16   Rac:    An'- li:ke I go:t a card at Christmas [an' stuff
17   Sar:                                          [Like Da(h)ve.
18            °Heh heh heh heh heh .hhh°
19   Rac:    [I love him!] Apple man!
20   Sar:    [A p p l e!  ]
21   Sar:    I [kno:w, I love Dave as well.]
22   Rac:      [They've all got their own  ] like little uh:m
23            nicknames an' stuff .hh bu::t there's this one woman >I
24            mean like I been serving her for like< worked nearly two
25            years an' stu:ff, .hh a::n' don't- >you know< you don't
26            really get to know anyone's names an' stuff c'z-
27            [(they/you) don't have name badge on or whatever,]=
28   Lou:    [No(h). (They just look like everyone              )]
29   Rac:    =they're j'st like a face an' you say ('oh hiya/who
30            are ya') they'll tell you- like their life sto:ry an'
31            stuff an' what's going on .hh an:uh: I got this-
32            Christmas ca:rd off 'er, .hh an' it said something-
33            .hh °What was it?° .hh It was li:ke 'to the gi:rl who
34            (0.6) [brightens the DRAbbest DA::[ys'.
35   Sar:          [Pt.                        [Aa:::::::[hh.
36   Rac:                                               ['The- the
37            drabbest mornins' or somethin' in the shop an' I jus'
38            thought 'ah, that's dead NIce' because (.) if you think
39            like sit- Liverpool City Centre sorta think, [it's- (.)=
40   Sar:                                                   [Yeah.
41   Rac:    =like completely (0.2) like a face in the crowd an'
42            stu:ff .hh an' that- y- I don't know anyone who:se li:ke
43            th't- gets- (.) cards like (.) because they're the shop
44            girl. [In the mor]ning (I'd do/get) like >a pile a'=
45   Sar:          [Y e : a h.]
46   Rac:    =Christmas cards< that high, I got a bottle o' wine,
47            I got chocolate,
48   Sar:    ↑Re::ally.
49            (0.4)
50   Rac:    ((Cough)) I got thirty pounds off
51   Sar:    °Fucking [hell°
52   Rac:             [that °kidney° patient guy.
53   Lou:    Nhh hhh
```

There are several interesting things to note about the way the praise is delivered in this extract. First, recall that in Extract 1 the self-praise was delivered
by Rachel directly, on her own behalf, as an A-event statement whose focal
action was to evidence something positive about her abilities at college. In this

extract, by contrast, Rachel embeds the positive assessment (that she '<u>br</u>ightens the <u>DRA</u>bbest DA::ys', line 34) within the written compliment of a third party; a woman she met in the course of her work in the hospital shop (lines 32–4 and 36–7). Hence, instead of delivering the praise in order to illustrate something positive about herself as speaker, here the third party attribution is delivered at the culmination of a scene-setting, experiential narrative in the form of an announcement (Terasaki, 2004) in the service of another, more focal action; in this case, to evidence something positive about her work experiences and the actions of this 'one woman' whose words Rachel is reporting. The praise (that she '<u>br</u>ightens the <u>DRA</u>bbest DA::ys') still comes through, but it is subsidiary to this focal task.

Second, Rachel presents the actions of the complimenting party (and hence the compliment itself) as contrary to her expectations and knowledge about what is normative for 'shop girls' in Liverpool City Centre (lines 38–9 and 41–4). Indeed, the woman's actions are made 'storyable' by virtue of being unusual, unexpected or surprising. Just as in other situations where the veracity or investment of the speaker in what they are saying may be in doubt (e.g., see Jefferson, 2004c), here, by presenting the woman's actions (and hence the compliment) as contrary to her expectations, Rachel manages the subject side of her description, presenting herself as a normal and rational perceiver of the world, not necessarily someone predisposed to seek or report compliments or praise on her own behalf, or invested in doing so. Indeed, the compliment is remembered and quoted very carefully by Rachel to be exactly 'as it was written' (lines 33 and 36–7), as factually accurate evidence for what 'this one woman' (line 23), and not Rachel herself, thought. The downgraded 'The- the drabbest mornin's' or somethin' (lines 36–7) shows her to be concerned to be precise about the description, at the same time as displaying that she is not especially personally invested in its specifics.

Third, the use of the third party attribution represents a shift in Rachel's inter-actional footing (Goffman, 1981; Levinson, 1988). Goffman argued that for any piece of speech one needs to distinguish between its 'principal' (that is, the person whose position the talk is meant to represent), the 'author' who scripts or composes the words that are used, and the 'animator' who says the words. In direct self-praise the current speaker is the principal, author and animator of the talk. By contrast, when reporting the compliment of a third party the speaker is the author and animator of the talk, but not its principal. The principal in such cases is the non-present third party whose compliment is being cited.

As Clayman (1992; 2007) and Clayman and Heritage (2002) observe in respect of news interview discourse, footing shifts achieved via the use of direct reported speech or summary are commonly used to display a speaker's neutral-ity on matters that may be deemed controversial. Indeed, one of the virtues of such shifts is that the speaker is able to 'place some degree of distance between themselves and their more overtly opinionated remarks' (Clayman & Heritage, 2002: 152), hence managing (and typically decreasing) their accountability in relation to their talk. The shift in footing casts the speaker as a neutral conduit for the opinion and 'as one who is merely reporting' (2002: 154) or animating the view(s) of a third party, hence increasing the description's credibility. When the third party is an expert witness on the subject of the compliment or the assessable, as indeed a regular shop customer may be in this case, then it makes it especially tricky for a recipient to dispute or undermine the reported view, opinion or attitude about the speaker (Clayman & Heritage, 2002: 166).

Fourth, the footing shift embodied in third party attributions may be bound up in managing the epistemological status of the positive assessment. Thus, Rachel is not claiming rights to self-assess, or necessarily implying that she would say this about herself, on her own behalf (e.g., 'I brighten up people's drabbest days'). Certainly, in direct contrast to Extract 1, the third party compliment is delivered here as something which originated (i.e., at the time it was initially uttered) as a B-event statement with the woman who complimented her, who had primary epistemic rights (in Sacks's (1984b) terms, she had the 'entitlement') to notice and assess such things.

Fifth, the reported compliment may be interactionally 'safer' than praising oneself, because it opens up additional response options not available to recipients of direct self-praise. Thus, with direct self-praise of the kind we saw in Extract 1, the recipient can respond by agreeing or disagreeing, aligning or disaligning with the assessment. (I take disalignment to include withholding a response and problematizing, sanctioning or detoxifying the assessment.) By contrast, with reported third party compliments, as we have seen, the embedded character of the praise means that the speaker is not claiming rights to self-assess or say this on their own behalf. It follows that the assessable (i.e., the claim that the speaker 'brightens the DRAbbest DA::ys', line 34) is not up for agreement or disagreement, alignment or disalignment, in quite the same way that a direct self-assessment might be.

So what options are available to recipients of reported attributions? An initial trawl of instances in my corpus suggests they can respond in the following ways, separately or in combination:

1 Recipients can respond to the embedded assessable in the same way as if it were delivered directly, by agreeing/disagreeing, aligning/disaligning with its content (they could note 'you do', for example). In order to respond in this way, the speaker must have direct access to the assessable.

2 Recipients can treat the reported compliment as an announcement, or as the punchline of a story, responding with news receipts and/or surprise reaction token(s) (Heritage, 1984a; Wilkinson & Kitzinger, 2006).

3 Recipients can respond by evaluating the complimenting action of the third
party.

Although each of these response options and combinations thereof are evidenced in my data, the nature of third party attributions may lean the recipient more heavily towards option (3), possibly combined with option (2). This
is because the embedded character of the praise tends to focus the recipient
on the actions of the 'principal' or originator of the praise, to use Goffman's
terms, and not on the substance of the compliment itself. Additionally since
third party attributions in my data are often cited when the recipient of the
report does not have independent access to the assessable, this makes it less
likely in such circumstances that the recipient will respond as in (1) above.

Extract 2 bears out these claims in that although Sarah *does* have at least some
access to the assessable (Rachel's personality or character) she chooses (3),
positively evaluating the actions of the customer who paid Rachel the compliment ('Aa::::::hh', line 35). Note that it is only *after* Rachel has secured
Sarah's positive participation that she offers her own perspective on the third
party attribution, aligning with Sarah by positively assessing the actions of the
customer ('an' I jus' thought 'ah, that's dead NIce', lines 37–8).

So far I have used evidence from conversation to explore some of the differences between self-praise that is delivered straight off by the speaker on
their own behalf, and praise that is embedded in the reported compliment
of a third party. I have shown that 'direct' self-praise is treated as problematic and is sanctioned and detoxified by recipients. By contrast, self-praise
delivered through the vehicle of a reported, third party compliment creates
epistemic distance between the speaker and the praise. This allows speakers to evidence and get on record positive things about who they are as a
person, and show they possess desirable attributes, while avoiding the kinds
of orientations, sanctions and efforts at detoxification noted in respect of
Extract 1. It is in this way that the praise still comes through (that Rachel
is so nice she brightens the 'drabbest mornings' of relative strangers, for
example), and Rachel shows that she accepts such praise, but since it is
subsidiary to the focal task with which the speaker is currently engaged,
and lodged in the opinion of a third party, it appears more objective. It follows that the substance of the reported compliment (that is, whether or not
Rachel does indeed brighten the drabbest of mornings) is protected against
the kinds of problematic recipient orientations and sanctions that are risked
with direct self-praise.

In the remainder of this chapter I consider how the phenomenon of reported,
third party compliments operate in the talk of transsexual patients, for whom,
as I noted earlier, they may have special relevance.

Evidence from the Gender Identity Clinic

Extract 3 comes from a video-taped assessment session between a male psychiatrist and a 'male-to-female' transsexual patient (i.e., a natal male) who in this
session presents as a man. The patient's wife is currently dying of cancer, and
we join the interaction as the psychiatrist asks the patient how he sees things
evolving from here on.

Extract 3 Speer Video 3 16.28 mins

```
 1   Psy:   So how do you see all this evo:lving now.
 2   ((43 lines omitted))
 3   Pt:    Both my children now know, I've told my son. Uhm: he:
 4          has had (0.6) uh- h- he's having some problems with
 5          that. [My dau:]ghter
 6   Psy:        [How  s-]
 7   Psy:   How surprised was your son.
 8          (2.0)
 9   Pt:    He had no idea. [Let me put it that way.]
10   Psy:                   [Okay. .h h h h  That']s
11          (pretty/very) surprised, yeah?
12   Pt:    Yeah.
13          (0.2)
14   Pt:    Uh:m, .hhh but- (0.4) when I said, you know, 'how do
15          you feel about it', he just said, '↑we:ll, you know,
16          what is ↑is,' uh:m,
17   Psy:   Okay, [good.
18   Pt:          [So, that- that was good. My daughter i:s very,
19          very supportive indeed.
20   Psy:   Mm:,
21   Pt:    Uhm, especially when she foun:d we both take the same
22          size sho:es so(h)hh heh th[ere's -  ] there's a=
23   Psy:                             [(O- oh.)]
24   Pt:    =lovely sort of rappo:rt there in a sense an' that
25          was .hhh (0.5) there was something very special about
26          that.=The first time she met me as Sarah:, she wanted
27          to meet me: at th[e:: commu- City Centre=
28   Psy:                    [Yeah:.
29   Pt:    =Community Church, an' we meet on neutral ground, .hhh
30          she came up to me, gave me a hug and said, 'you look
31          reallhy lovelyh'.
32   Psy:   >°Ho[w nice.°<
33   Pt:        [<And- (0.8) .hhhh I can't-
34   Psy:   That's very [nice.
35   Pt:                [I can't really put into words,
36   Psy:   (°T[hat's nice.°)
```

```
37   Pt:      [what that meant to [me.         [You knohw. [Uh:m,
38   Psy:                    [((coughs)) [Sure.       O[kay.
39   Pt:      Uhm:, she has no problem with hugging me, uhhm: an:'
40   Psy:     Good.=
41   Pt:      =just being with me (°you know. [Really°)
42   Psy:                                    [Okay.
43            (.)
44   Pt:      .hhhh An' there's a sense in which, (1.0) I suppose
45            given: the present circumstances, .hhh (0.4) I feel I can
46            be a [far better m: mu:m to her (.) than I can a da:d,
47   Psy:          [Fh:h h h h h h h
48   Psy:     Mmhm,
49   Pt:      I can never replace her mum:, (0.8) but=
50   Psy:     =(Correct/Right).
51   Pt:      I f- feel that I could actually bring somethi:ng (0.8)
52            of that motherly love [to her.]
53   Psy:                           [Oka:y,]
```

This instance shares several features with Extract 2. As before, the positive assessment (that the patient looked 'reallhy lovelyh' when dressed in role, lines 30–1), is not delivered by the speaker directly, on his own behalf (cf: 'when I met my daughter for the first time I looked really lovely'). Rather, it is embedded within the reported compliment of a third party, in this case the patient's daughter. The patient presents his daughter's actions (and hence the compliment itself) as pleasantly surprising, and contrary to his expectations, making them storyable by virtue of their unexpected nature. He does this in part through the use of the intensifiers 'very, very' (lines 18–19) and 'indeed' (line 19), and through positively contrasting the daughter's actions with his son's comparatively negative, unenthusiastic response (lines 3–16). By presenting his daughter's actions in this way, the patient manages the subject side of his description, simultaneously decreasing his accountability for the praise and presenting himself as someone who is not necessarily predisposed to seek or report such compliments or praise on his own behalf, or invested in doing so. He thus adds credibility to what he is saying.

Here again, the third party attribution is delivered at the culmination of a scene-setting, experiential narrative in the form of an announcement in the service of another, more focal action; in this case to evidence the 'lovely rapport' and special relationship that the patient has with his daughter,[9] and her positive treatment of her father. Once again, the footing shift represented by the third party attribution allows the patient to get the positive (and in this instance, gender-relevant) description of himself on record, without claiming epistemic rights

---

[9] Note also that 'really lovely' is arguably precisely the kind of assessment individuals orient to as one delivered by men or women to other *women* (Speer & Green, 2007, n. 23).

to self-assess, or implying that he might say this on his own behalf. Indeed, as before, the third party compliment originated as a B-event statement with the daughter, who had primary epistemic rights to notice and assess such things.

Just as in Extract 2, the reported compliment opens up an additional response option not available to recipients of direct self-praise. Here the psychiatrist responds in a similar fashion to Sarah (Extract 2, line 35), by evaluating the complimenting action of the daughter ('>°How nice.°<', line 32, 'That's very nice', line 34, and '(°That's nice.°)', line 36), before closing down this particular interactional sequence (e.g., lines 38, 40 and 42).[10]

In a similar manner to Rachel (Extract 2, lines 37–8), once he has secured the positive participation of the psychiatrist, the patient offers his own perspective on the reported compliment, aligning with the psychiatrist by positively assessing his daughter's actions. He does this by formulating his inability to 'put into words' what it meant to him to have his daughter act in this way (lines 35 and 37). Once again, in this extract the arguably gendered substance of the reported compliment (that is, whether or not the patient does indeed look 'reallhy lovelyh' dressed in role) is protected against the kinds of problematic recipient orientations and sanctions that we see with direct self-praise.

Evidence from a research interview

The next example comes from a one-to-one telephone research interview between myself and a male-to-female transsexual patient. Prior to the start of this extract, the patient describes her experience of her first appointment at the GIC. She reports that she was nervous about attending because it involved her going through London on her own on the train, dressed in role. Although she arrived with 'no problems', she was none the less anxious that someone might identify her as trans and 'go off on one' at her during her journey.

Extract 4 Speer Telephone Interview 17. 05.10.07 19.45 mins

```
1   SS:   Right.=How long was your first session.=
2   Pt:   =About half an hour I think.
3   SS:   'Kay.
4         (0.6)
5   Pt:   Uh:m, an' then I had uh: bloods taken.
6   SS:   Ri:ght. .hh
7   ?:    pt.hh
8   Pt:   Which ostensibly was- (.) was a::: a- (.) a full work
9         up.
```

---

[10] Note that this extract differs from the prior to the extent that the psychiatrist does not have independent access to the assessable (i.e., he did not see the patient dressed in role). Therefore it would be impossible for him to agree or disagree with the daughter's assessment.

```
10        (.)
11  SS:   Uh hu:h,
12  Pt:   .hh hu:hm: (0.6) which I >had no problem with< because
13        I- y'know- (0.6) my body issue - my weight issues and
14        everything else.
15  SS:   Hm:,
16  Pt:   An:: (.) other bits 'n >pi-=y'know,<
17  SS:   Mm
18  Pt:   Liver function an so on:,
19  SS:   Right.
20  Pt:   Uhm::, an' the woman who took the bloods actually said
21        'you're about the most convincing one I've seen'.
22  SS:   O(h)h rea(h)llyhhh[h h h h h h h h h
23  Pt:                     ['in: about six months'.
24  SS:   .hhh Brilliant! [h h h h
25  Pt:                   [Which was great coz: I'm like (.) I'd
26        only just started doing this, this is the first time
27        I'[ve (        )
28  SS:     [YEa::h.    Yea::e [h.
29  Pt:                       [You know.
30        (.)
31  Pt:   On- you know- alo:ne, without having someone else-
32        you know do makeup and everything (an'),
33  SS:   Yeahh.
34  Pt:   Uh:m, which was great!
35  SS:   Mmhm.
36  Pt:   Uhm:: and then basically I went home.
```

This extract shares a pattern of features with Extracts 2 and 3. The positive assessment, that the patient is the 'most convincing' transsexual (line 21), is embedded within the reported compliment of a third party, in this case 'the woman who took the bloods' (line 20). In an even stronger fashion than in prior extracts, the speaker talks 'so as to be heard as imparting *surprising* information' (Wilkinson & Kitzinger, 2006: 155; emphasis in original), marking the actions of the complimenting party (the nurse), and hence the compliment itself, as contrary to her expectations. She does so in the course of reporting the attribution, through the use of the word 'actually' (line 20; Clift, 2001), as well as after it, by noting that this was the 'first time' she had done her own makeup and travelled to the clinic alone dressed in role (lines 25–6 and 31–2). It is in this way that the patient manages the subject side of her description, reducing her accountability for the praise, and simultaneously showing herself to be someone who is not necessarily predisposed to seek or report such praise on her own behalf, or invested in doing so. The patient adds the increment 'in: about six months' (line 23; Schegloff, n.d.). This re-completes her initial description and downgrades its strength, perhaps showing attentiveness to its credibility in view of the interviewer's, possibly doubtful, reaction (line 22) (Edwards, 2000). Like Rachel in Extract 2 (lines 36–7), she here demonstrates her concern to be precise about the compliment, at the same time as displaying that she is not especially personally invested in its specifics.

Here again, instead of delivering the third party attribution in order to illustrate something positive about herself as a person, her appearance, attributes or character, the patient delivers the praise at the culmination of a scene-setting, experiential narrative in the form of an announcement in the service of another, more focal action, in this case to evidence something positive about the patient's experiences after her first assessment session and the actions of the nurse whose words she is reporting. Once again the footing shift represented by the third party attribution allows the patient to get a positive (and gender-relevant) view of herself on record, without claiming epistemic rights to self-assess, or implying that she might say this on her own behalf. The third party compliment originated as a B-event statement with the nurse, who, as someone who sees many transsexuals in the course of her work, has primary epistemic rights – indeed, an institutional entitlement – to notice and assess such things.

The recipient's response to the reported attribution in this extract is slightly different from that we observed in Extracts 2 and 3. Perhaps because the reported attribution appears strongly 'designed to elicit surprise' (Wilkinson & Kitzinger, 2006: 156), the interviewer reacts initially with a surprise token ('O(h)h rea(h)lly', line 22; Wilson & Kitzinger, 2006: 170), treating the nurse's actions as humorous news (line 22; Heritage, 1984a) and thus in terms of option (2) above. This serves to register the (in this case positively valenced) 'unexpectedness of information conveyed in a prior turn at talk' (Wilson & Kitzinger, 2006: 154); it aligns with the patient's treatment of it as surprising, and promotes elaboration of the narrative. As I noted above, the increment (line 23; Schegloff, n.d.) attends to the credibility of the compliment by downgrading it. At the same time, it creates a further slot in which the interviewer can positively assess the actions of the complimenting party (option (3) above), and hence provide the missing assessment, which she does here at line 24: '<u>Br</u>illiant! h h h h'.[11] Once she has secured the positive participation of the recipient, the patient offers her own perspective on the third party attribution, aligning with the interviewer by positively assessing the nurse's actions 'Which was <u>great</u>' (line 25; see also line 34).[12] Once again, in this extract the arguably gendered substance of the reported compliment (that the patient is one of the most convincing transsexuals

[11] Note once more that, since this is a telephone interview, the interviewer does not have independent access to the assessable and is not, therefore, in a position to agree or disagree with the nurse's assessment.

[12] Although this assessment comes sequentially *after* the interviewer's reaction, the word 'which' marks it as grammatically continuous with the increment, and shows her to have reached her view *independently of* the interviewer's reaction.

to attend the clinic) is protected against the kinds of problematic recipient orientations and sanctions that are risked with direct self-praise.

So far, I have demonstrated that reported, third party compliments represent one means by which speakers can perform the subsidiary action of evidencing that they are a certain sort of person (and in the last two cases, a gendered person) and that they possess positive, desirable attributes, whilst engaging in other, more focal actions not concerned with complimenting themselves or doing gender. In each case, the praise still comes through – but since it is lodged in the opinions of other people, it appears more objective. However, in order to gain analytic purchase on my claim that reported third party compliments are selected by speakers specifically in order to *avoid* the kinds of sanctions and orientations associated with direct acts of self-praise that I highlighted in respect of Extract 1, we need to show participants themselves orienting to the norm against direct self-praise, and to the interactional virtue of embedding self-praise within the compliment of a third party. Extract 5 demonstrates just such an orientation.

Participants' orientations to the norm against overt self-praise

Extract 5 comes from a psychiatric assessment session between a male-to-female transsexual patient and a second male psychiatrist. After discussing a reality television star who is transsexual, the psychiatrist notes that there is more to the patient than managing her gender role.

Extract 5 Speer Audio 125 11.57 mins

```
 1  Psy:   An' you'd describe yourself as a successful independent
 2         ↑businesswoman wouldn't you, first o[f    all.]
 3  Pt:                                       [Pt.hhh] (.)
 4         Yes:uhm::
 5  ((15 lines omitted))
 6  Pt:    [Pt.hhhhhh  I've always workedhhhh and uhm I
 7         enjoy this job.
 8         (.)
 9  Pt:    [And    ] you meet- it's exciting, you never=
10  Psy:   [(°Mm°)]
11  Pt:    =quite know what's gonna happen.
12         (.)
13  Pt:    And its uh- you doh haveh some ve- laughs as well.
14         (0.4)
15  Psy:   Sure but
16  Pt:    I mean, [you know,
17  Psy:           [it wouldn't be worthwhile doing it if you
18         d[idn't. Would it?]
19  Pt:    [Oh :  I  love it.] It's a jo:b, it's the onl[y job]=
20  Psy:                                               [Ye:ah.]
21  Pt:    =that I wanna d[o.       [And uhm, ye a h.]
```

22   Psy: [It's what [it's for is pa:rt]ly is (.)
23   Pt: .hhh
24   Psy: [(not] just) making [money is it.]
25   Pt: [<An-]   [A n : d a] lot of it as
26   well you've gotta be able to (0.2) pt.hhh I've-
27   I can laugh at myself.
28   (0.5)
29   Pt: I'm not- an en- entertainment, but if I go to Tesco I'm
30   not .hhh in the queue entertaining the customers, I
31   didn't 'ooh look there's that man whose- becoming a-
32   pt.hh[hh ooh'   you know. [There's] a freak show.=
33   Psy: [(°Ooh yeah°).   [Y ea h.]
34   Pt: =I mean there are people sadly who are- a little bit-
35   .hhh (1.0) like that.**=I come across as- pt.eh- (0.7) fhhh**
36   **I- other women say to me well I come across as a**
37   **woman.** .hhh [uh : m,] coz they- because they've=
38   Psy: [>Yeah.<]
39   Pt: =never met anybody::- they've only seen people(h)
40   o(h)n te(h)levision [or read t]he News of the Wor:ld=
41   Psy: [Yeah, or-]
42   Pt: =or- [y o u know.]
43   Psy: [(Jusht realih]zhed. (That's a/Dreadfully) poor
44   sa:mple. I mean you have to ask yourself of course, .hh
45   what sort of people want to go on telly. .hhh

The patient is describing how she can laugh at herself but that she is not a 'freak show', and she uses the reported third party compliment 'other women say to me well I come across as a woman' (lines 36–7) in the course of an experiential narrative to evidence this. The particularly interesting feature of this instance is that the patient begins as though to launch a positive *self*-description – 'I come across as' (line 35) but then aborts the utterance mid-TCU, halting its progressivity in order to initiate repair (twice) on it (Schegloff *et al.*, 1977), eventually shifting her footing to insert the reported third party attribution – 'other women say to me well I come across as a woman' (lines 36–7).

Clayman and Heritage (2002) comment on the use of these kinds of self-repairs in news interview discourse. They note that repairs in which an interviewer '*begins to launch into an assertion, but then aborts and revises it so as to invoke a responsible third party*' (2002: 158–62; emphasis in original) are not addressed to the 'correctness or coherence of the utterance' (Clayman, 1992: 173), but provide 'some of the clearest evidence that interviewers are working to sustain a neutralistic footing' (Clayman & Heritage, 2002: 158). Of course, Extract 5 is different from those Clayman and Heritage consider in that it involves a self-repaired assessment rather than a question. However, just like the instances Clayman and Heritage cite, this self-repair entails an abrupt shift to a more neutralistic footing, creating greater epistemic distance between the speaker and the praise, and lessening the speaker's accountability for the description. Once more, the third party compliment originated as a B-event statement with 'other women', who, *as* women, are entitled to notice and assess such things. Here we see the speaker's explicit orientation to the norm against direct self-praise, and her choosing one interactionally neutral description, over and above another, potentially problematic, less neutral, more invested description.

The psychiatrist's response to the third party attribution in this case differs from that of the recipients in prior extracts. Here, instead of assessing the actions of the complimenting party (as in Extracts 2–4), the psychiatrist responds by agreeing with the content of the compliment in terms of response option (1), described above: ('>Yeah.<', line 38). There are at least three possible interactional reasons for this. First, the reported compliment is delivered in an environment where the psychiatrist is already complimenting the patient and hence *treating her as a woman* (lines 1–2). In this respect, the patient is not situating the actions of these women as surprising or contrary to her expectations, but is simply offering evidence that warrants and embellishes the psychiatrist's existing perspective (indeed, unlike those in Extracts 3 and 4, the patient here explicitly indexes a gender category in the course of her attribution). Second, since the patient's self-description is *initiated* as a direct self-description (even if the repair means that it does not end up as one), it leaves open the possibility that it will be responded to as one, with agreement or disagreement. If this is the case, then although this technique – shifting footing midway through a self-description – clearly shows participants' orientations to the norm against self-praise, it is interactionally less robust than delivering a reported third party compliment 'straight off', as in Extracts 2–4. Indeed, since the reported praise in this instance is delivered as a summary of what other women say, rather than as direct reported speech, the speaker's accountability for the description is not reduced to the same extent as it is in Extracts 2–4. Third, unlike Extracts 2–4, where the recipient has either no access (as in Extracts 3 and 4) or partial access (Extract 2) to the assessable, in this extract, since the patient is sitting directly in front of him dressed in role, the psychiatrist has full independent access to the assessable, and can therefore respond on that basis with an assessment of it.

Discussion

In this chapter I have analysed instances in which speakers describe positive features of their experiences using reported third party compliments. There is a potentially infinite range of ways in which speakers could perform the same action – they do not *have* to report their experiences in this way, using reported third party compliments that 'just happen' to index positive (and in some cases gender-relevant) features of their identity. To do so involves their making a choice between myriad possible formulations.

I suggested that speakers appear to use *this* way to describe their experiences, embedding positive self-assessments or praise in the compliment of a third party, because self-descriptions are complex matters for speakers, bound up with inter-actional norms concerning who has epistemic rights to assess our appearance or character, and comment objectively on who we are as a person. Here we have, in action, a norm that posits that it should be other people, and not the speaker, who can rightfully praise, and comment authoritatively on, aspects of the speak-er's appearance, attributes or character (their identity). Embedding praise within reported speech or summary represents a means by which a speaker can objec-tively evidence and get on record positive comments on who they are as a person, without engaging in direct self-praise or bragging. The latter, as demonstrated in Extract 1, represent actions that typically risk the problematic orientations and sanctions of recipients. I argued that reported third party compliments allow the speaker to avoid bragging, in part because the embedded character of the com-pliment, and the footing shift it entails, create epistemic distance between the speaker and the praise, or the subject and the object of the compliment. In other words, the speaker is not claiming rights to self-assess (Heritage & Raymond, 2005), but is simply reporting what some, arguably more objective person (who *does* have epistemic rights to assess them) happened to say about them. Since the praise in a reported attribution originated as a B-event statement and derives from the views of another or others, and since the speaker is no longer the 'prin-cipal' of the assessment, to use Goffman's (1981) terms, the praise does not appear quite so invested or self-serving. The praise still comes through, but since it is subsidiary to the focal task with which the speaker is currently engaged, and lodged in the opinions of other people, it appears more objective, and the speaker's accountability for the praise is thereby reduced.

The final extract adds weight to some of these observations in that it high-lights both the strength of the norm against direct self-praise and participants' orientations to the interactional virtue of embedding praise within the compli-ment of a third party. Just as repairs from individual to collective self-reference (e.g., 'I' to 'we') are bound up with 'resolving (and thereby exhibiting) sources of troubles associated with speaker epistemic authority and responsibility for described actions' (Lerner & Kitzinger, 2007b: 526), so too self-repairs from direct self-praise to reported compliments are bound up with managing potential troubles associated with epistemic responsibility for positive self-assessment. Repairs from 'self' to 'other' descriptions constitute one means by which speakers manage and orient to the telling of descriptions that, epis-temically, should originate with, and derive from, someone else. Through them they transfer epistemic responsibility to a third party, and back away from their commitment to what they are saying.

One of the interesting things about the way the embedded compliments appear to function in these extracts is that they open up a range of possible response options for recipients, not available with direct self-praise. Indeed, none of the recipients disputes the veracity or facticity of the reported compliment *or* engages in actions that question the motives or character of the speaker (cf. Extract 1). Far from sanctioning the speaker, or else working to detoxify the reported compliment, the recipients either agree with the praise (as in Extract 5) or positively assess the actions of the complimenting party (as in Extracts 2–4). This paves the way for the speaker themselves to show that they accept or align with the praise.

Of course, it is important to note that reported third party compliments are not foolproof. As Clayman and Heritage note in respect of news interview discourse, 'although third-party attributed statements are less vulnerable (compared to unattributed assertions) to charges of bias, they are by no means invincible' (2002: 180). In Goffman's (1981) terms, since the current speaker is both 'animator' and – more importantly – 'author' of the words purportedly uttered by a non-present 'principal', the reported compliment is still susceptible to claims of self-interest. Reported attributions therefore lessen, but do not remove, the speaker's accountability for the description. Indeed, in Extract 5, the very act of repairing the problematic self-description in favour of a less problematic reported attribution, and the marked caution associated with doing so, may alert the recipient to the potentially controversial status of the claim (Clayman & Heritage, 2002: 161). Further work is needed to establish what constitutes a misaligning response in such instances (see Speer, forthcoming).

A related reason why embedded attributions seem to help the speaker to avoid bragging is that reporting the compliment of a third party is generally not the primary or '*focal action*' of the talk with which the speaker is currently engaged. Instead, reported, third party compliments are usually, in my data, embedded within narratives and deployed as subsidiary actions in the service of other, primary or focal tasks (for more on this see Kitzinger, 2008a: 200–3, and Speer & Green, 2007: 362). For example, in the data I examine in this chapter these focal tasks include evidencing a positive work experience (Extract 2), illustrating the special relationship that the speaker has with his daughter (Extract 3), documenting the speaker's experiences after their first assessment session (Extract 4), and describing how the speaker can laugh at themselves and are not simply entertainment for others (Extract 5). Crucially, as subsidiary actions, speakers can use the phenomenon of reported third party compliments as *vehicles* for evidencing objectively their male or female status. Through them they can *do gender* (or some other identity they value) in the interaction, and evidence objectively that, for example, they pass outside this setting as 'real' men or women, whilst engaging in *other*, more focal actions not concerned with doing gender (Jackson, this volume; Kitzinger, 2007b; 2008a; Speer & Green, 2007: 362; Stockill & Kitzinger, 2007). It is no coincidence that, in each case in the GIC and patient interviews, the category of person who is reported by the speaker to have performed the attribution is female (a daughter, a female nurse, 'other women') – people who have the entitlement to notice female attributes/another woman when they see one!

That the patient's attempts to pass and be treated by the psychiatrist as a woman may be subservient to these other, more focal activities does not mean that gender and passing are not relevant here, or that gender is not getting done, indexed or oriented to. Indeed, in the GIC and patient interviews, gender is a fairly pervasive category that gets indexed and talked about *much of the time*. Indeed, if gender is an omnirelevant category (see Klein, this volume), then it makes sense that doing, indexing and orienting to gender co-exist with, and get woven relatively seemlessly into the texture of, interactional slots whose primary purpose is the accomplishment of *other* actions (Speer & Green, 2007: 362). More work needs to be done to tease apart the relationship between focal and subsidiary actions, and their role in 'doing gender' (Kitzinger, 2008a).

I want to end by noting a methodological implication of these findings, and of a CA approach to gender more broadly (for more on this see Speer & Stokoe, this volume). An examination of self-assessment practices and their oriented-to avoidance can provide a route to understanding social structural norms concerning the presentation and management of speaker identities and 'face'. In particular, if reported third party compliments are oriented to by speakers as a relatively 'safe', socially acceptable way to get on record positive things about oneself, and are interactionally easier to manage than direct self-descriptions, then, just as there is an interactional *preference* for offers over requests and noticings over announcings (Schegloff, 2007a), there may be an oriented-to interactional preference for self-descriptions to be reported in *this* fashion, rather than delivered by the speaker 'straight off', on their own behalf. In his discussion of preferred and dispreferred first pair parts, Schegloff (2007a: 82) observes that: 'in achieving the official and explicit registering of some feature of the environment of the interaction affiliated to or identified with one of the participants – and "positively valued" features in particular – there appears to be a preference for noticing-by-others over announcement-by-"self" (where "self" is the one characterized by the feature)'. I want to argue that the preference organization of self-praise (i.e., the assessment of a positively valued feature of the self) is bound up with this preference for noticing over announcing. Extract 5 exhibits just such a preference in action. Feminist researchers and others examining gender identity need to be attuned to this, and especially careful when adopting methods and procedures (interviews, for example) that might involve posing questions to participants about identity matters that require them to reflect explicitly on or 'describe' their identity in the here and now, and in ways that may be interactionally non-normative. Conversation analysis provides one means by which we can analytically scrutinize, and reflexively examine, such moments.

9 'D'you understand that honey?': Gender and participation in conversation

Jack Sidnell

Introduction

This chapter focuses on a single turn-at-talk produced during the course of a backyard barbecue. I argue that this turn, 'D'you understand that honey?', can be seen not only to invoke the relevance of the recipient's gender but also, simultaneously, to formulate the kind of talk it refers to by 'that' – a dirty joke – as designed for an exclusively male audience. Though the talk in question contains no explicit mention of 'men' or 'woman' or 'girls', etc. – that is, though it contains no explicitly gendered referring expressions – it nevertheless serves to highlight this aspect of the context. In this chapter, then, the gender of the participants is conceptualized as a feature of the context which is always available but not always relevant. Rather, I suggest that it takes work to push gender from the taken-for-granted, seen but unnoticed backdrop into the inter-actionally relevant foreground of oriented-to features of the setting (Hopper & LeBaron, 1998). One way this happens is by talk, such as 'Do y'understand that, honey?', which links the organization of participation in the activity of the moment – here reception and appreciation of a dirty joke – to larger, socially significant categories such as those of 'men' and 'women'.

Prompted in part by Schegloff's (1997; 1998b) reply to Wetherell, as well as by Schegloff's earlier programmatic papers on 'social structure' (1991), a number of recent studies have advocated a specifically conversation analytic (CA) approach to gender which attends to participants' displayed orientation to gender-relevant categories as these are revealed in their own conduct (see inter alia Kitzinger, 2000a; 2005b; Sidnell, 2003; Speer, 2002a; 2005a; 2005b; Stokoe, 1998; Stokoe & Smithson, 2001; West & Zimmerman, 1987).[1] The point that gender can be studied in relation to participants' own displayed orientations is now well established. What is less clear, it seems to me, is, first,

I'd like to thank Susan Speer and Elizabeth Stokoe for exceptionally detailed and helpful comments on an earlier version of this chapter. I thank Chuck and Candy Goodwin for allowing me
to use the 'auto discussion' recording and Clare MacMartin for creating the figures.

[1] Kitzinger (2006) makes the inverse point that use of an explicitly gendered category term (e.g.,
'women') need not necessarily invoke gender *per se* and can be used in the service of quite other
kinds of interactional work.

183

the interactional work that gets accomplished through such displayed orientations to gender, and, second, the logical relationships between the categories so invoked (inclusion–exclusion, marked–unmarked, dominance, difference, etc.). I argue here that, in the case I analyse, the logical relationship implied by the invocation of the categories 'men' and 'women' is akin to the model of 'separate cultures' developed by Maltz and Borker (1982). In another context a quite different model might be implied by participants' conduct.

So in this chapter I hope to contribute to a growing body of CA-inspired work on gender in three ways. First, I describe the way in which the invoked categories of men and women fit into and co-implicate a larger framework of 'genders as separate subcultures'. Second, I show how gender is invoked as part of a larger course of action – here accounting for the behavior treated as evidence of an understanding failure. Third, drawing on video-taped, co-present interaction, I broaden the frame of gender-in-CA-studies (though see M. H. Goodwin, 2006; Speer & Green, 2007; Stokoe, 2006) to take into account not just the talk of the participants but also their gesture, gaze and body orientation. The focus on gaze and body orientation in co-present interaction leads me to consider different ways of participating in an activity and the possibility that this may be related to both issues of recipient design and the oriented-to gender of the participants.

I will begin by describing some aspects of the encounter within which the joke is embedded before turning to consider the joke itself and specifically its punchline and reception by the participants. I then move to examine in more detail the way in which body position and gaze are used to construct a participation framework which provides an interpretive context for the co-occurring talk. This leads directly into an analysis of the focal utterance. The final sections of the chapter consider the Maltz and Borker model of male–female miscommunication as well as the notion of 'peripheral participation'.

The setting

The fragment of talk to be examined comes from a film recording known as 'auto discussion' made by Charles and Marjorie Goodwin in the early 1970s (for analyses based in whole or in part on other portions of this recording see, inter alia, Ford et al., 1996; 2002; C. Goodwin, 1986a; 1986b; 1987a; 1987b; Schegloff, 1992a). The recording is of a backyard barbecue hosted by Curt and Pam. Two other couples, Mike and Phyllis and Gary and Carney, are present as well as several children (and a dog, Bo). During the portion of the recording to be examined Curt, Carney, Gary, Mike and a child are seated at a picnic table.

As can be seen in Figure 9.1, Curt, Gary and Mike sit more or less facing each other, forming together what Goffman described as a focused encounter (1961) and, elsewhere, as a situated activity system (1964). Carney, in contrast, has seated herself between Curt (her cousin) and Gary (her husband) facing

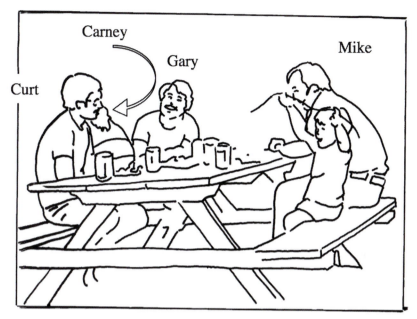

Figure 9.1

in the opposite direction. This makes her face inaccessible to the participants when they are engaged with one another. By the alignment of her body in relation to those of the other participants, Carney suggests that she is disattending and not engaged with the talk in progress. As we will see later in this chapter, however, things turn out to be considerably more complicated than this.

Among English-speaking North Americans, sitting around a picnic table, drinking beer while talking about cars and telling dirty jokes is likely to be recognized as stereotypically 'male' behaviour. Is the 'maleness' of this activity – this setting – simply imposed from without by eyes (and ears) predisposed to see (and hear) these activities as gendered male? Or do the participants themselves actively produce this talk to have it come off as an exclusively male activity, and, if so, how do they do this?[2]

---

[2] In a paper on 'audience diversity', Charles Goodwin, considering some of the same data as examined here, observes (1986a: 296):

> After the automobile discussion Mike, Curt and Gary start telling dirty jokes. The obscenity of the jokes (as well as more specific themes in them such as male competition) again locate the domain of discourse as one whose prototypical participants are male. Nonetheless one of the women, Carney, becomes engrossed in the jokes and wants to listen to them. However, when she joins the men, she seats herself at the picnic table with her *back* to the rest of the group. Thus, while she is physically present and able to act as a recipient to the jokes, she vividly marks that her participation status in the telling is quite different from that of the men seated with her.

The sequential context of the utterance 'D'you understand that honey?'

The turn to be examined in detail comes at the conclusion of a joke-telling by Curt. This joke is itself embedded in a round of jokes, all of them characterizable as 'dirty' in so far as they are about sexual exploits, male anatomy and so on (on 'rounds' see Lynch, 2001; Sacks, 1992: 281–91). In the wake of an appreciation of the previous telling, Curt starts his joke at line 2 with 'There's these-two-deaf'n dumb guys.' Curt thus introduces the protagonists of his joke in a way that turns out to be consequential for the telling.[3]

Extract 1 Auto Discussion, pp. 41–3

```
01   Gar:      heh-eh-eh! ˙hhh
02   Cur:  →   There's these-two-deaf'n dumb guys. drivin'
03             down the stree:t,
04                    (1.0)
05   Cur:      And, they pass these two girls, .hh on the
06             corner.
07                    (0.7)
08   Cur:      °A:nd uh, (thee-)/(he-) ( ) guy says t'the
09             other one'n sign language 'e taps im on
10             the shoulder'n 'e says,
11                    (1.0)
12   Cur:      Been out with the one before.
13                    (0.7)
14   Cur:      And.
15                    (0.4)
16   Cur:      It's a sure thi:ng. 's pick 'em up. 'n eez
17             sayin' it y'know ih- with his ha:nds. Can't
18             talk.
19                    (0.8)
20   Cur:      The other guy siz okay.
21                    (0.5)
22   Cur:      With iz hands.
23                    (0.7)
24   Cur:      So they- pull back in, pick'm up,'n away
25             they go:. They're drivin down the street'n,
26                    (0.5)
27   Cur:      Pretty soon this one chick starts playin'
28             with the other guy in the back seat y'know
29             en: Hahhhhhh! The guy in the front seat's
```

---

[3] The video-recording captures seven jokes – four told by Mike and three told by Curt. Curt's first attempt at a joke (the second in the round) is aborted when Mike tells Gary, 'Y'know w'th funniest part about it is? I know w't th'punchline i:s,'. In addition to being recognizably 'dirty' several of the jokes feature explicitly racist themes.

```
30              doin too- justabout as goo:d'n ˙hhh so they
31              decide they're gonna haftuh stop'n get some
32              rubbers.
33                      (0.7)
34    Cur:    [Tch!
35    Gar:    [Hnh! hnh-hn[h-hnh-hnh=
36    Cur:              [So(h)o,
37    Gar:    =hnh-hnh-nh-nh-ah!ah!ah!ah!ah!
38            [ah!  ah!  ah!  a!  a!  a  !a!a!]a!a:.
39    Cur:    [Goes intuh the drugstore.]
40    Gar:    .hunh! (Y'not (allerg[ic)/(a virg[in))
41    Cur:                          [An'uh:: about
42            fifteen minutes later 'e comes back out
43            just madder'n hell'n s,
44                      (0.2)
45    Cur:    The guy s'what's wro:ng. gez aw::: 'e says
46            Christ I, pounded on the,
47                      (0.7)
48    Cur:    Pounded on the::: counter en pointed et my
49            dick en: evrything else I couldn' make that
50            -uh=
51    Car:    =hh[hnh!
52    Cur:       [dumb asshole understand what the hell
53            I wannid in there,
54                      (0.3)
55    Car:    °hn-hn-[-hn
56    Cur:           [Guy siz we:ll, give me the fifty
57            cents'n I'll go in. S'e takes fifty cents'n
58            about half,
59                      (0.2)
60    Cur:    'Bout fifteen minutes later 'e comes back
61            out boy he's just m:madder'n all get out.
62                      (0.2)
63    Cur:    What the hell happened. .hhh Guy:z well,
64                      (0.7)
65    Cur:    I wen' in there, flopped my dick onna table
66            threw down fifty cents, guy flopped his
67            dick out beat me by half inch'n took
68            m(h)y fif[t(h)y ce(h)e(h)nts=
69    Mik:            [hn -hn hah-hah-[-hah-ha[h- h a
70    Cur:                            =[hn- hn [h .hh!
71    Gar:                                    [ha-ha:
72    Mik:    h- hah-      [-hah-hah
73    Cur:    ha:h   ha:h[hah!   ].hh!=
74    Gar:    =ha-ha-ha-[huhhuh]
75    Car:            [uh: : : : ]
```

```
76    Mik:    =[h  [eh-heh-huh-huh-hah-ha-ha:h =
77    Gar:    =[ah![ah! ah! ah! a! a a!a!a a a!=
78    Cur:          [heh heh heh.
79    Mik:    =[huh .hhnh!
80    Gar:    =[a!a!a!a!a!a!a!a![a!a!a!a! [a!a!a!a!
81    Cur:     [huh-uh huh   [        [
82    Mik:                    [a a : :h [hu:h hu:h
83    Cur:                              [huh-uh huh
84    Mik:    hu:h hu:h ˙hhh
85    Cur:    hu[:h huh
86    Mik:       [oooooo!
87    Cur:       [he:hhu:h[huh
88    Gar:                 [a!a!a!
89                     (.)
90    Mik:    .hnnh!
91    ?:      .hnnh
92    Mik:    .hh You heard d'one about=
93    Gar: →  =D'you understand that [honey
94    Mik:                            [eh heh [hhh
95    Cur:                                    [eh
96            [ha ha hha hah
97    Gar:    [(      tell you about it.)
98    Mik:    [.ehhh!
99    Cur:    [Too deep, ehhhah=
100   Mik:    =bout the guys et the ba:r y'know en,
101                 (0.5)
102   Mik:    ehheh! Ehh ((cough)) They w'r all
103           drinkin' pretty heavily, they decided well
104           they're gonna have a dick measuring contest
                  ((Joke continues))
```

I will not devote too much attention to the joke itself since the focus of the
analysis that follows is specifically on its reception. Briefly, it can be noted
that the story consists of a series of events – the two guys are driving down the
street when they see two women one of whom is known to one of the guys. The
women are 'picked up' (line 24) and the four continue driving. At a certain point
the guys 'decide to get some rubbers' (lines 31–2). This leads to an encounter
in the shop in which one of the guys attempts, unsuccessfully, to communicate
with the shopkeeper. In the last episode of the story, the second guy goes into
the shop. When he comes out again he is visibly distressed ('madder'n all get
out', line 61) occasioning the inquiry 'What the hell happened' (line 63). The
punchline is produced as an answer to this question.

The joke then turns on a miscommunication – the 'deaf 'n dumb' man 'flops
his dick' (line 65) on the table in an effort to convey his desire to purchase condoms but the shopkeeper understands this action as instigating a challenge – a
challenge to see which of the two has the larger penis. When the shopkeeper

'wins' the contest, he takes the money and the 'deaf 'n dumb' man's attempt to purchase the condoms is frustrated.

There are various themes at work in the joke. Some of these are conveyed by the categories used to partition the people into groups. Most important here are the categories which distinguish between hearing and non-hearing and male and female. Moreover, within the joke-world, an action such as 'flopping one's dick out' does not unambiguously convey a single communicative intention. Rather, although intended as the sign of a desire to buy condoms, the shopkeeper sees it as a challenge. Notice that in recounting what happened, the 'deaf 'n dumb' man does not have to explain to his listeners (and Curt does not have to explain to his audience) that this action was misinterpreted (e.g., by saying something along the lines of 'he thought I meant …'). Rather that this has been misconstrued as a challenge is shown simply by the reciprocal action of the shopkeeper.

So an action intended to initiate a commercial transaction is misunderstood as the initiation of a challenge. By treating the action in question as ambiguous – as the possible initiation of a challenge – the story presents the activity of competitive measuring as a routine and easily recognizable occurrence.

The 'punchline'

The key to any joke is its punchline – the point in the telling at which the 'laughable' occurrence, event or action is revealed. In the present case this begins with the word 'guy' at line 66.

Extract 2 Auto Discussion – 'punchline', p. 42

```
65  Cur:  I wen' in there, flopped my dick onna table
66         threw down fifty cents, guy flopped his
67         dick out beat me by half inch'n took
68         m(h)y fif[t(h)y ce(h)e(h)nts=
69  Mik:        [hn -hn hah-hah-[-hah-ha[h- h a
70  Cur:                =[hn- hn [h 'hh!
71  Gar:                      [ha-ha:
```

Some activities require equivalent or at least similar contributions by each participant while others require complementary or reciprocal contributions. For instance, in a footrace each competitor runs in the same direction for an established distance. In comparison, in a game of baseball the pitcher throws the ball towards the batter, who attempts to hit the ball somewhere into the field, and so on. This joke hinges on just such a distinction. An exchange such as takes place between a customer and vendor in a shop requires complementary or reciprocal contributions by each party. The customer indicates what it is they wish to purchase and produces the money to pay for it. The vendor, recognizing what it is the customer is after, locates the item, hands it over and takes the money. Such is the nature of an exchange. In Curt's joke, the vendor responds to the first part of this action sequence not with the complementary actions required in order to

Figure 9.2

accomplish an exchange but rather with the equivalent actions constitutive of a competition. The punchline then is produced where this treatment of the customer's action sequence becomes recognizable to the audience – at lines 67–8. The punchline itself can be seen to consist of multiple components:

1   Guy flopped his dick out
2   Beat me by half inch
3   'N took my fifty cents

According to the transcriber the first inkling of laughter is embedded in the production of 'my' in 'm(h)y fift(h)y ce(h)e(h)nts=' (line 68). The first recipient to laugh is Mike and this is produced as Curt says 'fifty cents'. Gary's laughter is somewhat delayed, occurring after Curt has finished the telling and has begun to join with Mike in an appreciation of it (see Jefferson, 1979).[4]

Laughter, body and participation in the reception of the joke

If we take Mike's laughter at line 69 as the onset of the joke's reception and his beginning to tell a next joke as the first move to close it down, the intervening activity of reception/appreciation lasts more than eight seconds. Not only

---

[4]   'Auto discussion' was transcribed by Gail Jefferson from a version of the film of much higher quality than is currently available.

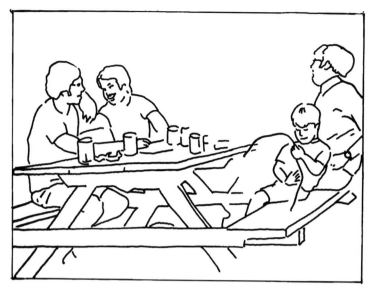

Figure 9.3

is the activity of receiving and appreciating the joke quite extended, it is also complex, incorporating multiple actions by the various participants. Although it appears on the transcript as one more-or-less continuous block of laughter, examination of the video-record and especially the gaze and body positioning of the participants suggests that the joke's reception can be divided into four units or phases.

In the first of these Mike and then Gary begin to laugh in response to the completion of Curt's joke, marked as we noted by a laugh token embedded in the word 'my' (line 68). In this first phase, Gary and Mike engage in mutual gaze while Curt apparently looks at both of them (Figure 9.2).

In the second phase, Mike continues to look at Gary. Gary, however, reorients the upper part of his body and brings his gaze around towards Carney (Figure 9.3). Eventually his head is completely obscured by Carney's as he brings his face in front of hers. Carney appears to reorient so as to receive his gaze (Figure 9.4). Curt brings his gaze to rest on Mike.

In the third phase, Gary discontinues the engagement with Carney and brings his gaze back to Mike, who appears to be still gazing at him. Curt reorients slightly towards Gary (Figure 9.5).

The fourth and final phase of the joke's reception sees Gary and Mike looking back to the teller (Curt) who is momentarily gazing down at the child (Figure 9.6). Both Gary and Mike respond by momentarily withdrawing and apparently appreciating the joke in solitude (Figure 9.7) before Gary visibly

Figure 9.4

Figure 9.5

bends his upper body to catch Curt's gaze and to shoot a quick glance back at Carney (Figures 9.8 and 9.9; see Schegloff, 1998a).

Each of these phases is marked by a discrete burst or wave of group laughter and each involves a particular configuration of participants engaging one another.

Figure 9.6

Figure 9.7

The basic framework of participation here involves the teller (Curt) and the two primary addressed recipients (Gary and Mike) and can be represented schematically as in Figure 9.10. However, Gary's attempts to draw in Carney effect a transformation resulting in a pattern more like that shown in Figure 9.11.

Figure 9.8

Figure 9.9

I will argue that by adjusting his gaze and body position, Gary dramatically alters the basic participation framework of the ongoing activity in such a way as to make Carney's laughter conditionally relevant and her not-laughing a noticeable absence (see below).

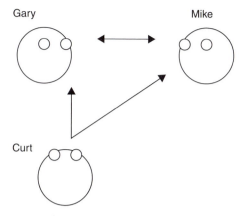

Figure 9.10

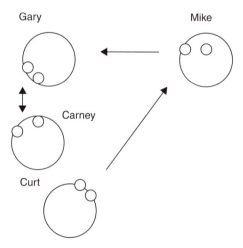

Figure 9.11

Understanding displays and their pursuit

A basic finding of conversation analysis is that, in conversation, understandings are displayed in subsequent turns-at-talk by addressed recipients (see Heritage, 1984b; Heritage & Atkinson, 1984; Moerman & Sacks, 1988; Sacks *et al.*, 1974). Where some display of understanding is relevant but not forthcoming its production may be pursued (Pomerantz, 1984c). A pursuit such as 'yihknow?' can be occasioned by a lack of uptake from the addressed recipient, this absence evidencing a possible failure to understand or appreciate what has been said. Such pursuits take various forms. One possibility is shown in Extract 3.

Extract 3 Geri and Shirley, p. 15

```
01   Shi:      .hhhh I s'd not only tha:t, .hh but the fact remains that
02             it is against the law, en thet yer jeopardizing. .hhhh not only
03             Jack's liquor license, .hh b't also, his means of (.) of
04             income. .hh en evrybuddy else's means of income who works here.
05      →     (0.4)
06   (S):      .pt.hhh
07   Shi: →   Yihknow,
08             (0.3)
09   Ger: →   Y[e:[ah,]
10   Shi:      [.h[I s]aid, (.) if (.) yihknow I s'd if yer so god da:mn,
```

Here, then, Shirley has been telling Geri a story about a mutual acquaintance
who came into the bar where she was working and started drinking alcohol
despite being under age. The story then is the vehicle for a complaint and at
lines 1–4 Shirley is making the complainable matter explicit by reporting her
own speech to the under-age drinker. Notice that this is delivered in a series
of instalments – the first ending on line 2 at 'law', the second ending on line
4 at 'income.' and the third ending on line 4 with 'here.'. Geri might have
responded with some display of understanding or token of affiliation at any of
these points. When she does not, a silence emerges at line 5. This is eventually
broken by Shirley's pursuit with 'Yihknow', which elicits from Geri a 'yeah,'.
Pursuits such as this are common in conversation and take a variety of forms.

The example to be examined here – Gary's 'D'you understand that honey?' –
differs from the one above in a number of crucial respects. First, in terms of
design, although 'yihknow' and 'yih know what I mean' and 'D'you understand that honey?' seem to share a focus on 'understanding', in the latter but
not the others that focus is made explicit. A failure to understand may be more
the fault of a speaker (because he used the wrong word, spoke too fast, had just
taken a bite of steak) or more the result of the recipient (because she was paying attention to the football game on television rather than listening, because
she is not a native speaker of the language, etc.). Given this situation, it may
be that by explicitly naming the trouble ('understanding') a pursuit such as
'D'you understand that honey?' locates responsibility for that trouble more
with the recipient than the speaker in comparison with a pursuit such as
'yih know', which may be neutral or 'unmarked' in this regard.

Another way Gary's utterance differs from the more familiar pursuits of
which the 'yihknow' in Extract 3 is an instance is in terms of the way it maps
onto the categories of speaker and hearer. The example from Geri and Shirley
comes from a telephone conversation. There we see that Shirley is telling Geri
something – Shirley is the speaker and Geri the recipient of this talk, and the
pursuit clearly maintains this configuration. In contrast, in the example from
'auto discussion', 'D'you understand that honey?' is said by someone other
than the speaker of what 'that' refers to, to someone who was not among the

addressed recipients for the referent of 'that'. There are reasons for supposing
that this difference may be consequential for the participants' understanding
of the utterance. Non-addressed recipients are neither required nor expected
to speak in a subsequent position and thus to display any understanding of
the talk. As such, an absent display of appreciation is just that – since it is not
conditionally relevant it is not missing in any obvious sense.

As an anthropologist, I was struck by the way Gary's question to Carney
('D'you understand that, honey?') is similar to one frequently asked of the eth-
nographer. Here is an example from my research in Guyana, a former British
colony bordering Venezuela, Brazil and Surinam in South America. The
recorded encounter in Extract 4 took place near the beginning of my fieldwork.
A group of us are sitting outside by the road chatting. Amir joins us and begins
to question Tony (line 1), his younger cousin, asking why Tony told another
young man named Derrick something. In response, Tony claims innocence,
initiating repair of the accusation with a partial and questioning repeat (line 7;
Tony repeats and thereby targets for possible repair 'tell Derrick' in line 1). He
then instructs Amir to ask Derrick himself (line 10) and finally gives a rather
detailed account of his recent activities, claiming in the process not to have
seen Derrick for some time. In the transcript, the first line consists of a broad
phonemic transcription, while the second (in italics) is a gloss that attempts to
convey the gist of what is being said.

Extract 4 GUYANA_T5b.mp3@3-00.mov

```
01   Amir:      Wai yu (kova/kom) op an tel Derik?
                Why did you go and tell Derrick?
02                       (1.6)
03   Tony:      We::?
                Whe::n?
04                       (0.2)
05   Tony:      [Mi kom bak
                [I came back
06   Amir:      [(            ) fos pat gu gu tel yu=
                [(            ) first part went and told you=
07   Tony:      Mii tel Derik?
                I told Derrick?
08                       (0.8)
09   Tony:      hHool on yu ga kom out a rood an tak tu him
                Hold on – you have to come out in the road and talk to him.
10   Tony:      Yu aks Derik
                You ask Derrick
11   Tony:      Mi na riich bak Derik sins a dee mi goo
                I haven't seen Derrick since the day I was
12              out (Gobin de) bak a-a-a bakdam.
                over by Gobin's in the backdam area.
13                       (0.4)
```

14 Tony: [(an miit Wewe an' a Stinka:)
                [*and I met Wewe and Stinker there)*
15 ?:   [(   )
16 Pamila: Ha heh ha
17 Pamila: → Yu ondastan wa hii a taak?
                Do you understand what he is saying?

At the conclusion of the stirring self-defence Pamila, one of several non-addressed recipients, laughs (line 16), thus displaying an appreciation of what has been said and specifically, it seems, the particularly animated way in which the talk was produced. She subsequently turns to me and asks 'Do you understand what he is saying?'[5]

In this situation, the fact that I do not display any appreciation of Tony's talk is taken as a possible indication that I have failed to understand what he is saying. By formulating this in the way she does Pamila simultaneously proposes a reason for my not understanding – specifically, Pamila suggests that Tony's talk (and my very partial competence in the variety) has resulted in my not understanding what he has said. By extension, Pamila's question implies a categorization of the people present – a division between those competent in the language variety, who can thereby understand what Tony is saying, and those not competent who cannot (i.e., me) (see also Egbert, 2004, for discussion of a similar phenomenon). The question then highlights a categorical distinction between separate groups, communities or, one might say, cultures. The point I want to draw from this example is that an understanding check of this kind can convey a categorization of the participants *since category membership* (in an ethnic or linguistic group) *is often treated as prerequisite to understanding.*

Equivocal participation

An understanding of Gary's question at line 93 (Extract 1) turns crucially on a more basic understanding of the participation framework within which it is embedded. I want to suggest that, despite Gary's attempt through the use of his body, and especially his gaze, to provide a context for his utterance that includes Carney, the participation framework for the larger spate of talk that encompasses Curt's joke can be understood in one of two ways. If Carney is understood to be one of the ratified participants for Curt's joke – and not as an overhearer, to employ Goffman's (1981) terms – her laughter at the joke's completion is conditionally relevant. Since Carney does not produce any laughter, on this understanding of the participation framework, it is noticeably absent. One possible account for the non-occurrence of Carney's laughter might be that she did not understand or, alternatively, did not appreciate the joke, these being

---

[5] My response to Pamila's question is difficult to hear on the tape.

not entirely independent considerations, since, in many cases at least, not appreciating a joke just is to not understand it. Call this the 'Carney in' condition.

If, on the other hand, Carney is understood not to be one of the ratified participants, if she is treated as a Goffmanian overhearer, her laughter at the joke's completion is not conditionally relevant. Although no laughter is produced it is not noticeably absent, since its occurrence was not made relevant by the preceding talk. On this treatment of the participation framework, no laughter or display of appreciation is missing and thus no account for its non-occurrence is required. Call this the 'Carney out' condition.

The matter is ambiguous precisely because the signs which make a participation framework visible in the first place – to the participants – are equivocal (see C. Goodwin, 2002; C. Goodwin & Goodwin, 2004). On the one hand there is Carney's body orientation, which surely suggests that she is not participating in the joke-telling (see Figure 9.2, for instance). Indeed, at certain points she appears to be talking to someone else off-camera. On the other hand, she is clearly in such a position that hearing the joke (talk) is inevitable whether she is listening to it or not. Moreover, as we have already noted, Gary does some elaborate work with his body at a crucial moment to reconfigure the participants and to establish a participation framework which includes Carney in the activity (see Figures 9.2–9.9). Finally, there is the design of Gary's question itself. Specifically, Gary's 'that' indexically presupposes the joke as an already established referent. That is to say, this formulation strongly suggests that Carney should be able to pick out what it is that is being referred to by 'that', which in turn clearly presupposes that she heard the preceding talk as a bounded unit (a 'that').

There is good evidence that this ambiguity in the participation framework is real for the participants themselves. Thus, just before Carney comes to sit down at the picnic table Mike announces (Extract 5, line 1), 'Hey I started t'tell you a joke'. When Carney sits down she remarks 'I gotta hear this' (Extract 5, line 17), accounting for joining the group at the table by reference to the projected joke-telling.[6]

Extract 5 Auto Discussion, p. 29

```
01   Mik:    [Hey I started t'tell you a joke ]
02           (thet you never)
03   Gar:    Oh we never did getcher jo:ke,
04                   (0.5)
05   Gar:    Ready fer the joke now¿
06                   (0.4)
07   Mik:    Ah you ready fer the joke=
```

---

[6] This extract comes several minutes and several jokes *before* the telling of Curt's joke. 'This' in 'I gotta hear this' refers to Mike's first joke and not to 'Curt's', which is the focus of the current analysis.

```
08   Cur:    Re'y f[er the joke, [yea(h)h.
09   Mik:         [Ehhhh      [hha hha
10   Gar:    Heh-heh
11   Mik:    Uh.
12   Cur:    Ehh[heh
13   Mik:       [Stage fright. I'm [not gonna tell it.
14   Cur:                         [Ahhh hih ha ha:
15           [ha:. ah  ha  ha ] heh heh=
16   Gar:    [Hahaha! haha eh!]
17   Car: →  =I gotta hear this.
18   Cur:    Ahh ha loo[kit'er it brought 'er
19   Mik:             [heh heh heh
```

Here Carney's 'I gotta hear this' surely suggests that she is joining the group
as a participant (an understanding reinforced by Curt's talk at line 18). At the
same time, however, the way she positions her body, facing in the opposite direction, suggests otherwise. This combination of talk and body positioning in
fact conveys a kind of peripheral participation, which Carney sustains throughout the round of jokes.

Further evidence that the participants themselves orient to the equivocality
of Carney's participation is provided later when Curt, Carney's cousin, is telling a joke which he presents as a true story about the time that he and Mike
were captured by the enemy in Vietnam. Gary, the primary recipient for the
joke, expresses doubt saying, in Extract 6, line 7, 'Mike en I?' and then in, line
13, 'Oh:: horseshit,='.[7] In response to these repeated displays of doubt, Curt
attempts to enlist Mike with 'Didn' we. r'member Mike?' at lines 21–2. At this
point, Carney turns to her cousin Curt and says 'You ferget I'm here' (line 31).

Extract 6 Auto Discussion p. 45
```
01   Cur:    =D'd I ever tell you about th'time Mike
02           en I were in Vietnam en' got captured by
03           the enemy¿
04                  (0.4)
05   Mik:    Oh [:: come o::n.]
06   Cur:       [Mike en I en,] Y[eah.
07   Gar:                       [Mike en I?
08   Cur:    Mike en [I yeh
09   Gur:           [Mackina:w?
10   Gar:    [(Mike'n I.)]
11   Cur:    [ N o  m e ]'n Mike wz in Vietnam we got
```

---

[7] Gary also seems to be initiating repair on the phrase 'Mike and I'. It is not clear what Gary
   means to treat as problematic about this, but, to hazard a guess, it may be that he finds the use of
   the (grammatically correct) nominative pronoun in this position 'presumptuous' – 'putting on
   airs' as it were. If so, this is a rather interesting case in which the 'incorrect' form is oriented to
   as the appropriate one. It may also be that Gary hears this as 'formulaic' and thus by initiating
   repair of it means to be highlighting its status as an index of the story's inauthenticity.

```
12              captured by the Me['n Mike 'n,
13  Gar:                    [Oh:: horseshit,=
14  Cur:    =Ye::s we di:d!
15              (0.7)
16  Cur:    'N we wz in- en there wz me'n Mike en,
17              en another guy en,
18  Gar:    Alright, kee[p goin Curt,
19  Cur:                [Ennuh:::
20  Gar:    [Keep bullshittin]   a w a y ,]
21  Cur:    [ W e   d i : d ? ] Didn'  we.] r'member
22              Mike?
23  Car:    ( [ )
24  Gar:      [R'member Mike?
25  Mik:    Dah,[yeh, sure enough,
26  Gar:              [You remember Mike, he wz
27              [pretty nice (           ).]
28  Cur:    [Remember we wz in there]
29              he [s a y[s-
30  Gar:        [.uhh![
31  Car: →            [You ferget I'm here.
32  Cur:    Ulright,
33  Car:    [Teh hhah hah hah
34  Cur:    [Mhh hehh heh[heh
35  Mik:                  [heh-heh-heh hah-hah
36              [hah heh heh
37  Cur:    [ehh heh heh
38  Car:    Go o:n,
39  Cur:    We:ll? We wz just in there et the
40              prison camp ennuh,
```

With her turn at line 31, Carney suggests that she can disconfirm what Curt is saying. Indeed, Curt, who has persevered in the face of multiple challenges by Gary, here appears to acquiesce to Carney. Not only does he suspend the telling in progress, saying 'ulright', he joins with Carney in a bout of laughter. In this way, Curt displays that he has been 'caught out' by Carney and does not in fact proceed with the telling until Carney instructs him to with 'Go o:n,' (line 38).

Notice also that in formulating this in the way she does, Carney characterizes her own participation as something that has been treated by others as equivocal, ambiguous or peripheral – as someone, who though present, can be, and has been to this point, disattended, in fact, forgotten.[8] So, to summarize, these examples evidence an orientation by the participants to the equivocal character of Carney's participation in the activities at the table. I will argue in

---

[8] Interestingly, with this turn Carney invokes not the categories of men and women but those of cousin and cousin. As Curt's cousin, Carney would presumably have heard if he and Mike had been captured by the enemy in Vietnam (Sacks, 1992, suggests some reasons why this is the case).

the conclusion that this equivocality is carefully managed by the participants and especially by Carney, in such as way as to avert potential recipient-design problems implicated in the telling of dirty jokes.

'D'you understand that honey?'

In his consideration of 'the course of a joke's telling', Sacks (1974: 345) suggests that in the case of jokes, a recipient 'needn't remedy failures of understanding in order to respond appropriately since there is available a general way to appropriately respond which can be used whether one understands or not, i.e. laughter produced at the recognized completion'. In the case of jokes, then, 'failures of understanding are concealable'.

Furthermore, for jokes and dirty jokes in particular, but not for stories generally, there are grounds for avoiding the assertion of occurred understanding failures. Jokes, and dirty jokes in particular, are constructed as 'understanding tests.' Not everyone supposably 'gets' each joke, the getting involving achievement of its understanding, a failure to get being supposable as involving a failure to understand. Asserting understanding failures can then reveal, e.g. recipients' lack of sophistication, a matter that an appropriately placed laugh can otherwise conceal. (Sacks, 1974: 345–6)

Sacks's argument can, I think, be pushed one step further: if laughter is available as a generally usable method for concealing a failure to understand, not laughing can be heard as actively displaying non-appreciation. In other words, because a recipient can laugh and thus conceal an understanding failure, not-laughing invites inferences other than that the non-laughing person didn't understand. Specifically, a non-laughing recipient may be understood to be showing not that they did not understand the joke but, rather, that they did not find the joke funny, which is to say they did not appreciate it.

Now although Sacks later goes on to argue, in accounting for a delayed reaction to a joke, that 'each recipient is not obliged to laugh' (1974: 348), it seems clear from the data and from his remarks quoted above that, at a joke's completion, a recipient's laugher is made conditionally relevant and therefore, where not produced, is noticeably and accountably absent. And note that where laughter is not produced an account for its non-production (or delayed production) may be formulated in terms of an understanding failure (e.g., 'I don't get it'). Sacks's own materials may be cited in this respect. Here the punchline is delivered as a question 'Why didn' ya say anything last night' and answer 'W'you told me it was always impolite t'talk with my mouth full' pair at lines 1–2 (see Sacks, 1978, for an analysis of the joke and the complete transcript).

Extract 7 GTS: From Sacks (1974: 339) (transcription updated)

```
01   Ken:    why didn' ya say anything last night. W'you told me
02           it was always impolite t'talk with my mouth full,
03                  (2.0)
```

```
04  Ken:     hh hyok hyok,
05               (1.0)
06  Ken:     Hyok.
07               (3.0)
08  Al:      HA-HA-HA-HA
09  Ken:     Ehh heh heh [hehhh
10  (Al):                [hehhhehhheh hhh
11  Roger:   Delayed reactio(h)n
12  Al:  →   hehh I hadtuh think [about it awhile you know?
13  Roger:                       [hhh heh
14               (1.0)
15  Roger:   Hehh hh hehh hhh you mean the deep hidden meaning
16           there doesn't hitcha right awa(hh)y heh heh
```

Here, then, Al accounts for his delayed reaction by saying (apparently ironically) that he 'had to think about it'. That is, the interval between the joke's completion and Al's reaction (during which time he was not laughing) is explained
by virtue of his not immediately understanding the joke. Notice also that Al
provides a basis (again apparently ironically) for his not understanding – in
saying that he 'had to think about it' Al suggests that an understanding of
the joke required some kind of mental computation. As Roger moments later
suggests, that 'deep hidden meaning' didn't hit him 'right away' – some work
was required to flush it out, as it were. Among other things, Sacks (1974)
shows, then, that failure to laugh at a joke's completion (or delay in doing so)
may occasion an account formulated in terms of problems in understanding.

Returning to the reception of the joke from 'auto discussion', we can see that
Gary positions his body and gaze in order to construct a participation framework
in which Carney is one of the recipients for the joke. In so doing he makes her not
laughing an accountable event, and in asking 'D'you understand that honey?' he
names a possible account for her not laughing in this position – i.e., not understanding. The question, along with Gary's elaborate body work which provides
its context, can thus be seen to highlight a basic difference in the ongoing behaviour of those present at the completion of the joke – Mike, Gary and Curt laugh
vigorously while Carney does not. It is important to note in this respect the way in
which Gary works to 'squeeze' his question into the ongoing response activity:[9]

Extract 8 Auto Discussion, p. 43
```
85  Cur:     hu[:h huh
86  Mik:     [oooooo!
87  Cur:     [he:hhu:h[huh
```

[9] Susan Speer (pers. comm.) asks why it is Gary and not Curt (the joke-teller) who checks Carney's
   understanding. While this is probably not answerable without drawing on a larger collections
   of such cases, here Gary's understanding check is occasioned by his prior attempt to draw her
   into the framework of participation and specifically the activity of appreciation. So the question
   would have to be why does Gary and not Curt do *this*.

```
 88   Gar:                [a!a!a!
 89                       (.)
 90   Mik:    .hnnh!
 91   ???:    .hnnh
 92   Mik:    .hh You heard d'one about=
 93   Gar: →  =D'you understand that [honey
 94   Mik:                           [eh heh [hhh
 95   Cur:                                   [eh
 96           [ha ha hha hah
 97   Gar:    [(    tell you about it.)
 98   Mik:    [.ehhh!
 99   Cur:    [Too deep, ehhhah=
100   Mik:    =bout the guys et the ba:r y'know en,
101                  (0.5)
102   Mik:    ehheh! Ehh ((cough)) They w'r all
103           drinkin' pretty heavily, they decided well
104           they're gonna have a dick measuring contest
                ((Joke continues))
```

Here we see that at lines 85–91 the activity of appreciating the foregoing joke appears to be winding down. Mike then begins with an appropriately positioned next activity in a round of jokes – a next joke. Gary, however, interrupts this turn before it can reach possible completion and thus establish the relevance of an answer to the question which it is projectably in the course of delivering. In so doing, he manages to extend the response activity a little further. This is important, for it is precisely within the context of Mike, Gary and Curt producing their appreciation of Curt's joke that Gary's question to Carney has the force that it does. Within this context, Gary's question picks up on an emergent yet witnessable difference in the participation of the different parties and makes something out of it.

Consider in this respect Gary's use of the endearment term 'honey'. Note that the address term does not seem to be required in order to establish the intended recipient, since this is already displayed through Gary's gaze, his body positioning, and the fact that Carney is the only person at the table not laughing at this point (and thus the likely recipient for the understanding check). In his discussion of methods for selecting next speaker Lerner (2003: 184) writes:

If one wants to direct a sequence-initiating action unambiguously to a particular coparticipant, then one can address that participant with a personal name or other address term, such as a term of endearment ('honey') or a categorical term of address ('coach') that applies uniquely to them on that occasion. Although this is arguably the strongest form of address available, that does not mean it has the widest use. ... address terms are far from ubiquitous, even though their use is rather unconstrained in turn-constructional terms. In fact, they seem to be used primarily under specific circumstances in which they are deployed to do more than simply specify whom the speaker is addressing. In other words, *this is a form of addressing employed when considerations beyond addressing are involved.* (emphasis added)

Lerner goes on to show that whereas pre-positioned address terms are frequently deployed where a speaker can anticipate potential problems of recipiency, post-positioned terms of address, such as Gary's 'honey', 'are regularly employed as a device to demonstrate a particular stance toward or relationship with a recipient under circumstances where that demonstration is particularly relevant' (2003: 185). Lerner goes on to say:

> In these cases, addressing usually is first indicated by gaze and/or tacit forms of address, and then a name is appended to the sequence-initiating action. Of course, this also can be done when the success of other methods used over the course of a turn's talk is questionable. However, adding a post-positioned address term does not generally seem to be reparative in this way; rather, it upholds the (already adequately established) intended recipient. As such, it underlines the very act of speaking expressly to the already addressed recipient. Moreover, to use an address term is always to say something about the addressed party. When the speaker is thus freed from the necessity of addressing, post-positioned address terms – coming in a turn TCU terminal position that carries virtually no grammatical restriction on its occurrence – can be employed selectively. (Lerner 2003: 185)

So what, in addition to addressing, might Gary be doing by including the endearment term 'honey'? One obvious observation is that it invokes the 'couple' relation between the speaker (Gary) and the recipient (Carney). In his use of 'honey', then, Gary displays an orientation to Carney's status as his wife. In this society (at this time) a 'wife' is normatively a woman, and thus, in so addressing her, Gary simultaneously draws attention to her gender (see Kitzinger, 2005a, for further discussion of this normative usage). The implication appears to be that Carney does not laugh because she does not understand and she does not understand because she is a woman. Let's also note that this formulation – in this context – is condescending. 'Honey' might be described as a 'pet name' just as well as an 'endearment term', and there is something clearly patronizing about its use here.

It is worth noting the various other ways in which Gary might have formulated his question here, since in asking specifically whether Carney *understood* the joke, Gary proposes one of several possible accounts for her not laughing. Asking either whether she *heard* or *liked* the joke would have been to propose quite different accounts for her not laughing. Indeed, it seems that what makes Gary's question here worthy of appreciation in its own right – an appreciation displayed especially by Mike discontinuing what he had started in order to laugh – is the proposal that Carney's not laughing is a result of her not understanding. Not laughing can, of course, convey that a recipient did not understand the joke and thus locate responsibility for the failure with the recipient. But, as noted earlier, not laughing can also convey that a recipient did not find the joke funny and thus attribute responsibility for the failure to the joke-teller. Here, in proposing an account which is specifically alternative to another perhaps more obvious one – that she did not laugh because she did not find the joke funny – Gary can be seen to be simultaneously mocking Carney and setting her up as a target for Mike and Curt's laughter. This then establishes a particular alignment of the participants – a transformation of the activity from one in which the group is appreciating the joke and laughing *with* Curt to one in which Gary, Mike and Curt are laughing *at* Carney. In his discussion of laughing *with* and laughing *at*, Glenn (2003a) discusses a strikingly similar example in which a joke-teller makes a hearer's displayed failure to understand into a laughable, 'thus transforming the interactional environment from laughing *with* to laughing *at*'. What shows a given occurrence of laughter to be laughing *at* as opposed to laughing *with*? Of the four keys that Glenn suggests typically distinguish these, the first seems most relevant to the present case. He writes:

> Of the broad class of conversational laughables ... certain types appear likely to make *laughing at* relevant. Specifically, in laughing at environments, the *laughable appoints/ nominates some co-present as a butt*. Participants may act as perpetrators of such laughables by ridiculing, teasing, or making fun of co-present others. The butt may collaborate in this alignment, ... by producing overbuilt turns that make teasing relevant, errors, unintentional double entendres, talk or actions revealing a naïve or otherwise sanctionable state, etc. (Glenn, 2003a: 113)

Gary, then, effects the transformation of participant alignments into an activity of laughing at by revealing a sanctionable possible understanding failure on Carney's part.

Curt's utterance 'too deep' (line 99) elaborates Gary's account for Carney's not laughing by proposing a possible reason for her failure to understand based on the joke's content. But while Curt thus appears to align with Gary, his remark here can also be heard as self-deprecating. 'Too deep' is clearly ironic – as Speer points out (pers. comm.), it is not clear that there is anything much in the joke to *not* understand, let alone anything particularly 'deep'. In that sense this is a negative assessment of the joke with which Curt appears to be inviting the others to redirect their laughter away from Carney and towards him. While aligning with Gary he is also, in a sense, undercutting Gary's attempt to poke fun at Carney.

A question arises as to how Carney herself responds to both the joke and Gary's question. At the joke's completion, Carney is facing away from the table and appears to be completely disengaged from the telling. When Gary repositions his body so as to invite and eventually establish mutual gaze with Carney, she adjusts slightly in his direction. As the laughter is beginning to fade, Carney readjusts again, turning her head noticeably to the right towards Gary. This alignment is sustained as Mike begins his joke but as Gary starts the turn that will eventually become the question 'D'you understand that honey?', Carney withdraws her gaze from him and appears to re-engage the off-camera party. Carney can thus be seen specifically to disattend Gary's question, refusing to treat it as a serious inquiry worthy of a response. Moreover, by re-engaging the off-camera participant, Carney shows that she is not, in fact, a participant in the activities at the table.

The separate cultures model of gender: An invokable participants' model?

In their well-known paper, 'A cultural approach to male–female miscommunica-tion,' Maltz and Borker (1982: 196) suggest that 'the general approach ... devel-oped for the study of difficulties in cross-ethnic communication can be applied to cross-sex communication as well'. These difficulties, they assert, are 'two exam-ples of the same larger phenomenon: cultural difference and miscommunication' (1982: 196). Maltz and Borker then argue that because men and women learn how to communicate in the predominantly same-sex groupings of childhood and adolescence, they end up in adulthood with rather different communicative prac-tices, repertories and competencies (see also Gray, 1992; Tannen, 1990). Women, for instance, display a greater tendency 'to ask questions' and 'to make use of positive minimal responses'. In general women are more cooperative and sup-portive, are less competitive, and 'criticize and argue ... without seeming overly aggressive, without being perceived as either "bossy" or "mean"'. Men, on the other hand, are more likely to 'interrupt the speech of their conversational part-ners', 'challenge or dispute their partners' utterances' and 'ignore the comments of the other speaker'. Moreover, men 'use more mechanisms for controlling the topic of conversation' and 'make more direct declarations of fact or opinion than do women' (Maltz & Borker, 1982: 198). Maltz and Borker trace these differ-ences to the distinct subcultures of childhood and adolescence. They write:

We have rules for friendly interaction, for carrying on friendly conversation. What is striking about these ... rules is that they were learned not from adults but from peers, and that they were learned during precisely that time period, approximately age 5–15, when boys and girls interact socially primarily with members of their own sex. (1982: 203)

In cross-sex conversation problems arise because 'Women and men have dif-ferent cultural rules for friendly conversation and ... these rules come into con-flict when women and men attempt to talk to each other as friends and equals in casual conversation' (1982: 212). This 'cultural approach' to language and gender has been thoroughly criticized and the many good arguments against it need not be rehearsed here (see Eckert & McConnell-Ginet, 2003; chapters in Holmes & Meyerhoff, 2003; Kitzinger, 2000a; as well as important critiques in M. H. Goodwin, 2006; Speer, 2005a).

The 'cultural approach', then, will clearly not serve, as its authors intended it to, as an account of the way the world works. What it does give us, I think, is a particularly pervasive set of ideas about the world. That is to say, while conversations do not work in the way Maltz and Borker suggest, conversation-alists not uncommonly understand them in just these terms. In the data from 'auto discussion' which we have been examining, there are at least two ways in which a 'separate subculture' is implicated.

First, within the story itself, men are portrayed as a highly competitive bunch; so much so that when one of them attempts to buy condoms, his ostensive signing is taken as the initiation of a challenge. Maltz and Borker tell us that 'the social world of boys is one of posturing and counterposturing' (1982: 207) and, moreover, that 'practical jokes, challenges, put-downs, insults, and other forms of verbal aggression are a ... feature of men's speech, accepted as normal among friends ... challenges rather than statements of support are a typical way for men to respond to the speech of other men' (1982: 212). I contend that although these assertions will have limited applicability to the real world, they well describe the world of Curt's joke.

Second, within the activity of telling the joke and responding to it, these participants, and Gary in particular, appear to invoke just such a separate-cultures model in order to explain and account for the very different behaviours of the male and female participants. Carney, as we have seen, has been disattending the joke-telling. However, by virtue of some rather elaborate gymnastics within the response section of the larger telling, Gary manages to draw Carney momentarily into the interaction just enough to create a context for his question, 'D'you understand that honey?', and by this to highlight and make noticeable the fact that Carney is not laughing. With 'honey', as I have noted, Gary further draws attention to Carney's gender and, in combination with the position of the question within the response sequence, conveys one possible basis for her not understanding – the fact that she is not a man and therefore cannot appreciate what has been designed for a male audience. In this way, then, Gary invokes 'separate subcultures' as an account for Carney's not understanding (or, at least, not displaying an appreciation). Indeed, it is precisely failures of understanding such as that which Gary imputes to Carney that Maltz and Borker's model seeks to explain.

Conclusion

By way of conclusion let me reiterate that I am not recommending the Maltz and Borker model of male–female miscommunication. The problems with this approach to conversation (largely quantitative in a 'X does Y more than Z'-type mode) and gender (separate subcultures) are legion. Rather, what I have suggested is that the Maltz and Borker analysis gives a fairly accurate account of the model of gender difference that Gary invokes in the case I have examined.

An understanding of the turn 'D'you understand that honey?' depends on an analysis of its sequential positioning within the activity of responding to a joke. That activity is itself embedded within the larger organization of a round of jokes. I have focused here on Carney's peripheral participation in that activity. The ambiguity or equivocality of her participation is accomplished not only through her talk but also through the way she organizes her body and gaze in relation to the other participants. Moreover, her peripheral participation is co-constructed, Gary's actions being crucial to the way in which Carney's participation is manifested and becomes consequential for the unfolding course of action. I have provided some evidence to suggest that in the details of their talk and bodily comportment these participants reveal an orientation to gender as a relevant feature of the unfolding context. I want briefly to consider here the larger implications of this. What is at stake in participation, and why would one person carefully manage things so as to occupy a peripheral position within an activity?

Approaching an ongoing activity, a newcomer will necessarily need to determine the current 'state of play', as it were. Just as partings typically make essential reference to what is happening at the moment in the activity from which the one parting is taking their leave, so enterings will be sensitive to what is already in progress (see C. Goodwin, 1987b). We saw earlier in this respect that when Carney joins the group she accounts for doing so by saying, in reference to a projected joke-telling, 'I gotta hear this' (Extract 5, line 17). In this way, Carney displays a detailed understanding of what is happening at the table – that a joke is about to be told. Moreover, in saying 'I gotta hear this', Carney indicates the part she intends to play in this activity (a hearer but not a reciprocal teller; compare 'I gotta get in on this'). At the same time, by orienting herself away from the group, Carney does not make overt demands on the teller to be recognized as a recipient. Now this may be quite consequential since jokes – like other tellings – are recipient-designed. The range of participant characteristics to which a given utterance (or joke) may be sensitive cannot be specified in advance in general, trans-situational terms (see Sacks *et al.*, 1974). In one case the height, age, race or gender of a recipient may be relevant and in another not. However, it is at least possible that for dirty jokes in particular, the gender of the recipients may be relevant to the design of their telling. What I am suggesting, then, is that, in managing her peripheral participation in this round of jokes, Carney may be anticipating a possible complaint to the effect that she, as a woman, is hampering the men's enjoyment, is preventing the telling of jokes not suitable for mixed company and so on. As a peripheral participant, on the other hand, Carney can simply disattend talk which shows itself to be designed for male recipients.

Gary's question, then, works to make explicit what is ambiguous and equivocal. By drawing Carney more immediately into the ongoing activity it questions her competence and ability to act as a full participant. In so doing it not only makes relevant Carney's gender but simultaneously invokes a model of male–female miscommunication.

10   Bids and responses to intimacy as 'gendered' enactments

Wayne A. Beach and Phillip Glenn

Introduction

Gender may or may not be treated by speakers as central to the interactional activities in progress. Kitzinger (2005a: 228), for example, has recently suggested that moments of 'sexual joking, banter, reports of (hetero)sexual activity, and innuendo' are frequent and explicit occurrences of (hetero)-sexual talk comprising everyday conversation. Yet on other occasions, gender remains implicit and backgrounded throughout: 'the utterly banal and commonplace nature of these heterosexual performances...simply getting on with the business of their lives, treating their own and others' heterosexuality as entirely unremarkable, ordinary, taken-for-granted and displaying it incidentally in the course of some other action in which they are engaged' (Kitzinger, 2005a: 255).

The fundamental issues may be summarized as follows: what are the primary social actions being managed throughout any given spate of interaction? Is gender explicitly foregrounded as a key focus of social activity, and if not, how does gender remain present yet implicit and thus subordinate to 'the business of their lives'? In this chapter we address these questions directly by examining how gender is constructed in the midst of *pursuing and responding to bids for intimacy*. The analysis reveals how participants embed 'gender' in the midst of *invitation → acceptance/rejection sequences*, how they show themselves to be engaged in these as primary social actions, and how foregrounding/back-grounding of gender is contingent upon how these sequences get expanded through affiliation, or, conversely, inhibited as speakers avoid and withhold pursuit of 'gendered' topics (e.g., physical appearance and mannerisms).

Our point of departure harks back over twenty years to an article entitled 'Notes on laughter in the pursuit of intimacy', an infrequently cited but, we believe, monumentally important contribution by Jefferson *et al.* (1987).[1] When this paper has been referenced, it has been utilized primarily as a key resource for understanding how speakers rely on laughter to pursue affiliation

[1] We acknowledge the phenomenal contributions and always illuminating insights made by Gail Jefferson, who passed away from cancer as final revisions of this chapter were under way.

from recipients (e.g., Glenn, 2003a; Haakana, 2001; Jefferson, 2004c). What has received only scant attention, however, is a related and empirically fundamental observation addressed in the study: how do speakers invite and recipients respond to potential 'improprieties', i.e., sensitive or inappropriate matters involving a wide range of topics or events?

One set of practices through which speakers produce possible improprieties is to draw on 'gender' as an interactional resource, actions working as invitations to act in collusion. Recipients may respond by affiliating and even escalating. Together, participants may continue producing talk about otherwise 'improper' matters through an evolving sequence, culminating in and constituting a display of intimacy (e.g., see Beach, 2000; Bergman, 1993; Bergman & Linnell, 1998). In contrast, recipients may minimally acknowledge or even directly reject prior speakers' actions as having produced an interactional breach – i.e., as having engaged in some kind of unsuitable, outlandish or even disgusting action. These moments reveal how speakers' offers may well have assumed too much, pushing the intimacy beyond what recipients are able and/ or willing to affiliate to, support or even excuse.

That a participant or person being referenced is a 'man' or 'woman' may get built as central to the main action of a turn-at-talk or series of turns. Alternatively, speakers may subordinate gendered identities in favour of other categories of person reference more germane to the actions getting done (e.g., bids for reassurance, or collaborating to attribute blame and fault to others). At such moments, although speakers may provide opportunities to foreground gender as they invite and solicit recipients' involvement in talk about possible delicate or even improper topics and events, they do so indirectly (if at all). What speakers assume, or know, and/or treat as shared knowledge about a particular woman or man, or men and women in general, is thus only hinted at en route to producing other contingent actions. That is, gender in these instances is 'present' and hearable, as with terms such as 'Mom' and 'Dad' that carry the heteronormative order noted by Kitzinger (2005a), lexical resources that could be utilized for improprieties, affiliation and/or intimacy. However, we will show contrasting instances where, at least in our core collection, participants let such opportunities pass in favour of what they treat as the principal and thus most important actions in play (e.g., accepting or declining opportunities to criticize another's demeanour).

The following questions are central to the ensuing analysis:

- How does gender figure into and thereby shape the initiation and unfolding of invitation sequences?
- What kinds of demonstrable evidence exist that the organization of interactional conduct, in particular the pursuit of intimacy, shows participant orientation to gender?

We address these questions by examining a series of excerpts, drawn primarily from phone calls between family members, in which invitations and responses to proposed actions occur during the telling and receiving of stories. These interactions involve five related features: (1) various combinations of male and female speakers; (2) invited opportunities to address others' gender, among other characteristics; (3) expanded affiliation sequences; (4) neutral and disaffiliating responses (i.e., declining opportunities to expand and affiliate with prior speaker); and throughout, (5) activities whereby speakers claim *entitlement* to initiate and respond to various *contingencies* of social action across different topics and relationships (e.g., see Curl, 2006; Curl & Drew, 2008). Moves that foreground gender, imply it or disattend it altogether occur as participants manage the social epistemics of roles and relationships (e.g., see Beach, 2009; Heritage & Raymond, 2005; Raymond & Heritage, 2006).

Brief examination of a 'gendered' and expanded affiliation sequence

We begin with an instance that shows a highly gendered, even sexualized *expanded affiliative sequence* (Jefferson *et al.*, 1987). In Excerpt 1, two male university students, W and T, talk in their dorm room. W begins a highly gender-marked reporting about 'Meli:ssa'.

Extract 1 SDCL: Two Guys: 5–7[2]
((Two university students are talking in a dormitory room.))
```
1    W:   >I went out with Meli:ssa las(t) ni:ght.<=
2    T:   =↑T'uh hu:[:  h ?  ]
3    W:            [We: we]nt to: u:h. (0.2) >In n'Out?<
4    T:   Uh huh.
5    W:   pt .hhh An(d) uh >she's all like<
6         ↑I'm uncomfortable in my dre:ss:
7         le'me go ho:me and $cha:[    :ng:e$     !!!]
8    T:                          [$Uh HAH HAH]
9         HAH ↓ HAH HAH HAH HAH HAH HAH HAH HAH HAH
10        HAH$!!! .ehh(gh)? =Too: much
11        cle:av[a g e ? ]
12   W:         $[Y:(h)es.]$=
```

In response (line 2), T's '=↑T'uh hu::h?' with marked stretching and intonation treats W's prior announcement as newsworthy and encourages W's bid for an extended telling. W continues, performing Melissa (lines 6–7) in a high-pitched, whiny voice as she complains about being uncomfortable in her dress and asks to go home and change. T's prolonged laughter suggests what his

---

[2] This and an extended excerpt are examined in more detail in Beach's (2000) analysis of how two men collaborate when talking about an absent woman.

earlier '=↑T'uh hu̲::h?' projected: that at least one of Melissa's noteworthy features is her 'cle̲:ava̲ge?'. W's reporting is already deeply *gendered*, as coming from a (supposedly heterosexual) male who 'went out' with 'Melissa' who wanted to change her dress. With the big laughter and 'cleavage' reference, T explicitly *sexualizes* the talk about Melisssa. By incrementally shifting from going out to clothing to female body parts (an example of 'dissector' talk that reduces women to supposedly desirable body parts; see Hopper, 2003: 149), T contributes to a 'precipitously initiated escalation … designed for two parties familiar with the phenomenon' (Jefferson *et al.*, 1987: 187). In overlap (line 12), W's '$Y:(h)es̲.$' affirms T's escalation by prosodically echoing T's coarse depiction of Melissa's 'cle̲:ava̲ge?'. Through choral resonance (see Lerner, 2002) W shows himself co-implicated in the sexualized talk.

Two features distinguish this stretch of talk. First, this instance illustrates an expanded affiliative sequence through which participants create and sustain escalating improprieties and appreciative laughter as a way to display intimacy. Second, by their references to a non-present woman, these speakers constitute themselves as heterosexual males. They work to elevate themselves as privileged speakers, having the right to be derogatory towards women – one bit of evidence of how gender 'creeps' into talk-in-interaction (see Glenn, 2003b; Hopper & LeBaron, 1998). Such moments, when participants co-produce expanded affiliation sequences revealing distinctly gendered orientations, appear routinely. It is not surprising that gendered talk provides one resource for producing improprieties and affiliating. For example, Kitzinger (2005a: 228) reports that moments of sexual joking, banter, reports of (hetero)sexual activity and innuendo are often the most explicit occurrences of (hetero)sexual talk in everyday conversation.

In contrast, in the following instances gendered identity displays are evident in talk, yet participants routinely orient to the doing of such gender work as *subordinate* to other primary social actions. That a speaker or person being referenced is a 'man or woman', or that the speaker implicitly positions his or her own gender vis-à-vis a co-participant or person referred to, appears as a background action. Even when speakers provide opportunities to let gender 'creep' into talk through initiating improper, sexual talk, recipients may decline both invitations to affiliate and opportunities to foreground gender.

Invitations and declinations across three contiguous 'cigarette' stories

Below we examine, in more detail, three contiguous stories about 'cigarettes'.[3] These serial events occur across three phone calls within a period

---

[3] These data excerpts, and several others in this chapter, are adapted from a chapter entitled 'Stories in-a-series: tellings and retellings about cigarettes, devastation, and hair'. These data appear in Chapter 11 of *A Natural History of Family Illness: Interactional Resources for Managing Illness* (Beach, 2009).

of one day. Each overviewed story reveals speakers' practices for organizing continuity in everyday affairs, i.e., ways of updating others on notable occurrences and linking them together into a series of ongoing involvements within a family. The interactions are variously gendered across speakers: an initial telling (by dad to son), and two retellings by son (each to different women in his family). The first story is told by a dad (about his wife) to a son (about his mom). In subsequent calls, the son twice retells alternative versions of dad's initial story, of which he was the recipient, to his aunt (mom's sister) and ex-wife.

In each story, speakers enact gendered roles, employ gendered reference terms (e.g., 'mom', 'dad', 'she', 'he'), and at times prosodically enact others' voices in gendered ways to portray events and demeanours. In each instance, in the ways the tellers (dad and son) report an incident about mom's smoking and actions, they create opportunities to criticize her actions – as a mom, family member and smoker – in expanded affiliative sequences. Yet on all three occasions, *recipients decline to affiliate with and pursue these improprieties*, displaying a marked unwillingness to talk about a woman (wife, mom, sister, ex-mother-in-law) who is undergoing cancer treatment. Thus gendering of the scene remains implicit.

Dad's initial reporting: '>Jesus Christ ya forgot my cigarettes.<'

Prior to Extract 2 (below) dad had just informed son that, since mom's medical condition due to cancer had stabilized, he should not travel to visit her and the family. However, dad urges son to remain in a state of readiness, since it is imminent that he will receive a call to travel in the near future. As evident in line 1, marked by laughter, son receives this news with troubled disbelief. He then states 'This is- this is weird. hhh'.

Extract 2 SDCL: Malignancy #12:3[4]

```
1       Son:    =$.hhh huh huh hh hh .hhh$ This is- this is weird. hhh=
2       Dad:    =Yeah [(        )] >I mean ya know< ya go=
3       Son:         [ O:y vey:.]
4       Dad:    =home at night and (.) ya cry yourself to sleep
5               thinkin' °w::ell this is the end of it.° Ya come back
6   →           the next day and she says- ((mimicking wife's voice))
7   →           >Jesus Christ ya forgot my cigarettes.<
8       Son:    $Humphhhh .hh$=
9       Dad:    =O:::h gimme a break.=
10  →   Son:    Yeah. hhh .hhh heah .hh So what'd the doctor have to
```

---

[4] In this and subsequent excerpts, 'SDCL' = San Diego Conversation Library; 'Malignancy' denotes a series of sixty-one phone calls involving family members talking through cancer over a period of thirteen months; call numbers and pages of transcriptions are also noted (e.g., '12:3').

```
11              say specifically anything.=
12    Dad:      =We:ll. (0.2) Th- the thyroid is too high, the pa:in:
13              is tremendous and it will just slowly keep
14              accumulating. They will leave her o:n (0.8) u::h the
15              morphine stuff.
16              (0.4)
17    Dad:      But it will be pill form instead of this drip system
18              and they will just keep the pain under control.
19              (0.8)
20    Son:      Okay. [.hh hhh hhhh hhh hh ]
```

With 'weird', son depicts being embroiled in bizarre circumstances: His prior and considerable efforts to arrange travel plans are put on hold in the face of mom's uncertain illness trajectory. With his next 'O:y vey:.' (line 3), son invokes a traditional Yiddish expression for dismay, exasperation, shock or sorrow.[5] With 'O:y vey:.', son encapsulates his experience of being embroiled within unpredictable problems associated with his mom's changing health condition.[6]

In response, dad extends son's prior 'weird' with his own story. He provides a *my-world* or *my-side telling* of similar troubling events (see Heritage, 1984a; 1998; 2002b; Pomerantz, 1980; 1984a),[7] speaking directly about stark and troubling contrasts anchored in his own life experiences. By employing the generic 'ya' three times (lines 2, 4 and 5), dad includes son but also situates his experience as unique (see Sacks, 1992: 349). Dad describes a scenario in which he arrives home (presumably from visiting mom at the hospital). With his 'ya cry yourself to sleep' (line 4), he reports the emotional turmoil of facing his wife's apparent and looming death ('°w::ell this is the end of it.°', line 5). By shifting to the next day (again, presumably, when he returns to the hospital), with 'she says-', dad directly reports what mom said by mimicking her voice (see Buttny, 1997; 1998; Holt, 1996; 1999; 2000; Holt & Clift, 2007b):

---

[5] As summarized in Wikipedia: 'Oy vey! (Yiddish: אוי וויי) is an exclamation of dismay or exasperation meaning "woe is me" or "oh, no".'

[6] This sequential environment also reveals one version of a normalized interactional practice: 'at first I thought, but then I realized' (see Halkowski, 2006; Jefferson, 2004b; Sacks, 1992). In these moments, son's 'This is- this is weird. hhh=O:y vey:.' (lines 1 and 3) contrasts his thoughts and feelings about what was going to happen (i.e., travelling home for mom's dying) with the strange realization that he must deal (indeed *is now dealing*) with the consequences of an unexpected event (i.e., mom's stabilization). As the improvement of her health is not treated as good or bad, but as unexpected news, son orients to hearing the news as an odd *rupture* of his expectations (see Maynard, 2003). In a very short period of time mom's looming death has been postponed, and thus so too have son's plans to travel home.

[7] Technically, this is not the kind of moment described by Pomerantz (1980) in her study of how speakers tell about an experience to 'fish' or elicit information from recipients. What dad does do, however, is proceed immediately to offer a revelation about his unsettling daily experiences with mom, and the kinds of troubling consequences arising as her illness progresses. It is in this specific sense that his story is characterized as a *my-side telling*, immediately following son's 'weird' formulation about a present and trying experience.

'>Jesus Christ ya forgot my cigarettes.<' (line 7). His performance of mom in several ways treats her behaviour as not just unexpected but uncalled for and even insensitive (especially contrasted to his own grief, which he has just expressed): sick in the hospital with cancer, she greets her visiting husband with intense language ('Jesus Christ'), rapid and animated prosody, and an accusation ('ya forgot my cigarettes'). In this way, dad produces a candidate *impropriety:* criticizing the actions (through his performance of them) of his wife, the mother of his interlocutor, a dying woman.

Following introduction of improprieties into talk, a number of responses become relevant. Jefferson *et al.* (1987) posit these as a continuum ranging from least to most affiliative, including (1) overt *disaffiliating* from the impropriety, (2) *declining to respond*, (3) *disattending* the impropriety while responding to some innocuous part of the utterance, (4) *appreciating* the impropriety with laughter and/or talk, (5) *affiliating* to the impropriety by replicating it in a next utterance and (6) *escalating* with a new impropriety. Laughter and laugh-like sounds represent a mid-point on this continuum. Laughter can show appreciation of the impropriety, but when laughter is produced on its own without other more clearly affiliating actions, the speaker's stance towards the laughable is equivocal.

With '$Humphhhh .hh$' (line 8), son aligns himself as receptive to dad's own quandary, but does not comment further on it. In the absence of any further elaboration by son, dad summarizes his reaction to Mom with a marked 'oh-prefaced' and incongruous '= O:::h gimme a break. =' (line 9; see Beach, 1996; Heritage, 2002b). Treating mom's action as absurd, and in the absence of a more specific upshot provided by son, dad makes his own case that he deserves special understanding: as a husband undergoing uncertain and grievous circumstances, he deserves a 'break'. Although son has another opportunity to affiliate or even escalate, he again passes on (1) making dad out to be blameless in this delicate situation, (2) holding mom accountable for her actions or (3) in other ways pursuing her possible tendencies to be (at times) moody, bitchy or difficult. His brief acknowledgment token 'Yeah.', subsequent laugh particle 'heah' (line 10), and shift *away* from dad's story about mom – i.e., to soliciting news about what the doctor reported – draw attention back to biomedical updating information, which dad provides (lines 12–18). In this way, the expanded affiliative sequence closes down.

The subordination of gender to other primary social activities

In this telling, the son repeatedly *withholds* further commentary on dad's story, bypassing opportunities to acknowledge, elaborate upon or collaborate with dad's report of wrongdoing by mom. Dad's appeals for commiseration, and providing of opportunities for son to be critical of his mother, are receipted by son in a manner reflecting a *neutral* stance (see Wu, 2004): no pursuit is made of potentially complex relationships between mom's reported demeanour, her smoking behaviours, her cancer or how the family has dealt with her ongoing addiction to cigarettes. Son's withholding, however, does not display (and dad does not treat it as) failure to hear or understand the significance of dad's story about mom. Rather, as recipient of dad's reporting, son is placed in a potentially conflicting situation: aligning with dad about his dying mother's (alleged) behaviour, yet simultaneously avoiding further criticism of her actions.

Contrasting this instance to the one presented at the beginning of this chapter allows for noticing what might have happened but did not. In both cases, hearably 'male' speakers engage in talk that features one party as teller about a non-present 'female' known to both. In both cases, the teller performs the non-present female, including prosodic gender markings, in ways that constitute her gender (and theirs) while setting her up as an object of possible ridicule. In the first, participants go on to gender (and even sexualize) the talk explicitly; in the second, they bypass that opportunity. In the first, through the deployment of laughables and laughter, they create an expanded affiliative sequence; in the second, son's responses shift them away from that possibility. Gender is thus present in this talk between dad and son, but it remains in the background.

Son's first retelling: 'given 'em hell'

In a call with his aunt (mom's sister) later that same day, son tells her about dad's original 'cigarette' story:

Extract 3 SDCL: Malignancy #17:2

```
1        Aunt:   [What'd-] did Dr. Wylie ↑say to him (.) >do ya know?<
2                (0.8)
3        Son:    No not <really.> hh u:m hhh (.) Ya know that they were
4                gonna radiate these tumors in her le:g and that- they
5                were gonna put 'er on ↑pill form morphine (.) .hhh
6                after a while n:: .hhh u::h
7                (0.4)
8        Son:    An'that was about it. An' that there no >there wasn't
9                quite the immediate danger they thought there was last
10               ni:ght an' that's basically,< .hhhh a:ll::.
11               (1.0)
12  →    Son:    ↓Ya know dad said °ya know° last night (.) .hhh <it was
13  →            one way an'> this morning she's m- .hh given 'em hell
14  →            for forgettin' her cigarettes (.) ya know. pt hh An' so
15  →            $hhh hhh hh .hhh$=
16  →    Aunt:   =Okay. So she was much better this m[orning.]
17       Son:                                       [Ye: ah.] Much
18               better apparently.
```

19	Aunt:	↑I'll take every day I c'n <u>get</u> without your mother
20		suffering.=
21	Son:	=↑Ye:ah.
22		(0.6)
23	Son:	hh .hh ↓Yeah. I- I agree.

In lines 1–10 son responds to aunt's query, requesting an update (via dad) from the doctor.[8] Son responds by summarizing the treatments done and mom's condition as less dangerous than thought the night before. With no immediate uptake from aunt (line 11), son begins telling a version of dad's 'cigarette' story. Several noticeable contrasts or 'transformations' (Ryave, 1978: 131) can be observed between dad's first telling and son's retelling. Offering his account as direct reported speech ('dad said'), in lines 12–13 son references '<u>last</u> night (.) <it was <u>one</u> way'. Next, however, he does *not* describe dad's reported emotional turmoil ('ya cry yourself to sleep' in Extract 1, line 4) about facing mom's death. Rather, son portrays dad's version of mom's action this morning, which dad had originally reported as '><u>Jesus</u> <u>Christ</u> ya forgot my cigarettes.<' (Extract 2, lines 6–7). But in his own terms, son reports that mom was 'given 'em <u>hell</u> for forgettin' her cigarettes' (Extract 3, lines 13–14). Son's 'given 'em <u>hell</u>' makes explicit the action achieved through dad's original '><u>Jesus</u> <u>Christ</u> …' reporting. Son constructs dad as recipient of a hard-line action by mom, an action left unarticulated in dad's original story as well as son's response to it. Son does not prosodically construct his 'given 'em <u>hell</u>' version with a voice resembling dad's '><u>Jesus</u> <u>Christ</u> …' personification of mom's upset or crass demeanour. Rather, son leaves it for aunt to determine the orientation mom was taking in her talk-in-interaction (as dad did for son in Extract 2, above).

This telling links to the prior report, building on the marked contrast between mom's condition last night and this morning: her 'given 'em <u>hell</u>' is hearable as evidence of her somewhat improved condition. At the same time, it introduces a possible impropriety, through a laughable (and possibly critical) depiction of mom: a soon-to-be dying mother, diagnosed with lung cancer precipitated (at least in part) by excessive smoking, chastising her husband for forgetting to bring her cigarettes – and to the hospital, of all places. Aunt declines to respond, and son prompts her with 'ya <u>know</u>. pt hh' (Extract 3, line 14). He further pursues laughable treatment of the telling and affiliation with 'An' so $hhh hhh hh .hhh$' (lines 14–15). He stops short of providing a particular point, upshot or moral to the story that would commit him to a particular, possibly

---

[8] In lines 1–10 no consideration was given to 'Dr. Wylie' being a woman, or any particular aspect of her care being related to her gender. Dad was referenced as 'him' in an unproblematic way. And in lines 3–10, reference was drawn away from 'Dr. Wylie' and towards the generic 'they' (e.g., see Beach, 2006) when describing both mom's medical care and any danger she may be in due to her failing health.

derisive *stance* (see Wu, 2004) towards mom. Instead, he provides another slot in which aunt might collaborate in an expanded affiliative sequence.

With her response ('=Okay. So she was <u>much</u> better this m[orning.', line 16), aunt briefly acknowledges son's retelling but immediately shifts attention towards mom's current state of health. In this way, aunt avoids addressing mom's potentially moody or inappropriate behaviour, or related features known in common about her, in favour of how mom's current health had stabilized so quickly from a near-death experience. In addition, following son's acknowledgement that mom was apparently better (lines 17–18), aunt further clarifies the basis of her priorities by reporting '↑I'll take every day I c'n <u>get</u> without your mother suffering.=' (lines 19–20). With this utterance, aunt does not explicitly reject the opportunity to collaborate with son about the inappropriateness of mom's actions. Rather, as Drew (1984: 146) observed:

> From what is reported the inviters/proposers are enabled to see for themselves that their invitation is being declined. Thus through just reporting, recipients not only manage to avoid outrightly or directly doing a rejection; particularly, they also have speakers (coparticipants) collaborate in seeing that, objectively or reasonably, an acceptance is not possible.

Indeed, as evident in son's repeated agreement (lines 21–3), aunt makes it clear that even though mom may well be engaging in some questionable actions, such possible behaviours pale in significance when compared to what's at stake: the fundamental importance of attending to mom's fragile health and *minimizing her suffering*. Indeed, the design of her utterance in lines 19–20, '↑I'll take every day I c'n <u>get</u> without your mother suffering.=', evidences her willingness to tolerate a wide range of occurrences that are trivial when compared with mom's suffering. This priority is treated as dwarfing other possible interactional opportunities to pursue mom's alleged wrongdoing, openings for criticizing and even ganging up on mom in her absence. Thus aunt's response makes available to son two distinct alternatives: (1) further pursuing collaboration from aunt in making mom out to have conducted herself in a questionable manner; or (2) aligning with aunt's priorities about mom's health and suffering. From his overlapping response to aunt's prior query about mom getting better (lines 17–18), and subsequent agreement (lines 21–3), his actions reveal that he chose alignment.

As in the previous story, these participants enact gendered family roles: son talking to an aunt about his mother, the aunt's sister; aunt responding to her nephew about her sister, his mother. However, the gendered roles remain in the background. At the same time, these participants create opportunities for an expanded affiliative sequence when son invites collaboration in criticizing the mom/sister. With aunt's decline of the invitation and the subsequent talk, these participants foreground the contingencies of health and pain as trumping other possible concerns about mom's cigarette-driven (mis)conduct.

Son's second retelling: '↑>Where are my cigarettes $anyw(h)ay .hh hhh$'

Son again retells dad's original telling about mom's 'cigarettes' in the next call that same day. He informs his ex-wife Gina that mom remains in the hospital, could live for a few more weeks, and is 'incoherent'. Extract 4 occurs next.

Extract 4 Malignancy #18:2

```
1       Son:    But they think that they're gonna >get her ba:ck< to
2               where she's- hhhh she floats in an' o:ut.
3               (0.2)
4       Gina:   °Mm hm.°=
5  →    Son:    =U:hm (0.2) and I guess she- .hhhh sh- at one point
6  →            $dad said$ that (ch')a:ll of a sudden she said (0.8)
7  →            ((mimicking mother's voice)) ↑>Where are my cigarettes
8  →            $anyw(h)ay .hh hhh$ >.hh An' he said< sounds like she's
9  →            back to normal again for a little bit there.=So .hhh
10              S[he-
11 →    Gina:    [>Who'd ya talk- who'd ya talk to toda:y.<
12      Son:    pt .hh U:h (0.8) Just da::d this morning.
```

In lines 5–10, son transitions away from describing mom's prognosis and coherence by initiating a second retelling. He begins one report with 'I guess she-', which marks an uncertain stance towards what is to follow; he abandons this in favour of reporting what dad said, and this leads him into the cigarette story.

Although this telling differs from the previous versions in several ways,[9] it still works like previous moments in deploying an impropriety as a possible

---

[9] In this second version, son continues to reduce emphasis given to the *temporal unfolding* of the event. In Extract 2, dad's original description included his emotional turmoil of being 'home at night'. In Extract 3, these details were glossed, becoming 'last night (.) it was one way' in son's retelling to aunt. For Gina, son simply states 'at one point $dad said$ that (ch')a:ll of a sudden she said'. Thus, from one retelling to the next, the particular sequential events leading up to mom's '>Jesus Christ ya forgot my cigarettes.<', and dad's surprised reaction, became not only diminished but *dispensable* (see Schegloff, 2004). But son's retelling also alters what dad reported that mom had actually said to him (as with Extract 3). Second, the laughable '$dad said$' framing, though different from the way dad originally reported mom's utterance, and dad's reaction to it, seems designed to solicit Gina's hearing and attention as story recipient. And as this is a second retelling, not a first (i.e., for aunt), son can rely on his prior experiences and adjust his story accordingly. In Extract 3, it was shown how aunt's '=Okay. So she was much better this m[orning.]' (line 16) acknowledged but decidedly shifted away from any sense of collusion *against* mom. This reaction by aunt did not explicitly reject, but neither did it overtly affirm or further encourage, son's story. One upshot of aunt's response is son's subsequent adaptation for a second retelling (to Gina). It is not uncommon for stories to become increasingly streamlined and tailored across repeated retellings (see Beach & Lockwood, 2003; Norrick, 1997; Sacks, 1992; Schegloff, 2004). Just as story formats can be altered to enhance the likelihood of receptivity, son may have shaped this retelling, *as laughable*, to boost Gina's acceptance of a not-yet-delivered story.

start-up to an expanded affiliative sequence. Prefacing the telling with the smile-voiced '$dad said$' frames the event as *presently* laughable. Son shifts intonation and prosodically mimics mom's voice as '(ch')a:ll of a <u>sudden</u>' she asks, '↑><u>Where</u> are my <u>ci</u>garettes $anyw(h)ay. hh hhh$' (lines 7–8). Again, the family member sick with terminal lung cancer is depicted as harshly demanding cigarettes in her hospital bed. Son further marks his own humorous stance towards mom's utterance with smile-voice and laugh particles '$anyw(h)ay .hh hhh$', inviting the interlocutor (in this case, her ex-daughter-in-law) to join in treating her behaviour critically and laughably. Gina bypasses this opportunity, remaining silent (middle of line 8). Son quickly shifts to a non-laughing, impropriety-free assessment of mom, attributed to dad: 'An' he said< <u>sounds</u> like she's <u>ba</u>ck to normal again for a little bit there'. Gina responds with '>Who'd ya <u>ta</u>lk- who'd ya<u>talk</u> to toda:y.<' (line 11). Like aunt, Gina next and also draws attention away from son's story about mom's 'cigarettes' to seeking information about whom he has been in touch with. She offers no acknowledgement of any point son might have been making about mom's behaviour (as possibly harsh, inappropriate or insensitive in her reported response to dad). Gina avoids participating in talk that might lead to escalating improprieties about mom. Once again, gender roles are present but not foregrounded; opportunities to display intimacy through shared improprieties and laughter get declined in favour of displaying serious uptake of mom's health news.

As storytellers, dad and son invite *recipient* collaboration about mom's smoking, her illness and her overall demeanour. Dad's original telling to son, and two subsequent retellings by son (to aunt and Gina), yielded only minimal acknowledgement from recipients, no belittling collaboration, and marked shifts *away* from the focal point of the initial story. In the original telling, son's laughter showed appreciation for dad's story about mom and the cigarettes, but he provided only brief acknowledgement to dad's '= <u>O</u>:::h <u>gi</u>mme a <u>break</u>.=' (Extract 2, line 9) before asking what the doctor had to say. Similarly, aunt and Gina responded minimally to son's critically comical depictions of mom, instead taking up talk about mom's treatment and condition. As evident in Extracts 2–4, *recipients* dealing with mom's dying – son, aunt and Gina alike – displayed little interest in corroborating, in any derogatory way, about a mom in the final few weeks of her life. These choices reflect the moral nature of such moments. As Bergman (1993: 99) has observed regarding *gossiping*, there is a 'morally contaminated character' inherent in talk about absent others' personal and private lives (see also Bergman & Linnell, 1998). Simply because the focus of talk is about intimate others – even beloved family members facing terminal cancer – does not mean that problems inherent in managing possible indiscretions will mystically go away. These moments are implicitly gendered – through role enactments, pronouns and prosodic performances – but that gendering, as a resource participants could draw on in expanding comical depictions of mom, remains in the background.

Pivotal moments: The initial acceptance/ declination of a playful impropriety

When sequences get expanded, allowing for such matters as 'gender' to become a progressive focus of co-present speakers, some triggering action occurs that is marked by an invitation and affiliative response by next speaker. Returning to Extract 1, note that the following pair of actions occurred.

Extract 5 SDCL: Two Guys: 5-15
((Two university students are talking in a dormitory room.))
1   W: >I went out with Meli:ssa las(t) ni:ght.<=
2   T: =↑T'uh hu:[: h ?]

This gives rise to an escalation involving W's whiny and complainable portrayal of Melissa, T's reference to Melissa's cleavage, and W's choral confirmation. That is, T's playful uptake marks W's announcement as newsworthy and establishes his affiliation with the improper position that is projected. These expansions stand in marked contrast with previously examined, non-sexualized Extracts 2–4. During these interactions, all three recipients (son, aunt and Gina) decline affiliation through minimal acknowledgements and shifts of attention away from prior invitations to collaborate:

Extract 6 SDCL: Malignancy #12:3
10 → Son: Yeah. hhh .hhh heah .hh So what'd the doctor have to
11   say specifically anything.=

Extract 7 SDCL: Malignancy #17:2
16 → Aunt: =Okay. So she was much better this m[orning.]

Extract 8 Malignancy #18:2
11 → Gina: [>Who'd ya talk- who'd ya talk to toda:y.<

At these pivotal moments, recipients decline the invitation to participate in improper talk about a non-present other. In all the instances, gendered materials are present and available to employ as resources in pursuit of interactional intimacy. However, gendering the scene is not necessary to creating an expanded affiliative sequence. In the following section we contrast instances of expanded affiliative sequences, both involving objectifying talk that treats non-present others as inanimate objects. One is deeply gendered and sexualized; the other achieves playful intimacy through increasingly gendered references to a female's appearance. The contrast allows us to see the interplay of these features, which we take up in the closing discussion.

Two contrasting instances: Playful expansions of objectifying talk

The following bit of blatantly demeaning and sexist talk comes from a telephone call between two males who are university students (see Glenn, 2003b):

Extract 9 (SIUC S1)

```
1    Stan:    and then I was uh at my brother's wedding last
2             weekend.
3             (0.8)
4    Dave:    There's a lot of wool at weddings.=Y'know that?=
5    Stan:    =I know.=You wouldn't believe all the coot that was
6             up there.
7    Dave:    ↑Ohhoh khhh ((guttural, throat clearing sound))
8             [(take me)
9    Stan:    [They make these girls looks like dog meat.
10            (0.8)
11   Dave:    Haw::::hhh ((guttural sound))
12   Stan:    These girls have no (0.7) These girls look like shit
13            down here compared to girls up there,
14            I'm tellin' [ya.
15   Dave:                [Aw ↑hell yeah,
16            (0.9)
17   Dave:    Well they're easy to grease down here.=Up there 'er a
18            challenge.
19   Stan:    I know but they have an attitude.khh
20            (0.3)
21   Dave:    Hey I don't know whyhh,
22            (2.0)
23   Dave:    Maybe if they drop fifteen or twunny I'd start
24            lookin' around again.
25   Stan:    kheh heh huh °eh eh uh° .h=
26   Stan:    =It's the food they eat over here. .hh
27   Dave:    What is it feed?
28   Stan:    hhh eh eh [hh
29   Dave:              [Tryin' to beef 'em up for Thanksgiving?=
30   Stan:    =Yeah really.
31   Dave:    hh₁h hnh heuh heuh kh [.hh
32   Stan:                         [What iuh (.) What do ya wanna
33            do for fall break?
```

At line 4, Dave responds to Stan's otherwise benign reporting about his brother's wedding with 'There's a lot of wool at weddings.=Y'know that?='. This reference to 'wool' makes relevant further talk about weddings as occasions for observing good-looking women. Stan pursues this trajectory, as his reference to 'coot' implicates himself as a collaborator in producing this form of 'gendered' talk about women. With Dave's next '↑Ohhoh khhh ((guttural, throat clearing sound)) (take me)' (lines 7–8), they launch subsequent talk that expands 'wool' and 'coot' to other terms attributed to women (e.g., 'shit', 'dog meat' and comparison to livestock) – objects treated as 'easy to grease' (line 17), with 'an attitude' (line 19) and overweight (lines 23–4).

In short, these two men demonstrate an objectifying male gaze through colloquial and reductionistic references to women. Their collaborative pursuit of crass and sexualized versions of women evidences a form of shared and normalized intimacy, enacted through an expanded affiliation and explicitly 'gendered' sequence of activities. That neither participant treats their talk as improper or immoral thus reveals their (perhaps hyper-) heterosexual orientations to talk. This is further evident when in lines 32–3, Stan's query 'What do ya wanna do for fall break?' makes clear that prior talk about women and weddings is not distinct from other routine daily activities, such as discussing future social plans.

Extract 10, again from the corpus of family cancer calls, resembles the preceding instance in that two male participants objectify non-present female(s) via metaphoric body references as improprieties that lead to expanded affiliative sequences. In this case it concerns mom's lack of hair due to chemotherapy and radiation treatments.

Extract 10 Malignancy 37: 3

```
1    Son:   .hh Is her hair growing back yet?
2    Dad:   $Heh heh$ No:[:.
3    Son:                  [$Heh heh heh heh.$=
4    Dad:   =She does have a little stubble up there, cuz I
5           kissed her goodbye last night and I got whisker
6           burns.
7    Son:   $Heh heh heh$ .hh Well tell her she should sha:ve.
8           You >gotta get her one of those electric-< like a-
9           .hh a Norelco or somethin.=
10   Dad:   [[ [ Yea::h. ]
11   Son:   =[[ [She could] b'fffph over her hea[d.
12   Dad:                              [Remington.
13   Son:   Yeah yeah, there you go. .hh Or an Epilady for your
14          head huh? $Hh [heh heh heh heh.$]
15   Dad:                 [$Heh  heh  heh.$ ] Right.=
16   Son:   =Heh. O(h)ka:y.
17   Dad:   But other than that I don't have time to do anything
18          else, so nothing else seems to change much [u:h-] =
```

Dad laughs in response to son's question about mom's hair. Son laughs along, and the shared laughter projects joint willingness to treat this issue playfully. Dad reports that mom has 'a little stubble up there' and that he got 'whisker burns' from kissing her head (lines 4 and 5–6). This possibly improper reference

to their cancer-suffering family member gets met by more laughter and an esca-
lated impropriety from son in the form of a joking suggestion. They make more
jokes along these lines, affiliating in their treatment of the issue. In lines 17–18,
dad shifts away from further play and back to reporting about his lack of time
and the status quo nature of caring for mom as her cancer progresses. Here, the
taken-for-granted gendering of the scene appears in bald jokes, a male reporting
'whisker burns' from kissing and the shift in names of razors to 'an Epilady for
your head' – a product explicitly named for and marketed to females.

We bring our analysis to a close with a similar and final instance, further involving mom's lack of hair, but here in the context of dad reporting about how difficult
it is to give her a bath. Prior to the excerpt below, dad had reported how he kept
forgetting that mom had no hair by doing dumb things like retrieving the sham-
poo. Son also reported forgetting that she had no hair. At line 6, son invites dad's
playful collaboration by proposing 'You need a bowling ball washer, huh?'

Extract 11 Malignancy 41: 5–6

```
1    Dad:   =°Heh he heh.° ↑Yeah. So I went back and I got the
2           wa:sh cloth and soap =
3    Son:   $Uh hu [heh heh heh heh heh heh heh$ hhh.]
4    Dad:          [(                ) you know. °I said°]
5           ↑O:h God (      ).
6    Son:   You need a bowling ball washer, huh?
7           $hhh [hhh heh   heh.$]=
8    Dad:        [$Heh heh heh.$]
9    Son:   =Don't tell her I said that, [okay?]
10   Dad:                              [No:  I] won't (tell).
11   Son:   $Heh heh heh$ .hh hh .pt Bla:h. ((heavy swallow))
12          Yeah you could just get a- a little pledge an a- kind
13          a dust cloth an' chika=chika=chika right?
14   Dad:   Polish it [  up.]
15   Son:             [Buff] it up.=
16   Dad:   =Uncle Tom's car buffer: [an-
17   Son:                            [$Yeah heh [heh ha.$
18   Dad:                                       [Few of those and
19          the- the- then bo:y it'd be shiny!=
20   Son:   =Ts:::h::: I:=li:ke it. .hh U:gh.
21   Dad:   A::gh:.
22   Son:   .hhh So- so what- what's she doing I me:an-
23   Dad:   °A:h:°, less and less:.=
24   Son:   =Less [and  le]ss.=Oka:y.
25   Dad:         [U::hm ]
26          (0.3)
27   Dad:   She got up for a whi:le yesterday. She fe::ll:-
28          (1.2)
29   Dad:   O::h: hell F:riday morning.
```

Though it is immediately followed by their shared laughter, son and dad display recognition (lines 9–10) that what they are doing qualifies as an impropriety. Dad agrees not to tell mom about his suggestion, and it is only following dad's confirming promise not to tell that they expand the playful sequence. Following another flurry of expanded affiliation, dad and son work together to produce how 'Pledge' (a furniture polish) might be used on mom's head and how her head might be polished and buffed, including the use of 'Uncle Tom's car buffer:' (line 16). Soon thereafter (line 22), son shifts back by querying dad about what mom has been doing and, once again, dad reports more serious and countering 'bad news' (see Maynard, 2003) that mom is doing 'less and less' (line 23) and fell after getting up Friday morning.

For dad and son, discussions about strategies for shaving and polishing mom's bald head are incidental ways of reporting on daily circumstances involving caring for and living through a family cancer experience. What is fundamental – not only for dad and son, but for all interactions comprising social life – is that invitations to collaborate are routinely formulated, accepted or rejected, and that sequences get subsequently expanded or constrained depending on just how these co-produced actions get interactionally managed. In each of these instances, gendered resources are present and available for generating expanded affiliative sequences. Those same resources may remain in the background, however, as participants instead pursue alternative contingencies and displayed orientations.

Discussion

The instances analysed in this chapter reveal participants managing possibilities that involve gendering the talk, and pursuing bids for intimacy, through expanded affiliative sequences. In two separate instances of college males engaging in sexist talk, such talk gets triggered by initial improprieties which recipients next affiliate to and even escalate. In the first three instances of family cancer talk, speakers offer possible improprieties that recipients disattend, opting instead to pursue serious uptake of cancer news. In the final instances, participants employ improprieties and shared laughter that allow them to display intimacy.

Joking and laughter occur within sequential environments conducive to producing gendered talk. A first joke or humorous remark, prompting laughter, provides a sequential warrant for any speaker producing another such to extend the laughter (Glenn, 2003a). A second speaker producing a next humorous or playful impropriety both forwards the laughing environment and ratifies like-mindedness.

In all of these instances, features of the talk show implicit gendering: pronoun references, embodied performances of non-present others and body talk that carries gendered assumptions. This gendering is part of the hetero-normativity of everyday talk that Kitzinger discusses:

The apparent ease with which the speakers produce and understand this locally initial *he* as Mrs. Hooper's [an ill woman] husband displays (for us as analysts) the extent to which coping with a wife's illness is an activity category bound to husband, and that this category boundedness is a *resource* that is relied on by the speaker who deploys – and the recipient who makes sense of – the locally initial proterm … Through the invocation of husbands and wives with locally initial proterms (we, he, she), speakers treat the existence of such persons as a taken-for-granted feature of their social worlds. (Kitzinger, 2005a: 252)

In the materials we have examined, gender appears as a resource that analysts may notice, but the participants may or may not foreground in the course of activities such as telling and affiliating. Moments involving *invitation* → *acceptance/declination* sequences provide one critical lens for explaining how talk about 'gender' – as sexualized and/or as focused on others' actions and demeanour – gets initiated, responded to, and expanded or inhibited.

When 'gender' becomes an explicit and sexualized focus for speakers, *playful conduct is demonstrable as flurries of concerted intimacy.* Speakers act in collusion by 'doing being men (or women)' together, positioning themselves as sufficiently confident with one another to talk about the physical appearance or other sexual possibilities made available by formulating members of the opposite (or same) sex in particular ways. They do so in an escalating manner that sexualizes, or at least envisions, actions with and about non-present others that are treated as humorous, laughable, momentarily entertaining and somehow edifying for involved parties. Yet even when expanded affiliation sequences are produced, as with dad and son in Extracts 10–11, talk may become gendered without being sexualized. *Bids and confirmations or declinations of intimacy are both locally occasioned and relationally idiosyncratic.* When a dad and son humorously manage a family cancer journey, they do so as consequential members sharing a distinctive relational history. Both rely on these lived experiences when claiming and demonstrating being significantly impacted by mom's cancer diagnosis, treatment and prognosis. They enact their history and experience as mirrored male–male interactional involvements – particular ways of raising and responding to specific topics, initiating and expanding playful actions, imposing and adhering to tolerance thresholds evidenced through shifts away from play and back to more serious discussions about mom's condition and how best to care for her maladies. These actions yield inherently privatized interactions that might not occur in other moments, relationships and/or in the presence of other participants.

Though instances have been identified here where speakers momentarily 'catch' themselves as having constructed some impropriety, and/or impose boundaries by routinely shifting topics and attention away from further talk on potentially sensitive topics, such noticings and corrections do not expunge the fact that a normative heterosexual order is firmly entrenched in the social fabric of everyday living. Bids and responses to intimacy are equally ingrained as rich environments for understanding how or whether speakers construct others, or themselves, as 'gendered' in the actions they produce together.

Part IV

Gender identities and membership
categorization practices

11   Accomplishing a cross-gender identity: A case of passing in children's talk-in-interaction

Carly W. Butler and Ann Weatherall

Introduction

Garfinkel's (1967) account of the methods used by a transsexual to pass as a woman, Agnes, was groundbreaking with respect to the then existing social theories of gender. Through analysis of the practices Agnes reported using to accomplish membership as a woman, Garfinkel proposed that gender was a joint social achievement routinely produced in the course of everyday interactions. Motivated by ideas of gender as a situational accomplishment (see also Kessler & McKenna, 1978; Speer, 2005a; Speer & Green, 2007; Weatherall, 2002a; West & Zimmerman, 1987), in this chapter we present a case study of a 6-year-old boy, William, who, for a brief time at least, assumes an identity as a girl called Charlotte. Our aim is to illuminate some of the interactional practices used by William and his classmates to support and challenge William's identity as Charlotte.

The data were drawn from a larger corpus of audio-recordings of 6- to 8-year-old children at a New Zealand school (see C. W. Butler, 2008; C. W. Butler & Weatherall, 2006).[1] Most of the recordings in this corpus are of conversations between children outside of their interactions with adults. Written consent for participation was received from the children's parents, and children received an information sheet and were asked for verbal consent prior to wearing the mini-disc recorder. Children were free at any time to ask for the recording to be stopped, or for a part of the recording to be deleted from the disc.

The episode presented in this chapter was recorded in the classroom while the students were engaged in a teacher-assigned activity of writing and drawing about an arts festival the school had held the previous evening. They were free to talk amongst themselves while doing this task. A mini-disc recorder was placed on a group of desks with four students: Tara, William, Benjamin and Tanya (all names and identifying information have been changed). A few minutes into the assigned task, in an apparently out-of-the-blue announcement, Tara introduced William (sitting beside her) as Charlotte. The identification of William as a girl named Charlotte was a thread in the desk group's conversation

---

[1] Financial support for the study was provided by the New Zealand Tertiary Education Committee (TEC, formally FRST).

for around forty minutes of recording. To the best of our knowledge this was Charlotte's first and only appearance.[2]

Conversation analytic methods are used to describe some of the practices used by the children to generate, maintain and ignore William's new identity as Charlotte. The analysis considers *when* and *how* Charlotte was made relevant in the children's ongoing course of talk. We consider three pervasive ways in which Charlotte was produced: the management of epistemic status (i.e., access to and use of information, belief and knowledge), through person references (e.g., use of names and pronouns), and with gender references and categorizations (Kitzinger, 2007b; Stokoe, 2006).

We begin with two extracts from the opening sequences of this episode, in which Tara first introduces William as Charlotte. These extracts illustrate some of the identity and categorization work that we consider in more detail in the remainder of the chapter.

'This is Charlotte': Proffering an identity

The episode was initiated, apparently randomly, when Tara made an announcement – 'This is Charlotte'. Extract 1 represents this first recorded instance of William being identified as Charlotte. Whilst it is possible that William had been called Charlotte at some earlier stage, I (C.B.) observed and recorded many of William's informal interactions over the course of a month and did not hear any other reference to Charlotte.

Extract 1 (1:45–2:16)

```
1    Tara:      <This is Cha:rlotte>
2               (2.6)
3    William:   My- yesterday my hair was up ↑ta °here
4               (1.0)
5    William:   Bu:t (0.4) m=[my ↓mum] cut it.
6    Tara:                   [Fo' rea:l? ]
7               (0.4)
8    William:   My mum cut it up to he↑re >in=my
9               bR↑o[th
10   Tara:          [N↑O:::[:.
```

---

[2] At other times William did take on a cross-gendered membership (not typically with a 'name'), and at those times both he, and other children, oriented to his proper gender membership as somewhat ambiguous. For instance, it was not unusual for William to be referred to as 'her' in the playground when no apparent cross-gender identity had been accorded him (these references were also occasionally repaired). It is unclear how this bears on the interaction presented here, as the children have access to a social history and shared understanding that cannot be fully available to us. However, while the switched identity might well be understood by reference to a history of William having a cross-gender identity, we still have a record of how *this* cross-gender identity was established *this* time.

```
11  William:                    [.h ↑Yes: u:m my: um m (.) William's
12              hair is [s:o:: sho:rt?
13  Tara:                [↑Yous are
14  Tara:       Yous arem jus making up that ↓sto:ry:
15              you: ↑are?
```

Tara's utterance 'This is Charlotte' can be described as an identification prof-fer, which according to Sacks (1992) is different from, say, making an identi-fication. He suggested that:

> for proffering identifications, it's quite irrelevant whether you're correct, for example, but the issue is, again, whether it's relevant that you're correct, or whether some other identification is, or is assumed to be, more relevant than the one you propose. (Sacks, 1992, I: 306)

The identification of William as Charlotte could be treated as relevantly correct, or less relevant than some other identification (such as 'William'). Whether or not William is to be recognized as Charlotte depends on whether this identifi-cation is accepted by the other members of the desk group – including William himself. If this identification is not treated as relevant, then William is not Charlotte. The relevant correctness of the identification of William or Charlotte was an ongoing matter throughout the episode. The identity of Charlotte was in a sense proffered in each instance of talk in which an identification was made or used.

As far as we know, the identity was up until this point not known by any-body, so Tara's announcement offers the other members some new informa-tion. As an introduction, the announcement opens up the possibility of a spate of talk between the co-present parties (Sacks, 1992, II: 68). The desk group members Benjamin and Tanya, along with William, are invited to take part in identifying William as Charlotte. The introduction also serves as a mapping move in a game – the application of a player category to a person (C. W. Butler, 2008; C. W. Butler & Weatherall, 2006; Sacks, 1992). If a play sequence is to ensue, Tara's mapping has to be accepted by William and/or the other children in a consistent second move, such as greeting Charlotte.

After a silence of 2.6 seconds William responds (line 3) with a story about having his hair cut. There is no indication that William is talking as Charlotte until lines 8–9, where he begins to make reference to a brother that he is known not to have. Then at line 11 William repairs the reference to his brother with the name 'William'. Technically, William is referring to himself as an absent third person, but this is done in order to do 'not being William', and displays an identity as William's sister – Charlotte. In this way William orients to the relevance and correctness of the proffered iden-tity, and performs a consistent second move in the sequence of play that was initiated by Tara.

Tara's identification of Charlotte attributes a change in gender for William. By telling about a hair cut, William narrates a personal and family history that can be heard to account for his appearance. It is noteworthy, even if coincidental, that in his first display of membership as Charlotte, William accounts for his hair length. Experimental and interview-based research has found that when asked to attribute a gender to a person, the responses of both children and adults indicate that hair length is fundamental to the act of gender attribution (Bem, 1993; Kessler & McKenna, 1978). Hair length is an important index or attribute of gender category membership and William demonstrates his attention to the accountability of that aspect of his appearance. There is no explicit identification of William as a girl but this is inferred in the selection of a feminine name, and through William's accounting work. Personal name and hair length can be heard as attributes bound to gender categories, which are invoked by the resonance of gender as a cultural framework.

Despite William's apparent alignment with Tara's initial action (i.e., identifying William as Charlotte), Tara expresses disbelief about the story of the haircut, claiming it to be made up (lines 10, 13–15). This sequence then lapses, and over the next forty seconds attention turns to using and borrowing stationery equipment and sharpening pencils. Then, shown in line 4 of Extract 2, overlapping an on-task question by William, Tara repeats her earlier identification – 'this is Charlotte'.

Extract 2 (2:55–3:22)

```
1    William:   Why: [does it need a h-
2    Tara:            [Thi:s i::s Cha:rlo:tte
3               (4.9)
4    Tara:      <Di:d you:r bro:the:r> what did your bro:tha
5               s:a:y:?
6               (0.6)
7    William:   Say about what.
8               (1.5)
9    Tara:      Kapa Ha:ka: group?
10              (1.0)
11   William:   I d↑unno:.
12              (2.3)
13   William:   He: just said they were si:nging.
14              (1.7)
15   Ben:       Si:ngi:ng and what were the:y d↑oing?
```

Tara's full repeat of her earlier turn 'this is Charlotte' (line 2) suggests her orientation to the failure of the first introduction to produce the expected next action. In Schegloff's words, Tara introduces Charlotte for 'another first time' (Schegloff, 1996c: 455). The restarting may demonstrate that the first attempt had failed to produce the kind of response that Tara had proposed or intended.

The second introduction also seems to fail, in the sense that a next speaker does not appear to self-select (line 3). Instead, Tara asks a question which is addressed to Charlotte – 'what did your brother say?' (lines 4–5). Tara restarts her turn in line 4 in order to reformulate her question – the use of 'what did ...' invites a more detailed response than her initial formulation starting with 'did' (which could be answered with a yes/no answer). The use of the relational reference 'your brother' serves to emphasize Charlotte's closeness and Tara's distance from William, something which may more strongly implicate the expectation that, as the sister of William, Charlotte has some access to information about William's experiences (Stivers, 2007).

In the clarification in lines 7–9 it is established that a report of Kapa Haka[3] was expected. William initially responds to Tara's question with 'I dunno' (line 11), and then after a delay adds 'he just said they were singing'. This is a relatively minimal account of what happens at Kapa Haka performances, and accordingly William's initial claim of no knowledge might be heard to be a reflection of the inadequacy of his brother's report, rather than a display of his non-participation or alignment in the pretence.

In this sequence, Tara aligns with William's earlier proposal that William is Charlotte's brother, one which she had appeared to express doubt about in Extract 1. In Extract 2 she is treating William as Charlotte, and Charlotte as William's brother. Benjamin's request for elaboration at line 15 displays his orientation to the relevance of the changed identity, and is the first time he participates in the activity of identifying William as Charlotte. In the immediately subsequent turns (not shown here), attention to Charlotte lapses as once again talk turned to stationery and the task at hand.

Over the following thirty minutes, William's identity as Charlotte was repeatedly invoked in the course of the ongoing interaction and recurrently oriented to as a locus for collective action and shared understanding. Extracts 1 and 2 offer examples of some of the practices used to generate a new identity for William: person reference (the personal name, relational categories), epistemics (Charlotte's access to knowledge about William) and gender membership (the use of a feminine name, hair length). In the remainder of the chapter we examine how these practices were used to establish the relevance of 'Charlotte' over the course of the interaction.

We begin by considering how knowledge and information about William, Charlotte and the classroom were invoked and managed in this episode – that is, how epistemic rights and responsibilities were relevant in establishing the identity of Charlotte. Tara initiated the episode, and throughout she establishes herself as someone who knew more than anybody else (perhaps even more

---

[3] A group who perform Maori dance and songs – William was a member of the school Kapa Haka group who had performed the previous evening at the arts festival.

than William himself) about the identity, and also as someone responsible for informing others of the identity change. We also show how the status of William's knowledge was shaped by his membership as Charlotte.

In the following section we discuss the organization of person reference in this episode, focusing on the use of the names 'William' and 'Charlotte', and the use of indexical references ('she', 'he', etc.). We discuss how the selection, positioning and form of personal names occasioned the ongoing production and recognition of the fictional identity. The analysis shows how the use of one reference form over another was sensitive to the sequence in which it occurred, and was used to manage locally situated action.

The next section presents instances of gender references and categorizations. Gender membership was ascribed, resisted, noticed, made (ir)relevant, challenged and defended in the course of establishing William's identity as Charlotte. Gender categorization activities also served as tools for doing particular kinds of social actions, and were implicated, for example, in the way that a tease sequence is produced and understood.

Epistemic management

Participation in the interaction relied on identifying and recognizing William as Charlotte, which was in turn dependent on knowing about his new identity. Tara's initial naming of Charlotte in the opening minutes of the episode displayed her access to information about Charlotte, and her offer of this information to the other members opened up the possibility for others to participate. There, and throughout the episode, Tara positioned herself as someone with both a right and responsibility to tell others (and know *more* than them) about Charlotte's identity. In many ways, this was Tara's game; she started it and it was she who reinvoked the relevance of the identity if it happened to lapse.

One of Tara's methods for inviting participation from other children into her game, and invoking the relevance of William's new identity, was to announce the identity switch to visitors to the desk group. In the following extract, Amber – a passer-by – was informed about William's new identity as Charlotte.

Extract 3 (18:25–18:44)

1	Tara:	You [know Amber .h that >she is=
2	Oscar:	[>No↑myfa- m.
3	Tara:	=actually a gi:rl?
4		(2.4)
5	Amber:	(Him) William?
6		(1.3)
7	Ben:	Ch:a[:rlotte
8	Tara:	[Her na:me is not William=

```
9    William:    =I' is (.) <Charlot[te>
10   Tara:                        [Yah because you: kno:w hi-
11               (.) her bro:ther?, the:y >they are-< (0.6) thar
12               tentical twi[ns?
13   William:                [I:d[entical
14   Amber:                       [(Don't) (get it)?
15   Tara:       Identical twi:ns?
```

The description of Charlotte that Tara offers Amber ('you know Amber that she is actually a girl?') is designed as an announcement. The token 'you know' (line 1) suggests that the information to follow will be news to Amber, demonstrating how participation and non-participation in this pretence could be managed in terms of displaying and offering access to the correct and relevant information. Tara's use of 'actually' at line 3 treats the information being offered in this turn as counter to Amber's assumed understanding (see Clift, 2001) that the person she sees is a boy.

Amber displays her state of knowledge and understanding in her request for clarification at line 5, where (if heard correctly) she identifies the referent 'she' as 'him William'. The other desk group members orient to Amber's identification as a source of trouble, and display their access to the correct name (lines 7–9). Benjamin offers the replacement name 'Charlotte', and in overlap Tara says 'her name is not William', which is latched onto and completed by William ('It is <u>Charlotte</u>'), establishing a collaboratively produced turn (Lerner, 2004). Amber, however, explicitly claims a lack of understanding ('don't get it', line 14). The failure to establish a shared understanding of William as Charlotte has implications for the trajectory of action projected by Tara in her informing, and the potential for Amber to support the new identity. Indeed, Amber's only involvement in the episode after this was to challenge the legitimacy of William's membership as a girl named Charlotte (see Extract 12).

In the following extract, states of knowledge are implied and made relevant following an identification of Charlotte as William.

Extract 4 (6:56–7:10)
```
1    Ben:     But he':s Wi:ll (.) i- (.) that's William
2             (.)
3    Tara:    No:
4             (0.2)
5    Ben:     (Will-)=
6    Tara:    =His real name is actually Charlotte ↓aye
7             William.
8             (1.4)
9    Tara:    Aye?
10            (0.8)
11   Tara:    Charlotte.
```

```
12                  (1.3)
13   Tara:          [A:nd she: is actually a girl and you=
14   William:       [(Yeah) (it i:s)
15   Tara:          =don't kno:w.
```

Tara's repair of Benjamin's identification (line 1) attends to his use of the personal name 'William' as displaying a lack of understanding about what 'his real name is actually'. After seeking agreement from Charlotte, Tara continues to inform Benjamin with 'and she is actually a girl and you don't know' (lines 13–15). In this extension to her turn, Tara addresses a further misunderstanding inferred on Benjamin's behalf – that, like Amber, he thought 'William was a boy'. Although Benjamin does not explicate this understanding, Tara attributes it to him on the basis of his incorrect identification at line 1, and his lack of knowledge is explicated when Tara claims 'you don't know' (lines 13 and 15). Here, as in Extract 3, 'actually' is used to correct an inferred understanding.

A fundamental aspect of Charlotte's biography and personal history is that she is a new person in the classroom, and thus has limited access to information about past events and classroom members (recall that Charlotte had only been introduced a few minutes prior). Knowledge, or lack thereof, was made relevant in the way William organized his talk with respect to what Charlotte would or would not know about, as part of doing being Charlotte, a newcomer to the classroom. However, membership as William's sister gave Charlotte limited, second-hand access to some information about the members and activities of the classroom.

Epistemic rights and access are associated with a person's identity or social relations – for example, membership in a family can provide an account for having access or not having access to particular information (see Heritage & Raymond, 2005; Kitzinger, 2005b; Raymond & Heritage, 2006). Recall from Extract 2 that Tara's question regarding what William said about Kapa Haka rested on assumptions about what could and should be known by family members. As William's sister, Charlotte has both rights and obligations to know about her brother and have some access to things he knows about.

In Extract 5 (starting after a 10-second lapse in the conversation), Tara makes an assessment of the likelihood of their class group (or desk group) receiving a prize of ice cream for performance at a task. William's assessment of this claim invokes the matter of how much Charlotte can know about the classroom history.

Extract 5 (7:19–7:37)

```
1   Tara:        Aw we:re gonna lo::se we're not gonna get an
2                i:ce crea::m
3                (0.8)
4   William:     So? we:ve had a lot of i- (0.7) ha:ve we?,
5                (0.3)
6   William:     My bro:ther said (1.0) we've ha:d a lot?
```

7   (3.6)
8   Tara: We wo:n ↓every time bu'=I think they're gonna
9   win toda:y

William begins to question the significance of Tara's prediction ('We're gonna lose, we're not gonna get an icecream') with the retort 'So? we've had a lot'. Use of the collective proterm 'we' maps the speaker as a member of the classroom – but this is problematic, as this is Charlotte's first time in the class. Showing he notices the problem, William's projected account of a collective history is cut off, and he reformulates his turn into a question with 'have we?' This makes the display of knowledge uncertain and invites others to confirm or deny. In a next turn, William accounts for his claim to know something by reporting the speech of 'her' brother, who as a long-term classroom member has access to information regarding how many ice creams had been won. Attributing the information to her brother establishes that Charlotte did not acquire the knowledge first-hand (cf. Sharrock, 1974).

The next extract is very similar to the previous one in terms of the way William attends to, repairs and formulates his epistemic access and limitations as Charlotte.

Extract 6 (20:19–20:29)
1   William: ↑Rose's name is a:cshaly Rosa- (1.3) my: brother
2   said that this gi::rl? .hh her name is
3   Ro:say?

William begins his turn at line 1 with an assertion, offering information about another member of the class (not a member of the current interaction). As with the examples presented earlier (Extracts 3 and 4), 'actually' is used in a turn where the provision of information runs counter to the assumed understandings of the other members (Clift, 2001). William's epistemic claim is cut off and reformulated in a repair that downgrades the status of the knowledge as being second-hand, passed on by her brother. With this repair, William also reformulates his recognitional reference to Rose to the non-recognitional reference 'this girl'. The initial use of the personal name suggests that the talked about person is known to both speaker and recipients (Sacks & Schegloff, 1979). The non-recognitional reference formulation 'this girl' indicates that the person is unknown to the speaker, and in this way Charlotte again positions herself in relation to other class members as new and unfamiliar (see Stivers, 2007).

William's reparative work in Extracts 5 and 6 accomplishes a shift in the epistemic status of the utterance, and the epistemic access of the speaker. By cutting off a still incomplete turn, restarting, and referencing a brother, William's identity as Charlotte is relevant and he downgrades the claim to know about the ice creams, or 'this girl's name'. The sibling relationship to William provides for Charlotte some access to information about the classroom (families talk about their days and the people they talk to with each other), albeit limited by being second-hand. William orients to Tara's epistemic authority with respect to classroom information, with her extended first-hand experience as a classroom member.

The management of epistemic access and claims in this episode demonstrates that and how people 'can be placed within or outside of a particular knowledge domain or territory' (Stivers, 2007: 34), and this epistemic work was accomplished by 'exploiting the structure of both the language and the cultural system'. For instance, linguistic features such as epistemic markers (e.g., 'do you know' and 'actually') were deployed in addition to a cultural framework for knowledge management (e.g., the rights and obligations to 'know' that family membership offers). The production of Charlotte was in this way integrated into the ongoing action, and the relevant correctness of 'her' identity was invoked in the procedures for the management of knowledge.

Referring to and addressing Charlotte

During the interaction both 'Charlotte' and 'William' were used as terms of address and reference. The selection of either name could be used to generate and demonstrate one's orientation to the relevance of the identity switch (or not). Both names do adequate and possibly correct reference to the same person, but the use of one or the other might be seen as relevantly correct (Sacks, 1992) for the purposes of particular instances of interaction.

Even where a person does not have two personal names, the selection of a particular term of address for them involves an orientation to the specific circumstances in which that address is used (Sacks & Schegloff, 1979). A shift from the default form of person reference (typically, a real, given-at-birth personal name) can indicate that the speaker is doing something interactively over and above referring (Schegloff, 1996c). Such references have been termed alternative recognitionals, 'are designed to be fitted specifically to the action in which they are embedded and therefore to work to convey the action and/or account for it' (Stivers, 2007: 31), and can also be used to manage relationships and 'epistemic territories' (p. 34).

Extract 7 demonstrates the kind of trouble caused by William having two possibly relevantly correct personal names. It begins with a complaint by Tara regarding Charlotte's non-attendance at the arts festival the previous night, whereas William 'needed to go'.

Extract 7 (6:35–7:06)

```
1    Tara:   But it's no:t unfair because (.) m:y lovely .h
2            cause Cha:rlotte didn't get to go:
3            (1.6)
4    Tara:   B't Wi:lliam needed to ↓go:.
```

```
5              (1.0)
6     Tara:    Ha:te your brothe:r
7              (2.1)
8     Ben:     Hates- (0.5) you mean you hate William?
9              (2.1)
10    Tara:    But Cha:rlotte's all ri:ght to me.
11             (0.5)
12    Ben:     But he:'s Will(.)i- (.) that's William
13             (.)
14    Tara:    No:
15             (0.2)
16    (Ben):   (Will-)=
17    Tara:    =His real name is actually Charlotte ↓aye
18             William.
19             (1.4)
20    Tara:    Aye?
21             (0.8)
22    Tara:    Charlotte.
```

In Tara's turn at lines 1–2, she appears to begin a positive assessment of Charlotte,[4] which is contrasted in line 6 with a strong negative assessment of William. William is referred to with the marked person reference form 'your brother', suggesting Tara's orientation to Charlotte's relationship with William, and emphasizing their social affiliation as siblings. The emphasis on the affiliation may also serve to distance Tara from William (see Stivers, 2007), and potentially serve to implicate a second assessment by William more strongly in the next slot.

After a 2.1-second silence, Benjamin reformulates Tara's turn – 'you mean you hate William' (line 8). Benjamin is referring to the person in their desk group, but William is also the name of Charlotte's brother – the absent third party to whom Tara was referring. Accordingly Tara appears to give tacit confirmation or acceptance of Benjamin's formulation with her subsequent contrasting assessment, 'but Charlotte's all right to me' (line 10). The possible correctness of both Charlotte and William for doing reference means establishing which of these names is relevantly correct and the framework within which references are to be made sense of (Sacks, 1992). In this case, the ambiguity of references has resulted in a lack of convergence in terms of the identifications being made by Tara and Benjamin, and this is attended to in the subsequent turns.

In pursuit of an intersubjective understanding, Benjamin counters Tara's response with a direct identification of William – 'but he's Will- (.) that's William' (line 12). The indexical reference 'he' is repaired to 'that', suggesting

[4] The abandoned 'my lovely' was possibly intended to be completed with 'sister'. In extracts not discussed here, Tara mapped herself as Charlotte's sister and pursued this throughout the episode. Due to space, and the added complexity that this adds to the episode, we have not addressed Tara and Charlotte's sibling relationship in this chapter.

an orientation to the problems in referring to gender in this case, as, like the names, both 'he' and 'she' could be correct (see below). The replacement with a gender-neutral reference could also address the problems in making a locally subsequent reference following Tara's use of 'Charlotte' (Schegloff, 1996c). The proper indexical to use here would be 'she', which would contradict the identification of William the boy. The pro-term 'that' works in this case as a unique and non-ambiguous indexical reference and identification.

Tara rejects the identification offered by Benjamin (line 14), and informs him that 'his real name is actually Charlotte' (line 17) (the possibly incorrect gender reference, 'his', is not noticed in this instance). Tara invites verification of this by seeking agreement from William (line 17–18). An agreement is not made, and is pursued by Tara with the repeat of her prompt 'aye' (line 20). Tara then adds the name 'Charlotte' as a delayed increment at line 22. The replacement repair displays Tara's understanding that her address term was a source of trouble – the lack of response was due to her incorrect use of 'William' – and that a response (and alignment) may be contingent on the correct name being used. Tara's repair attends to the possibility that the absent response and agreement are because 'Charlotte' has not been properly referred to, and has not technically yet been invited to speak next.

As indicated by Benjamin's repair of the pro-term 'he's' in Extract 7, indexical reference to William (or Charlotte) could be problematic due to the ambiguity of his gender membership. Like the names 'William' and 'Charlotte', both the pro-terms 'he' and 'she' can possibly be relevantly correct for doing reference to William, and thus this everyday practice for referring can become a point of trouble.[5] On the other hand, the use of 'she' and 'her' in making reference to William served to display that the pretend, female identity of Charlotte was being referred to, and was thus relevant for establishing and maintaining the identity switch. In this way indexical reference served as a resource for the organization of action and understanding within the sequence.

That either 'he' or 'she' could be considered to be relevantly correct was observable in instances of repair with which members corrected their own or others' gendered pro-term use. In Extract 8, Tara is telling Amber about Charlotte for the first time, and initiates repair on her own pro-term usage:

Extract 8 (18:37–18:41)
1   Tara: Yah because you: kno:w hi- (.) her bro:ther?,
2   the:y >the:y are-< (0.6) thar tentical twins?

Tara begins to say 'his', but this is cut off before completion, and then replaced with 'her'. The self-repair is accomplished with minimal disruption to the

---

[5] See Kessler and McKenna (1978) for a discussion of problems with referring to people with a cross-gender identity.

trajectory of her turn. While it ensures an attention to the use of the correct identity, the displayed relevance of gender in this extract is to do correct reference (Kitzinger, 2007b).

In other instances, repair of an indexical reference was initiated by someone other than the speaker of the reference, and such cases typically caused more disruption to the progression of the turn or sequence in progress. In such cases, the progression of the sequence rested on first establishing and applying a relevantly correct reference for William/Charlotte (see Heritage, 2007).

Extract 9 (17:09 – 17:23)

```
1   Tara:       He is so: y=y=yeah you a::re: so so so so (.h)
2               so::: not gonna tell them cos he's coming to my
3               ↑house
4               (1.1)
5   Tara:       ↑Aye Will[i-
6   William:             [She:
7               (0.5)
8   Tara:       Cos she is coming to (our) hou=↑aye
9               Charlotte.
```

In this case, repair of a gendered pro-term is other-initiated, when at line 6 William notices Tara's use of 'he' at lines 1 and 2. William's noticing of Tara's indexical reference is somewhat delayed – it is not until Tara begins to invite a next turn from William with a prompt for agreement (line 5) that William initiates repair on the pro-term used earlier. He does so in overlap with Tara, which effectively ignores and cuts off her turn in progress, and the action she was launching with it. It is interesting that William repairs the pro-term reference, rather than the similarly 'incorrect' personal name reference, projected in Tara's turn at line 5. By going back to the initial incorrect reference ('he', lines 1 and 2), the repair indicates that the progression of the sequence (and alignment with Tara) will be conditional on correct reference being made first. In doing the repair (lines 8–9), Tara recycles the last unit of her prior turn (lines 2–3), and uses the repaired indexical in her reformulation. She also repairs the address form – replacing 'William' with 'Charlotte'. By repairing the incorrect reference and address forms Tara gets the action of the sequence back on track.

Selection of one of two possible personal names, or of a masculine or feminine pro-term, was one way in which William as Charlotte was displayed and made relevant for the organization of the local social action. References to William/Charlotte or him/her displayed understandings and stance with regard to participation in the episode of pretence. In the extracts discussed so far, gender is invoked in terms of the feminine name, the account for short hair, and doing correct person reference.

Gender reference and categorization

In addition to the relevance of membership in the category *girl* for doing identification and correct reference, William's membership as a girl was also consequential for his performance as Charlotte. William, like Agnes (Garfinkel, 1967), could not simply declare himself to be female, but had to work actively to accomplish membership in this category. It was suggested that William's account for having short hair (in Extract 1) displayed an orientation to the relevance of his gender membership, and was used to do being a girl. Membership as a girl invokes a range of attributes and activities that are expectedly done by members of this category. In this section we discuss how the children attended to William's membership in the category *girl* and to the adequacy of his performance of the associated category-bound activities and attributes.

Extract 10 contains an assessment regarding what 'Charlotte' sounds like, and invokes William's membership as a girl – and potentially also his membership as a *pretend* girl.

Extract 10 (14:01–14:20)

```
1    William:   .H ↑↑o:w
2               (0.4)
3    Ben:       .hh
4    Tara:      .hhHH (.) .hh↑↑hhhhhhh
5    William:   kHH::!
6               (1.9)
7    Tara:      Charlotte, (1.1) you sound luk- a b:o::y
8               (0.5)
9    William:   You sound like a aWo:ma:n.
10              (0.8)
11   William:   .hh
12   Ben:       [.h
13   Tara:      [I a:m a wo:ma:n
14              (0.6)
15   William:   I said O::ld woma:n
```

Tara notices and assesses how Charlotte sounds at line 7 – 'like a boy' (possibly with reference to the sounds at lines 1 and 5). The assessment involves an orientation to an inconsistency between category membership (girl) and attribute (sound of voice), making gender noticeable, accountable, relevant and consequential. As Tara's turn is addressed to Charlotte, it could be heard as being done within the bounds of the pretend identity. However, it also makes this pretence somewhat vulnerable – William's performance of a girl has been noticed to be inadequate, and in a next turn William might need to defend either his legitimate membership as a girl, or the adequacy of his performance as a girl.

Either way, the assessment requires that William should establish or maintain his relevantly correct gender membership in a next turn. If William is to 'do being Charlotte', he needs to display this membership by 'doing being a girl'.

William responds at line 9 with 'you sound like a woman'. The response mirrors the formulation used by Tara, that is '*you sound like X, you are not an X*'. Tara's assessment could potentially be disagreed with (i.e., 'I'm not a boy' or 'I don't sound like a boy') but instead William issues a return or a retort, a second insult which recycles the formulation of the first, and in which 'the truth value of a statement is not at issue, a prior move is responded to with a reciprocal action' (M. H. Goodwin, 1990: 152; see also Evaldsson, 2005).

West and Zimmerman (1987) noted with respect to Agnes that one of the challenges she faced was preserving her gender categorization as female. The possible threat to William's identity as a girl, made by Tara, is avoided by William's attention to the *action* rather than the content of the utterance. The retort at line 9 treats the turn *as an insult* rather than an assessment, and in this way the second insult can be used as a 'way of giving a special characterization to the first insult as something that is not serious and is not going to be heard as serious' (Sacks, 1992, I: 160). By making insulting rather than categorizing as the relevant action orienting to, William characterizes Tara's turn as a non-serious challenge to his gender membership. He preserves his categorization as a girl without having to assert his membership directly or account for how he sounds.

William is further rebutted by Tara's declaration that she is 'a woman', a retort that may make use of the apparent flexibility of the use of age-based gender categories (i.e., 'girls' can refer to a group of 50-year-old women). This retort also confirms the formula for the insult, and the non-serious nature of attributing membership to a category one is not a member of. However, William's return in this case has invoked the matter of truth, and is treated as something to be disagreed with by Tara. With a reformulation at line 15, William claims that he had used another category – 'old woman'– which, by specifying 'stage-of-life', is one that Tara really cannot claim membership in.

In the turns following Extract 10, Tara and William have a play-fight in an extension of the tone of this particular sequence (note that Tara says 'just jokes' in line 2 in Extract 11). The resolution of this is presented in Extract 11, lines 2 and 4, after which Benjamin reinvokes the earlier sequence and the assessment of what Charlotte sounds like.

Extract 11 (14:48–15:08)

```
1   William:    .hhhhh[h
2   Tara:             [Ju:st jokes.
3               (0.4)
4   Tara:       'Kay le:t's just get on.
5               (1.1)
6   Ben:        You sou:nd like Willia:m, (0.2) Cha:rlo:tte
```

7		(4.4)
8	William:	.HHihih
9	Tara:	A gi:rl does not go like that Charlo:tte
10		(1.6)
11	William:	And a bo[::(u):y goes like
12	Tara:	[A (big)(el) is <u>lovely</u>

At line 6 Benjamin initiates a new action sequence with his assessment, 'you sound like William, (0.2) Charlotte', which alludes to the earlier sequence by recycling Tara's insult (Extract 10, line 7). Like Tara's, Benjamin's assessment is addressed to Charlotte.[6] However, while Tara assessed William's performance as a girl, Benjamin can be heard to be assessing William's more general identity performance as Charlotte. To sound like another person is not accountable in the way that sounding like a member of another gender category is – unless, as is the case here, the relevant and correct identity of a person is potentially ambiguous. In this sense, Benjamin's assessment could possibly undermine the achieved status of 'William as Charlotte'.

In response to William's small giggle at line 8, or to some non-verbal action during the preceding 4.4-second gap (line 7), Tara says 'a girl does not go like that Charlotte'. This turn involves a shift in the formulation of the insults so far, and by reinvoking Charlotte's gender membership Tara uses a different categorization device from that used by Benjamin. Tara's turn may also be heard to maintain Charlotte's identity in the face of a potential challenge to it posed by Benjamin. While Benjamin's turn alluded to Charlotte's 'real' identity as William, Tara retains the pretence by orienting to William as a girl – albeit not a very good one. In this sense, the attention to gender, although critical, may serve as safer territory in that it preserves the pretence, and the identity of William as a girl called Charlotte.

It could be argued that Tara in the previous two extracts is, in some way, instructing William in the ways of being a girl – correcting, rather than undermining his performance. Seeing William not doing a good job of doing being a girl is seeing William's behaviour as a gender performance. C. W. Butler (2008) has described other instances of 'noticed inadequacies' in performances in a pretend role such as teacher or student. One does not necessarily have to be convincing as a member of a category in order to display and maintain membership in that category; but others may monitor one's activities as a member of that category, and call one to account for not meeting category-bound expectations. In this way, membership in pretend categories is monitored and regulated.

William's response at line 11 ('and a boy goes like') appears to downgrade the relevance that Tara's declaration has for him personally and for the sequence

---

[6] See Lerner (2003) on how post-positioned personal names can be used to highlight the relevance of the person being addressed for the action being done in a turn.

of action. The use of the conjunction 'and' to tie the turn to Tara's generates a collaboratively produced two-part list of 'attributes of category members'. Although William's turn might be heard constructively to be extending an action initiated by Tara, in the context of the ongoing interaction it actually appears to shift the action launched by Tara's turn. William shifts attention away from his inadequate performance as a girl by invoking the relevance of masculine behaviour and membership. The category *boys* is used by William *to do categorization* – essentially, to make a general description about what members of this category do – and this categorization work appears to be used to avoid the particularization that Tara's turn seemed intended to do (Schegloff, 2007a).

Throughout these potential challenges to William's cross-gender identity, we might argue that William manages to preserve his categorization as female through his management of the prior turns and responses. Attention to the truth as to whether William really was a girl was diverted by means of hearing and doing an insult. Following a few inaudible turns of talk after Extract 11, William is explicitly categorized as a boy, shown in Extract 12.

Extract 12 (15:12–15:30)

```
1    Tara:       mBo::ys.
2                (2.0)
3                [X    X  ((banging on a desk))
4    William:    [.Hi.hi that's you Ben
5                (.)
6    Ben:        No:
7                (0.3)
8    Ben:        Wi:lliam
9                (1.0)
10   Ben:        Ma:y[be:
11   Amber:          [And you Wi:llia:m
12                (1.8)
13   Ben:        Ch[a:rlotte
14   Tara:         [No::::
15                (2.3)
16   Amber:      Because he's a bo::y (.) an he is'in'a gi::rl
```

Given the problems hearing the preceding turns, it is unclear what Tara's 'boys' at line 1 is in reference to, but following this William identifies Benjamin as a member of this category, 'that's you Ben' (line 4). William's identification of Benjamin as a boy invokes his own non-membership in this category – the category membership *boys* does not apply to 'her', Charlotte. Benjamin's disagreement ('no') is somewhat ambiguous, but is followed by use of the name 'William', presumably mapping him into the category *boy*. This suggests that Benjamin's disagreement may be orienting to the cross-membership that was implied in William's turn – that by identifying Benjamin as a boy, William identified himself as *not a boy*. Amber also orients to the self-exclusion invoked by William's categorization of Benjamin with her incremental turn unit, 'and you William' (line 11). Amber's turn is tied to William's at line 4 ('that's you Benjamin'), with the conjunction 'and', which uses the mapping of Benjamin to serve as the start of a list, and William's absence from this list as noticeable and accountable. By including William as a member of the category *boys*, Amber offers a candidate categorization of William and possibly invites a clarification or repair from him with respect to his alluded-to exclusion.

Tara negates this categorization (line 14), and Benjamin appears to make a repair of Amber's reference to William, with the replacement 'Charlotte'. Amber, however, continues with an account for her inclusion of William – 'because he's a boy and he isn't a girl' (line 16). The use of 'because' ties the categorization done here to the earlier mapping of William in line 11, and does not directly attend to the relevance of Tara's just-prior negation. Amber's account or argument for William's inclusion is explicit and somewhat extended – asserting not only what 'he is', but also 'what he is not'.

In Extract 12, then, gender is made relevant for the purposes of doing categorization, of explicitly describing membership in a gender category. This work is similar to that done by Tara in informing newcomers of William's new identity – identification of Charlotte and participation in the pretence required recognition of the relevantly correct gender membership. It might be argued that categorization per se is less problematic for the maintenance of Charlotte's identity than the ongoing matter of 'doing gender'. Whether or not William/Charlotte is a girl or boy can in this case be treated as a matter of knowledge, belief and game participation; but more central to the recognition of the correctness of either gender membership is to be able to 'pass' as one or the other.

Closing comments

We have described a number of ways in which William's identity as a girl called Charlotte was generated and made relevant in a stretch of interaction. Shared understandings about Charlotte, and absences of these, were demonstrated throughout the episode in practices such as informing, referring, describing and categorizing. The analysis has drawn on past conversation analytic (CA) findings to identify practices for organizing this particular episode of action, and shown how these practices were used in a locally contingent and relevant way to establish a cross-gender identity. The chapter follows recent CA approaches to the study of gender, which are grounded in the analysis of the action sequences in which gender references and relevancies are deployed and are consequential for what happens in, and/or what is to be understood of, that particular sequence (e.g., Kitzinger, 2007b; Speer, 2005a; Stokoe, 2006;

Weatherall, 2002a). The nature of our data offers a rare glimpse into a case of gender being made relevant, consequential and accountable in an interaction generated by its members.

Our attention has been drawn to those 'trivial but necessary social tasks' that Garfinkel (1967: 108) suggested doing gender involved. The analysis has considered how tasks such as the management of personal history and knowledge are made relevant and invoked in everyday interaction. We have shown that the quite remarkable claim of a change in identity and gender was accomplished by rather ordinary conversational procedures. Furthermore, it was in everyday practices such as description and reference that Tara and the others made the identity of Charlotte known about and relevant for the interaction.

We might consider Garfinkel's description of Agnes's passing activities in relation to William's passing as Charlotte:

> The scrutiny she paid to appearances; her concerns for adequate motivation, relevance, evidence and demonstration; her sensitivity to devices of talk; her skill in detecting and managing 'tests' were attained as part of her mastery of trivial but necessary social tasks. (Garfinkel, 1967: 108)

Charlotte's scrutiny of appearances evidenced in her hair-cut story, her concern for adequate motivation and so on in terms of managing knowledge and the relevance of correct reference, and a 'sensitivity to devices of talk' evident in her attention to indexicals show that and how 'trivial but necessary social tasks' were managed in this episode. Charlotte's management of assessments or insults, for example, demonstrated her skill in noticing and dealing with what might be considered tests to her correct and relevant gender identity. The tasks that Agnes described in her biographical account of her daily life are illustrated here over the course of a 30-minute interaction.

While Garfinkel had only Agnes's accounts for how her gender membership was made relevant in the course of her everyday interactions with others, these data demonstrate how that interactional relevance might play out in everyday conversation. Whatever gender membership William (or Tara) claimed was correct was largely irrelevant if the other members did not share an understanding and recognition of this membership as being relevant and correct. In this sense, the relevance and performance of Charlotte's gender membership were far from an individual responsibility; 'doing gender' was a collaborative accomplishment.

Engendering children's play: Person reference
in children's conflictual interaction

Marjorie Harness Goodwin

Introduction

This chapter examines how children employ gendered membership categories in the midst of their everyday talk. Feminist conversation analysts have
devoted considerable attention to explicating the issues entailed in providing
grounded analyses of how gender is invoked, negotiated and oriented to in
conversational exchanges,[1] how it 'creeps into talk' (Hopper & LeBaron, 1998:
32–3). Making use of work by Harvey Sacks (1972; 1992, I) on membership
categorization analysis,[2] Stokoe (2008a) has recently called for a close examination of the kinds of actions being done with membership categories in close
association with analysis of the sequential environments in which such categories repetitively occur. Stokoe (2009) argues that the particular categories that
are selected from an array of possibilities[3] are significant because through their
choices[4] people orchestrate social actions (Hester & Eglin, 1997); for example,
accusation, justification, praise, etc.

Work on children's language and gender for some time was dominated
by the notion of contrastive male and female personalities, an idea put forward by Maccoby and Jacklin (1974) in the 1970s, revitalized by Maltz and
Borker (1982) with their separate-world hypothesis in 1982 (for a thoughtful
review of the controversy see Kyratzis, 2001a), and buttressed by Gilligan's

---

[1] For a review of the debates between Schegloff, Wetherell and Billig regarding how gender
relevance in interaction must be demonstrated in the participants' orientations, see Stokoe and
Wetherall (2002a). See also Speer (2005a), Kitzinger (2000a; 2006) and Benwell and Stokoe
(2006: 84–5).

[2] Explicating the distinction between membership categorization analysis (MCA) and conversation analysis (CA), Benwell and Stokoe (2006: 38) argue, 'Whereas CA focuses on the turn by
turn sequencing and organisation of talk, MCA also pays attention to the situated and reflexive
use of categories in everyday and institutional interaction, as well as in interview media and
other textual data.'

[3] Early work by cognitive anthropologist Ward Goodenough (1965) argued for the relevance of
identity selection from a set of possibilities. Goodenough used the term 'identity' to refer to an
aspect of self that makes a difference in how one's rights and duties distribute to specific others.
Goodenough's work was read and cited by Sacks in his thesis (1966).

[4] Work which examines membership categorizaton from an ethnomethodological perspective
among children includes C. D. Baker (2000) and Danby (1998).

Ethnographic background: An implicit hetero-normative social order

The neighbourhood and school settings I have observed differed with respect to the social arrangements of participants. The Maple Street neighbourhood in Philadelphia provided a very rich setting for interaction; there a range of different categories of children – younger and older, girls and boys – are co-present while participating in a number of diverse activities, for example chores and babysitting, that intersect with play. During such caretaking activities girls display their authority with respect to younger children. In North American schools, by way of contrast, children generally play in same-age and same-sex groups (an arrangement that is atypical of peer groups worldwide; Harkness & Super, 1985). Gender separation is influenced by children's own preferences as well as by teachers' notions of appropriate group divisions (Thorne, 1993).

The children I studied on Maple Street in Philadelphia in 1970–1 (M. H. Goodwin, 1990), as well as those I studied in Los Angeles during the late 1990s (M. H. Goodwin, 2006), displayed an orientation towards an implicit heterosexual social order (Kitzinger, 2005a: 222; 2006: 165) in their folklore and play.[10] In his *Lectures on Conversation* Sacks (1992, I: 249) describes the nature of *category-bound activities* by stating, 'Many activities are taken by Members to be done by some particular or several particular categories of Members where the categories are categories from membership categorization devices.' While playing jump rope (skipping) in same-sex groups, the popular rhymes in both girls' and boys' groups[11] at the middle-class Hanley School, Los Angeles, depicted the category-bound activities (Sacks, 1992) of male/female romantic relationships; for example, 'Cinderella, dressed in yella, went upstairs to kiss a fella. Made a mistake and kissed a snake. How many doctors did it take?' Category-bound activities entailing heterosexual relations were also featured in the rhyme 'Ice Cream Soda, Vanilla Berry Punch. Tell me the name of your Honey Bunch.' Following this rhyme, spectators recited the alphabet from A to Z until the jumper missed. When this occurred, the spectators in the girls' group would yell, 'Oh, you marry Tommy (a boy's name)!' while, in the boys' group, jumpers 'married' girls: 'You marry Carrie (a girl's name)!' At Hanley School among fourth grade girls, the text of a favorite underground song called 'The Bedroom Song' made reference to heterosexual relationships with the

---

[10] J. Butler (1990a: 140) considers folklore a 'ritual social drama' and discusses it as the 'stylized repetition of acts'.

[11] Lanclos (2003: 84) reports that in Belfast clapping and skipping games are chanted or sung almost exclusively by girls. On Maple Street in Philadelphia (M. H. Goodwin, 1990) this was true as well. However, at Hanley School boys enjoyed playing jump rope, as it was part of the school sports curriculum.

refrain 'It felt like heaven', and 'Let's do it again.' The pro-terms used specified 'he' taking off 'her' shoe and 'he' kissing 'her' knee.[12]

While playing house, a hetero-normal social order was oriented towards in the depiction of role relations as well. Though boys seldom played house with girls at Hanley School, girls constituted heterosexual role relationships as primary to their 'house' identity. In the midst of organizing play both Lisa and Janis competed for the same boy (Jason, a classmate) to be the partner they were 'married to' or their 'boyfriend'.[13]

Extract 1

1	Lisa:	Yeah. I'm married to him.
2		You're married to his brother.
3	Janis:	They're exactly the same.
4	Nichole:	YOU GUYS!
5	Janis:	Jason's my boyfriend. ((chanting))

Henley (1995) and Cameron (1998b) have argued that we need to consider how gender interacts with other kinds of identity categories; for example, class and age. As playing house got under way the girls all wanted to be teenagers with boyfriends. Class as well as gender proved to be relevant to the development of roles in category-bound activities. When Janis specified that the girls would have to 'say your life, your future', Ruth interpreted Janis's directive as requiring both a specification of what type of car she drove and who her boyfriend was.

Extract 2

1	Janis:	Okay. I point to you, you guys have to say your name,
2		Your life, your future, and junk like that.
3		Okay. Ruth. Go. Shh. Silence. Go Ruth.
4	Ruth:	My name's Monique,
5		No actually- what's my name.
6	Janis:	Just use Monique.
7		Just use Monique.
8	Ruth:	Okay fine. My name's Monique,
9		And I have a black Corvet,
10		A::nd, my boyfriend is, you know who.

Heterosexual relationships were also oriented-to features in the talk of fourth grade boys at Hanley School; they discussed girls as people they liked to 'flirt with' in paired relationships.

---

[12] The full text of the song is given in the appendix to this chapter.
[13] Data are transcribed according to the system developed by Gail Jefferson, outlined in Sacks *et al.* (1974: 731–3).

Extract 3

1	Alan:	Eh. What else.
2	Dan:	Oh Denzel- Denzel flirts with Aretha,
3		*((pats Denzel on back))*
4	Denzel:	*((play hits Dan))*
5	Dan:	Okay. I flirt with Emi, *((puts arm around Denzel's*
6		*shoulder))*
7	Denzel:	Here comes Melissa.
8	Dan:	And Alan flirts- I mean Bruce flirts with Melissa.
9		And we usually like-
10		Walk around, sayin' like- funny stuff.

Thus boys as well as the girls displayed in their talk an orientation to a taken-for-granted heterosexual world (Kitzinger, 2005a; Stokoe & Smithson, 2002), one in which boys 'flirt with' girls, and individuals kiss, marry and 'do it again' with members of the opposite sex.

'Girl' and 'boy' as terms of reference in comparison sequences

The terms 'girl' and 'boy' constituted a major set of identity categories in terms of which children differentiated group members. While Maple Street boys were sitting together on the front steps they would compare the activities of girls with those of boys (rather than, for example, using age or neighbourhood as a feature of differentiation).

Extract 4

1	Malcolm:	The girls do the same thing all the time.
2		Play rope.
3	Ossie:	That's why Bea always go in the-
4		my house and wanna play with my top.
5	Malcolm:	Different times of year
6		<u>we</u> do different things.
7	Ossie:	Boys' games <u>better</u> than girls'.

Speer and Potter (2002: 159) argue that one of the ways that participants 'do gender' is observable 'in the way they present it (and certain behaviours or "category bound activities" (Sacks, 1992)) as normative'. In Extract 5, boys attempt to 'make non-normative or "transgressive" behaviours *morally accountable*' (Speer, 2005a: 119) by attempting to lay claim to particular activities as exclusive to their gendered cohort. When girls returned from turtle hunting and began to describe their adventures falling in the creek, boys were quick to critique girls, arguing that girls were doing 'boys' stuff'. In response, girls produced counters, challenging the boys' categorization.

Extract 5

*((Bea has just returned from hunting for turtles in a city
creek))*

1	Bea:	Ruby felled in the water.=
2		Her <u>sneak</u>ers flew way over there!
3		Eh heh-heh!
4	Chopper:	Girls doin' boys' <u>stuff.</u>
5	Sister:	Girls doin' // <u>boys'</u> stuff,
6	Bea:	Like <u>what.</u>
7	Chopper:	Goin' down the park.
8		Getting in that water.
9		Collectin' <u>rocks</u>!

Competition between girls and boys was also evident in the practices girls used
actively to conceal what they were doing from boys, and prevent them from
entering into their activities. In Extract 6, Martha (age 10) discusses how she
wanted to prevent boys from finding out about a secret activity of the girls,
making rings from glass bottle tops.

Extract 6

((Girls planning strategy to keep ring making secret from boys))

1	Martha:	If the boys try to follow us here,
2		Let's tell 'em-
3		Let's act just like we don't even know.
4		*h Just say "<u>N:o</u>." You know.

In the Hanley School group I studied, the terms 'girl' and 'boy' were also used
to make reference to categories of person who were positioned in adversarial
arrangements. Explicit mention of the division of competing teams by gender,
for example, occurred in the talk about play among third graders (children age
8–9) at Hanley School. As Sandra and Vanessa were talking about basketball
teams that were being organized in opposing teams ('girls against boys'), girls
were formulated as agents and boys as the recipients of the girls' victorious
actions.

Extract 7

1	Sandra:	Am I gonna be on <u>your</u> team? *((to Vanessa))*
2	Vanessa:	And <u>Kath</u>y and <u>Madi</u>son. In other words it's girls a-
3		<u>Girls</u> against <u>boys.</u>
4	Sandra:	Oh great. We <u>smoosh</u> boys.
5		Girls <u>smoosh</u> boys.

In the neighbourhood of Philadelphia as well as the playgrounds of Los
Angeles, and across various age groups I have studied, the terms 'girl' and
'boy' were used to designate members of groups situated in oppositional
arrangements.

Borderwork, power and the collaborative construction of gendered oppositional groups

With respect to how social space is defended in a Guyanese rumshop, Sidnell (2003: 330) argues, 'It is clear that the "all-male" or "all-female" character of an interactive setting is not something that simply happens – rather, it is an accountable and contingent accomplishment requiring several different kinds of interactional work.' As a feature of their competitive play, the girls I studied organized their groups in terms of same-sex divisions, and actively worked to defend their space from boys.[14] Thorne (1993) reports that boys in the playground frequently interrupt girls' games or violate their social space; I found that Latina girls in downtown LA actively worked to keep boys from intruding into their hopscotch grid (M. H. Goodwin, 1998: 25), using direct commands such as 'Get out of the way!' or 'Go back! Go back!' With respect to forms of 'borderwork' (Thorne, 1993: 64–88) among the peer group at Hanley School, while the girls were jumping rope, boys made use of mitigated requests to enter into the girls' arena; these were answered by flat refusals from the girls:

Extract 8

1	Stephen:	*((makes a nonverbal bid to join the group))*
2	Janis:	Stephen we're having a contest.
3		[We're having a contest.
4	Stephen:	[Can I try it?
5	Janis:	Well not <u>really</u> because-
6	Melissa:	Because there's <u>three</u> against- one.

An asymmetry of power developed with respect to boys attempting to enter the girls' game, and girls rejecting them. In Extract 9, occurring 20 seconds later, the boys were momentarily permitted into the girls' play space (lines 3–5). However, when one of the group members argued that the game should be exclusively 'us', Janis revised her granting of permission and stated 'Oh <u>yeah</u>. =You're not part of our gang. So you can't.' (lines 10–11), and the boys were excluded.

Extract 9

1	Denzel:	Can you guys just- turn the rope?
2		eh heh-heh!
3	Janis:	Okay <u>fine</u>. You can <u>play</u>.
4		You can play.
5		[You can <u>play</u>.
6	Stephen:	[Hey. Can I play if I-
7	Emi:	<u>No</u>:: <u>us.</u> *((shaking head))*

---

[14] Sidnell (2003) discusses how social space is defended as exclusively male in a Guyanese rumshop.

8	Denzel:	I don't want to do that
9		Mexi[co thing
10	Janis:	[Oh yeah. =You're not part of our gang.
11		So you can't.
12	Boys:	((remain silent in the play space, then move))

With respect to the operative situational identities (Zimmerman, 1998)[15] in this example, Stephen (line 6) makes use of a request, a highly mitigated (Labov & Fanshel, 1977) way of asking to play, as it constitutes an action which seeks permission rather than demanding the right to play. What he gets in response is a flat defiant refusal, with Emi's utterance 'No:: us' accompanied by a lateral head-shake (line 7). A form of asymmetry of role relations unfolds, with boys making use of polite actions that request, and girls (as initiators of the play and more skilful players), with their ability to grant or refuse admission to the game, displaying a position of power vis-à-vis the boys. In her account for refusing permission – 'You're not part of our gang. So you can't.' – Janis formulates the operative identity categories as 'our gang' and outsiders to her gang. In response, the boys remain silenced on the sidelines for a while, and eventually move away. The responses to the account prohibiting access to the game provide a way to investigate the emergent local identities of requesting party-denying party.

Asymmetrical relationships of power are thus observable in the way the game is played (though not the types of asymmetry generally assumed by proponents of dominance theory (Lakoff, 1973), with boys responding to their being excluded by becoming silent and later leaving the scene). In this example the right to control the game is not exclusively based on gender, but rather is largely dependent on skill in the game; in fact, a month later, after the boys practised hard and became skilled players as well as competent organizers of the group, both boys and girls delivered bald imperatives to one another in the course of a game.

Later during the lunchtime period when the girls permitted boys to play with them, they once again made use of bald imperatives to tell boys how they should locate themselves in space, and what they needed to do with the rope. In the process of orchestrating this activity the terms 'girl' and 'boy' were used to differentiate teams, tell who was required to hold the end of a rope, and indicate how team members were to be positioned spatially.

Extract 10

((Organizing the game))

1	Sarah:	KAY! GIRLS ON THIS SIDE,
2		Girls on this side,

---

[15] See Sacks (1992, II: 327) and Benwell and Stokoe (2006: 74–8) for a discussion of 'operative identities' in the midst of an offer sequence.

3	Janis:	Here. Get it!
4		*((referring to the end of the rope))*
5	Denzel:	What the heck <u>is</u> it.
6	Janis:	ONE BOY! // HERE! Hold the end.
7		Hold it! *((throwing rope to Denzel and pointing))*
8	Melissa:	<u>BOYS ON THAT</u> SIDE!
9		Get on the other <u>side</u> .
10	Boys:	*((Move to the side Melissa directs them))*

In Extracts 9 and 10, girls displayed a clear ability to tell the boys what to do; this in part was because girls, as more skilled players, controlled access to the game. However, after a month's intensive practice the boys became almost as competent as the girls in jumping rope. One lunch period the boys and girls agreed to compete to see who could jump the longest. On this occasion the terms 'girl' and 'boy' were used to differentiate specific team groupings. In Extract 11, Angela constructs the participants who are 'racing against' one another as 'we' and 'you two'. Malcolm subsequently transforms this utterance into 'two girls versus two of the boys' and makes explicit the categories the pronouns reference in his proposal for how opposing teams should be constituted.

Extract 11

1	Angela:	Okay, We'll racing against you two.
2	Malcolm:	Okay. Me and Ron versus two- (.) <u>girls</u>.
3		Two <u>girls</u> versus two of the <u>boys</u>.

As the boys organized practice for the contest Malcolm used the terms 'girl' and 'boy' to orchestrate relevant spatial divisions in the group. More explicitly, Malcolm gave instructions that designated boys and girls as distinct groups, tied to separate territories, producing a form of gender exclusivity.

Extract 12

		((The girls have practiced several minutes))
1	Malcolm:	All the girls have to go bye bye.
2	Girls:	*((Girls start to move to another area))*
3	Malcolm:	Okay. Now the <u>boys</u> get to practice.
4	Ron:	This is our home <u>field</u>.

By complying with the instructions that Malcolm gave them, the girls demonstrated their shared orientation to gender as a relevant feature of the local scene. Later that day girls celebrated their victories in the jump rope contest with elaborate high-five handslaps, while exclaiming '<u>Yeah</u> the girls are winning!' Teams of girls against boys were clearly oriented towards in the children's talk during the activity of competitive jump rope.

Gender in disputes over rights and justifications

The previous examples demonstrate how girls and boys may explicitly differentiate their groups along gendered lines in the midst of competitive exchanges, disputes between teams or talk about competition. Gender categories were also invoked to lay claim to certain (naturalized) rights that adhered to particular types of activities, in attempts to exert positions of power. By examining such practices we can take stock of how cohorts of individuals attempt to achieve domination over others.

J. Butler (1990a: 140), discussing the playground as a site for the performance of gender, proposes that the 'stylized repetition of acts' in an exterior space can inform us about local notions of gender. As Speer (2005a: 63–5) cautions, though Butler talks about discourse and iterability, she does not analyse actual features of interaction in specific contexts to examine how participants constitute their gendered social worlds. Sociologist Thorne (1993: 82–3), investigating the play patterns of boys in the USA, has documented how in school playgrounds boys control as much as ten times more space than girls, if one considers large playing fields and basketball courts.

Example 13 provides a striking example of how both fifth grade boys and girls at Hanley School orient to gendered categories as relevant features differentiating groups in the midst of a dispute on the soccer field. The sequence occurs during school lunchtime as a group of eight fifth grade girls decide they will forgo their usual thirty minutes of eating and talking in favour of securing a soccer ball and beating the boys onto the field. As they begin to organize their teams on the soccer field, boys arrive, and the following debate occurs. In a move arguing his position that the soccer playing field rightfully belongs to an exclusive category of persons, boys, Miguel provides his justification with the account, 'It's more boys than girls.' (line 3).

Extract 13

((Ron, Miguel and Manuel approach the girls on the field.))
1 Emi: We have it today.
2 Ron: We play soccer every day.= okay?
3 Miguel: It's more boys than girls.
4 Emi: So? Your point?
5 Ron: This is our field.
6 Emi: It's not your field. Did you pay for it? No.
7   Your name is not written on this land.
8 Kathy: Mine is. K-A-T-H-Y! *((writing in the dirt))*

The players who are in contention for the field are identified with respect to their gender (line 3); Miguel argues that the difference in number of participants of his gender cohort playing soccer legitimates use rights to the field. His account affiliates with Ron's immediately prior statement. Ron's account for why the field belongs to the boys formulates gender as associated with habitual activity, in what might loosely be considered a form of 'adverse possession', keeping out others and physically occupying it exclusively and openly as if it were their own for an extended period of time: 'We [the boys] play soccer every day.=okay?'

An alternative type of justification for rights to play occurs in what follows in Emi's talk. The 'so?' in the initial part of Emi's next turn (line 4) provides a dismissive stance, what Halliday and Hasan (1976: 207–17) describe as a ' "disclaimer" (an action that denies the relevance of a prior action rather than disagreeing with it)' towards the previous utterance; here the 'so' treats the prior act as irrelevant. Emi in line 6 refutes Ron's statement that 'This is our [the boys'] field.' Emi's move interprets the boys' arguments as ill founded, as lacking legitimacy or a 'point'. In her response countering Ron and Miguel, Emi invokes another possible criterion legitimating use of the field when in line 6 she argues, 'Did you pay for it?' Here, in opposition to Miguel and Ron, who argue that the power to control adheres in a category that is gendered and legitimated through continuous possession, Emi counters, undermining this justification, by arguing that this matter should be determined with respect to whose parents have paid for the field, indexing access to wealth as the relevant criterion.

To understand better the types of explanations given here we need to examine the cultural underpinnings of certain types of accounts and categorizations. Evaldsson (2005), for example, in her analysis of categorizations among a multi-ethnic peer group in Sweden, finds it essential to make use of ethnographic knowledge of children and school settings to understand children's insults. She argues that 'categorizations are bound up with particular actions (category-bound activities) or characteristics (natural predicates) that both constitute and reflect conventional expectations of normative behaviours within a specific group and setting' (p. 768). Evaldsson found that in making negative assessments, possessions, clothing, limited language proficiency in Swedish, ethnicity and sexuality were all-important topical concerns relevant within the frame of insults. In order to understand why particular aspects of self were viewed in a negative light – for example, why Swedish-language proficiency was evaluated in a particular way – she found it important to make use of her ethnographic knowledge of the language ideology in the school setting. Indeed, Stokoe and Smithson (2002: 84) argue that despite claims to an 'unmotivated "analytic mentality"' researchers working within the conversation analysis framework 'use their background knowledge, either acknowledged or unacknowledged, in the process of doing analysis'.

The particular trope the boys utilize is one regularly invoked by those in authority in the playground. On the day of the soccer dispute, gender differences were clearly oriented towards in the explanations that the male aide, the authority figure on the scene, gave to the girls for why they should vacate the field. The male college-aged playground assistant took the side of the boys, and addressed the girls explicitly with statements such as 'GIRLS! LET THE BOYS HAVE THEIR FIELD!' In Extract 14, we see that the playground assistant formulates the activity of the girls' standing up for their rights as 'giving me an attitude'.

Extract 14

```
1   Aide:    Listen to me. And stop giving me an attitude.
2            Do you understand? (0.4) Do you understand?
3            Listen. I'm not gonna take this attitude.
4            You girls came out here on Monday and left the field.
5            The boys couldn't play soccer.
```

In Extract 15, the male playground assistant addressed the groups of protagonists as 'girls' (lines 1, 28) and 'boys' (line 2) and provided an account (indexing a category-bound activity) that affiliated with the reason provided by the boys: 'The boys are always here playing soccer' (line 25).

Extract 15

```
1    Aide:     GIRLS! Go somewhere else.
2              The boys are coming to play
3              and you took over their field.
4              That's not cool.
5    Girls:    NO!! ((raucous screaming for several seconds))
6    Melissa:  Miss Harper said we could!!
[30 seconds omitted]
25   Aide:     The boys are always here playing soccer.
26             You can go over there and play soccer?
27             They can't go on the black top.
28             You girls can go anywhere.
29             And do what you're doing.
30             Am I right or am I wrong.
31   Melissa:  Why can't they go anywhere.
32   Aide:     They can't go anywhere.
33             They can't go onto the blacktop and play soccer.
34             Somebody's gonna fall and
35             [break their knee.
36   Sandra:   [Well that means [we-
37   Kathy:                     [Well neither can we!
```

The aide provided descriptions of the two groups that differ with respect to routine category-bound activities as well as spaces; boys require a particular kind of space (because of the potential danger of falling), whereas girls can go 'anywhere'. The girls, however, do not go along with these depictions; Kathy (line 37) explicitly challenges the aide, stating that girls as a group are subject to the same sorts of potential dangers of falling as are the boys.

Equally important with respect to the forms of justifications that are given are the types of sequencings that occur in the dispute. Emi (Extract 13) did not let stand the account that Miguel and Ron put forward regarding the boys' entitlement to space; instead she provided her own counter-explanation. Kathy (Extracts 13, 15) also took up an oppositional stance to the account justifying boys' rights to the soccer field. The girls' ability to deliver a return volley (Extracts 13, 15), and negotiate a definition of the situation, demonstrates that female participants to this interaction do not envision themselves as occupying an inferior status. Instead they demonstrate they can challenge hegemonic claims to social space, thus countering many gender stereotypes.

'Girl' as an epithet or stance carrier during conflict talk

Gendered address forms may occur in counter-moves during conflict talk. For example, during a game of hopscotch among African American migrant children, when a player attempted to usurp another's turn, the term 'woman' was used in the counter-move by the complainant/referee: 'My go woman!' In the terminal position of a counter-move, the gendered address term does not function as a summons or a vocative, and neither is it required. Instead, it appears to function as a form of intensifier or a 'post-completion stance marker' (Schegloff, 1996b: 90–2) (an added segment that displays a 'retrospective or retroactive alignment toward' the completed utterance). Thus, when among Latina children playing hopscotch a jumper took exceptionally large steps rather than the small baby steps that are permitted when one's token is located at the far end of the hopscotch grid, a referee used the term 'niña' as she yelled, 'QUÉ TIENES QUE METERTE EN LA RAYA DE AQUÍ LOS DOS JUNTI::TOS AL OTHER PIE NIÑA!' ('You have to put yourself on this line with both feet very close together to the other foot girl!'). Here 'woman' and 'niña', used in terminal position during adversarial interaction in hopscotch, accompany actions that display a strong stance, functioning as intensifiers.

The term 'girl' can be used to mark an oppositional stance in cross-sex adversarial interaction as well. In Extract 16, 'girl' appears near the beginning rather than at the end of the turn. In line 11 the term 'girl' is used as an epithet while locating a prior action as an infraction in a dispute resulting from a co-ed basketball game among third graders. At the end of the game Ken complained that Kathy had fouled him a number of times (lines 1–4). Sandra subsequently initiated a counter with 'You know what Ken?' Before she could complete her turn, Ken opposed her: '°Just shut up please.' Paul's next move, allying with Ken, made use of features of opposition turns within children's games

(M. H. Goodwin, 1998) – response cry + person descriptor + formulation of
the offence: 'oh' + 'girl' + 'big talker' (lines 11–13). Following these moves
the dispute developed into a series of insult/insult return sequences (M. H.
Goodwin, 1990: 185–8) in lines 21–46.

Extract 16

		((Kids are seated on the curb of basketball court
		after a game discussing fouls))
1	Ken:	*((looking pained))*
2		I know that I got fouled by Kathy, (0.4)
3		almost ten *((hand gestures emphasizing beats))* (.)
4		or eleven times
5		[in this one game.
6	Sandra:	[You know what Ken?
7	Sandra:	[It's-
8	Ken:	[°Just shut up please.
9	Donna:	Heh heh heh!
10	Sandra:	*((smiles and gazes at Donna))*
11	Paul:	Oh girl you-=
12	Ken:	=Just shut up.=
13	Paul:	=Big talker. Man you-
14	Paul:	What size mouth do you wear.=
15	Ken:	=Is it any of your business? No::.
16	Ken:	Was I talking to you?
17	Ken:	Is this any of your business? No::::.
18		I [wasn't-
19	Sandra:	[I wasn't saying (more.)
20	Paul:	*((leaning into Sandra's face))*
21		Come on Sandra. What size mouth do you wear.
22		(1.0)
23	Sandra:	*((turns to Paul))* You know-
24		You don't have a size mouth.
25		*((dramatic head movements punctuate talk))*
26		You come with- *((dramatic hand movements))*
27		What you (.) were born with.=
28	Paul:	Batteries not included- eh heh-heh! *((looks at Ken))*
29		(2.0)
30	Vanessa:	Oh. Please! Come on. Pau::l,
31	Ken:	Can I take your batteries out (of this thing)?
32		*((Moves to Vanessa and makes movements on her back))*
33	Vanessa:	What kind of- what size- NOSE do you wear.
34	Ken:	Nose?
35	Vanessa:	You have a big nose.
36	Ken:	Do I have a big nose? *((said turning to Paul))*
37	Paul:	(Kind of)
38	Vanessa:	Eh heh-heh hah-hah hah-heh!

39	Isaac:	You were shooting that three per cent nose.
40	Vanessa:	Do you buy your ponytail at <u>Thrif</u>ty? *((to Ken))*
41	Paul:	You should see her <u>Mom's</u> nose boy.
42		*((does large motion with hands))* Dnh dnh!
43	Vanessa:	<u>My</u> mom's nose,
44	Paul:	Looks like a <u>sow's</u> nose to <u>me</u>.
45	Vanessa:	No it's <u>YOUR</u> nose that's the mouth
46		(mouse) was just stickin' out of the sky.

Here the person formulation 'girl' introduces a sequence that subsequently becomes a series of insult/insult return moves that entail not only gender, but also loquaciousness (indexed by size of mouth), size of nose and hairstyle. Sandra's initial move of objection ('You know what Ken?') is responded to with another question – itself an insult: 'What size <u>mouth</u> do you wear' (line 21). In her reply to Paul, Sandra counters with 'You know- You don't <u>have</u> a size mouth. You come with- what you (.) were <u>born</u> with.' (lines 23–7). Sandra treats Paul's move as serious and animatedly corrects him. With his phrase 'Batteries not included' Paul appends talk to Sandra's; his added segment (C. Goodwin, 1981) both reinstates the topic of Sandra's mouth, and (jokingly) provides a characterization of it as battery-operated (line 28).

In ritual insult sequences (Labov, 1972b) insults are responded to with counter-insults, in 'exchange and return' (Pomerantz, 1975: 16) paired moves. The recipient of an initial ritual insult (an insult about an attribute of the target known not to be literally true) must utilize the scene described in the prior speaker's talk to produce a second description which turns the initial insult on its head and is even more outrageous.[16] The most artfully done insult sequences make minimal semantic shifts using the format of the prior utterance (M. H. Goodwin, 1990: 185–8). Here Paul and Ken act as a team (Goffman, 1959: 77–105) in the production of moves answered by the team of Vanessa and Sandra. Vanessa (in contrast to Sandra) plays the language game of ritual insult. Making use of the format provided in Paul's insult ('What size mouth do you wear?'), Vanessa ties her utterance to Paul's; she replaces 'mouth' with 'nose', asking, 'What size nose do you wear' (line 33). Introducing a second insult she asks Ken 'Do you buy your ponytail at <u>Thrif</u>ty?' (line 40). Paul (not Ken) responds and insults Vanessa's mom by comparing her nose with a sow's (lines 41, 44). Vanessa's next turn transforms Paul's move and makes him rather than her mother the target of the insult (line 45) about big noses.

Though typically described as an all-male genre (Kochman, 1981; Labov, 1972b), the ritual insult sparring that occurs between third graders Vanessa and Paul demonstrates a form of language game in which both female and male

---

[16] For a critique of this formulation of sequencing in ritual insult sequences see Kochman (1981).

players participate on an equal footing. The type of competitive interaction developed here has resonances with the ways in which fifth grade girls at the same school took up opposition to the boys' claims to symbols of power, and eventually succeeded in restructuring the use of the soccer field from an exclusively male domain to one that was shared by both girls and boys (Extracts 13–15). Girls display their ability to provide adversarial moves that run counter to many stereotypical notions about the nature of girls' same-sex interactions as essentially cooperative.[17] Typically cross-sex interactions are viewed in the context of male power and female subordination (Henley & Kramarae, 1991).[18] Girls here, as in other contexts (see M. H. Goodwin, 1990; 2006), demonstrate an orientation towards pursuing rather than inhibiting moves expressing oppositional stances. With respect to the interaction at hand, girls hold their own in cross-sex interaction.

'Girl' as an intensifier in an assessment sequence

In Extract 16, we saw that the term 'girl' displayed a negative valence when used in adversarial interaction. However, the term 'girl' can also display a positive alignment with one's interlocutor. In Extract 17, the terms 'girl' and 'girlfriend' (used in the USA as a friendly or intimate form of address between women[19]) are used by co-participants as intensifiers or 'post-completion stance markers' (Schegloff, 1996b: 90–2). The terms occur in self-congratulatory celebratory commentaries by girls on their negative assessment of Sean and Janis, who have excluded everyone but Janis's best friends from the softball game. Girls consider the activity of talking about other people, particularly those who offend them, as enjoyable. In fact when girls have nothing in particular to do and activities such as playing a game or sport are proposed, girls opt for the activity of complaining about others, with utterances such as 'I like sitting here and being mad and talking about people.'

In the following extended example, Aretha, Sarah and Angela are upset because Janis's boyfriend Sean excluded them from a game of softball; in addition they are mad at Janis for her attitude of superiority, for example thinking she's better than others because she wears the latest fads. After explicating their complaints to each other about Sean and Janis, and contrasting their own perspective on Janis's need to be trendy, the excluded girls yell insults about

---

[17] See Maltz and Borker (1982) and Coates (1996; 1997; 1998b).

[18] While researchers concerned with dominance relations seek to avoid the essentialist explanations often present in deficit and difference views, Stokoe (2000: 554) notes they can unwittingly perpetuate dichotomized notions of male and female practices, 'blending a constructionist stance with cultural (essentialist) feminism'.

[19] See http://encarta.msn.com/dictionary_/girlfriend.html.

the ugliness of Janis's clothes in her direction (lines 13–15), though they are not demonstrably attended.

Extract 17

1	Angela:	Tell me naturally
2		[Do you really like Janis?
3	Aretha:	[Janis does everything that's trendy.
4		She thinks that she's so popular
5		[Cause she stays up to date.
6	Sarah:	[Look at her now.
7		(2.0)
8	Sarah:	I don't <u>like</u> being trendy.
9	Angela:	She's not even matching
10		To tell [you the truth.
11	Sarah:	[I got this three years ago.
12	Sarah:	Trust [me.
13	Aretha:	[I HATE THOSE <u>PANTS!</u>
14		(0.8)
15	Aretha:	THEY'RE <u>UGLY</u>!!
16		(0.8)
17	Sarah:	Ooooo! Girl<u>frie::nd</u>!
18	Aretha:	They <u>are</u>! <u>Look</u> at 'em!
19		They look like some <u>boys'</u> shorts.
20	Angela:	They look-
21	Angela:	Okay.
22	Angela:	They [look like- Shaka Zulu.
23	Aretha:	[You know how boys wear their shorts?
24		They look like she's trying to be like-
25		She wants to- *h <u>match</u> <u>Sean</u>! *((eyeball roll))*
26		(0.8)
27	Aretha:	So she's wearing some tren[dy-
28	Sarah:	*((chanting))* [Sean has a
29		shirt like that! Sean has a shirt like that!
30		*((high fives Aretha))* Girl Girl <u>Girl</u>!
31		(0.4)
32	Sarah:	<u>Girl</u>! <u>Girl</u>! (0.3) <u>Girl</u>! eh heh-heh!
33	Sarah:	Gi(hh)rl°frien-! *((continuing to clap hands))*

In response to the insults Aretha yells towards Janis (lines 13–15), Sarah produces a response cry 'Ooooo!' and the person formulation 'Girl<u>frie::nd</u>!' (line 17). The 'Ooooo!' response cry in the initial part of the turn takes up a stance of joyful disbelief about Aretha's boldness in delivering such a direct insult. Sarah treats Aretha's insult as something unbelievable and risky to have said (as evidenced by Aretha's subsequent reaffirmation of her own talk in line 18). A second component of the turn, the address term 'Girl<u>frie:::nd</u>!', is produced with heightened affect, and displays a close alignment with Aretha and her commentary about Janis and Sean. As the girls continue with their negative assessment, saying that Janis's shorts look like boys' shorts, and that she is attempting to match Sean's clothing (lines 19, 24–5), Sarah produces the address term 'girl' (lines 30–2), a shortened version of 'Girlfriend' (line 33), six times. In association with their talk, Sarah and Aretha execute elaborate high-five handclaps to celebrate their common worldview about someone they are gossiping about. In the midst of the clapping Angela raises her arms over Sarah's body to co-participate in the activity (see Figure 12.1).

In both Extracts 16 and 17 the address term 'girl' that is used functions as a *stance carrier*. Different forms of affect can be conveyed through the intonation and the gestures performed with the term, as well as through rhythm and repetition. The gestures that accompany the exclamation 'girl' in Extract 17 provide a way to say 'Bravo' or 'Good job' by slapping hands together in the air.[20] The activity of physically clapping, resembling girls' handclapping games (Gaunt, 2006), seals the pact that the girls have against the absent parties who offend them. Repetition provides further intensification of the action.

The girls' congruent view of events, expressed through the embodied way in which they joyfully produce the word 'girl', differs dramatically from the way in which the word 'girl' is produced in Extract 16; there 'girl' prefaces a turn in which opposition and insult are achieved while taking up a stance of derision with respect to co-present rather than absent parties. We see from Extracts 16 and 17 that the meaning of a term such as 'girl' depends very much on the actions in which it is embedded and the context in which it is used. While it has a pejorative valence when used in complaining directly about something done in someone's presence, the term can also have a positive connotation when congratulating someone about what she has said (in the present case, in response to a complaint about an absent offending party). The same person formulation can have very different meanings depending on the interactive context in which it emerges, as it takes its meaning from the activity-in-progress being produced through its utterance.

Discussion

This chapter has investigated some of the ways in which gender becomes observably oriented towards in the midst of children's spontaneous talk. We have examined the ways in which children take for granted, in both their folklore and dramatic play, a heterosexual ordering of females and males. Gender constitutes one of the important dimensions that is used for person formulations during adversarial talk that accompanies 'borderwork', maintaining the

---

[20] See www.englishdaily626.com/slang.php?063 for a definition of 'high five'.

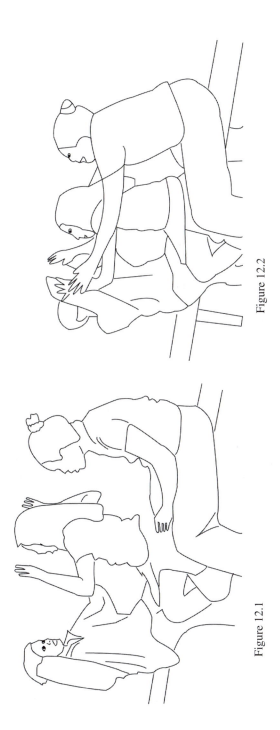

Figure 12.2

Figure 12.1

boundaries of their group. When boys intrude on girls' spaces, they go to considerable lengths to defend their social groups and spaces they occupy from others who differ with respect to gender. Girls and boys position themselves on opposing teams of 'girls versus boys' or 'girls against boys' in contests such as basketball and jump rope. Person references that are used as intensifiers obtain their meanings from the activity in progress, as well as the position of the term in the turn. The very same term ('girl') can be used to produce a stance that displays either heightened affiliation or derision.

Two different trajectories in dealing with disputes were observable in the younger and older mixed gender groups. Younger boys and girls enjoyed competitive co-ed sports such as basketball, and their disputes led to playful ritual insult sequences as a way of elaborating (and dissipating) complaints about sportsmanship. Older children, by way of contrast, competed for a place on the soccer field in heated, serious disputes. When boys produced accounts that made claims to exclusive entitlement based on gendered habitual use, girls countered such claims and argued about entitlement based on their parents' monetary contributions to the school. The different trajectories that develop from disputes related to sports are arguably related to how play and the 'other' are viewed at different points in the life cycle, with younger children maintaining more 'easeful'[21] relations with each other, permitting playful rather than antagonistic argumentation.

An ethnographic approach combined with a close investigation of language in use permits us to examine the ways that cultural concerns enter into the accounts and genres through which dispute is performed and conduct is sanctioned. Social anthropologist Sigurd Berentzen (1984), investigating the social organization of a Norwegian nursery school (children ages 5–7), found that a girl who was thought to 'act so smart all the time' by bragging about the praise she had received from a teacher was eventually ostracized. This negative sanctioning demonstrates a clear orientation to a behaviour deemed inappropriate, though it is not specifically labelled as a gendered form of behaviour by the children themselves. Similarly, with respect to male groups Berentzen (1984: 32–3) found that by attending to how boys comment on their own and others' behaviour, he could locate particular classifications that the children themselves attend to; for example, 'tough' and 'dull' were used as assessment adjectives by males with respect to male persons. Ranking with respect to these attributes was observable in how queues were formed, who had to make offers of gifts (objects) in order to gain access to a playgroup, etc. Though the boys did not themselves explicitly locate these activities as distinctively 'male',

---

[21] According to Schofield (1981: 72), 'boys' and girls' awareness of each other as possible romantic and sexual partners, concern about rejection in such relationships, and strong sex-typing of interests and activities result in a great deal of informal segregation of the sexes and rather ritualized and constricted types of behavior when cross-sex interaction does occur'.

their behaviour displayed a clear orientation to them as relevant phenomena in their social world.

In this chapter I have investigated how one aspect of person formulation, gender, is explicitly oriented towards by participants of a peer group. Indeed, both gender and age[22] constitute important dimensions of borderwork. Yet while these dimensions of identity are significant, by far the most ubiquitous forms of comparison (and ones that are consequential for girls) are those conducted among same-age, same-sex members of the group. In the midst of their talk with each other, girls vigilantly monitor the actions of their peers and patrol their moral behaviour (M. H. Goodwin, 2002a; 2002b; 2006). However, they do not explicitly label their activities as 'girls'' activities. Ethnographic description is important because it allows us to examine how forms of interaction not only vary with context (Danby & Baker, 1998; M. H. Goodwin, 1990) and may change over time (M. H. Goodwin, 2001; Kyratzis, 2001b), but, most importantly, matter for the participants.

Appendix

The full text of the song is as follows:
One by one, the *fun* has just begun.
In the *bed*room, dah dah, *dah*-dah dah-dah
Two by two, he *took* off her shoe. [Refrain}
Three by three, he *kissed* her knee. [Refrain}
Four by four, we *knocked* on the door. [Refrain}
Five by five, we *saw* a beehive. [Refrain}
Six by six, we *picked* up sticks. [Refrain}
Seven by seven, it *felt* like heaven. [Refrain}
Eight by eight, we *closed* the gate. [Refrain}
Nine by nine, the *twins* were fine. [Refrain}
Ten by ten, let's *do* it again. [Refrain}

---

[22] For example, blocking the intrusive and insulting actions of older girls (sixth graders) constitutes a critical concern of fourth grade girls at lunchtime, made explicit in complaints such as, 'You guys prove a lot of things to make fun of- kids who are younger than you.'

13 Being there for the children: The collaborative construction of gender inequality in divorce mediation

Angela Cora Garcia and Lisa M. Fisher

Introduction

The problem of gender inequality is often conceived in terms of relationships between variables, social forces, socialization, power and so on. These analyses beg the question of how inequality is created in particular instances in everyday life. It is through talk that much of the construction of gender inequality occurs and is perpetuated. However, research on gender inequality that compares the interactional styles or behaviours of males with females ignores the fundamentally interactional nature of human action. Rather than focusing on whether males or females typically perform different types of actions, or how individuals construct gender, researchers should study how gender inequality is collaboratively constructed by participants in interaction (e.g., Kitzinger, 2000a; Stockill & Kitzinger, 2007).

The social process of divorce mediation is a particularly salient context in which to examine how participants in interaction make gender relevant, because it is a situation in which the family is in transition. Participants use their experiences of family and the range of typical family structures that occur in their culture as background assumptions to shape and justify their actions. Participants construct and use links between gender and spousal and parental roles as they make claims and justify positions. These connections are not mechanistic; they are constructed by participants in the course of the interaction.

In this chapter, we will show how participants' actions in a divorce mediation session led to an instance of inequality in which the wife was disadvantaged during the interaction relative to the husband. This inequality centred on the ability to define the terms of the debate, in this case, what it meant to 'be there' for the children. The issue of whether each parent was capable of 'being there' for the children after the impending divorce became central to the negotiation process. The spouses' marital and parental roles were used as resources to argue positions in the mediation session. The wife's version of being there

We would like to thank Brent Shannon and Jennifer Baker Jacobs for transcribing the tapes, and the mediators and mediation participants for allowing us to record their mediation sessions. NSF grant SBR # 9411224 from the Law and Social Sciences Program provided the funds for data collection.

(physically present to provide care for the children) was trumped by the husband's version of being there (financially supporting and arranging for the care of the children). This outcome weakened the wife's ability to argue for shared residential custody during the mediation session.[1]

As in other single-case analyses (e.g., Garcia & Parmer, 1999; Stockill & Kitzinger, 2007; Whalen et al., 1988; see also Schegloff, 1987b; 1990; 1993), we use conversation analytic research findings to support our interpretation of this interaction, revealing how a problematic outcome was collaboratively achieved. In this chapter, we describe our methods and data, use excerpts from the mediation session to illustrate our analysis, and conclude with a discussion of implications for the study of gender in interaction.

Analytical approach

The role of gender in interaction has been the subject of numerous studies (see Speer, 2005a, and Stokoe, 2006, for critical discussions of this body of research). While focusing on gender can illuminate experiences and social processes which are not visible without this attention, there is a risk that privileging gender over the whole stream of behaviour which participants create may result in a distorted view of the interaction.[2] Interaction *in situ* is produced by participants for each other – they are not 'doing gender' for the convenience of researchers, but for the course of action in which they are engaged (Schegloff, 1997). The best approach to the study of gender inequality may be to examine the interaction as a whole rather than searching for specific points at which gender is 'made relevant' or made observably relevant.

Schegloff (2007d) argues that simply being a member of a category (e.g., age, gender) is not enough to argue that that category is relevant for the participants in the talk at that point in time. There must be evidence in the talk itself that the category is relevant. However, as Schegloff (1997) also acknowledges, showing an 'orientation to gender' can be done in ways that do not involve talking about gender. Gender, therefore, can be relevant for an interaction without being mentioned in the interaction. This perspective is supported by Garfinkel's (1967) study of a transsexual who was trying to

---

[1] After a total of four mediation sessions and a number of court dates, the couple did eventually work out a shared parenting agreement specifying that the children would split their time between the two households. The focus of our analysis is on the interactional production of inequality in specific interactions, rather than the disposition of the case as a whole, which depends on a number of factors and events.

[2] Similarly, in Schegloff's (2007d) analysis of how person reference and membership categorization are done in conversation he argues for an analytical approach in which investigation of the phenomena of interest is accomplished through the analysis of the interaction as a whole. Schegloff analyses two episodes of interaction in this paper, 'episodes whose analysis is not restricted to observations about person-reference but is shaped by the exigencies of getting the analysis of the interactional episode right, whatever it takes' (Schegloff, 2007d: 434).

hide her lack of a female biography. Garfinkel (1967) describes how Agnes learned to cook by asking her boyfriend's mother to teach her how to cook special dishes for him, thus concealing the fact that she lacked the knowledge (expected for a female in her generation and social location) of how to cook. Therefore, much of the work of doing gender in an interaction may be making it invisible. This observation is analogous to Sacks's work on membership categorization (which in effect assumes that there are 'default interpretations' of categories). For example, in Sacks's (1992) well-known discussion of the story 'The baby cried. The mommy picked it up', he argues that when two categories from the same 'device' (in this case 'family') are used, the listener hears them as belonging to the same unit unless there's something in the story that indicates otherwise. So, in this example, the hearer assumes that the mommy in the story is the mother of the baby that she picks up (see also Schegloff, 2007b: 471).

Enfield (2007) describes the work done to achieve the ordinary in everyday life (see also Sacks, 1984b). He gives the example of how 'default' choices of clothing can make that clothing unremarkable and unnoticeable. The clothes of a male plumber who shows up at work wearing overalls would not be noticed, but if he had shown up wearing a dress, this would be visible and accountable:

> When we follow a default course of action in this way, we are in one sense not doing anything special; indeed we may be taken not to be 'doing' anything at all. But since it takes work to pull off the invisible appearance of ordinariness, even when our manners of behaviour are rendered literally unremarkable by their conformity, we are nevertheless always doing something by choosing just those manners of behaviour. (Enfield, 2007: 97)

We argue that there are also 'default interpretations' of gender (and gendered terms) in a given culture and in specific social contexts or interactions. The analyst can therefore also rely on these taken-for-granted default interpretations, and observe when participants actively work to construct meanings that differ from default assumptions about the gendered nature of the social world to which they belong, or use the default interpretations strategically (for an analogous argument regarding person reference see Stivers *et al.*, 2007).

According to West and Zimmerman (1987), just about any social occasion provides a forum for doing gender, and participants are evaluated according to the congruence of their behaviour with normative conceptions of what is appropriate masculine versus feminine behaviour. West and Zimmerman also note that if one 'does gender' appropriately, the social order is legitimated, and gender remains invisible as long as it remains unremarkable, as Garfinkel (1967) states. We prefer to speak of social orders rather than 'the' social order, because the meaning of gender may vary depending on how participants treat it in a given interactional context, social location or historical period. Participants in an interaction may not share the same sense of how gender is attached to social roles, the division of labour in the family or the assumed 'essential nature' of the participants; these differences can become the subject of explicit or implicit negotiation in the course of interaction.

We argue that analysts of gender inequality must not ignore the actions, assumptions and behaviours relied on by participants which may contribute to the unfolding events in a given social situation. Garfinkel's (1967) breaching experiments show us that the procedures used to organize and understand actions in everyday life become invisible because they are routine and taken for granted. When norms are broken or violated (whether in a breaching experiment or in real life), the routine practices become visible. In this chapter we will show how participants used the gendered spousal and parental roles in their 'traditional' marriage as background assumptions, thus enabling them to make arguments based on gender-differentiated parental roles without necessarily referring to gender.

Our analysis relies on a combination of a conversation analytic perspective with an interpretive analysis of the interaction based on shared cultural knowledge. Gender is not just an interactional phenomenon. It is a part of who we are and a part of every person's experiences, relationships and history. West and Zimmerman (1987: 131) write that 'Agnes's case makes visible what culture has made invisible – the accomplishment of gender.' Gender is therefore potentially relevant whether it is displayed in the talk as relevant or not (e.g., explicitly discussed or labelled as gender-relevant).

Our perspective is consistent with Enfield's (2007) argument that even 'unmarked' or 'default' references imply a choice and carry meaning beyond the term itself (see also Kitzinger, 2007b). We show how participants construct and use shared, commonsense understandings and background assumptions about the gendered nature of parental and marital roles during the interaction to advance local interactional goals.

Talk in mediation

Previous research on talk in institutional settings (e.g., Boden & Zimmerman, 1991; Drew & Heritage, 1992b) has shown how the interactional organization of talk varies by context. For example, while in ordinary conversation, turn type, turn length, turn topic and turn exchange are locally managed and free to vary (Sacks *et al.*, 1974), one or more of these parameters are typically constrained in the speech-exchange systems of talk in institutional settings. Greatbatch's (1988; see also Clayman & Whalen, 1988/9) study of television news interviews found that interviewers spoke first, asked questions and controlled the topic of talk, while interviewees spoke second and answered questions. Interviewers were able to control the floor without interruption in order to produce sometimes extensive background material to set up their questions.

The interviewees typically refrained from speaking during this material, even to the extent of withholding minimal responses and continuers.

The speech-exchange system of mediation also differs from that of ordinary conversation. Garcia (1991) found that disputants in mediation sessions routinely direct their remarks to the mediator rather than to each other and are expected to wait to speak until given the floor by mediators.[3] Disputants in turn are typically given extended periods of time to 'tell their story'; these extended turns are typically followed by questions from the mediators. Turn transition is thus not relevant at every possibly complete unit type, as it may be in oral conversation.[4] The opposing disputant is then given a chance to tell their story and respond to the first disputant's version of events. Therefore, actions which would typically be adjacent in ordinary conversation (such as accusations and denials) are routinely separated in mediation talk.

One of the challenges facing mediators is how to be fair to both parties and create a neutral setting for interaction. Unlike court proceedings, the mediation context is a 'non-adversarial' alternative to litigation in divorce and child custody cases (Saposnek, 1983). The mediator is supposed to remain neutral in the dispute, and acts as a facilitator rather than a judge or decision-maker. Because disputants may come to mediation with different levels of power or skill, mediators often must work to empower the weaker disputant.[5] The issue of gender bias is perhaps even more sensitive in divorce mediation than in other types of mediation because of the gendered nature of spousal and family relationships. The common belief that divorce courts favour mothers when there are children involved is directly referred to by the husband in this session. The prevalence of this belief could lead divorce mediators to work to avoid disadvantaging the male. In the case studied here, the mediators' efforts to allay the husband's fears of gender bias against him may lead to a situation in which the wife does not feel adequately supported. As the wife reveals towards the end of the mediation session, the relationship between the spouses during their marriage was one in which conversations turned into arguments, and the wife felt powerless and unheard (see Extract 6 below).

---

[3] Mediation programmes differ in their structure and conventions; see, for example, Greatbatch and Dingwall (1997) on British mediation.

[4] Although note that even in ordinary conversation a possibly complete unit type, while a necessary component of a transition relevance place, does not alone define it. Timing, intonation and non-verbal behaviour such as gaze direction and gestures all work together to communicate when a speaker is 'done' and when a transition in speakership is relevant. See Sacks et al. (1974); C. Goodwin (1984).

[5] See S. Cobb (1993), Dingwall (1988), Garcia (1995) and Garcia et al. (2002) for discussions of empowerment in mediation. Briefly, empowerment is a technique mediators can use to attempt to balance the power between disputants where there is a potentially consequential difference in power, status or knowledge by helping the weaker party (Barsky, 1996; Neumann, 1992; see also C. B. Harrington, 1985; Regehr, 1994; Tjosvold & Van de Vliert, 1994; Wall, 1981).

Data

The 90-minute mediation session examined in this chapter was video-taped in 1995 as part of a larger project.[6] In this family mediation programme, each session is led by two mediators, one experienced and the other a trained mediator seeking certification. Although many of the couples participating in the programme have been referred by the courts, the mediation process is voluntary. The mediators do not have the right to make decisions for the couple or enforce the law. Their job is to help the divorcing spouses discover whether they can resolve contested issues. In a divorce agreement, legal custody (the right to make decisions regarding the children) and residential custody may be shared or assigned to one parent. When parents share residential custody and decision-making about the children, this is referred to as a 'shared parenting plan'. The mediators in this session follow the policies of the courts in favouring shared parenting arrangements.[7] Shared parenting arrangements are consistent with a family structure in which parental roles are not distinguished on the basis of gender. The mediators thus start out encouraging parenting plans which assume parents' equal participation in childcare.

The session analysed here was the first of four mediation sessions participated in by a divorcing couple ('John' and 'Susan') and two female mediators. John and Susan have two children. The trainee in this case ('Mediator B') was a family therapist. A disjuncture between the participants becomes visible early as the mediators support the idea of shared parenting both explicitly and implicitly (e.g., by expressing approval of the parents' current equal division of the children's time, by asking questions supporting Susan's claims to continue to be a residential parent, and by reframing John's complaints to suggest he also wants to continue shared parenting), even though the divorcing couple seems to be oriented to a 'traditional' breadwinner/homemaker family model. As the session unfolds, John reveals that he is seeking sole residential custody of the children, and this goal proves to be a formative force on the interaction. John acts in numerous ways to support his claim for sole residential custody, including criticizing Susan's competence and suitability as a mother. While Susan does at times actively defend her role as caretaker of the children and contest John's attacks, she also often fails to do so. She eventually explains her silence as a habitual response to ongoing conflict in their relationship. In this chapter, we show how the participants use gender strategically, and how their combined actions serve to create gender inequality in the interaction between the participants in the session, thereby compromising the wife's position in their struggle over residential custody of the children.

[6] See Garcia (2000) and Garcia et al. (2002) for further descriptions of the data.
[7] Regehr (1994) found that mediators tend to favour shared parenting rather than having the children live with one of the parents.

Being there for the children

Divorcing couples with 'traditional' marriages, in which the husband has been the breadwinner and the wife has been the full-time caretaker of the children, face post-divorce decisions about whether and how to change their gendered spousal and parental roles as they divide into two households. In this mediation session, John works to justify his position that he should have sole residential custody of the children. He complains that his wife has started drinking since their separation (in their religion, alcohol consumption is considered wrong), stopped attending church and introduced her boyfriend to the children, even letting him stay overnight. After an extended period of discussion in which John presents his concerns about Susan's behaviour since the separation, the mediators ask him to specify how his concerns are relevant for the custody issue. In the middle of an extended turn in which he makes even more serious allegations, John draws an upshot or conclusion of his criticisms of Susan (Extract 1). The extract begins as he is stating that his wife 'deserves' her children:[8]

Extract 1

```
1  J:  An' sh:e deserves °them.° (0.5) She deserves them! (0.9)
2      But I worry (0.6) °if they deserve° °°her.°° (0.8) That's my
3      concern. (0.8) If .h (0.3) that she: can be (1.4) th'
4      kin'=uh parent that will, an' I'm not sayin' have uh good
5      time! She- .h I worked °most uh thuh time, I understood!
6      She spent uh lot uh time with thuh kids.° .h (0.5) °But
7      that she will be thuh- kin' uh°°k-°° °parent that can raise
8      them?° .h (0.9) A:n' (0.9) be there fer them? An' .h things
9      like that?
```

This complex utterance is carefully constructed in mitigated fashion to place the main criticism of Susan at the end of a series of compliments, explanations and assertions. After a couple of false starts and hesitations, John says 'She- .h I worked °most uh thuh time' (line 5). The use of repair format (a repairable followed by a cut-off, a hesitation and a replacement of the trouble source; Jefferson, 1974) shows John first using the pronoun 'she' to refer to his wife, and then replacing it with the first person pronoun ('I worked most of the time').[9] John goes on to say 'She spent uh lot uh time with thuh kids' (line 6).

---

[8] This extended turn is constructed of multiple unit types. During John's speech, his ex-wife and the two mediators sit back in their chairs, bodies relaxed and still, exhibiting listening posture. John holds his hands up in front of his chest during the whole speech (including the portion shown in Extract 1), with the fingers touching each other. This sustained gesture indicates that he is not done with his 'story', and has not given up the floor (C. Goodwin, 1984).

[9] See Schegloff (2007d) and Lerner and Kitzinger (2007b) regarding the use of pronouns for person reference.

This revised ordering of the 'facts' of their family life during the marriage, which lists his contribution first and hers second, accomplishes two things. First, it references a marriage in which sharply demarcated parental roles (male as provider, female as caretaker of the children) are both described and presented as unremarkable and as a normal, natural state of events (cf. Garfinkel, 1967). Second, since Susan's contribution to the family is described only after his own contribution is described, John's provider role becomes a 'frame' for the time she has spent with the children. John's work is his account both for not physically 'being there' and for how Susan was able to be there for the children. After acknowledging that Susan spent more time with the children than he did because he was working, John says he is not sure 'that she will be thuh- kin' uh° °°k-°° °parent that can raise them?° .h (0.9) A:n' (0.9) be there fer them? An' .h things like that?' (lines 7–9).

The phrase 'being there' can have two meanings: physically being there or being supportive. In this utterance, John is constructing a natural state of events in which he can 'be there' for the children without physically being there (because he has been working to provide for the family), while at the same time calling into question Susan's ability to 'be there' for the children despite her long-term history of physical presence with them.

In this extract John is complaining about or criticizing Susan's performance of her parental role. Note that in lines 4 and 7 John uses the gender-neutral term 'parent' to refer to Susan, instead of the gendered term 'mother' which he had used earlier in the session. In our culture the term 'mother' has connotations of nurturing, caring and close emotional connection with the children which are not conveyed by the term 'parent'.[10] By this lexical choice, John works to minimize Susan's past contributions and to challenge her future role as a nurturer. This formulation also allows John to avoid stating that he wants his children to be 'motherless', which might have made him appear insensitive to the emotional needs of his children.[11] He thus constructs his complaint as a contrast between two parents rather than a contrast between 'mother' and 'father'.

In short, this extract illustrates John's strategic use of referents to his wife at various points in the mediation session. When the use of a gendered parental term (such as 'mother') would support his interests (as in Extract 5, discussed below), John uses the term 'mother' or 'mom'. When the use of a gendered parental term would support his wife's interests rather than his own, he chooses the gender-neutral term 'parent'. John works to create a local gender order in which the cultural context of the gendered parental terms works

---

[10] See Pomerantz and Mandelbaum (2005: 150) on how participants convey 'shared assumptions about incumbents' by using relationship categories.

[11] See Edwards (2005) on how people produce complaints while at the same time managing impressions made by their performance of the act of complaining.

to his advantage. Which term is the 'default' term may therefore vary with the local interactional context.[12]

Later on in the session, John uses the gendered term 'Daddy' to refer to himself and his relationship with his children (Extract 2, line 5), in contrast to the term 'parent' he had just applied to Susan.[13]

Extract 2

```
1   J:    Those °are th' things° °°I'm concerned with!°° (0.4) °I'm
2         just,°<I w:orry?> (1.0) An' love? (0.6) °my children.° (0.6)
3         °An' just wanna see thuh very best for them.° (1.5)
4         °An' that's th' part° °that=I think that° .h (1.0) °through:°
5         °°An' I'm not s-°° °sayin' I'm thuh best Daddy in thuh world
6         but just-° (0.7) °°in 'is particular case°° °°°I think I'm
7         thuh best parent right now.°°°
8              (.)
9   MA:   °Okay.°=
10  J:    =°s-° (0.4) But I don't know that (we'll [(           )]
11  MA:                                    [NOW YER] HOM:E
12        (0.6) every day Susan?
13             (0.3)
14  S:    °Mm hm?°
15             (.)
16  MA:   And um (1.2) th'children are in school all day.
17             (0.4)
18  S:    °Right?°
19             (0.5)
20  MA:   So, what happens after school.
21             (1.5)
22  MA:   M- Will=you be=at work after school John?
23             (1.0) ((Susan nods in silence.))
24  S:    °Y[es. °]
25  J:     [U:h ] there uh uh time when I am now-. (0.6) Susan='as:
26        left out uh couple things. She was working? (0.5) °A:n'°
27        (0.6) °she?° (1.0) °u:m° .h (1.2) >quit, got laid off, how
28        [ever=you=wanna=s-]
```

---

[12] Stivers (2007: 80) notes that 'when speakers depart from the use of a default referring expression, they convey that they are doing more than just referring'. See also Land and Kitzinger (2007: 499) on how choices of terms 'draw on cultural members' taken-for-granted understandings of the attributes associated with these categories, and use them in pursuit of the action in which they are engaged'.

[13] As C. Goodwin (1984) notes, participants telling 'stories' use non-verbal behaviour to indicate transitions in the talk. Note that John's utterance in lines 1–7 is an extended turn constructed of multiple unit types. John uses non-verbal behaviour to indicate that his extended turn is not complete. He holds his hands in front of his chest, with the fingers touching, for lines 1–6. In the middle of line 6 he starts moving the fingers back and forth quickly in a swishing motion – the

When talking about his love and concern for his children, John does not just say father, or Dad, he says 'Daddy' (line 5), the most endearing and juvenile form of the word, which connotes a close connection with and certain vulnerability of the children. Thus, he strengthens his position strategically by claiming the term 'Daddy' from the gendered pair 'Mommy/Daddy' for himself, while withholding the term 'Mommy', with its connotations of a close relationship with the children, when referring to Susan (as in Extract 1 above).

John continues gesturing through the turn from line 3, indicating that he has not given up the floor at the possibly complete unit type in line 3 (Sacks *et al.*, 1974; C. Goodwin, 1984).[14] John then adds an assessment: 'I'm not saying I'm the best Daddy in the world but just in this particular case, I think I'm the best parent right now' (lines 5–7).[15] While assessments often indicate a speaker is 'opening up closing' (Schegloff & Sacks, 1973), John keeps gesturing, indicating that he has not given up the floor (C. Goodwin, 1984).

Pomerantz (1984a; see also Schegloff, 1987b: 106; 1997) notes that assessments make agreement or disagreement with the assessment a relevant next action. Although Mediator A responds very quickly to John's turn, producing a quiet 'Okay.' in line 9, she neither agrees nor disagrees with his assessment. Withholding agreement is consistent with the role of a neutral party (Garcia *et al.*, 2002). Although the use of 'okay' in contexts such as these often indicates a pre-closing move (see Schegloff, 2007a), John then immediately speaks again. Mediator A then interrupts him by loudly talking over him (line 11). John drops out almost immediately after the interruption (see Schegloff, 1987a: 215–16).

Recall that the speech-exchange system of mediation discourages disputants from selecting themselves to speak unless given the floor by the mediators (Garcia, 1991). John thus benefits from an interactional context in which Susan would be seen as speaking out of turn if she spoke up to disagree with his assessment of his superior parenting abilities, or assert her own desire to have the best for their children. Thus John's statement that he wants to see the very best for his children stands alone.

In line 11 Mediator A shifts the focus to Susan. Mediator A's 'Now you're home every day Susan?' addresses Susan's ability to 'be there' for the children, thus indirectly challenging John's construction of the 'being there' issue. Note

---

transition from the stable position to the initiation of this motion indicates he is moving towards finishing his turn. In line 7 he moves his hands outwards in an 'open' position, then puts them in his lap, indicating that he is giving up the floor.

[14] Recall that in the turn-taking system of mediation disputants have the floor for an extended turn to tell their stories – not just one unit type. Turn transition does not therefore become relevant at the end of each unit type, but rather at the end of the disputant's 'story'. When the disputant does reach completion of their 'story', not all co-present parties are equally free to select themselves as next speaker – only the mediators are (Garcia, 1991).

[15] Self-praise is interactionally problematic (Pomerantz, 1978; see also Speer, this volume). John mitigates the effect of his self-praise by prefacing it with a disclaimer.

that this question has a preference for agreement (Sacks, 1987). While Mediator A is doing work here to balance the power between the two disputants, by getting Susan's side of the 'being there' issue on the table, she does not provide a space for or solicit Susan's response to John's criticisms and accusations. Note also that in Extract 2, Susan does not take advantage of having the floor in lines 14 and 18 to disagree with or challenge John. She restricts herself to one-word answers to the mediator's questions. Susan thus passes on two opportunities to disagree with John's framing of the issues. The absence of direct challenges to John's positions is thus produced both by the mediators and by Susan.

When Mediator A asks 'Will you be at work after school, John?' (line 22), Susan side-steps the convention that disputants should wait until they are addressed by a mediator to speak. She first nods (line 23), and then says 'yes' (line 24). In John's response (lines 25–8), which overlaps Susan's short utterance, he begins by saying that sometimes he's at home when the children get home from school. He then cuts himself off, pauses and switches to a response to Susan's claim that she is 'there every day': he discloses that she worked also (for at least some of the time), thereby challenging her claim that she is and has been a full-time mother. Note that John's notions about the value of paid work are gendered: while previously (and elsewhere) he valorized his provider role in the family, in this context 'work' is problematic in Susan's life because it detracts from her ability to 'be there' for their children. It is here that John raises the issue of Susan's job.

In sum, in this segment of the session, the participants act in ways which show their adherence to the gendered frame John constructed to support his version of 'being there'. John makes several claims which support his suitability to be the residential parent. The mediators try to elicit Susan's side of the issue, and indirectly suggest that John cannot always physically be there to care for the children, but do not explicitly or openly challenge John's claims. Susan speaks up once to answer a question which displays John's inability to 'be there' physically for the children after school, but does not otherwise intervene or challenge John's claims. Susan 'passes' on two opportunities to respond to John's claim that he is the best parent, or otherwise disagree with his assertions. The mediators take the space where Susan could have responded and use it to ask questions about her availability for childcare after the children come home from school.

Gendered family roles and 'being there' for the children

This next series of extracts illustrates the relationship between the shared history of the participants (the type of marriage they had and the gendered nature of their parental and spousal roles) and the ability of each party to construct images of themselves as suitable residential parents. For John, there is the continuing challenge of not having been the one to provide childcare during the marriage, along with his work commitments, which often prevent him from being physically present. For Susan, the challenge is how to maintain the status of caretaking parent when the post-divorce family situation will make it essential for her to get paying work. In Extract 3, Mediator A makes several attempts to get Susan to articulate her work plans (lines 1–2, 4, 8 and 12–13).[16]

Extract 3

```
1    MA:   °Okay.° .h (.) So are you looking fer employment now
2          or=[what-]
3    S:       [Tch  ] I'm goi[n' to.      ]
4    MA:                     [What=wou]ld be yer situation.
5                (.)
6    S:    I'm going to at thuh first uh thuh year.
7                (0.8)
8    MA:   An' would that be full time er part time?
9                (.)
10   S:    Tch (0.3) U:h, I don' know! (0.4) °>>I dunno ye'.<<°
11               (0.9)
12   MA:   If you could get full time wouldju be s:eeking it d'you
13         think? er=
14   S:    =>I dunno.<
15               (0.6)
16   MA:   °Okay.°
17               (0.2)
18   S:    I'd rather be home with 'em.
19               (0.7)
20   MB:   When=th[ey come=home.]
21   S:           [When='ey-   ] When 'ey come [home ] from school
22   MB:                                       [Yeah.]
23               (.)
24   MB:   What about [summers.]
25   J:               [Mm.    ]
26               (2.5)
27   MB:   What about summers an' spring break, an' Christmas break
28         an' things like that.
29               (1.1)
30   MB:   Ho:w wouldju propose to=it- um (0.8) have someone available
31         fer thuh children.
32               (2.4) ((Susan glances at John during the end of this
33         silence.))
34   J:    As far as myself I- I mean as far as thuh children self .h
35         (.) is: (1.0) Care will be provided. (0.7) U:m (0.5) Right
```

[16] Susan's use of a non-conforming-type response to a yes/no question (Raymond, 2003; Schegloff, 2007a; MA's lines 1–2) allows her to avoid having to appear delinquent in her responsibility to gain employment after the divorce. By saying 'I'm going to.' (line 3) Susan focuses the discussion on her intent to seek work rather than on the fact that she has not yet begun to seek work.

36   now? (0.5) Thuh children (0.7) have? (0.3) (uh note of) me
37   they have (0.7) twenny four °uh° hour day <u>care</u>! (0.6) An'
38   that is with (0.5) An' an' yes, I do utilize family? °An'
39   grandparents° that .h (0.3) °uh-° As of right now °I'm°
40   stayin' with until our (0.6) <u>housing</u> situation is
41   [straightened out.]

Susan displays her uncertainty about her work plans by saying 'I don't know'
three times (lines 10 and 14), providing a sharp contrast with John's earlier confident portrayal of himself in the provider role. Mediator A backs off and produces a non-committal, delayed, minimal response in line 16. Susan then selects
herself to speak in line 18 ('I'd rather be home with 'em.'), suggesting that she
would rather not take a full-time job. Susan does not present her (future) work
role as a natural event; she presents it as something uncertain, problematic and
in conflict with her desire to be there for the children. Susan thus defines taking
care of her children as requiring physical presence.[17] While at this point Susan
does not suggest that John should be physically present too, later on in the session she does criticize him along these lines (Extract 4, discussed below).

Susan and John construct very different senses of what 'being there' for the children means. For Susan, throughout her marriage, being there for the children has
meant not just taking primary responsibility for their care but literally, physically
being there, in the home, available first and foremost to meet their needs. John's
version of being there is not tied to physical presence, and is instead a commitment
to responsible provision of support. Since the separation, he has taken responsibility for arranging for the children's care when they are at his house (although
generally by proxy). These different concepts of what it means to 'be there' for the
children are not directly resolved by the mediators. This may disadvantage Susan
in the mediation session by implicitly devaluing her contributions to the family,
and allowing John's framing of his contributions to go unchallenged.

Mediator B asks a series of questions about Susan's ability to be physically
present for the children in the future (lines 24, 27–8 and 30–1). Note that each
subsequent question is an other-initiated repair of Susan's absent answer to
the previous question, thus making Susan's inability to respond visible (Sacks
et al., 1974; Schegloff, 1980; 2007b: 474, n. 3; Schegloff et al., 1977). When
Susan does not respond to the first two queries, Mediator B reframes her question 'How would you propose to … have someone available for the children.'
In one sense, this is a challenge to Susan, especially given her apparent inability to answer questions about her future availability for childcare. But in this
third formulation, Mediator B gives Susan a hint about how to answer it: she
does not have to be physically present all the time; she can make arrangements

---

[17] Eicher-Catt (2004) argues that mothering in our culture is essentially tied to 'being there'
physically.

for the children's care at times, just as John does. However, a 2.4-second silence elapses (line 32) without Susan producing an answer to this question. Her inability to explain how she would provide care becomes visible to all. After Susan's silence in line 32, she glances at John. John selects himself to speak and answers the question which was directed at her.

John prefaces his turn with 'As far as myself' (line 34), thus explicitly contrasting his ability to provide care with Susan's failure to answer the question. After some hesitation and reframing John produces a strong statement: 'Care will be provided' (line 35). He then reveals that he does 'utilize family and grandparents' to provide at least some of this 'twenty four hour day care' (lines 36–9). Implicit in his answer is the assumption that being there for the children can be done without his presence.

After Extract 3, John describes his childcare arrangements in detail. When the children are in his custody, he is at work (sometimes bringing them to work with him, where the children watch television or play video games), he is at church (bringing them with him), his father is caring for them or picking them up from the bus, or his 'parents' are caring for them until he comes home from work. Even with his employer 'helping him out' by letting him leave work early, he does not arrive home until six to seven at night.

In short, John is often not physically present with the children when they are in his custody, and even when he is physically present his schedule goes on essentially uninterrupted, with the children merely accompanying him.

In this extract, therefore, John (with the help of the mediators) has solidified his version of being there for the children, especially when contrasted with Susan's inability to provide an answer as to how she would provide care. Susan's inability to provide care is also made visible by the actions of the mediators, through their questions. Thus all participants, acting together, produce the privileging of John's version of being there for the children over Susan's.

There are occasions in the data when Susan does speak up for herself and challenges John's claims. Extract 4 shows Mediator B helping Susan to express disagreement with John by noticing her shake of the head and soliciting her explanation of her disagreement. Susan uses her turn to challenge John's account of the amount of time he spends with the children (lines 8–11).

Extract 4

```
1   J:    So I'm always there .h (0.3) u:m (0.5) when they get home?
2         °An'° ((Susan begins shaking her head here.)) (0.3) °In thuh
3         day er whatever.°
4                (0.5)
5         °A:n'°=
6   MB:   =Yer not agreeing with him.
7                (.)
8   S:    No 'e's not always home. He's usually gone hunting? Or .h
```

9   (.) gone tuh work out before they go tuh school because
10   'ey call me in 'uh mornings tuh- .h (.) if they need
11   somethin' or in th' evenin's when they get home.

John is living with his parents now, so perhaps there is another adult there when John is away. But Susan's claim that the children call her and ask her to come to John's parents' home suggests that the grandparents do not or cannot adequately meet the children's needs. Susan thus implies that John may be leaving the children unattended or that the children prefer her brand of 'being there' to his.

Gendered spousal roles

As the session continues, John defends himself against Susan's assertion that he is not always home and available to care for the children. He uses the traditional nature of their marriage as a resource to define the meaning of the time he spent with (or absent from) the family during the marriage, an argument that relies on the gendered nature of the couple's spousal and parental roles. Their shared history thus becomes a resource for John as he works to create a reality in which his absence still qualifies as 'being there'.

At this point in the session, John has made many criticisms and complaints about Susan's performance of the role of parent. Mediator A asks Susan whether she wants to respond to 'what John talked about', or whether she would rather talk to the mediators alone. Mediator A thereby works to integrate Susan's perspective into the debate, while at the same time displaying sensitivity to her apparent reluctance to speak; perhaps also out of a feeling that John's accusations delve into sensitive personal topics. After several long pauses, Susan explains that she and John always argue, and 'have never been able to talk to one another'. She says that she has 'been there' for her family 'ninety nine point nine percent of the time'. John and Susan then contest each other's history of 'being there' for the children. John reminds her that there was a time when she worked, too. Susan counters that even when she was working she always got the children on the bus because John would go out hunting or to the gym. John's silence seems to concede Susan's point.

Later, when Susan is explaining why she likes their current plan of sharing the children's time equally, she argues that the children benefit by spending more time with their father now than they ever did during the marriage. A few minutes later, John responds to Susan's implied accusation that he did not spend enough time with the children. John first denies that he was there as seldom as Susan claims, but then goes on to describe a work scenario during the marriage in which he was hardly ever in the home. He worked ten or twelve hours a day, including weekends, at times only getting home in time to say goodnight to the kids. John's account of his participation in family life during the marriage sounds pretty close to 'never being there'. But he embeds these facts in claims about what they meant. He claims that he was a good provider, and he worked long hours not for selfish reasons but for his family's benefit and 'nice life-style'. He always told his family that he loved them, and he was not 'an abusive man'. Without talking directly about gender, he orients to a traditional model of marriage in which the male provider role is central. Thus, he implies that he should get credit for being there, because he did it for his family.[18]

John admits that he did go out hunting and fishing, presumably taking even more time away from the family, on top of his long work hours. But he presents these absences in a positive light, by describing these trips as 'hobbies'. Hobbies are considered normal, natural things for adults to do. Since hobbies tend to be gendered in our society (hunting vs. knitting, for example), he can claim these hobbies as part of his normal, natural male gender. The hobbies of hunting and fishing require that he be absent from the home for significant periods of time. John's choice of these particular hobbies diminishes even further his ability to be there for the children, but in the logic of his 'gender order' they are normal and justified.

John is therefore able to use the traditional marriage he and his wife shared as a resource to claim a different standard of 'being there' for the children from the one Susan is held to. In this mediation session, it is not clear whether Susan realizes she is holding herself to a higher standard of 'being there' than John does.

However, while the mediators do not challenge John's construction of the 'being there' issue, there are points in the session where they work to encourage John to accept shared parenting rather than try to get sole residential custody. As the session continues, the mediators question John about his desire to gain full residential custody. Mediator A asks John 'Would it be fair to say that you would be in favor of a shared parenting plan if you could have more comfort with the concerns that you raised in terms of …'. After a 0.8-second silence, John begins his answer to this question with a strong agreement ('Oh I think definitely'), but then adds more criticisms of Susan's performance as a mother which work to justify his position further (Extract 5).

Extract 5

```
1   J:   I was scared t'death. Because .h (0.3) when it goes
2        in? an' it's (0.9) Dad against Mom? I mean it's like
3        (0.7) h! Dad!'s done! (0.6) An' I told 'er I said I:
4        will not, I can not? I cannot live without my kids, I
5        cannot live with seein' 'em .h (0.3) two days on 'uh
6        weekend, an' then as (0.5) time progressed an' things
```

---

[18] Christiansen and Palkovitz (2001) argue that just as women's housework is invisible labour, because it is unpaid, men's provision of financial resources for the family has become invisible because it takes place outside of the home. Provision is a manifestation of love for the children which is often ignored in discussions of family life. In traditional families, with men providing financially and women providing most of the childcare, men's contribution to the care of the children has often been devalued.

```
7        (0.8) mm (0.7) CAME T' LIGHT an' things: were (1.4)
8        >Some uh th' lifestyle chang- I mean wh' we first
9        separated?< .h (0.5) There's w's things I didn't
10       know! (0.5) an' it was: I mean it was (0.3) >Things I
11       di'n' know thing I did know an' it was< .h (0.8) It
12       was y'know I- h! I HAVE NO question! (0.6) I have no
13       question in my mind °that she loves 'em! ° (1.8) But
14       thuh QUESTihhon=hinh! .h (.) Thuh quehhstion I <have
15       is that> (1.1) eh- an' I do (1.3) of- of that? (1.8)
16       major of uh lifestyle change whether? .h (0.9) she-
17       >li'=I=said< doesn't make any dif- whether it's
18       CASUAL er whether that people have had tuh help her
19       home! (0.6) That (0.6) Y'know? .h (0.5) But that
20       does! he- It CANnot be that uh child's raised, eight
21       an' thirteen years in an environment that .h (0.3)
22       these things are wrong? (0.6) °>An' these thing-<°
23       .h (0.3) RIGHT er WRONG! (1.2) W- Or whether y'
24       'gree er not! .h (0.4) Then all of uh sudden now that
25       (0.4) °that's okay! ° (0.6) Y'know there was (0.4)
26       there was uh gen'lemen introduced (0.6) tuh my
27       children? (0.8) One week after (0.9) we separated!
28       (1.1) That (0.8) >spent thuh night< °there?° (0.3)
29       (Susan shakes her head in pause.) >Things like
30       that!< (0.6) An' I have (0.5) I did not (0.7) answer
31       questions fer thuh children but thuh questions °came! °
32       (0.7) An' I referred 'em t' their mother. (0.6) °Ask
33       yer Mom! ° (0.9) °I don't know if I c'n help. ° .h (0.2)
34       Those things were concerns tuh them? (0.7) They
35       would- They asked thuh questions. (0.7) They did ask
36       °thuh questions. °
```

John begins by describing his initial fears that because he was the male parent the courts would decide that the children should live with their mother (lines 1–3). While at some points in the mediation session (discussed above) John used the gender-neutral term 'parent', here it is to his strategic advantage to use the gendered terms 'Mom' and 'Dad', because the use of 'Mom' evokes shared background assumptions about mothers' special relationship with their children which justify his belief that 'Moms' get preferential treatment from the courts. This choice of the term 'Mom' may also serve to set up what happens in the next few lines of his extended turn, in which John again criticizes Susan's alcohol use (lines 17–19) and claims that she had her boyfriend sleep over at the house (lines 25–8). While earlier in the session (see Extract 1 above) he used the term 'parent' to refer to Susan when it was to his strategic advantage to do so, in lines 32 and 33 he uses the terms 'Mom' and 'mother' instead of saying 'Susan' or 'her'. The use of this term implicitly challenges Susan's ability to be a good mother by setting up motherhood and sexual behaviour as incongruent. As White (2002: 414) points out, 'if "mother" is associated with nurturance and care, a description of behaviours departing from these expectations will serve to reference deviance'.[19]

Susan does not intervene verbally to respond to these criticisms, but she does shake her head in line 29. While in ordinary conversation, accusations have a preference for disagreement (the next expected action after an accusation would be a denial of the accusation; Pomerantz, 1984a), in this mediation programme an opposing disputant is not supposed to speak until they have been selected to speak by the mediators (Garcia, 1991). Thus denials will not typically be placed adjacent to accusations. The interactional organization of mediation prevents arguments by eliminating adjacent placement of oppositional utterances which can escalate into disputes (Garcia, 1991).

In this mediation session, there are several instances in which John interrupts Susan or even argues with her to insert his side of the issue into the conversation, not always waiting for his turn to speak. The mediators generally do not challenge these deviations from mediation format (Extract 2 above is an exception). While Susan hardly ever speaks out of turn, she does shake her head at times to register her disagreement with what John is saying while conforming to the mediation rules. By restricting herself to non-verbal gestures, Susan makes her denials of accusations not as strong as John's verbal responses. In sum, part of the 'doing' of gender in this session, and Extract 5 in particular, may be Susan's compliance with the rules and procedures of mediation, and deference to John as a function of their family interactional norms.

Later on, Susan provides an account for her failure to speak up for herself consistently during the mediation session.

Extract 6

```
1    MA:   So d'you have any um (1.7) Anything that chu wanna
2          say tuh John about, um, yer relationships?
3                (0.6)
4    MA:   That, would help to allay his fears about thuh
5          children?
6                (0.2)
7    S:    It doesn't matter. (0.3) Whatever I say he doesn't
8          believe anyway. (0.8) I try tuh tell 'im stuff that-
9          (0.3) just like thuh drinkin'? He thinks that I do it so
10         mu:ch an' .h (0.2) An' I'm drunk? An' all this stuff
11         an' it's not true? (1.0) He can thin- An' he's gonna
12         think what he wants 'uh think. (.) It dudn't matter
13         what I tell I'm. He won't believe me.
```

[19] See also Stokoe (2006); Stokoe and Edwards (2011); Land and Kitzinger (2007). Stivers *et al.* (2007: 17) note that when reference techniques other than a person's name are used, 'they are

Here Susan clarifies why she has been relatively silent during the session, for the most part letting John set the agenda and only occasionally challenging his claims and accusations. We learn here that her relative silence is apparently a deliberate response, arisen out of hopelessness of being able to communicate with John (lines 7–8, 12–13). Susan's statement this late in the mediation session indicates that the mediators' efforts to put the discussants on an equal footing has not been entirely successful, in spite of the mediators' clear preference for an egalitarian solution to their childcare conflict, which coincided with Susan's wishes. Susan has expressed both here and elsewhere in the transcript (not shown) that she felt silenced during the marriage and she feels silenced in mediation.

A few minutes later, the mediators make another attempt to move John in the direction of accepting shared residential custody with Susan. Mediator A points out some areas of agreement between the spouses, and proposes that John does not really want custody:

Extract 7

```
1   MA:   So: it SEEMS LIKE (2.7) in many ways yer very
2         close. (0.9) um To: workin' out uh parenting plan.
3                (1.0) ((John rolls eyes up to ceiling during silence–
4         looks skeptical.))
5         U:m tch Closer than uh LOT uh people we see (0.8)
6         come in here an' somebody's (0.6) ADamant. I want
7         custody! um .hh=it doesn't sound like you want custody,
8         so much John as you would (2.0) uh like tuh have=hh (0.3)
9         asSURANCES that thuh children will °u:m° (0.8) tch (1.0)
10        hh!Be comfortable? Be: safe? Be: um (1.0) in an environment
11        that is: (1.1) that's good fer them.
12               (0.6)
13  MB:   An' be protected from some=uh=thuh=things °of which=you
14        don't° °°approve.°°
15               (1.1)
16  J:    °°tch Sure.°°
```

In Extract 7, Mediator A acknowledges that there is a difference of opinion between the disputants relative to the child custody issue. She calls upon her experience as a family mediator to characterize John's position as more concerned with ensuring the children are raised in a good environment than in securing custody for himself. However, John's response to this statement provides a very minimal level of support for it. First, in the silence after Mediator A's statement in lines 1 and 2 that they are 'very close' to working out a parenting plan, John rolls his eyes upward, indicating disbelief or scepticism.

openly choosing some attribute to pick out, or one of the possible attributes or kin relations to explictly associate the individual with'.

While Mediator A is only visible on the video-tape from the back and right side, it apears that she is looking down at this point and does not observe his expression. Second, after Mediator A has completed her turn and Mediator B has added her extension of this thought in lines 13–14, there is a 1.1-second silence. After this silence, John very quietly says '°°tch Sure. °°'. The delay and subdued volume indicate this is a very unenthusiastic agreement with Mediator B's statement. Subsequent events support the interpretation that John is not agreeing with this statement. This exchange is followed by a long sequence in which the mediators address the complaints John has brought up and try to find ways that John could accept these 'differences' and become reconciled to a shared custody arrangement. However, John steadfastly sticks to his position. When these efforts to lessen the distance between the disputants fail, the mediators turn to the technique of caucusing with each disputant individually. In their individual caucus with Susan, she again repeats her belief that there is no point in challenging John's complaints, because no matter what she says he will not believe her.

Thus the mediation session ends with an unresolved disjuncture between the disputants on the issue of residential custody of the children. They schedule another mediation session in which they plan to address these issues further.

Conclusions

In this chapter we have shown how participants collaboratively construct the local micro-political gender order through accounts of their personal histories, their use of person reference, and their representations of their parental and spousal roles. While our analysis supports the notion that participants collaboratively create local gender orders, this does not mean that all parties' interests are equally well served by their creation. John's ability successfully to negotiate background assumptions about gendered roles which support his goals proves to be an effective strategy.

In this divorce mediation session, the spouses contest each other's positions regarding the shared parenting plan and the suitability of the wife for shared custody of the children. They co-construct versions of 'being there' for the children that are based on gendered spousal roles: husband as provider, and wife as homemaker. Susan's version of 'being there' for the children means being physically available to meet their needs and treating them as her primary concern. John cannot claim to have 'been there' for the children in the same way as his wife was during their marriage. However, he accounts for his not being there by referencing gendered models of the family and the male provider role. His post-separation ability to continue to fulfil this 'ideal worker role' (Williams, 2000) is facilitated by his parents' provision of childcare, just as it was facilitated by Susan during their marriage. Since their separation, John's schedule essentially goes on uninterrupted by childcare responsibilities.

Susan, however, has shown that she expects to have a work schedule that matches her children's school and vacation schedule so that she can perform both breadwinning and care work on her own. The net effect is that Susan's post-divorce performance of the mothering role is revealed as inadequate as a breadwinner because of her childcare obligations, and inadequate as a parent because of her breadwinning obligations (Williams, 2000).

John, understandably, marshals every rhetorical device he can in support of his position. Susan, as she suggests because of the nature of her relationship with John, does not assert herself as frequently or as forcefully as she could to argue her case. At the end of the first session, John still holds out for full custody; his version of 'being there' is let stand because it has not been challenged by Susan or the mediators. Susan goes into the next session in a relatively weak position, which could be potentially consequential for the outcome of the mediation process.

We have attempted to demonstrate how inequality between males and females, in a particular interaction, was created and maintained through talk. This happened in spite of the efforts of the skilful and well-trained mediators, who worked on several occasions to elicit Susan's perspective and to challenge John's position. Perhaps the inequality in this interaction came about because of the delicate position the mediators were in of trying to empower the weaker disputant while, at the same time, avoiding the appearance of female bias against the male.

Our analysis of this mediation session suggests that the type of marriage participants have is likely to be consequential for their discussion of the issues under dispute in a divorce mediation session. Because of this, it may be helpful for mediators to elicit information from the spouses early on in the session (or from a brief pre-mediation questionnaire) about their habitual family patterns and parental roles. This information-gathering phase would enable mediators to address up front any differing expectations between the spouses or between the mediators and the spouses about the relative practicality and value of shared parenting. Through this process, information could also be obtained about typical communication problems or patterns that might impact on both spouses' participation in the mediation session. This type of activity could bring couples' gendered norms, expectations and communication patterns out in the open so they can be talked about explicitly rather than remaining tacit and invisible.

Inequality in this particular interaction was created partly through gendered rhetorical techniques, but more importantly by the whole stream of behaviour by all the parties. The participants' life histories, religious beliefs and previous relationships to each other are resources for this negotiation. Mediation does not start from a blank slate and create the world anew. Inequality (whether gendered or not) cannot be studied just by looking at gendered strategies or the actions of men as opposed to women; the whole stream of behaviour must be considered. Our job as analysts is not to find a scientifically verifiable way of studying gender, but to understand what happens in particular instances – for these people, right here, right now, how was this outcome achieved? At times the explicit use of gender, or at least a demonstrable orientation to gender, can be perceived in the talk itself. But to argue that these types of evidence are the only ways that gender is relevant in talk is to ignore the main points of Garfinkel's work: we must pay attention to the unseen, unnoticed background assumptions and routine practices and procedures through which we construct and reconstruct our shared social worlds.

14   Gender as a practical concern in children's management of play participation

Jakob Cromdal

Introduction

In everyday life, people act in ways that are observably gendered. That is to say, as members of society we are capable of understanding human behaviour in terms of (the two available) gender categories. What is more, as Garfinkel (1967) has pointed out, we are overwhelmingly prone to do so. According to Kessler and McKenna (1978), this process of gender attribution, albeit mostly unnoticed, forms one of the ways through which people crucially make sense of one another's actions. This can become acutely noticeable when, for instance, we find ourselves unable to tell a person's sex or, more often, when we notice people engaging in actions typically associated with the other gender. But the process of gender attribution does not merely concern (other) people: we sometimes conceive of certain actions, activities, traits, preferences and so on in terms of gender binaries. Here, researchers within ethnomethodology, and its allied disciplines of conversation analysis and discursive psychology, have come to articulate a view of gender as a form of social and cultural practice (see, e.g., Fenstermaker & West, 2002; Hopper & LeBaron, 1998; McIlvenny, 2002a; Nilan, 1995; Speer, 2005a; Stokoe, 2004; 2006; West & Zimmerman, 1987; Wowk, 1984, for some central discussions of an ethnomethodological approach to the study of gender). In this growing body of work we find, in a very general sense, a view of gender as something that emerges between people, rather than resides within them. When it emerges, it does so as a concern for participants engaged in some form of interaction, and therefore becomes observable in the ways through which they note, invoke or otherwise orient to gender as part of their ongoing

This chapter is partially based on a presentation given at the Second International Conference on Conversation Analysis, Copenhagen, May 2002. I wish to thank a number of colleagues who have generously commented on the data presented here: Derek Edwards, Katarina Eriksson Barajas, Rebecca Jones, Jane Montague, Ann Phoenix, Pam Shakespeare, Anna Sparrman, Susan Speer and Elizabeth Stokoe. Any remaining shortcomings are of course entirely my own. This work was partly prepared during my year as visiting research fellow with the Loughborough University Discourse and Rhetoric Group (DARG), financially supported through a scholarship from the Swedish Foundation for International Cooperation in Research and Higher Education (STINT).

business. In a nutshell, gender is viewed as a matter of social conduct. As a members' phenomenon, gender is an indexical, often fleeting and invariably locally produced feature of social action.

Against this backdrop, I examine in this chapter how children invoke cultural conceptions of gender by categorizing persons and their actions in certain ways, and how this practice serves to deal with local matters of participation in peer group activities. Drawing on a corpus of video-recorded recess activities of two groups of students attending grades 2 and 4 respectively (roughly corresponding to 8 and 10 years of age) at an English school in Sweden, I present two episodes of interaction in which the participants are pursuing different interactional projects with regard to play participation. In the first episode, two girls are collaboratively building their actions so as to enforce their territorial rights. The second extract shows how a group of girls strive to engage two boys in an upcoming play event. The analysis explores how, in pursuing these interactional projects, the participants invoke and exploit some culturally distributed notions of gendered behaviour. By examining the participants' categorization work, I demonstrate how gender stereotypes are brought about in the interaction to accomplish social action. In other words, the present chapter points at some ways through which gender relations as well as social and moral orders are invoked and locally produced in children's mundane interaction. By fleshing out the methods through which the participants accomplish this, the analysis adds to the existing body of work in ethnomethodology on gender-in-interaction. More generally, by analysing the interactional workings of membership categories, this chapter contributes to our understanding of how young people draw upon and exploit local orders – as well as those of society at large – to organize their ordinary activities. Hence, the analysis offers some of the empirically grounded insight into children's social worlds that is notably missing in the current sociological approach to childhood advanced by A. James and Prout (1990) and others (e.g., A. James *et al.*, 1998; Mayall, 1996; Qvortrup, 2005; see Cromdal, 2009, for a discussion).

Children, social interaction and gender

In his lectures on membership categorization, Sacks (e.g., 1992, I: 236; see also 1972) examined a short story of a nearly 3-year-old child to uncover the organizing principles that allow members to make sense of descriptions and other actions in culturally methodical ways. This categorization 'apparatus' (Sacks, 1972: 218) deals with how categories inferentially relate to one another as well as to typified traits and behaviours, or category-bound 'predicates' and 'activities'. While not solely an exercise in analysing gender – its scope and application were much wider than that – Sacks's work on membership categorization came to inform some of the earliest interaction-oriented explorations of how children come to behave in accountably gendered ways. For instance, Garnica (1979) examined how staff at a nursery centre would use gendered person terms when talking to young female children (aged 1–2 years). Garnica observed that staff often elaborated on the same-sex person term 'girl', supplying a number of attributes and activities that are commonly associated with the female gender (e.g., 'long hair', 'wearing a dress', etc.). In contrast, the cross-sex person term 'boy' was typically used without further elaboration. According to Garnica, these observations elucidate mundane ways through which very young children learn to associate attributes and activities with gender categories in ways that accord with what is commonsensically known and taken for granted in the adult community.

In Cahill's (1986) analysis of the language of social identification in preschool activities, he demonstrates how 2-year-old children drew upon parental kin categories such as 'mommy' and 'daddy' to identify animals, concluding that the 'family' device (comprising such categories as 'mommy', 'daddy', 'baby', etc.) 'often serves as the organizing framework for young children's collective activities' (p. 300). Cahill argues that children's use of this categorization device – its 'generative grammar of categorical identification' (p. 300) – serves as an important cultural resource for young children's gender socialization.

Garnica's and Cahill's work offers empirical demonstrations of the impact of language – through its role in social identification, categorization and mundane interaction – on young children's acquisition of gender identity. Subsequent studies of social interaction have focused on the *in vivo* accomplishment of gender relations in children's mundane activities. For instance, analysing the talk of preschool children, Danby and Baker (1998) show how a group of boys engaged in script-like acts of 'terror' when initiating younger boys to the activities of the 'block area' – a place designed for children to play with building blocks. According to the authors, such ritualized activities, including comments on and displays of bodily strength and threats of physical violence, revealed the older boys' notions of masculinity and served to produce and sustain the dominant social order of the block area. Following up on these observations, Danby (1998) shows in a single episode how a group of girls imitate boys' routine exchanges as a way of mocking and ridiculing one of the boys, while at the same time sustaining his interest in their interaction. Hence, Danby's study illustrates how the gendered orders of the peer group provide its members with local discursive resources, or *ethnomethods*, for carrying out interactional work.

In another study of cross-gender play, Weatherall (2002b: 775) shows how 4-year-old children struggle to 'come to grips with gender identity categories and the category-bound activities associated with them'. In particular, her analyses show how different occupations are linked up with gender categories, and how such categorial associations are explicitly brought to the fore and debated in the children's interactions. Children's use of the inferential order of membership category devices is further demonstrated by C. W. Butler and Weatherall (2006), who focus on members' procedures for 'mapping' (Sacks, 1992, I) oneself and others into relevant sets of categories in role play episodes, for instance when playing 'family'.

In teenage groups, gender often becomes intertwined with matters of romance and sexuality. For instance, Tholander (2002) shows how Swedish teenagers invoke romantic themes to build sequences of teasing, and that teasing actions are typically directed at members of the other sex, regardless of the nature of the precedent action that has given rise to the teasing. This leads him to conclude that the adolescents' choice of cross-sex teasing targets testifies to the salience and interactional relevance of gender in their daily conduct. While this should perhaps remain an open issue, Tholander's (2002) as well as Weatherall's (2002b) studies point to an area that has recently caused some (conceptual, methodological as well as ideological) concern among scholars of social interaction, namely how to study gender-in-action, i.e., gendered identities, relations and norms from within interactional exchanges, without imposing the analyst's own – often ideologically motivated – notions of gender upon the participants' unique understandings of their conduct.

Studying gender as a members' accomplishment

The focus of ethnomethodological inquiry on the witnessably accountable properties of participants' practical actions, gendered or otherwise, has led to a scholarly debate on the compatibility of a feminist research agenda with a participant-oriented approach to social interaction as known from ethnomethodology and conversation analysis (e.g., McIlvenny, 2002b; Speer, 1999; 2002a; Stokoe, 2006; Stokoe & Smithson, 2001). One of the obvious concerns has to do with the conceptualization of feminism. According to Stockill and Kitzinger (2007: 233), the intellectual task of a feminist conversation analysis is to 'expose[] the ways in which gender is constructed in everyday interaction'. Now, if this is taken to imply an analytic interest that reaches beyond the (demonstration of) members' own orientations to gender as an accountable feature of their actions, then such a position can only be maintained at the price of compromising some of the basic principles of ethnomethodology (cf. Wowk, 2007). If, on the other hand, we set out to examine the observable-reportable features of members' 'gendering work' (Eglin, 2002) as part of their *in situ* practices of reasoning – hence retaining the ethnomethodological concern with analysing the situated nature of social organization in terms of participants' own displayed understandings of their joint conduct – then the uniquely feminist contribution seems less obvious: in what way would such an approach differ from other forms of ethnomethodological inquiry not prefaced by the label 'feminist'?

While recognizing the relevance of this discussion to the wider field of discourse studies, in this chapter I try to stay indifferent to such considerations. Rather, the chief concern of the analysis to follow is with the ways in which young persons make relevant culturally available notions of gender in their peer group interactions. Taking Sacks's (1992) work on membership categorization as a point of departure, and particularly the notion of category-bound activities and predicates, I wish to entertain the *possibility* that certain activities, habits, traits or preferences may be associated with – among other things – gender categories. It is worth pointing out that this is a possibility not only – not even primarily – for the social theorist, but rather for the members themselves. That is to say, in situated interaction, it is a possibility for members to *treat* the activities, habits, preferences and so on *as* naturally bound to gender categories. This, of course, happens on some occasions, while not on others. This may be of little controversial value, but it is what makes it a *possibility*; a members' option in social interaction. It is this option, the possibility for members to *notice gender* in one way or another, and for various local purposes in talk, that I will be exploring in this chapter (see Stokoe, this volume, on relevance and repair of gender in membership categorization).

Treating activities and attributes bound to gender categories is sometimes thought of, in vernacular terms, as gender stereotyping. Such stereotypes are, in Schutz's (1973) terminology, commonsense-based typifications and generalizations of gender. For the ordinary member of society, they provide *possible* shorthand understandings of actions, persons and events – they form a class of members' methods for practical reasoning. However, such understandings are not always treated as contextually appropriate options, such that conversationalists may be held accountable for showing an understanding of a person or her actions based on gender stereotypes. For instance, some analysts have shown how participants at talk orient to, and deal with, the possibility of being heard as sexist (Speer, 2002b; Stokoe & Smithson, 2001) or heterosexist (Speer, 2005a; Speer & Potter, 2000). As a matter of contrast, the analysis at hand will focus on practices of unmitigated, publicly displayed, gender-stereotyped inferencing. It will attempt to show how members – in this case schoolchildren – invoke such typified, culturally available, notions of gendered behaviours, traits and dispositions to pursue specific interactional goals.

Gender and the practicalities of managing participation in play

Several studies of interaction located in the playground have highlighted the work in which children engage to organize participation in peer activities.

For instance, studies of children's procedures for entering ongoing events (Björk-Willén, 2007; C. W. Butler, 2008; C. Cobb *et al*., 2009; Corsaro, 2005; Cromdal, 2001; Danby & Baker, 1998) show how candidate participants produce samples of locally relevant competence – demonstrating knowledge of the rules, displaying relevant and/or desirable artefacts, invoking adequate or even superior physical capacities, and the like – and conversely, how players sometimes produce and trade on local orders to counter such entry bids, thus keeping the candidate children out of their activity.

Extract 1 shows how two girls, Jolanta and Magdalena, protect their play territory, a *koja*[1] or 'hideout', from potential intrusion of Steven, a non-member of the *koja*-team (cf. line 9), while at the same time sustaining the boy's attention and presence at the location (see Cromdal, 2001; 2004, for other discussions of this extract). The analysis begins with a set of observations about how the two female *koja*-members recurrently invoke gender categories in their exchange with Steven, then proceeds with an explication of the interactional work that the girls' use of membership categories is designed to accomplish. Just prior to this exchange, Steven had dropped his stick so that it landed in the *koja*, and the transcript begins with Jolanta picking it up and looking up at the boy. Since the data were collected in a bilingual environment,[2] with Swedish and English as the two languages chiefly spoken at the school, it may be pointed out that all transcripts show the language used in the original recordings. For utterances in Swedish (marked in bold), English translations (marked in italics) are supplied in the next unnumbered line.

Extract 1 (Lost stick. Lunch break, year 2)

```
01   Jol:         THAnk you ve:ry much!
02   Steven:      Ahm (.) I'm telling the [teacher.
03   Magdalena:                           [↑TATTLE ↓tale
04                ↑TAttle ↓tale ↑tattle↓tale ((teasing melody))
05   Steven:      Give it [back!]
06   Jolanta:             [The- ] the boys always call the girls
07                tattle (↑tellers).
08                        (1.0)
09   Magdalena:   If you: prom
ise (0.5) to leave us alone.
```

[1] The Swedish word *koja* translates literally into English as 'treehouse', 'hut' or 'shack'. However, I have no record of anyone (children or staff) using any of the English terms when referring to the children's hideouts. Instead, the Swedish equivalent was used in English speech, as a borrowed lexical unit. I therefore chose to stick to this term in the present text. During a period of my fieldwork, *koja*-play was the most frequent activity during recess at the school. Each episode starts as a team of players finds a suitable (often recurring) location, e.g., in a cleft or shelf in the rocks, up in a tree or behind some bushes. Having settled in, the *koja*-owners soon find themselves being raided by other teams of children. This organization of play makes *koja*-owners rather suspicious towards out-of-team visitors. It also leaves many possibilities for non-players to attempt enrolment as bouncers or *koja*-guards.

[2] For details concerning data collection see Cromdal (2001; 2004).

10		(1.5)
11	Jolanta:	You can sit there but you can't keep on
12		screaming at us like that.
13	Steven:	(I can do) worse (.) if I want >give us
14		the stick <u>back</u>.<
15	Jolanta:	An' you promise not to- that you wi[ll not-
16	Magdalena:	[(Well) DON't
17		give it BACK! ((*to Jolanta*))
18		(0.5)
19	Magdalena:	<u>Boys</u> are not allowed to (have) sticks (.) ok↑ay?
20	Jolanta:	((retrieves the stick)) Boys a[re stu:pid.
21	Steven:	[You ↑kno:w I'll
22		steal <u>all</u> your sticks.
23	Jolanta:	We don't <u>have</u> any=
24	Magdalena:	**=Du FÅR inte tillbaka pinnen (.) fattar [du inte de**
25		*=you can't HAVE the stick back don't [you get it*

As Jolanta picks up the stick, she looks up at Steven, sitting on top of a rock right above the *koja* (line 1), teasingly offering her gratitude for the stick. Steven's hearing of this action as mockery is evident in his next move: he counters Jolanta's action by threatening to tell on her to the teacher. This move is immediately exploited by Magdalena, the second *koja*-owner, who challenges Steven with being a tattle tale,[3] producing her turn in a conventional sing-song rhyme: '↑TATTLE ↑tale ↑TAttle ↓tale ↑t<u>a</u>ttle↓tale' (lines 3–4). In response to this, Steven produces an emphatically marked command, demanding his stick back. Note that Jolanta's next move builds on Magdalena's previous turn, picking up on the theme of tattling and pointing out that it is habitual for boys to accuse the girls of such behaviour. This testifies to the close collaborative organization of the girls' conduct: they are accountably acting as a team.

In addition to its collaborative design, Jolanta's turn in lines 6–7 offers some interesting insights into the local use – and usefulness – of membership categorization devices. Let us therefore consider this action in some detail. The first thing to note about Jolanta's turn is that it makes relevant the intersection of two category collections, or devices, which we may label peer group[4] and gender. Sack's first hearer's maxim (1992, I: 247) – which specifies that if two categories, drawn from the same population, can be heard as belonging to the same

---

[3] Indeed, we can see that Magdalena is able to project the turn as a threat to tell the teacher, allowing her to challenge Steven with tattling before he has had a chance to declare such an intention fully.

[4] This deserves a comment. Clearly, 'boys' and 'girls' are categories that may belong to several collections, such as *gender* and *stage of life*. Hence, we are hearably dealing with male and female individuals of relatively young age, persons that may be adequately categorized as 'children'. Furthermore, the definite article *the* preceding the two categories provides for a hearing of reference terms 'the boys' and 'the girls' as not just any collection of boys and girls but a definite one. Lacking any further specification, this particular collection of boys and girls is self-

categorization device, then that indeed is an adequate hearing of the categorization – allows us to hear the population as the local peer group, now partitioned into the two relational pairs by way of the gender device. It is important to note that not only are these two gender categories explicitly identified in Jolanta's turn, but crucially, a certain mutual relationship is being invoked between their incumbents, based on their joint relational history within the peer group: 'the boys always call the girls tattle(↑tellers)'. Hence, what is being formulated here is a form of social practice, a local but recurring activity – let us call it accusing peers of tattling for lack of a better term – in which one part of the population regularly sanctions the actions of the other part for being morally deplorable. And that practice systematically cuts across the population along the gender categories. Jolanta's formulation further invokes and ascribes to the boys a collective view of girls; as persons who are particularly prone to tattling. Sacks (1992, I: 249) introduced the notion of *category-bound activities*, proposing that 'many activities are taken by Members to be done by some particular or several particular categories of Members where the categories are categories from membership categorization devices'. In our example, Jolanta is ascribing to the boys a stereotypic notion of girls as tattle tales, hence treating tattling as a type of activity typically bound to the category 'girl'.

Let us explore this point further by considering Jolanta's membership categorization work in its local context. As several analysts of social interaction have shown, categories, as well as the predicates and activities that are routinely associated with their incumbents, may be used to accomplish accusations, allocations of blame and other action types in adversary exchanges (e.g., Drew, 1978; Jayyusi, 1984; Watson, 1978). In the present exchange, Jolanta's move needs to be considered as part of a collaborative rebuttal of Steven's threat to tell on the two *koja*-owners. We should note that Jolanta does not merely hold Steven accountable for violating the moral order of the peer group by tattling (or, technically, by threatening to do so). That has already been done by Magdalena in lines 3–4 and repeating the challenge would merely stress the alignment between the two *koja*-members, which, considering that they are already on the same team, might not contribute greatly to the exchange. Rather, Jolanta can be seen to mount her adversarial move on her team-mate's prior action; she has just witnessed Magdalena accusing Steven of being a tattle tale, and now she is confronting him with the observation that this is typically what the boys in the peer group do to the girls. This allows Jolanta to add a new dimension to the exchange: Steven is no longer merely accountable for violating a norm *of the peer group at large*. Jolanta's declamation highlights the disjuncture between Steven's current actions and the conventional predicates (viewing tattling as a

evidently known to everyone present, making Jolanta's turn hearable as a reference to the local peer group. Of course, the naming of the two gender categories serves to partition that population in specific ways, shaping the upshot of her action.

specifically 'girly' practice) and behaviour (sanctioning girls' tattling, whenever spotted) *of the boys in particular*. Thus, Steven's displayed intention to tell on the girls is construed as an infraction of a gendered order. Crucially, he is held accountable for engaging in a form of behaviour that his part of the population routinely treat as typical of the other gender. This move turns on Jolanta's partitioning of the peer group across the gender device, and the ascription to the two categories of that device a set of conventional behaviours and attributes, including the corresponding attitudes and stereotypic beliefs that the incumbents of one category hold towards those of the other.

This shows how gender categories may be used to invoke local gender stereotypes and how such conventionalized notions of gendered behaviour may serve to build oppositional actions in an ordinary play episode. Let us skip ahead in the transcript to consider the next instance of gender categories being made relevant. In lines 15–17, Jolanta is beginning to hand over the stick to Steven, trying at the same time to negotiate some form of peace treaty, following up on Magdalena's previous attempt to come to a deal in line 9 ('If you: promise (0.5) to leave us alone'). However, Magdalena stops her midway, prohibiting her team-mate from returning the stick (lines 16–17). Having stopped Jolanta from returning the stick, Magdalena goes on to propose a new rule that prohibits boys from using sticks (line 19). This proposition is partly built on a general schoolyard rule, according to which it is not allowed for children to play with (big) sticks, but Magdalena seems to suggest that this rule only applies to boys. Rule formulations typically rely for their sense on categorial inferencing (C. W. Butler, 2008; C. Cobb *et al.*, 2009). According to Sacks (1992, I: 40), membership categories are *inference rich*, such that members may hear categories as naturally related to certain behaviours and dispositions. This allows for a range of commonsense expectations related to conventional behaviours and preferences of any given incumbent of a certain category. In our current example, the category 'boy' together with the object 'stick' allows us to hear 'fighting' as the relevant activity, and the rule that Magdalena proposes can only make sense if the hearer recognizes 'boys use sticks for the purposes of fighting' as what Sacks would term a 'possible correct observation' (1992, I: 260).

Note that Magdalena's turn in line 19 is packaged so as to solicit her team-mate's explicit agreement with the rule she is proposing.[5] Now, whereas Jolanta's withdrawing of the stick (line 20) is clearly compliant with Magdalena's direct order in lines 16–17, it seems less clear whether her comment that 'boys are stu:pid' serves to ratify Magdalena's rule (recognizing its underlying categorization of boys as prone to using sticks to fight), or whether she is merely attending to the fact that boys as a group have been *somehow* categorized,

---

[5] This hearing of Magdalena's action rests on the terminal question inflected 'ok↑ay?', which makes relevant an agreement as the preferred next action.

adding another category-bound feature to the incumbents of this gender category. In any event, Jolanta is accountably aligning with Magdalena's previous action, both in picking up the relevant action format (gender categorization) and in continuing (or rather, resuming) the *koja*-team's adversary treatment of Steven (Cromdal, 2004).

Clearly, then, Extract 1 shows how the two *koja*-owners use the socially distributed knowledge of gender categories, their category-bound activities and predicates, to counter Steven's demands and threats. Notably, we have seen that gender stereotypes make available a set of distinct discursive resources: as commonsense typifications and generalizations of gendered behaviour and dispositions, they offer a set of normative expectations regarding the actions of incumbents of gender categories. In social interaction, participants may formulate such expectations as norms, and use them to construct certain actions as accountable – as recognizably at odds with established gender norms, thus posing a threat to the perpetrator's social identity (e.g., Nilan, 1995; Stokoe, 2003; West & Zimmerman, 1987; Wowk, 1984).

Let us elaborate this point through a second example. This extract was drawn from the first minute of an extended episode in which a large number of fourth grade children are preparing to play war. This usually involves such practicalities as teaming up, dividing up local roles and responsibilities (cf. Sacks's, 1992, I: 490, notion of 'mapping'; see also C. W. Butler & Weatherall, 2006), defining and partitioning a geographical space, and discussing and possibly debating local rules of play. Inherent to all this is the work of negotiating social relations: relations of friendship and of power as well as of gender, to name but a few aspects of human relations. Such negotiations involve participants drawing on, and displaying for each other, an array of culturally available notions of the social world. The analysis is mainly concerned with the participants' notions of gender-specific, category-bound predicates, as these are accountably invoked and made relevant to accomplish particular actions. The excerpt shows a group of girls trying to recruit three boys to play war. The transcript begins as several girls rush out of the school building shouting 'WAR!'

Extract 2 (Not going war. Lunch break, year 4)
```
01   Several:    YE:::::Y::
02   Beatrice:   WA::R=
03   Matilda:    =WHAA::!
04   Talia:      [YEE:::]
05   Ebba:       [YA:::: ]
06   Several:    [YA:::: ]
07   (Ebba):     WA:[::R
08   Beatrice:      [WA:::R
09   Several:    WHuh HAAahhah:: eh
10   Ebba:       (Va) är dom fortvarande inne och äter?=
```

		(Wha') are they still in there eating?=
11	Lara:	**=Ja vet de.**
		=I know
12	Beatrice:	Excuse me but- (.) GUST↑A::V!
13	Beatrice:	Are you guys with?
14	Gustav:	No::? ((*The other girls approach the bench*))
15	Lara:	The boys are ↑in there its not only all gi[:rls.
16	Ebba:	((to Lara)) [Yeh but
17		(.) they don't know if they wanna be with.
18	Beatrice:	[Yeh but-]
19	Boy:	**[Varför] komm[er alla hit?]**
		[*Why*] *is every* [*one coming here?*]
20	Matilda:	((smiling)) [↑I:: thi]nk they are
21		just humiliated cuz they were asked by g<u>ir</u>ls.
22		(0.5)
23	Ebba:	<u>HEHMPHh</u>
24		(2.5) ((*Gustav and Don turn their heads to the left*))
25	Beatrice:	But [e:h >there's a problem<] (.) we can't- we have=
26	(Lara):	[HHehhh ehha:hah]
27	Matilda:	=We have to have three boys,=
28	Beatrice:	=Three boys at least one or tw[o:>won't work< f]our=
29	Pete:	**[Herre Gu::d.]**
		[*Oh my Go::d*]
30	Beatrice:	=or three.
31	Matilda:	And it <u>will</u> work if <u>you</u> guys [(decide) to go (war)]
32	Pete:	[Come o::]:n
33		((*punches Gustav on shoulder*))
34	Beatrice:	((*gives Matilda a "look"*)) >Didn't think so.<
35	( ):	[( ) ( )] [( )]
36	Beatrice:	[(That's why)] we'll make a rule, I [( )]
37	Pete:	O:[:::hh]
38	Matilda:	[Are] you guys <u>dead</u> or what.

It is evident from the transcript that the teams are short on male participants, and so a group of girls engage collectively in persuading three boys to join the play (lines 13, 15, 20–1, 25–8, 31 and 38). Let us focus on the gender work that is accomplished as part of the girls' recruitment attempts. Approaching the bench where the three boys are seated, Beatrice asks if they want to join in, or 'be with'.[6] As Gustav emphatically declines the invitation, Lara explains that

---

[6] The phrase 'to be with' is a cross-linguistic phenomenon: it is a literal translation of the Swedish phrase used for asking to enter ongoing play events 'Kan ja va me?'/'Can I be with?' Notably, this was the default English phrase that all children at the present school would use when bidding for entry into ongoing activities. In other words, what would normally be treated as a non-idiomatic grammatical construction has become an established phrase in the children's everyday interactions. As such, it comprises an unmarked instance of language borrowing. See Cromdal (2001) for further discussion.

there are other boys involved in the planned activity who have not yet come into the school yard. She then assures the boys that it is not 'only all girls' (line 15). Hence, she is acting on the assumption that the three boys' reluctance to play has to do with the observable fact that at the moment only girls are involved in the war play preparations. In other words, Lara targets the unequal gender distribution of players as a potential source of trouble, and attempts to deal with it by suggesting that there will be other boys joining in soon. This, however, is immediately problematized by Ebba, who points out that the other boys may in fact not join in at all (lines 16–17). Clearly, this may prove counterproductive for the girls' attempt to recruit the three boys, and it seems that Beatrice begins to oppose this line of reasoning ('yeh but-', line 18), but drops her turn as it overlaps with a new participant, who is wondering why everyone has gathered in front of the bench (line 19). The floor is then immediately taken by Matilda, who suggests in lines 20–1 that the boys find it humiliating to have girls asking them to join in.

It is clear that gender *somehow* comprises an accountable feature of this episode, so let us inspect its interactional features by first considering some formal properties of Matilda's move, then by proceeding to examine its categorial organization. The first thing to note about Matilda's turn (lines 20–1) is that it is delivered as a personal opinion through the preface '↑I:: think they are …'. Second, her opinion is produced in a third person format: it is produced for the three boys to (over)hear, but it specifically does not address them as recipients. It is an opinion *concerning* the boys, but it is hearably addressed to anyone present at the scene who may find an interest in hearing her opinion on the matter. There is a tiny smile on Matilda's lips as she produces her talk, and she is looking sideways down at the boys, making her action unmistakably hearable as a challenge. Yet it does not make relevant any particular response, and it does not assign a next speaker to deliver one.

The challenging force of Matilda's action merits a few comments. Her turn ascribes to the boys a particular emotional state, humiliation, and that formulation is being publicly offered as an explanation for their unwillingness to join in. It also accounts for the boys' humiliation on the grounds that they have been 'asked by girls' to play war. Thus, Matilda's turn in lines 20–1 accomplishes at least this: it ascribes to the boys an emotional state and provides for its accountability at the same time. Having been challenged by girls to play war seems to count as a perfectly legitimate reason for boys to feel humiliated. How is this achieved? What is it about being 'asked by girls' to go war that makes humiliation a relevant emotional state?

In terms of membership categorization, Matilda's turn treats activities such as asking, inviting, challenging or otherwise engaging other people in physically violent behaviour – of which playing war is clearly a species – as bound to the category 'boy' (invoked by her identification of its standard relational category pair, 'girl'). In this sense, she can be seen to invoke a common gender stereotype of males as typically disposed towards fighting, aggression, warfare, etc. In our example, however, it is the girls who seem eager to play war, while the three boys on the bench seem overwhelmingly unwilling to engage in this activity. Thus, the membership categorization work accomplished by Matilda in lines 20–1 turns on the recognition of a gendered social order. That is to say, in order to see the girls' invitation to play war as humiliating for boys, one needs to recognize the commonsense expectations associated with gender categories. This involves knowledge of such category-bound behaviours, preferences, traits and dispositions as form the cultural fundaments of gender stereotypes.

Jayyusi (1984) and other scholars of social interaction (e.g., Hester, 2000; Osvaldsson, 2004; Stokoe & Edwards, 2011) have pointed to the close relationship between the categorial organization of actions at talk and the reflexive, local production of moral orders. Let us note that humiliation implies, by its definition, some form of moral misconduct, so by ascribing to the boys this emotional state, Matilda casts their failure to act in gender-appropriate ways as a transgression of the moral order. In fact, it is possible to hear Matilda's turn as both challenging and admonishing – as an instruction concerning how the boys *ought to* feel, or at least how any proper incumbent of the category 'boy' would feel having failed to accept an invitation to play war, especially when the inviting party is a girl.

Following upon Matilda's turn, we find that the so-far rather lively interaction suddenly goes very quiet. During the relatively lengthy pause (lines 22–4), broken only by Ebba's suppressed outburst of laughter in line 23, we get a glimpse of some of the participants' reactions to Matilda's comment. For instance, the video uptake of this sequence shows Lara's perplexed reaction, her mouth wide open as if taken by complete surprise – just before she bursts out laughing in line 26. Roughly at the same time, Gustav and Don turn away from the group of girls in front of them to face Pete, who is now standing up to their left. Judging from the other participants' reactions, then, Matilda's challenge to the boys in lines 20–1 constitutes something of an interactional peak, an unexpected kind of move.

The silence is broken by Beatrice, who takes a slightly different tack, presenting their situation as 'a problem' (line 25), which can only be solved by recruiting a minimum of three boys for their war teams. Matilda then spells it out clearly for the boys: 'it will work if you guys (decide) to go (war)' (line 31). Pete, who now seems eager to oblige the girls, punches Gustav on the shoulder (line 33) in an attempt to persuade his friend to join in. Neither Gustav nor Don seems to take notice of this, and we can see Pete letting out a frustrated 'o::::h' in line 37, followed by a new challenge by Matilda: 'are you guys dead or what' (line 38). In the end, the girls' attempts to enrol the three boys proves unsuccessful, and some minute later (not in transcript), Gustav and Don stand up and leave the area.[7]

The analysis has shown how issues of gender form an integral part of school-children's ordinary business: how children identify and make use of culturally available gender stereotypes by categorizing persons, events and actions in ways that allow them to pursue certain interactional goals by construing the actions of their interlocutors as dissonant with their relevant gender categories. Throughout the analysis I have striven to avoid relying on theories of gender, highlighting instead its practical accomplishment as oriented to in and through the participants' own conduct. Let us therefore move on to discuss some theoretical as well as methodological aspects of this work.

Discussion

It is possible to argue that ethnomethodology offers one of the most radical and empirically robust approaches to the study of gender. Garfinkel's (1967) notion of 'sexual status' as an omnirelevant feature of social conduct implies that gender constitutes *for members* 'an invariant but unnoticed background in the texture of relevances that comprise the changing actual scenes of everyday life' (p. 118). The ethnomethodologist's task, then, must be to examine and highlight the culturally available methods of practical reasoning and action by means of which members come to behave in accountably gendered ways.

One way of telling the gendered status of some behaviour is by investigating the ways through which people deploy and deal with membership categories (Hester & Eglin, 1997; Sacks, 1972; 1992; Stokoe, 2004; 2006; Watson, 1978) to produce their actions as socially intelligible in the situated unfolding of interaction. But the accomplishment of gender in interaction is an accountable matter. It is not merely an issue of local construction of meaning – it is, as Garfinkel (1967) points out, a question of moral conduct. As West and Zimmerman (1987: 27) proposed, '*Gender*...is the activity of managing situated conduct in light of normative conceptions of attitudes and activities appropriate for one's sex category' (emphasis in original). It follows, then, that failure to meet the expectations is sanctionable as a *moral* transgression (Jayyusi, 1991).

In this chapter, I have considered how young members of society deal with matters of gender as a practical concern in their mundane interactions, examining two extracts in which the participants' interactions can be glossed as 'managing participation in play'. The first extract presented a case of gatekeeping,

---

[7] In fact, the girls' search for more male participants and other preparations for the war play continued throughout the lunch break. When the bell rang some 25 minutes later, they still had not managed to set up satisfactory teams, and the war play that they were so meticulously planning was not resumed during the remaining months of my fieldwork.

with two *koja*-owners trying to assert their territorial rights by confiscating the stick of a potential intruder, while the second extract showed how a group of players attempted to recruit three prospective, yet thoroughly unwilling, participants to play war. Both events involved gender categories being invoked by female players, who elaborated and exploited the relevant category attributes to undercut the actions of their male peers. To accomplish this, they drew upon socially distributed gender stereotypes; that is, typified and generalized notions of the 'distinctive psychological and behavioural propensities' (West & Zimmerman, 1987: 127) associated with each gender category.

Through their categorization work, the girls invoked such normative forms of behaviour and contrasted them with the observed local actions (or lack thereof) of the boys. Clearly, publicly highlighting the gender incongruity in people's behaviour can be a powerful interactional resource, and may radically constrain the options available to them in the continuing interaction. Consider, for instance, the options available to Gustav and Don in Extract 2, after having been challenged by Matilda's comment that they are humiliated to be asked to play war by girls: clearly, admitting to being thus humiliated is not an appealing alternative. However, *not* feeling humiliated in a situation where the relevance of that emotional state trades on commonsense notions of gender may be seen as a failure to live up to the norms of one's own gender identity. In the light of this, it is hardly surprising to find the two boys working at 'being disattentive' towards the ongoing exchange (and shortly leaving the group altogether). In other words, if gender constitutes one of the 'seen but unnoticed' backgrounds of everyday human affairs, then it may also be subject to 'motivated noticing'. It affords members a set of methods for doing discourse work. The children's noticing of gender – of gender categories as well as their conventionally bound activities and predicates – as an interactional option, as a way of going about their ordinary business in socially accountable ways, is what Sacks (1972: 218) termed 'the fine power of culture'.

Is this all there is to gender in social life? A range of poststructuralist scholars taking a feminist approach to language and gender have pointed to a variety of practices through which gender- and sexuality-infused relations, differences and asymmetries are enacted and reproduced (e.g., Cameron, 1997b; Eckert, 2003; Wetherell & Edley, 1999; Wodak, 1997). It may be tempting for a critically oriented analyst of discourse to treat some of the data I have presented, yet left uncommented, as prime examples of gender-in-action. Consider, for instance, Extract 1, in which Steven is issuing orders (lines 5 and 13–14) and threats (lines 2, 13 and 21–2) while the two girls are repeatedly reaching out to arrive at a peaceful solution (lines 9, 11–12 and 15) – are these not, one might ask, verging on textbook examples of gendered behaviour?

There are various plausible answers to such questions. The analyses of gender work that have been discussed in this chapter do not aspire to give a complete sense of the children's understanding of gender relations. Nor does ethnomethodology make any claims to the ultimate understanding of gender in society. What it does provide is a competitive approach to how we may understand the practices through which members make sense of and produce various features of social life – whether gendered or not (for an elaborate debate see Schegloff, 1997; 1998a; Wetherell, 1998). Steven's actions in Extract 1 may well be seen as hegemonically masculine, just as Jolanta's and Magdalena's actions may be thought of as tokens of their female predisposition towards dialogue and relational concern, but that reading of the data can only be arrived at *via an* a priori *formulated theory of gender relations*, whether based on scholarly work or rooted in the analyst's own experience as a member in society. It is not, however, easily compatible with the participants' own displayed understandings of the unfolding interaction. While there is no doubt that the *koja*-owners treat Steven's actions as intrusive, hostile, perhaps even threatening, there seems to be little empirical grounds for claiming that the parties to that interaction understand Steven's behaviour as specifically masculine. If anything, some of the collaborative work of the *koja*-owners seems designed to question the gender appropriateness of Steven's actions – accountably using the boys' own yardstick!

Herein lies ethnomethodology's unique contribution to the study of gender: it comprises an effort to explore *whether*, and *in what ways*, conventional notions of gender relations inform members' situated conduct. Such vernacular conceptions of gender are, following Lynch and Bogen (1996), ubiquitous, and this chapter has pointed to some of the (ethno)methods through which these conceptions are identified, formulated, managed, brought to work – and thereby reflexively produced – by a group of schoolchildren. By examining in this way the commonsense reasoning of young persons, we learn about social organization as it is being accomplished moment by moment in the course of their daily life.

References

Ainsworth-Vaughn, N. (1992). Topic transitions in physician–patient interviews: Power, gender, and discourse change. *Language in Society, 21*, 409–26.

American Psychiatric Association (1994). *Diagnostic and Statistical Manual of Mental Disorders* (4th ed.). Washington, DC: American Psychiatric Association.

Antaki, C. (1999). Interviewing persons with a learning disability: How setting lower standards may inflate well-being scores. *Qualitative Health Research, 9* (4), 437–54.

   (ed.) (in press). *Applied Conversation Analysis: Changing Institutional Practices.* Basingstoke: Palgrave Macmillan.

Antaki, C., & Widdicombe, S. (1998). Identity as an achievement and as a tool. In C. Antaki & S. Widdicombe (eds.), *Identities in Talk*. London: Sage.

Aries, E. (1996). *Men and Women in Interaction: Considering the Differences*. New York: Oxford University Press.

Atkinson, J. M., & Heritage, J. (eds.) (1984). *Structures of Social Action: Studies in Conversation Analysis*. Cambridge: Cambridge University Press.

Baker, C. D. (2000). Locating culture in action: Membership categorization in texts and talk. In A. Lee & C. Poynton (eds.), *Culture and Text: Discourse and Methodology in Social Research and Cultural Studies*. London: Routledge.

Baker, P. (2008). *Sexed Texts: Language, Gender and Sexuality*. London: Equinox.

Baron, D. (1986). *Grammar and Gender*. New Haven, CT: Yale University Press.

Barsky, A. E. (1996). Mediation and empowerment in child protection cases. *Mediation Quarterly, 14* (2), 111–34.

Bauman, Z. (2004). *Identity*. Cambridge: Polity.

Baxter, J. (2003). *Positioning Gender in Discourse: A Feminist Methodology*. Basingstoke: Palgrave.

Beach, W. A. (1996). *Conversations about Illness: Family Preoccupations with Bulimia*. Mahwah, NJ: Lawrence Erlbaum.

   (2000). Inviting collaborations in stories about a woman. *Language in Society, 29*, 379–407.

   (2006). Who are 'they'? Speakers' practices for referring to known and unknown others. Manuscript.

   (2009). *A Natural History of Family Cancer: Interactional Resources for Managing Illness*. Cresskill, NJ: Hampton Press.

Beach, W. A., & Lockwood, A. (2003). Making the case for airline *compassion fares*: The serial organization of problem narratives during a family crisis. *Research on Language and Social Interation, 36*, 351–93.

Bem, S. L. (1993). *Lenses of Gender.* New Haven, CT: Yale University Press.

Benor, S., Rose, M., Sharma, D., Sweetland, J., & Zhang, Q. (eds.) (2002). *Gendered Practices in Language.* Stanford, CA: Centre for the Study of Language and Information.

Benwell, B. (2004). Ironic discourse: Evasive masculinity in brutish men's lifestyle magazines. *Men and Masculinities, 7* (1), 3–21.

Benwell, B., & Stokoe, E. (2006). *Discourse and Identity.* Edinburgh: Edinburgh University Press.

(2010). Identity in social action: Conversation, narratives and genealogies. In M. Wetherell & C. T. Mohanty (eds.), *Sage Handbook of Identities.* London: Sage.

Berard, T. J. (2005). On multiple identities and educational contexts: Remarks on the study of inequalities and discrimination. *Journal of Language, Identity and Education, 4* (1), 67–76.

Berentzen, S. (1984). *Children Constructing their Social World: An Analysis of Gender Contrast in Children's Interaction in a Nursery School.* Bergen Occasional Papers in Social Anthropology, No. 36: Department of Social Anthropology, University of Bergen.

Bergman, J. (1993). *Discreet Indiscretions: The Social Organization of Gossip.* Hawthome, NY: Aldine de Gruyter.

Bergman, J., & Linnell, P. (eds.) (1998). Morality in discourse. Special issue of *Research on Language and Social Interaction, 31* (3/4).

Bergvall, V. L., Bing, J. M., & Freed, A. F. (eds.) (1996). *Rethinking Language and Gender Research: Theory and Practice.* Harlow: Addison Wesley Longman.

Billig, M. (1999). Whose terms? Whose ordinariness? Rhetoric and ideology in conversation analysis. *Discourse and Society, 10,* 543–58.

Björk-Willén, P. (2007). Participation in multilingual preschool play: Shadowing and crossing as interactional resources. *Journal of Pragmatics, 39,* 2133–2158.

Boden, D., & Zimmerman, D. H. (1991). *Talk and Social Structure: Studies in Ethnomethodology and Conversation Analysis.* Berkeley and Los Angeles: University of California Press.

Boenke, M. (2003). Darn those new names and pronouns. PLAG Transgender Network. www.youth-guard.org/pflag-tnet/articles/pronouns.htm. Accessed 25 April 2006.

Bohan, J. S. (1993). Regarding gender: Essentialism, constructionism and feminist psychology. *Psychology of Women Quarterly, 17,* 5–21.

Bornstein, K. (1998). *My Gender Workbook: How to Become a Real Man, a Real Woman, the Real You, or Something Else Entirely.* New York: Routledge.

Boyd, E., & Heritage, J. (2006). Taking the history: Questioning during comprehensive history-taking. In J. Heritage & D. W. Maynard (eds.), *Communication in Medical Care: Interaction Between Primary Care Physicians and Patients.* Cambridge: Cambridge University Press.

Brooks, A., & Marianne, D. (2004). Biological sex and psychological gender as predictors of routine and strategic relational maintenance. *Sex Roles, 50* (9–10), 689–97.

Bucholtz, M. (1999). Series foreword. In M. Bucholtz, A. C. Liang, & L. A. Sutton (eds.), *Reinventing Identities: The Gendered Self in Discourse.* Oxford: Oxford University Press.

(2003). Theories of discourse as theories of gender: Discourse analysis in language and gender studies. In J. Holmes & M. Meyerhoff (eds.), *The Handbook of Language and Gender.* Oxford: Blackwell.

(ed.) (2004). *Language and Woman's Place: Text and Commentaries*. New York: Oxford University Press.

Bucholtz, M., & Hall, K. (2004). Theorizing identity in language and sexuality research. *Language in Society, 33*, 469–515.

(2005). Identity and interaction: A sociolinguistic cultural approach. *Discourse Studies, 7* (4–5), 585–614.

Bucholtz, M., Liang, A. C., & Sutton, L. A. (eds.) (1999). *Reinventing Identities: The Gendered Self in Discourse*. Oxford: Oxford University Press.

Burman, D. D., Bitan, T., & Booth, J. R. (2008). Sex differences in neural processing of language among children. *Neuropsychologia, 46* (5), 1349–62.

Butler, C. W. (2008). *Talk and Social Interaction in the Playground*. Ashgate: Aldershot.

Butler, C. W., & Weatherall, A. (2006). 'No, we're not playing families': Membership categorisation in children's play. *Research on Language and Social Interaction, 39*, 441- 70.

Butler, J. (1990a). *Gender Trouble: Feminism and the Subversion of Identity*. New York: Routledge.

(1990b). Performative acts and gender constitution: An essay in phenomenology and feminist theory. In S. Case (ed.), *Performing Feminisms: Feminist Critical Theory and Theatre*. Baltimore, MD: Johns Hopkins University Press.

Buttny, R. (1997). Reported speech in talking race on campus. *Human Communication Research, 23*, 475–504.

(1998). Putting prior talk into context: Reported speech and the reporting context. *Research on Language and Social Interaction, 31*, 45–58.

Buzzanell, P. M., Sterk, H., & Turner, L. H. (eds.) (2004). *Gender in Applied Communication Contexts*. London: Sage.

Cahill, S. (1986). Language practices and self definition: The case of gender identity acquisition. *Sociological Quarterly, 27*, 295–311.

Cameron, D. (1992). *Feminism and Linguistic Theory*. Basingstoke: Macmillan.

(1996). Rethinking language and gender studies. In S. Mills (ed.), *Language and Gender: Interdisciplinary Perspectives*. Harlow: Longman.

(1997a). Demythologizing sociolinguistics. In N. Coupland & A. Jaworski (eds.), *Sociolinguistics: A Coursebook and Reader*. Basingstoke: Macmillan.

(1997b). Theoretical debates in feminist linguistics: Questions of sex and gender. In R. Wodak (ed.), *Gender and Discourse*. London: Sage.

(ed.) (1998a). *The Feminist Critique of Language: A Reader*. London: Routledge.

(1998b). Gender, language, and discourse: A review essay. *Signs, 23* (4), 945–67.

(2005a). Language, gender, and sexuality: Current issues and new directions. *Applied Linguistics, 26* (4), 482–502.

(2005b). Relativity and its discontents: Language, gender and pragmatics. *Intercultural Pragmatics, 2* (3), 321–34.

(2007). *The Myth of Mars and Venus: Do Men and Women Really Speak Different Languages?* Oxford: Oxford University Press.

(2009). Theoretical issues for the study of gender and spoken interaction. In P. Pichler & E.M. Eppler (eds.), *Gender and Spoken Interaction*. Basingstoke: Palgrave Macmillan.

Cameron, D., & Kulick, D. (2003a). *Language and Sexuality*. Cambridge: Cambridge University Press.

(2003b). Introduction: Language and desire in theory and practice. *Language and Communication, 23*, 93–105.

Cameron, D., McAlinden, F., & O'Leary, K. (1988). Lakoff in context: The social and linguistic functions. In J. Coates & D. Cameron (eds.), *Women in their Speech Communities: New Perspectives on Language and Sex.* New York: Longman.

Chaitow, L. (1998). *Fibromyalgia and Muscle Pain.* London: Thorsons/HarperCollins.

Cheshire, J., & Trudgill, P. (eds.) (1998). *The Sociolinguistics Reader: Gender and Discourse* (Vol. 2). London: Arnold.

Chesler, P. (1972). *Women and Madness.* New York: Four Wall Eight Windows.

Christiansen, S. L., & Palkovitz, R. (2001). Why the 'good provider' role still matters: Providing as a form of paternal involvement. *Journal of Family Issues, 22* (1), 84–106.

Christie, C. (2000). *Gender and Language: Towards a Feminist Pragmatics.* Edinburgh: Edinburgh University Press.

Clayman, S. E. (1992). Footing in the achievement of neutrality: The case of news interview discourse. In P. Drew & J. Heritage (eds.), *Talk at Work: Interaction in Institutional Settings.* Cambridge: Cambridge University Press.

(2007). Speaking on behalf of the public in broadcast news interviews. In E. Holt & R. Clift (eds.), *Reporting Talk: Reported Speech in Interaction.* Cambridge: Cambridge University Press.

Clayman, S., & Heritage, J. (2002). *The News Interview: Journalists and Public Figures on the Air.* Cambridge: Cambridge University Press.

Clayman, S., & Whalen, J. (1988/9). When the medium becomes the message: The case of the Rather–Bush encounter. *Research on Language and Social Interaction, 22*, 241–72.

Clift, R. (2001). Meaning in interaction: The case of 'actually'. *Language, 77* (2), 245–91.

(2006). Indexing stance: Reported speech as an interactional evidential. *Journal of Sociolinguistics, 10* (5), 569–95.

Coates, J. (1996). *Women Talk.* Oxford: Blackwell.

(1997). Women's friendships, women's talk. In R. Wodak (ed.), *Gender and Discourse.* London: Sage.

(ed.) (1998a). *Language and Gender: A Reader.* Oxford: Blackwell.

(1998b). Gossip revisited: Language in an all-female group. In J. Coates (ed.), *Language and Gender: A Reader.* Oxford: Blackwell.

(1999). Changing femininities: The talk of teenage girls. In M. Bucholtz, A. C. Liang, & L. A. Sutton (eds.), *Reinventing Identities: The Gendered Self in Discourse.* Oxford: Oxford University Press.

(2003). *Men Talk.* Oxford: Blackwell.

(2004). *Women, Men and Language: A Sociolinguistic Account of Gender Differences in Language* (3rd ed.). Harlow: Longman.

Coates, J., & Cameron, D. (eds.) (1988). *Women in their Speech Communities.* Harlow: Longman.

Cobb, C., Danby, S., & Farrell, A. (2009). Young children as rule makers. *Journal of Pragmatics, 41* (8), 1477–92.

Cobb, S. (1993). Empowerment and mediation: A narrative perspective. *Negotiation Journal, 9* (3), 245–59.

Conefrey, T. (1997). Gender, culture and authority in a university life sciences laboratory. *Discourse and Society, 8* (3), 313–40.

Conrick, M. (1999). *Womenspeak*. Dublin: Marino Books.

Cook-Gumperz, J., & Szymanski, M. (2001). Classroom 'Families': Cooperating or competing – girls' and boys' interactional styles in a bilingual classroom. *Research on Language and Social Interaction, 34* (1), 107–30.

Corbett, G. G. (2005). Sex-based and non-sex-based gender systems. In M. Haspelmath, M. S. Dryer, D. Gil, & B. Comrie (eds.), *The World Atlas of Language Structures*. Oxford: Oxford University Press.

Corsaro, W. A. (2005). *The Sociology of Childhood*. Thousand Oaks, CA: Pine Forge Press.

Craib, I. (2000). Narratives as bad faith. In M. Andrews, S. Day Sclater, C. Squire, & A. Treacher (eds.), *Lines of Narrative: Psychosocial Perspectives*. London: Routledge.

Crawford, M. (1995). *Talking Difference: On Gender and Language*. London: Sage.

Cromdal, J. (2001). 'Can I be with?' Negotiating play entry in a bilingual school. *Journal of Pragmatics, 33*, 517–45.

(2004). Building bilingual oppositions: Code-switching in children's disputes. *Language in Society, 33*, 33–58.

(2009). Childhood and social interaction in everyday life: Introduction to the special issue. *Journal of Pragmatics, 41* (8), 1473–6.

Curl, T. S. (2006). Offers of assistance: Constraints on syntactic design. *Journal of Pragmatics, 38*, 1257–80.

Curl, T. S., & Drew, P. (2008). Contingency and action: A comparison of two forms of requesting. *Research on Language and Social Interaction, 41*, 129–53.

Danby, S. (1998). The serious and playful work of gender: Talk and social order in a preschool classroom. In N. Yelland (ed.), *Gender in Early Childhood*. London: Routledge.

Danby, S., & Baker, C. (1998). How to be masculine in the block area. *Childhood, 5*, 151–75.

Davis, K. (1986). The process of problem (re)formulation in psychotherapy. *Sociology of Health and Illness, 8* (1), 44–74.

(1988). Paternalism under the microscope. In A. Dundas Todd & S. Fisher (eds.), *Gender and Discourse: The Power of Talk*. Norwood, NJ: Ablex.

DeFrancisco, V. L. (1991). The sounds of silence: How men silence women in marital relations. *Discourse and Society, 2* (4), 413–23.

Devor, A. H. (1989). *Gender Blending: Confronting the Limits of Duality*. Bloomington: Indiana University Press.

Dingwall, R. (1988). Empowerment or enforcement: Some questions about power and control in divorce mediation. In R. Dingwall & J. Eekelaar (eds.), *Divorce Mediation and the Legal Process*. New York: Oxford University Press.

Drescher, N. L. (2006). Sex, roles, and register: A corpus-based investigation of sex-linked features in university settings. Dissertation Abstracts International, A: The Humanities and Social Sciences.

Drew, P. (1978). Accusations: The occasioned use of members' knowledge of 'religious geography' in describing events. *Sociology, 12*, 1–22.

(1984). Speakers' reportings in invitation sequences. In J. M. Atkinson & J. Heritage (eds.), *Structures of Social Action: Studies in Conversation Analysis*. Cambridge: Cambridge University Press.

(1987). Po-faced receipts of teases. *Linguistics, 25*, 219–53.

(2005). Conversation analysis. In K. L. Fitch & R. E. Sanders (eds.), *Handbook of Language and Social Interaction*. Mahwah, NJ: Lawrence Erlbaum.

Drew, P., & Heritage, J. (1992a). Analyzing talk at work: An introduction. In P. Drew & J. Heritage (eds.), *Talk at Work: Interaction in Institutional Settings*. Cambridge: Cambridge University Press.

(1992b). *Talk at Work: Interaction in Institutional Settings*. Cambridge: Cambridge University Press.

Drew, P., Chatwin, J., & Collins, S. (2001). Conversation analysis: A method for research into interactions between patients and health-care professionals. *Health Expectations*, *4*, 58–70.

Eckert, P. (2003). Language and gender in adolescence. In J. Holmes & M. Meyerhoff (eds.), *The Handbook of Language and Gender*. Oxford: Blackwell.

Eckert, P., & McConnell-Ginet, S. (1998). Communities of practice: Where language, gender and power all live. In J. Coates (ed.), *Language and Gender: A Reader*. Oxford: Blackwell.

(eds.) (2003). *Language and Gender*. Cambridge: Cambridge University Press.

Edelsky, C. (1981). Who's got the floor? *Language in Society*, *10*, 383–421.

Ediger, R. (1991). *Coping with Fibromyalgia*. Toronto: LRH Publications.

Edley, N. (2001). Conversation analysis, discursive psychology and the study of ideology: A response to Susan Speer. *Feminism and Psychology*, *11* (1), 136–40.

Edley, N., & Wetherell, M. (2001). Jekyll and Hyde: Men's constructions of feminism and feminists. *Feminism and Psychology*, *11* (4), 439–58.

Edwards, D. (1991). Categories are for talking: On the cognitive and discursive bases of categorization. *Theory and Psychology*, *1* (4), 515–42.

(1994). Script formulations: An analysis of event descriptions in conversation. *Journal of Language and Social Psychology*, *13*, 211–47.

(1997). *Discourse and Cognition*. London: Sage.

(1998). The relevant thing about her: Social identity categories in use. In C. Antaki & S. Widdicombe (eds.), *Identities in Talk*. London: Sage.

(2000). Extreme case formulations: Softeners, investments and doing nonliteral. *Research on Language and Social Interaction*, *33*, 347–73.

(2005). Moaning, whinging and laughing: The subjective side of complaints. *Discourse Studies*, *7* (1), 5–29.

(2006). Facts, norms and dispositions: Practical uses of the modal *would* in police interrogations. *Discourse Studies*, *8* (4), 475–501.

(2007). Managing subjectivity in talk. In A. Hepburn & S. Wiggins (eds.), *Discursive Research in Practice: New Approaches to Psychology and Interaction*. Cambridge: Cambridge University Press.

Edwards, D., & Potter, J. (1992). *Discursive Psychology*. London: Sage.

Edwards, D., & Stokoe, E. H. (2004). Discursive psychology, focus group interviews, and participants' categories. *British Journal of Developmental Psychology*, *22*, 499–507.

(2007). Self-help in calls for help with problem neighbours. *Research on Language and Social Interaction*, *40* (1), 9–32.

Egbert, M. (2004). Other-initiated repair and membership categorization: Some conversational events that trigger linguistic and regional membership categorization. *Journal of Pragmatics*, *36* (8), 1467–98.

Eglin, P. (2002). Members' gendering work: 'Women', 'feminists' and membership categorization analysis. *Discourse and Society*, *13* (6), 819–926.

Eglin, P., & Hester, S. (1999). 'You're all a bunch of feminists': Categorization and the politics of terror in the Montreal Massacre. *Human Studies, 22,* 253–72.

Eicher-Catt, D. (2004). Noncustodial mothering: A cultural paradox of competent performance – performative competence. *Journal of Contemporary Ethnography, 33* (1), 72–108.

Enfield, N. J. (2007). Meanings of the unmarked: How 'default' person reference does more than just refer. In N. J. Enfield & T. Stivers (eds.), *Person Reference in Interaction: Linguistic, Cultural and Social Perspectives.* Cambridge: Cambridge University Press.

Enfield, N. J., & Stivers, T. (eds.) (2007). *Person Reference in Interaction: Linguistic, Cultural and Social Perspectives.* Cambridge: Cambridge University Press.

Evaldsson, A.-C. (2002). Boys' gossip telling: Staging identities and indexing (unacceptable) masculine behaviour. *Text, 22* (2), 199–225.

  (2003). Throwing like a girl: Situating gender differences in physicality across game contexts. *Childhood, 10* (4), 475–97.

  (2004). Shifting moral stances: Morality and gender in same-sex and cross-sex game interaction. *Research on Language and Social Interaction, 37* (3), 331–63.

  (2005). Staging insults and mobilizing categorizations in a multiethnic peer group. *Discourse and Society, 16* (6),763–86.

  (2007). Accounting for friendship: Moral ordering and category membership in pre-adolescent girls' relational talk. *Research on Language and Social Interaction, 40* (4), 377–404.

Farris, C. E. P. (2000). Cross-sex peer conflict and the discursive production of gender in a Chinese preschool in Taiwan. *Journal of Pragmatics, 32,* 539–68.

Fausto-Sterling, A. (2000). *Sexing the Body: Gender Politics and the Construction of Sexuality.* New York: Basic Books.

Fawcett Society (2005). Money, money, money: Is it still a rich man's world? http:// fawcettsociety.org.uk. Accessed 22 May 2007.

Feinberg, L. (1998). *Trans Liberation: Beyond Pink or Blue.* Boston: Beacon Press.

Fenstermaker, S., & West, C. (eds.) (2002). *Doing Gender, Doing Difference: Inequality, Power, and Institutional Change.* New York: Routledge.

Fishman, P. (1978). Interaction: The work women do. *Social Problems, 25,* 397–406.

  (1983). Interaction: The work women do. In B. Thorne, C. Kramarae, & N. Henley (eds.), *Language, Gender and Society.* Rowley, MA: Newbury House.

Ford, C. E., Fox, B., & Thompson, S. A. (1996). Practices in the construction of turns: The TCU revisited. *Pragmatics, 6* (3), 427–54.

  (2002). Constituency and the grammar of turn increments. In C. E. Ford, B. Fox, & S. A. Thompson (eds.), *The Language of Turn and Sequence.* Oxford: Oxford University Press.

Foucault, M. (1972). *The Archaeology of Knowledge.* London: Tavistock.

Francis, D. (1994). The golden dreams of the social constructionist. *Journal of Anthropological Research, 50* (2), 1–22.

Fransen, J., & Russell, I. J. (1996). *The Fibromyalgia Help Book: Practical Guide to Living Better with Fibromyalgia.* St Paul, MN: Smith House Press.

Freed, A. F. (1996). Language and gender research in an experimental setting. In V. L. Bergvall, J. M. Bing, & A. F. Freed (eds.), *Rethinking Language and Gender Research: Theory and Practice.* Harlow: Addison Wesley Longman.

Freed, A. F., & Greenwood, A. (1996). Women, men, and type of talk: What makes the difference? *Language in Society, 23,* 1–26.

Frith, H. (1998). Constructing the 'other' through talk. *Feminism and Psychology*, 8 (4), 530–6.

Garcia, A. C. (1991). Dispute resolution without disputing: How the interactional organization of mediation hearings minimizes argument. *American Sociological Review*, 56, 818–35.

(1995). The problematics of representation in community mediation hearings: Implications for mediation practice. *Journal of Sociology and Social Welfare*, 12 (4), 23–46.

(1996). Moral reasoning in interactional context: Strategic uses of care and justice arguments in mediation hearings. *Sociological Inquiry*, 66 (2), 197–214.

(1998). The relevance of interactional and institutional contexts for the study of gender differences: A demonstrative case study. *Symbolic Interaction*, 21 (1), 35–58.

(2000). Negotiating negotiation: The collaborative production of resolution in small claims mediation hearings. *Discourse and Society*, 11 (3), 315–44.

Garcia, A. C., & Parmer, P. (1999). Misplaced mistrust: The collaborative construction of doubt in 911 emergency calls. *Symbolic Interaction*, 22 (4), 297–324.

Garcia, A. C., Vise, K., & Whitaker, S. (2002). Disputing neutrality: When mediation empowerment is perceived as bias. *Conflict Resolution Quarterly*, 20 (2), 205–30.

Garfinkel, H. (1967). *Studies in Ethnomethodology*. Englewood Cliffs, NJ: Prentice Hall.

Garnica, O. K. (1979). The boys have the muscles and the girls have the sexy legs: Adult–child speech and the use of generic person labels. In O. K. Garnica & M. L. King (eds.), *Language, Children and Society*. Oxford: Pergamon Press.

Gaunt, K. D. (2006). *The Games Black Girls Play*. New York: Teachers' College Press.

Gibbon, M. (1999). *Feminist Perspectives on Language*. Harlow: Pearson Education.

Gilligan, C. (1982). *In a Different Voice: Psychological Theory and Women's Development*. Cambridge, MA: Harvard University Press.

Glenn, P. (2003a). *Laughter in Interaction*. Cambridge: Cambridge University Press.

(2003b). On sexism in conversational joking. *Media and Culture*, 6. www. media-culture.org.au/0311/1-glenn-feature-sexism.html>.

Goddard, A., & Patterson, L. M. (2000). *Language and Gender*. London: Routledge.

Goffman, E. (1959). *The Presentation of Self in Everyday Life*. Harmondsworth: Penguin.

(1961). *Encounters: Two Studies in the Sociology of Interaction*. Indianapolis: Bobbs-Merrill.

(1964). The neglected situation. *American Anthropologist*, 66, (6, pt II), 133–6.

(1979). Footing. *Semiotica*, 25,1–29.

(1981). Footing. In E. Goffman, *Forms of Talk*. Philadelphia: University of Pennsylvania Press.

Golato, A. (2005). *Compliments and Compliment Responses: Grammatical Structure and Sequential Organization*. Amsterdam: John Benjamins.

Goodenough, W. H. (1965). Rethinking 'status' and 'role': Toward a general model of the cultural organization of social relationships. In M. Banton (ed.), *The Relevance of Models for Social Anthropology*. London: Tavistock.

Goodwin, C. (1979). The interactive construction of a sentence in natural conversation. In G. Psathas (ed.), *Everyday Language: Studies in Ethnomethodology*. New York: Irvington.

(1981). *Conversational Organization: Interaction Between Speakers and Hearers.* New York: Academic Press.

(1984). Notes on story structure and the organization of participation. In J. M. Atkinson & J. Heritage (eds.), *Structures of Social Action: Studies in Conversation Analysis.* Cambridge: Cambridge University Press.

(1986a). Audience diversity, participation and interpretation. *Text, 6* (3), 283–316.

(1986b). Gesture as a resource for the organization of mutual orientation. *Semiotica, 62* (1/2), 29–49.

(1987a). Forgetfulness as an interactive resource. *Social Psychology Quarterly, 50* (2), 115–30.

(1987b). Unilateral departure. In G. Button & J. R. E. Lee (eds.), *Talk and Social Organisation.* Clevedon: Multilingual Matters.

(2002). Time in action. *Current Anthropology, 43* (Supplement), 19–35.

Goodwin, C., & Goodwin, M. H. (1987). Concurrent operations on talk: Notes on the interactive organization of assessments. *IPrA Papers in Pragmatics, 1* (1), 1–52.

(2004). Participation. In A. Duranti (ed.), *A Companion to Linguistic Anthropology.* Oxford: Blackwell.

Goodwin, M. H. (1990). *He-Said She-Said: Talk as Social Organization Among Black Children.* Bloomington: Indiana University Press.

(1998). Games of stance: Conflict and footing in hopscotch. In S. Hoyle & C. T. Adger (eds.), *Kids' Talk: Strategic Language Use in Later Childhood.* New York: Oxford University Press.

(2001). Organizing participation in cross-sex jump rope: Situating gender differences within longitudinal studies of activities. *Research on Language and Social Interaction* (special issue), *34* (1), 75–106.

(2002a). Building power asymmetries in girls' interaction. *Discourse and Society, 13* (6), 715–30.

(2002b). Exclusion in girls' peer groups: Ethnographic analysis of language practices on the playground. *Human Development, 45* (6), 392–415.

(2003). Gender, ethnicity and class in children's peer interactions. In J. Holmes and M. Meyerhoff (eds.), *The Handbook of Language and Gender.* Oxford: Blackwell.

(2006). *The Hidden Life of Girls: Games of Stance, Status and Exclusion.* Oxford: Blackwell.

Goodwin, M. H., Goodwin, C., & Yaeger-Dror, M. (2002). Multi-modality in girls' game disputes. *Journal of Pragmatics, 34,* 1621–49.

Graddol, D., & Swann, J. (1989). *Gender Voices.* Oxford: Blackwell.

Gray, J. (1992). *Men are from Mars, Women are from Venus: A Practical Guide for Improving Communication and Getting What you Want in your Relationships.* London: Thorsons.

Greatbatch, D. (1988). A turn-taking system for British news interviews. *Language in Society, 17,* 401–30.

Greatbatch, D., & Dingwall, R. (1997). Argumentative talk in divorce mediation sessions. *American Sociological Review, 2* (1), 151–70.

Haakana, M. (2001). Laughter as a patient's resource: Dealing with delicate aspects of medical interaction. *Text, 21,* 187–220.

Haddington, P. (2004). Stance taking in news interviews. *SKY Journal of Linguistics, 17,* 101–42.

Halkowski, T. (2006). Realizing the illness: Patients' narratives of symptom discovery. In J. Heritage & D. Maynard (eds.), *Communication in Medical Care: Interaction between Primary Care Physicians and Patients*. Cambridge: Cambridge University Press.

Hall, K., & Bucholtz, M. (eds.) (1995). *Gender Articulated: Language and the Socially Constructed Self*. New York: Routledge.

Halliday, M. A. K., & Hasan, R. (1976). *Cohesion in English*. London: Longman.

Hammersley, M. (2001). Obvious, all too obvious? Methodological issues in using sex/gender as a variable in educational research. In B. Francis & C. Skelton (eds.), *Investigating Gender: Contemporary Perspectives in Education*. Buckingham: Open University Press.

Harkness, S., & Super, C. M. (1985). The cultural context of gender segregation in children's peer groups. *Child Development, 56*, 219–24.

Harrington, C. B. (1985). *Shadow Justice: The Ideology and Institutionalization of Alternatives to Court*. Westport, CT: Greenwood Press.

Harrington, G. S., & Farias, S. T. (2008). Sex differences in language processing: Functional MRI methodological considerations. *Journal of Magnetic Resonance Imaging, 27* (6), 1221–8.

Harrington, K., Litosseliti, L., Saunston, H., & Sunderland, J. (eds.) (2008). *Gender and Language Research Methodologies*. Basingstoke: Palgrave.

Harry Benjamin International Gender Dysphoria Association (2001). Standards of care for gender identity disorders (6th version). www.hbigda.org. Accessed July 2008.

Have, Ten P. (1999). *Doing Conversation Analysis: A Practical Guide*. London: Sage.
  (2007). *Doing Conversation Analysis: A Practical Guide* (2nd ed.). London: Sage.

Hawkesworth, M. (1997). Confounding gender. *Signs, 22* (3), 649–85.

Heap, J. L. (1990). Applied ethnomethodology: Looking for the local rationality of reading activities. *Human Studies, 13*, 39–72.

Henley, N. M. (1995). Ethnicity and gender issues in language. In H. Landrine (ed.), *Bringing Cultural Diversity to Feminist Psychology: Theory, Research, and Practice*. Washington, DC: American Psychological Association.

Henley, N. M., & Kramarae, C. (1991). Gender, power and miscommunication. In H. Giles, N. Coupland, & J. M. Wiemann (eds.), *'Miscommunication' and Problematic Talk*. Newbury Park, CA: Sage.

Hepburn, A. (2004). Crying: Notes on description, transcription and interaction. *Research on Language and Social Interaction, 37*, 251–90.
  (2005). 'You're not takin me seriously': Ethics and asymmetry in calls to a child protection helpline. *Journal of Constructivist Psychology, 18*, 255–76.
  (2007). Turn medial tag questions. Paper presented at National Communication Association, Chicago.

Hepburn, A., & Potter, J. (2007). Crying receipts: Time, empathy and institutional practice. *Research on Language and Social Interaction, 40*, 89–116.
  (2010). Interrogating tears: Some uses of 'tag questions' in a child protection helpline. In A. F. Freed & S. Ehrlich (eds.), *'Why Do You Ask?': The Function of Questions in Institutional Discourse*. Oxford: Oxford University Press.

Hepburn, A., & Wiggins, S. (eds.) (2005). Developments in discursive psychology. *Discourse and Society* (special issue), *16* (5), 595–601.
  (eds.) (2007). *Discursive Research in Practice: New Approaches to Psychology and Interaction*. Cambridge: Cambridge University Press.

Heritage, J. (1984a). A change-of-state token and aspects of its sequential placement. In J. M. Atkinson & J. Heritage (eds.), *Structures of Social Action: Studies in Conversation Analysis*. Cambridge: Cambridge University Press.

(1984b). *Garfinkel and Ethnomethodology*. Cambridge: Polity.

(1998). *Oh*-prefaced responses to inquiry. *Language in Society, 27*, 291–334.

(2002a). The limits of questioning: Negative interrogatives and hostile question content. *Journal of Pragmatics, 34*, 1427–46.

(2002b). *Oh*-prefaced responses to assessments: A method of modifying agreement/ disagreement. In C. E. Ford, B. A. Fox, & S. A. Thompson (eds.), *The Language of Turn and Sequence*. Oxford: Oxford University Press.

(2005). Conversation analysis and institutional talk. In K. L. Fitch & R. E. Sanders (eds.), *Handbook of Language and Social Interaction*. Mahwah, NJ: Lawrence Erlbaum.

(2007). Intersubjectivity and progressivity in references to persons (and places). In N. Enfield & T. Stivers (eds.), *Person Reference in Interaction: Linguistic, Cultural and Social Perspectives*. Cambridge: Cambridge University Press.

Heritage, J., & Atkinson, J. M. (1984). Introduction. In J. M. Atkinson & J. Heritage (eds.), *Structures of Social Action: Studies in Conversation Analysis*. Cambridge: Cambridge University Press.

Heritage, J., & Maynard, D. (eds.) (2006). *Communication in Medical Care: Interaction between Primary Care Physicians and Patients*. Cambridge: Cambridge University Press.

Heritage, J., & Raymond, G. (2005). The terms of agreement: Indexing epistemic authority and subordination in talk-in-interaction. *Social Psychology Quarterly, 68* (1), 15–38.

Heritage, J., Robinson, J. D., Elliott, M., Beckett M., & Wilkes, M. (2007). Reducing patients' unmet concerns in primary care: The difference one word can make. *Journal of General Internal Medicine, 22* (10), 1429–33.

Hester, S. (2000). The local order of deviance in school: Membership categorisation, motives and morality in referral talk. In S. Hester & D. Francis (eds.), *Local Educational Order*. Amsterdam: John Benjamins.

Hester, S., & Eglin, P. (1997). Membership categorization analysis: An introduction. In S. Hester & P. Eglin (eds.), *Culture in Action: Studies in Membership Categorization Analysis*. Boston: International Institute for Ethnomethodology and University Press of America.

Hollway, W., & Jefferson, T. (2000). *Doing Qualitative Research Differently: Free Association, Narrative and the Interview Method*. London: Sage.

Holmes, J. (1995). *Women, Men and Politeness*. Harlow: Longman.

(2007). Social constructionism, postmodernism and feminist sociolinguistics. *Gender and Language, 1* (1), 51–67.

Holmes, J., & Meyerhoff, M. (1999). The community of practice: Theories and methodologies in language and gender research. *Language in Society, 28*, 173–83.

(eds.) (2003). *The Handbook of Language and Gender*. Oxford: Blackwell.

Holt, E. (1996). Reporting on talk: The use of direct reported speech in conversation. *Research on Language and Social Interaction, 29*, 219–45.

(1999). Just gassing: An analysis of direct reported speech in a conversation between two employees of a gas supply company. *Text, 19*, 505–37.

(2000). Reporting and reacting: Concurrent responses to reported speech.

Research on Language and Social Interaction, 33 (4), 425–54.

Holt, E., & Clift, R. (eds.) (2007a). *Reporting Talk: Reported Speech in Interaction.* Cambridge: Cambridge University Press.

(2007b). 'I'm eyeing your chop up mind': Reporting and enacting. In E. Holt & R. Clift (eds.), *Reporting Talk: Reported Speech in Interaction.* Cambridge: Cambridge University Press.

Hopper, R. (2003). *Gendering Talk.* East Lansing, MI: Michigan State University Press.

Hopper, R., & LeBaron, C. (1998). How gender creeps into talk. *Research on Language and Social Interaction, 31* (3), 59–74.

Hutchby, I., & Wooffitt, R. (2008). *Conversation analysis* (2nd ed.). Cambridge: Polity.

James, A., & Prout, A. (1990). *Constructing and Reconstructing Childhood: Contemporary Issues in the Sociological Study of Childhood.* London: Falmer Press.

James, A., Jenks, C., & Prout, A. (1998). *Theorizing Childhood.* Cambridge: Polity.

James, D., & Clarke, S. (1993). Women, men, and interruptions: A critical review. In D. Tannen (ed.), *Gender and Conversational Interaction.* Oxford: Oxford University Press.

James, D., & Drakich, J. (1993). Understanding gender differences in amount of talk: A critical review of research. In D. Tannen (ed.), *Gender and Conversational Interaction.* Oxford: Oxford University Press.

Järviluoma, H., Moisala, P., & Vilkko, A. (2003). *Gender and Qualitative Methods.* London: Sage.

Jayyusi, L. (1984). *Categorization and the Moral Order.* Boston: Routledge & Kegan Paul.

(1991). Values and moral judgment: Communicative praxis as moral order. In G. Button (ed.), *Ethnomethodology and the Human Sciences.* Cambridge: Cambridge University Press.

Jefferson, G. (1974). Error correction as an interactional resource. *Language in Society, 3* (2), 181–99.

(1978). Sequential aspects of storytelling in conversation. In J. Schenkien (ed.), *Studies in the Organization of Conversational Interaction.* New York: Academic Press.

(1979). A technique for inviting laughter and its subsequent acceptance/declination. In G. Psathas (ed.), *Everyday Language: Studies in Ethnomethodology.* New York: Irvington.

(1983). Issues in the transcription of naturally-occurring talk: Caricature versus capturing pronunciational particulars. *Tilburg Papers in Language and Literature, 34,* 1–12.

(1987). On exposed and embedded correction in conversation. In G. Button & J. R. E. Lee (eds.), *Talk and Social Organization.* Clevedon: Multilingual Matters.

(1996). On the poetics of ordinary talk. *Text and Performance Quarterly, 16* (1), 1–61.

(2004a). Glossary of transcript symbols with an introduction. In G. H. Lerner (ed.), *Conversation Analysis: Studies from the First Generation.* Amsterdam: John Benjamins.

(2004b). A note on laughter in 'male–female' interaction. *Discourse Studies, 6,* 117–33.

(2004c). 'At first I thought': A normalizing device for extraordinary events. In G. H. Lerner (ed.), *Conversation Analysis: Studies from the First Generation*. Amsterdam: John Benjamins.

Jefferson, G., Sacks, H., & Schegloff, E. (1987). Notes on laughter in the pursuit of intimacy. In G. Button & J. R. E. Lee (eds.), *Talk and Social Organisation*. Clevedon: Multilingual Matters.

Johnson, S., & Meinhof, U. (eds.) (1997). *Language and Masculinity*. Oxford: Blackwell.

Jurik, N. C., & Siemsen, C. (2009). 'Doing gender' as canon or agenda: A symposium on West and Zimmerman. *Gender and Society, 23* (1), 72–5.

Karkkainen, E. (2006). Stance taking in conversation: From subjectivity to intersubjectivity. *Text and Talk, 26* (6), 699–731.

Kendall, S. (2008). The balancing act: Framing gendered parental identities at dinnertime. *Language in Society, 37*, 539–68.

Kessler, S. J., & McKenna, W. (1978). *Gender: An Ethnomethodological Approach*. New York: John Wiley.

Kitzinger, C. (2000a). Doing feminist conversation analysis. *Feminism and Psychology, 10*, 163–93.

  (2000b). How to resist an idiom. *Research on Language and Social Interaction, 33*, 121–54.

  (2002). Doing feminist conversation analysis. In P. McIlvenny (ed.), *Talking Gender and Sexuality*. Amsterdam: John Benjamins.

  (2005a). Speaking as a heterosexual: (How) does sexuality matter for talk-in-interaction? *Research on Language and Social Interaction, 38* (3), 221–65.

  (2005b). Heteronormativity in action: Reproducing the heterosexual nuclear family in after-hours medical calls. *Social Problems, 52* (4), 477–98.

  (2006). Talking sex and gender. In P. Drew, G. Raymond, & D. Weinberg (eds.), *Talk and Interaction in Social Research Methods*. London: Sage.

  (2007a). Feminist research practice: The promise of conversation analysis for feminist research. *Feminism and Psychology, 17*, 133–48.

  (2007b). Is 'woman' always relevantly gendered? *Gender and Language, 1* (1), 39–49.

  (ed.) (2007c). Special feature: Feminist conversation analysis: Research by students at the University of York, UK. *Feminism and Psychology, 17* (2), 133–236.

  (2008a). Developing feminist conversation analysis: A response to Wowk. *Human Studies, 31* (2), 179–208.

  (2008b). Conversation analysis: Technical matters for gender research. In K. Harrington, L. Litosseliti, H. Saunston, & J. Sunderland (eds.), *Gender and Language Research Methodologies*. Basingstoke: Palgrave.

Kitzinger, C., & Kitzinger, S. (2007). Birth trauma: Talking with women and the value of conversation analysis. *British Journal of Midwifery, 15* (5), 256–64.

Kitzinger, C., & Mandelbaum, J. (2007). Word selection and social identities in talk-in-interaction. Paper presented at the Annual Convention of the American Sociological Association. Chicago. August.

Kitzinger, C., & Peel, E. (2005). The de-gaying and regaying of AIDS: Contested homophobias in lesbian and gay awareness training. *Discourse and Society, 16* (2), 173–97.

Kitzinger, C., & Rickford, R. (2007). Becoming a 'bloke': The construction of gender in interaction. *Feminism and Psychology, 17* (2), 214–23.

Kitzinger, C., & Wilkinson, S. (in press). Identifying and remediating heterosexist talk. In C. Antaki (ed.), *Applied Conversation Analysis: Changing Institutional Practices*. Basingstoke: Palgrave Macmillan.

Koch, M. (2008). *Language and Gender Research from a Queer Linguistic Perspective*. Saarbrücken: VDM.

Kochman, T. (1981). *Black and White: Styles in Conflict*. Chicago: University of Chicago Press.

Koller, V. (2004). Businesswomen and war metaphors: 'Possessive, jealous and pugnacious'? *Journal of Sociolinguistics*, *8* (1), 3–22.

Korobov, N., & Bamberg, M. (2004). Positioning a 'mature' self in interactive practices: How adolescent males negotiate 'physical attraction' in group talk. *British Journal of Developmental Psychology*, *22*, 471–92.

Kulick, D. (1999). Language and gender/sexuality. *Language and Culture Mailing List: Online Symposium*. www.language-culture.org/archives/subs/kulick-don/index.html.

Kyratzis, A. (1999). Narrative identity: Preschoolers' self-construction through narrative in same-sex friendship group dramatic play. *Narrative Inquiry*, *9* (2), 427–55.

(2001a). Children's gender indexing in language: From the separate worlds hypothesis to considerations of culture, context, and power. *Research on Language and Social Interaction*, *34* (1), 1–13.

(2001b). Constituting the emotions: A longitudinal study of emotion talk in a preschool friendship group of boys. In B. Baron & H. Kotthoff (eds.), *Gender in Interaction: Perspectives on Femininity and Masculinity in Ethnography and Discourse*. Amsterdam: John Benjamins.

Kyratzis, A., & Guo, J. (1996). 'Separate worlds for girls and boys?' Views from U.S. and Chinese mixed-sex friendship groups. In D. Slobin, J. Gerhardt, A. Kyratzis, & J. Guo (eds.), *Social Interaction, Social Context, and Language: Essays in Honor of Susan Ervin-Tripp*. Mahwaw, NJ: Lawrence Erlbaum.

Labov, W. (1972a). *Sociolinguistic Patterns*. Philadelphia: University of Pennsylvania Press.

(1972b). Rules for ritual insults. In W. Labov, *Language in the Inner City: Studies in the Black English Vernacular*. Philadelphia: University of Pennsylvania Press.

Labov, W., & Fanshell, D. (1977). *Therapeutic Discourse: Psychotherapy as Conversation*. New York: Academic Press.

Lakoff, R. (1973). Language and woman's place. *Language in Society*, *2*, 45–79.

(1975). *Language and Woman's Place*. New York: Harper & Row.

(2003). Language, gender, and politics: Putting 'women' and 'power' in the same sentence. In J. Holmes & M. Meyerhoff (eds.), *The Handbook of Language and Gender*. Oxford: Blackwell.

Lanclos, D. M. (2003). *At Play in Belfast: Children's Folklore and Identities in Northern Ireland*. New Brunswick, NJ: Rutgers University Press.

Land, V., & Kitzinger, C. (2005). Speaking as a lesbian: Correcting the heterosexist presumption. *Research on Language and Social Interaction*, *38*, 371–416.

(2007). Some uses of third-person reference forms in speaker self-reference. *Discourse and Society*, *9*, 493–525.

Lazar, M. M. (ed.) (2005). *Feminist Critical Discourse Analysis*: *Gender, Power and Ideology in Discourse*. London: Routledge.

(2007). Feminist critical discourse analysis: Articulating a feminist discourse praxis. *Critical Discourse Studies*, *4* (2), 141–64.

Leap, W. (1996). *Word's Out: Gay Men's English*. Minneapolis: University of Minnesota Press.

Lerner, G. H. (1996). Finding 'face' in the preference structures of talk-in-interaction. *Social Psychology Quarterly*, *59* (4), 303–21.

(2002). Turn-sharing: The choral co-production of talk-in-interaction. In C. Ford, B. Fox, & S. Thompson (eds.), *The Language of Turn and Sequence*. Oxford: Oxford University Press.

(2003). Selecting next speaker: The context-sensitive operation of a context-free organization. *Language in Society*, *32*, 177–201.

(2004). Collaborative turn sequences. In G. H. Lerner (ed.), *Conversation Analysis: Studies from the First Generation*. Amsterdam: John Benjamins.

Lerner, G. H., & Kitzinger, C. (2007a). Introduction: Person-reference in conversation analytic research. *Discourse Studies*, *9* (4), 427–32.

(2007b). Extraction and aggregation in the repair of individual and collective self-reference. *Discourse Studies*, *9*, 526–57.

Lev, A. I. (2004). *Transgender Emergence: Therapeutic Guidelines for Working with Gender-Variant People and their Famillies*. Binghampton, NY: Haworth Clinical Practice Press.

Levinson, S. (1988). Putting linguistics on a proper footing: Explorations in Goffman's concepts of participation. In P. Drew & A. Wootton (eds.), *Erving Goffman: Studies in the Interactional Order*. Cambridge: Polity.

Liang, A. C. (1999). Conversationally implicating lesbian and gay identity. In M. Bucholtz, A. C. Liang, & L. A. Sutton (eds.), *Reinventing Identities: The Gendered Self in Discourse*. New York: Oxford University Press.

Litosseliti, L. (2006). *Gender and Language: An Introduction and Resource Book*. Oxford: Oxford University Press.

Livia, A., & Hall, K. (eds.) (1997). *Queerly Phrased: Language, Gender and Sexuality*. Oxford: Oxford University Press.

Lorber, J. (1994). *Paradoxes of Gender*. New Haven, CT: Yale University Press.

(2000). Using gender to undo gender: A feminist degendering movement. *Feminist Theory*, *1* (1), 79–95.

Lynch, M. (1993). *Scientific Practice and Ordinary Action: Ethnomethodology and Social Studies of Science*. Cambridge: Cambridge University Press.

(2001). Ethnomethodology and the logic of practice. In K. Knorr-Cetina, E.v. Savigny, & T. R. Schatzki (eds.), *The Practice Turn in Contemporary Theory*. London: Routledge.

Lynch, M., & Bogen, D. (1996). *The Spectacle of History: Speech, Text and Memory at the Iran–Contra Hearings*. Durham, NC: Duke University Press.

Macbeth, D. (2004). The relevance of repair for classroom correction. *Language in Society*, *33*, 703–36.

Maccoby, E. E., & Jacklin, C. N. (1974). *The Psychology of Sex Differences*. Stanford, CA: Stanford University Press.

Macpherson, D. A., & Hirsch, B. T. (1995). Wages and gender composition: Why do women's jobs pay less? *Journal of Labor Economics*, *13* (3), 426–71.

Maltz, D. N., & Borker, R. A. (1982). A cultural approach to male–female miscommunication. In J. J. Gumperz (ed.), *Language and Social Identity*. Cambridge: Cambridge University Press.

(1998). A cultural approach to male–female miscommunication. In J. Coates (ed.), *Language and Gender: A Reader.* Oxford: Blackwell.

May, K. (2002). Becoming women: Transgendered identities, psychosexual therapy and the challenge of metamorphosis. *Sexualities, 5* (4), 449–64.

Mayall, B. (1996). *Children, Health and the Social Order.* Buckingham: Open University Press.

Maynard, D. W. (1992). On clinicians co-implicating recipients' perspective in the delivery of diagnostic news. In P. Drew & J. Heritage (eds.), *Talk at Work: Interaction in Institutional Settings.* Cambridge: Cambridge University Press.

(2003). *Good News, Bad News: Conversational Order in Everyday Talk and Clinical Settings.* Chicago: University of Chicago Press.

Maynard, D. W., Houtkoop, H., Schaeffer, N. C., & van der Zouwen, H. (eds.) (2002). *Standardization and Tacit Knowledge: Interaction and Practice in the Survey Interview.* New York: Wiley Interscience.

McConnell-Ginet, S. (2003). 'What's in a name?': Social labeling and gender practices. In J. Holmes & M. Meyerhoff (eds.), *The Handbook of Language and Gender.* Oxford: Blackwell.

McElhinny, B. (2003). Theorizing gender in sociolinguistics and linguistic anthropology. In J. Holmes & M. Meyerhoff (eds.), *The Handbook of Language and Gender.* Oxford: Blackwell.

McHoul, A. W. (1987). An initial investigation in the usability of fictional conversation for doing conversation analysis. *Semiotica, 67* (1–2), 83–104.

McIlvenny, P. (2002a). Introduction: Researching talk, gender and sexuality. In P. McIlvenny (ed.), *Talking Gender and Sexuality: Conversation, Performativity and Discourse in Interaction.* Amsterdam: John Benjamins.

(ed.) (2002b). *Talking Gender and Sexuality: Conversation, Performativity and Discourse in Interaction.* Amsterdam: John Benjamins.

McMullen, L. M., Vernon, A. E., & Murton, T. (1995). Division of labor in conversations: Are Fishman's results replicable and generalizable? *Journal of Psycholinguistic Research, 24* (4), 255–68.

Menz, F., & Al-Roubaie, A. (2008). Interruptions, status and gender in medical interviews: The harder you brake, the longer it takes. *Discourse and Society, 19* (5), 645–66.

Mills, S. (ed.) (1996). *Language and Gender: Interdisciplinary Perspectives.* Harlow: Longman.

(2003). *Gender and Politeness.* Cambridge: Cambridge University Press.

(2008). *Language and Sexism.* Cambridge: Cambridge University Press.

Moerman, M., & Sacks, H. (1988 [1970]). On 'understanding' in the analysis of natural conversation. In M. Moerman (ed.), *Talking Culture: Ethnography and Conversation Analysis.* Philadelphia: University of Pennsylvania Press.

Moonwomon-Baird, B. (1997). Toward the study of lesbian speech. In A. Livia and K. Hall (eds.), *Queerly Phrased: Language, Gender and Sexuality.* Oxford: Oxford University Press.

Morgan, R., & Wood, K. (1995). Lesbians in the living room: Collusion, co-narration in conversation. In W. L. Leap (ed.), *Beyond the Lavender Lexicon: Authenticity, Imagination, and Appropriation in Lesbian and Gay Languages.* Amsterdam: Gordon and Breach.

Morrish, E. (2002). The case of the indefinite pronoun: Discourse and the concealment of lesbian identity in class. In L. Litosseliti & J. Sunderland (eds.), *Gender Identity and Discourse Analysis*. Amsterdam: John Benjamins.

Mullany, L. (2007). *Gendered Discourses in Professional Communication*. Oxford: Blackwell.

Nagle, J. (1995). Framing radical bisexuality: Toward a gender agenda. In N. Tucker (ed.), *Bisexual Politics: Theories, Queries, and Visions*. New York: Haworth Press.

Nakamura, K. (2001). Gender and language use in Japanese preschool children. *Research on Language and Social Interaction, 34* (1), 15–44.

Neumann, D. (1992). How mediation can effectively address the male–female power imbalance in divorce. *Mediation Quarterly, 9* (3), 227–39.

Newman, L. K. (2000). Transgender issues. In J. Ussher (ed.), *Women's Health: Contemporary International Perspectives*. Leicester: BPS Books.

Nilan, P. (1995). Membership categorization devices under construction: Social identity boundary maintenance in everyday discourse. *Australian Review of Applied Linguistics, 18* (1), 69–94.

Norrick, N. R. (1997). Twice-told tales: Collaborative narration of familiar stories. *Language in Society, 26*, 199–220.

Ochs, E. (1992). Indexing gender. In A. Duranti & C. Goodwin (eds.), *Rethinking Context*. Cambridge: Cambridge University Press.

Osvaldsson, K. (2004). 'I don't have no damn cultures': Doing normality in a deviant setting. *Qualitative Research in Psychology, 1*, 239–64.

Parks, J. B., & Roberton, M. A. (2008). Generation gaps in attitudes toward sexist/non-sexist language. *Journal of Language and Social Psychology, 27* (3), 276–83.

Pauwels, A. (1998). *Women Changing Language*. Harlow: Addison Wesley Longman.

Pellegrino, M. J. (1997). *Fibromyalgia: Managing the Pain* (2nd ed.). Columbus, OH: Anadem.

Pichler, P. (2009). *Talking Young Femininities*. Basingstoke: Palgrave Macmillan.

Pichler, P., & Eppler, E. M. (eds.) (2009). *Gender and Spoken Interaction*. Basingstoke: Palgrave Macmillan.

Plug, L. (2006). Speed and reduction in postpositioned self-initiated self-repair. *York Papers in Linguistics Series 2, 6*, 143–62.

Pomerantz, A. (1975). Second assessments: A study of some features of agreements/disagreements. Unpublished PhD dissertation, Division of Social Sciences, University of California, Irvine.

(1978). Compliment responses: Notes on the co-operation of multiple constraints. In J. Schenkein (ed.), *Studies in the Organization of Conversational Interaction*. London: Academic Press.

(1980). Telling my side: 'Limited access' as a fishing device. *Sociological Inquiry, 50* (3 and 4), 186–98.

(1984a). Agreeing and disagreeing with assessments: Some features of preferred/dispreferred turn shapes. In J. M. Atkinson & J. Heritage (eds.), *Structures of Social Action: Studies in Conversation Analysis*. Cambridge: Cambridge University Press.

(1984b). Giving a source or basis: The practice in conversation of telling 'how I know'. *Journal of Pragmatics, 8* (5–6), 607–25.

(1984c). Pursuing a response. In J. M. Atkinson & J. Heritage (eds.), *Structures of Social Action: Studies in Conversation Analysis*. Cambridge: Cambridge University Press.

(1986). Extreme case formulations: A new way of legitimating claims. *Human Studies*, *9*, 219–30.

Pomerantz, A., & Mandelbaum, J. (2005). A conversation analytic approach to relationships: Their relevance for interactional conduct. In K. Fitch & R. E. Sanders (eds.), *Handbook of Language and Social Interaction*. Mahwah, NJ: Lawrence Erlbaum.

Potter, J. (1996). *Representing Reality*. London: Sage.

Potter, J., & Hepburn, A. (2003). 'I'm a bit concerned': Call openings on a child protection helpline. *Research on Language and Social Interaction*, *36*, 197–240.

(2011). Somewhere between evil and normal: Traces of morality in a child protection helpline. In J. Cromdal & M. Tholander (eds.), *Morality in Practice: Exploring Childhood, Parenthood and Schooling in Everyday Life*. London: Equinox.

Precht, K. (2008). Sex similarities and differences in stance in informal American conversation. *Journal of Sociolinguistics*, *12* (1), 89–111.

Press for Change (2007). Response to draft good practice guidelines for the assessment and treatment of gender dysphoria. www.pfc.org.uk. Accessed January 2009.

Qvortrup, J. (2005). *Studies in Modern Childhood: Society, Agency, Culture*. Basingstoke: Palgrave Macmillan.

Raymond, G. (2003). Grammar and social organisation: Yes/no interrogatives and the structure of responding. *American Sociological Review*, *68*, 939–67.

Raymond, G., & Heritage, J. (2006). The epistemics of social relationships: Owning grandchildren. *Language in Society*, *35* (5), 677–705.

Regehr, C. (1994). The use of empowerment in child custody mediation: A feminist critique. *Mediation Quarterly*, *11* (4), 361–71.

Remlinger, K. (1999). Widening the lens of language and gender research: Integrating critical discourse analysis and cultural practice theory. *Linguistik Online*, *2* (1/99), 1–14.

Robinson, J. D. (2004). The sequential organization of 'explicit' apologies in naturally occurring English. *Research on Language and Social Interaction*, *37* (3), 291–330.

(2005). The concept of trouble responsibility in conversational repair and its implications for interactional organization and interpersonal alignment. Unpublished paper, University of California, Santa Barbara, CA.

Robinson, J. D., & Heritage, J. (2006). Physicians' opening questions and patients' satisfaction. *Patient Education and Counseling*, *60*, 279–85.

Rose, S., & Frieze, I. H. (1989). Young singles' scripts for a first date. *Gender and Sexuality*, *28* (9–10), 258–68.

Ryave, A. L. (1978). On the achievement of a series of stories. In J. Schenkein (ed.), *Studies in the Organization of Conversational Interaction*. New York: Academic Press.

Sacks, H. (1966). The search for help: No one to turn to. Unpublished doctoral dissertation, University of California, Berkeley.

(1972). On the analysability of stories by children. In J. Gumperz & D. Hymes (eds.), *Directions in Sociolinguistics: The Ethnography of Communication*. New York: Holt, Rinehart, and Winston.

(1974). An analysis of the course of a joke's telling in conversation. In R. Bauman & J. Sherzer (eds.), *Explorations in the Ethnography of Speaking*. Cambridge: Cambridge University Press.

(1975). Everyone has to lie. In M. Sanches & B. Blount (eds.), *Sociocultural Dimensions of Language Use*. New York: Academic Press.

(1978). Some technical considerations of a dirty joke. In J. Schenkein (ed.), *Studies in the Organization of Conversational Interaction*. New York: Academic Press.

(1979). A revolutionary category: Hotrodder. In G. Psathas (ed.), *Everyday Language: Studies in Ethnomethodology*. New York: Irvington.

(1984a). Notes on methodology (ed. G. Jefferson). In J. M. Atkinson & J. Heritage (eds.), *Structures of Social Action: Studies in Conversation Analysis*. Cambridge: Cambridge University Press.

(1984b). On doing 'being ordinary'. In J. M. Atkinson & J. Heritage (eds.), *Structures of Social Action: Studies in Conversation Analysis*. Cambridge: Cambridge University Press.

(1987 [1973]). On the preferences for agreement and contiguity in sequences in conversation. In G. Button & J. R. E. Lee (eds.), *Talk and Social Organisation*. Clevedon: Multilingual Matters.

(1992). *Lectures on Conversation* (Vols. I and II, ed. G. Jefferson). Oxford: Blackwell.

Sacks, H., & Schegloff, E. A. (1979). Two preferences in the organization of reference to persons in conversation and their interaction. In G. Psathas (ed.), *Everyday Language: Studies in Ethnomethodology*. New York: Irvington.

Sacks, H., Schegloff, E. A., & Jefferson, G. (1974). A simplest systematics for the organization of turn-taking for conversation. *Language*, *50* (4), 696–735.

Sanden, I., Linell, P., Startkammar, H., & Larsson, U. S. (2001). Routinization and sensitivity: Interaction in oncological follow-up consultations. *Health*, *5* (2), 139–63.

Saposnek, D. T. (1983). *Mediating Child Custody Disputes*. San Francisco: Jossey-Bass.

Schegloff, E. A. (n. d.). Increments. Unpublished manuscript.

(1972). Notes on a conversational practice: Formulating place. In D. N. Sudnow (ed.), *Studies in Social Interaction*. New York: Free Press.

(1979). The relevance of repair to syntax-for-conversation. In T. Givon (ed.), *Syntax and Semantics 12: Discourse and Syntax*. New York: Academic Press.

(1980). Preliminaries to preliminaries: Can I ask you a question? *Sociological Inquiry*, *50* (4), 104–52.

(1986). The routine as achievement. *Human Studies*, *9*, 111–51.

(1987a). Between micro and macro: Contexts and other connections. In J. Alexander, B. Giesen, R. Munch, & N. Smelser (eds.), *The Micro–Macro Link*. Berkeley: University of California Press.

(1987b). Analyzing single episodes of interaction: An exercise in conversation analysis. *Social Psychology Quarterly*, *50* (2), 101–14.

(1990). On the organization of sequences as a source of 'coherence' in talk-in-interaction. In B. Dorval (ed.), *Conversational Organization and its Development* (Vol. XXXVIII in the series Advances in Discourse Processes). Norwood, NJ: Ablex.

(1991). Reflections on talk and social structure. In D. Boden & D. Zimmerman (eds.), *Talk and Social Structure*. Berkeley: University of California Press.

(1992a). In another context. In A. Duranti & C. Goodwin (eds.), *Rethinking Context: Language as an Interactive Phenomenon.* Cambridge: Cambridge University Press.

(1992b). Repair after next turn: The last structurally provided defense of intersubjectivity in conversation. *American Journal of Sociology, 97* (5), 1295–345.

(1993). Reflections on quantification in the study of conversation. *Research on Language and Social Interaction, 26* (1), 99–128.

(1996a). Issues of relevance for discourse analysis: Contingency in action, interaction and co-participant context. In E. H. Hovy & D. R. Scott (eds.), *Computational and Conversational Discourse: Burning Issues – An Interdisciplinary Account.* New York: Springer.

(1996b). Turn organization: One intersection of grammar and interaction. In E. Ochs, S. Thompson, & E. A. Schegloff (eds.), *Interaction and Grammar.* Cambridge: Cambridge University Press.

(1996c). Some practices for referring to persons in talk-in-interaction: A partial sketch of a systematics. In B. Fox (ed.), *Studies in Anaphora.* Amsterdam: John Benjamins.

(1997). Whose text? Whose context? *Discourse and Society, 8* (2), 165–87.

(1998a). Reply to Wetherell. *Discourse and Society, 9,* 413–16.

(1998b). Reflections on studying prosody in talk-in-interaction. *Language and Speech, 41* (3–4), 235–63.

(1999). 'Schegloff's texts' as 'Billig's data': A critical reply. *Discourse and Society, 10* (4), 558–72.

(2001a). Accounts of conduct in interaction: Interruption, overlap, and turn-taking. In J. H. Turner (ed.), *Handbook of Sociological Theory.* New York: Kluwer Academic/ Plenum.

(2001b). Getting serious: Joke serious 'no'. *Journal of Pragmatics, 33* (12), 1947–55.

(2004). On dispensability. *Research on Language and Social Interaction, 37* (2), 95–149.

(2007a). *Sequence Organization in Interaction: A Primer in Conversation Analysis.* Cambridge: Cambridge University Press.

(2007b). A tutorial on membership categorization. *Journal of Pragmatics, 39,* 462–82.

(2007c). Conveying who you are: The presentation of self, strictly speaking. In N. Enfield & T. Stivers (eds.), *Person Reference in Interaction: Linguistic, Cultural and Social Perspectives.* Cambridge: Cambridge University Press.

(2007d). Categories in action: Person-reference and membership categorization. *Discourse Studies, 9,* 433–61.

(2007e). Interaction: The infrastructure for social institutions, the natural ecological niche for language, and the arena in which culture is enacted. In N. J. Enfield & S. C. Levinson (eds.), *Roots of Human Sociality: Culture, Cognition and Interaction.* London: Berg.

(2009). One perspective on conversation analysis: Comparative perspectives. In J. Sidnell (ed.), *Conversation Analysis: Comparative Perspectives.* Cambridge: Cambridge University Press.

Schegloff, E. A., & Sacks, H. (1973). Opening up closings. *Semiotica, 7,* 289–327.

Schegloff, E.A., Jefferson, G., & Sacks, H. (1977). The preference for self-correction in the organization of repair in conversation. *Language, 53* (2), 361–82.

Schleef, E. (2008). Gender and academic discourse: Global restrictions and local possibilities. *Language in Society*, *37*, 515–38.

Schofield, J. W. (1981). Complementary and conflicting identities: Images and interaction in an interracial school. In S. R. Asher & J. M. Gottman (eds.), *The Development of Children's Friendships*. Cambridge: Cambridge University Press.

Schutz, A. (1962). *Alfred Schutz: Collected Papers. Vol. I: The Problem of Social Reality*. The Hague: Martinus Nijhoff.

  (1973 [1953]). Common-sense and scientific interpretation of human action. In M. Natanson (ed.), *Alfred Schutz: Collected Papers. Vol. I: The Problem of Social Reality*. The Hague: Martinus Nijhoff.

Sclater, S. D. (2003). What is the subject? *Narrative Inquiry*, *13* (2), 317–30.

Scott, J. W. (1986). Gender: A useful category of histoical analysis. *American Historical Review*, *91* (5), 1053–75.

Sharrock, W. (1974). On owning knowledge. In R. Turner (ed.), *Ethnomethodology: Selected Readings*. Harmondsworth: Penguin.

Shaw, R., & Kitzinger, C. (2007). Memory in interaction: An analysis of repeat cells to a home birth helpline. *Research on Language and Social Interaction*, *40* (1), 117–44.

Shaw, S. (2000). Language, gender and floor apportionment in political debates. *Discourse and Society*, *11* (3), 401–18.

Sidnell, J. (2003). Constructing and managing male exclusivity in talk-in-interaction. In J. Holmes & M. Meyerhoff (eds.), *The Handbook of Language and Gender*. Oxford: Blackwell.

Siewierska, A. (2005). Gender distinctions in independent personal pronouns. In M. Haspelmath, M. S. Dryer, D. Gil, & B. Comrie (eds.), *The World Atlas of Language Structures*. Oxford: Oxford University Press.

Smith, D. E. (1978). K is mentally ill: The anatomy of a factual account. *Sociology*, *12*, 23–53.

Speer, S. A. (1999). Feminism and conversation analysis: An oxymoron? *Feminism and Psychology*, *9* (4), 417–78.

  (2001). Reconsidering the concept of hegemonic masculinity: Discursive psychology, conversation analysis and participants' orientations. *Feminism and Psychology*, *11* (1), 107–35.

  (2002a). What can conversation analysis contribute to feminist methodology? Putting reflexivity into practice. *Discourse and Society*, *13*, 783–803.

  (2002b). Sexist talk: Gender categories, participants' orientation and irony. *Journal of Sociolinguistics*, *6* (3), 347–77.

  (2002c). 'Natural' and 'contrived' data: A sustainable distinction? *Discourse Studies*, *4* (4), 511–25.

  (2005a). *Gender Talk: Feminism, Discourse and Conversation Analysis*. London: Routledge.

  (2005b). The interactional organization of the gender attribution process. *Sociology*, *39* (1), 67–87.

  (2007). Natural and contrived data. In In P. Alasuutari, J. Brannen, & L. Bickman (eds.), *The Handbook of Social Research*. London: Sage.

  (2009). Passing as a transsexual woman in the gender identity clinic. In M. Wetherell (ed.), *Theorizing Identities and Social Action*. Basingstoke: Palgrave Macmillan.

(2010). Pursuing views and testing commitments: Hypothetical questions in the psychiatric assessment of transsexual patients. In A. Freed & S. Ehrlich (eds.), *Why Do You Ask? The Function of Questions in Institutional Discourse*. Oxford: Oxford University Press.

(forthcoming). The epistemics of self-praise.

Speer, S. A., & Green, R. (2007). On passing: The interactional organization of appearance attributions in the psychiatric assessment of transsexual patients. In V. Clarke & E. Peel (eds.), *Out in Psychology: Lesbian, Gay, Bisexual, Trans and Queer Perspectives*. Chichester: John Wiley.

(2008). *Transsexual Identities: Constructions of Gender in an NHS Gender Identity Clinic*. End of Award report. Award No: RES-148–25-0029. London: Economic and Social Research Council.

Speer, S. A., & Parsons, C. (2006). Gatekeeping gender: Some features of the use of hypothetical questions in the psychiatric assessment of transsexual patients. *Discourse and Society*, *17* (6), 785–812.

(2007). 'Suppose you couldn't go any further with treatment, what would you do?': Hypothetical questions in interactions between psychiatrists and transsexual patients. In A. Hepburn & S. Wiggins (eds.), *Discursive Research in Practice: New Approaches to Psychology and Interaction*. Cambridge: Cambridge University Press.

Speer, S. A., & Potter, J. (2000). The management of heterosexist talk: Conversational resources and prejudiced claims. *Discourse and Society*, *11* (4), 543–72.

(2002). From performatives to practices: Judith Butler, discursive psychology, and the management of heterosexist talk. In P. McIlvenny (ed.), *Talking Gender and Sexuality: Conversation, Performativity and Discourse in Interaction*. Amsterdam: John Benjamins.

Spender, D. (1980). *Man Made Language*. London: Pandora Press.

Stivers, T. (2007). Alternative recognitionals in person reference. In N. J. Enfield & T. Stivers (eds.), *Person Reference in Interaction: Linguistic, Cultural and Social Perspectives*. Cambridge: Cambridge University Press.

Stivers, T., Mangione-Smith, R., Elliott, M., McDonald, L., & Heritage, J. (2003). Why do physicians think parents expect antibiotics? What parents report vs what physicians believe. *Journal of Family Practice*, *52* (2), 140–8.

Stivers, T., Enfield, N. J., & Levinson, S. C. (2007). Person reference in interaction. In N. J. Enfield & T. Stivers (eds.), *Person Reference in Interaction: Linguistic, Cultural and Social Perspectives*. Cambridge: Cambridge University Press.

Stockill, C. (2007). Use of alternative (non-)recognitionals: A marked practice to display social distance. Paper presented at the International Pragmatics Association Conference, Goteborg, Sweden, July.

Stockill, C., & Kitzinger, C. (2007). Gendered 'people': How linguistically non-gendered terms can have gendered interactional relevance. *Feminism and Psychology*, *17* (2), 224–36.

Stokoe, E. H. (1997). An evaluation of two studies of gender and language in educational settings. *Gender and Education*, *9* (2), 233–44.

(1998). Talking about gender: The conversational construction of gender categories in academic discourse. *Discourse and Society*, *9* (2), 217–40.

(2000). Toward a conversation analytic approach to gender and discourse. *Feminism and Psychology*, *10* (4), 552–63.

(2003). Mothers, single women and sluts: Gender, morality and membership categorization in neighbour disputes. *Feminism and Psychology*, *13* (3), 317–44.

(2004). Gender and discourse, gender and categorization: Current developments in language and gender research. *Qualitative Research in Psychology*, *1* (2), 107–29.

(2005). Analysing gender and language. *Journal of Sociolinguistics*, *9* (1), 118–33.

(2006). On ethnomethodology, feminism, and the analysis of categorial reference to gender in talk-in-interaction. *Sociological Review*, *54* (3), 467–94.

(2008a). Categories and sequences: Formulating gender in talk-in-interaction. In K. Harrington, L. Litosseliti, H. Saunston, & J. Sunderland (eds.), *Gender and Language Research Methodologies*. Basingstoke: Palgrave.

(2008b). Dispreferred actions and other interactional breaches as devices for occasioning audience laughter in television 'sitcoms'. *Social Semiotics*, *18* (3), 289–307.

(2009). Doing actions with identity categories: Complaints and denials in neighbour disputes. *Text and Talk*, *29* (1), 75–97.

Stokoe, E., & Edwards, D. (2007). 'Black this, black that': Racial insults and reported speech in neighbour complaints and police interrogations. *Discourse and Society*, *18* (3), 337–72.

(2011). Mundane morality and gender in familial neighbour disputes. In J. Cromdal & M. Tholander (eds.), *Morality in Practice: Exploring Childhood, Parenthood and Schooling in Everyday Life*. London: Equinox.

Stokoe, E. H., & Smithson, J. (2001). Making gender relevant: Conversation analysis and gender categories in interaction. *Discourse and Society*, *12* (2), 243–69.

(2002). Gender and sexuality in talk-in-interaction: Considering a conversation analytic perspective. In P. McIlvenny (ed.), *Talking Gender and Sexuality*. Amsterdam: John Benjamins.

Stokoe, E. H., & Weatherall, A. (2002a). Gender, language, conversation analysis and feminism. *Discourse and Society*, *13* (6), 707–13.

(eds.) (2002b). Gender, language, conversation analysis and feminism. *Discourse and Society* (special issue), *13* (6).

Streeck, J. (1986). Towards reciprocity: Politics, rank and gender in the interaction of a group of schoolchildren. In J. Cook-Gumperz, W. A. Corsaro, & J. Streeck (eds.), *Children's Worlds and Children's Language*. Berlin: Mouton de Gruyter.

Stringer, J. L., & Hopper, R. (1998). Generic *he* in conversation? *Quarterly Journal of Speech*, *84*, 209–21.

Sunderland, J. (2004). *Gendered Discourses*. Basingstoke: Palgrave.

(ed.) (2006). *Language and Gender: An Advanced Resource Book*. London: Routledge.

Swann, J. (1992). *Girls, Boys and Language*. Oxford: Blackwell.

(2009). Doing gender against the odds: A sociolinguistic analysis of educational discourse. In P. Pichler & E. M. Eppler (eds.), *Gender and Spoken Interaction*. Basingstoke: Palgrave Macmillan.

Tainio, L. (2003). 'When shall we go for a ride?': A case of the sexual harassment of a young girl. *Discourse and Society*, *14* (2), 173–90.

Talbot, M. M. (1998). *Language and Gender: An Introduction*. Cambridge: Polity.

Tannen, D. (1990). *You Just Don't Understand: Women and Men in Conversation*. London: Virago.

(ed.) (1993). *Gender and Conversational Interaction*. Oxford: Oxford University Press.

(1994). *Gender and Discourse*. New York: Oxford University Press.

(1997). Women and men talking: An interactional sociolinguistic approach. In M. R. Walsh (ed.), *Women, Men, and Gender: Ongoing Debates*. New Haven, CT: Yale University Press.

(1998). Talk in the intimate relationship: His and hers. In J. Coates (ed.), *Language and Gender: A Reader*. Oxford: Blackwell.

Tavris, C. (1994). Reply to Brown and Gilligan. *Feminism and Psychology*, *4* (3), 350–2.

Terasaki, A. K. (2004). Pre-announcement sequences in conversation. In G. H. Lerner (ed.), *Conversation Analysis: Studies from the First Generation*. Amsterdam: John Benjamins.

Tholander, M. (2002). Cross-gender teasing as a socializing practice. *Discourse Processes*, *34*, 311–38.

Thorne, B. (1993). *Gender Play: Girls and Boys in School*. Buckingham: Open University Press.

Thorne, B., & Henley, N. (eds.) (1975). *Language and Sex: Difference and Dominance*. Rowley, MA: Newbury House.

Thorne, B., Kramarae, C., & Henley, N. (eds.) (1983). *Language, Gender and Society*. Rowley, MA: Newbury House.

Tjosvold, D., & van de Vliert, E. (1994). Applying cooperation and competitive conflict theory to mediation. *Mediation Quarterly*, *11* (4), 303–11.

Toerien, M., & Kitzinger, C. (2007). Emotional labour in action: Navigating multiple involvements in the beauty salon. *Sociology*, *41* (4), 645–62.

Toerien, M., & Wilkinson, S. (2003). Gender and body hair: Constructing the feminine woman. *Women's Studies International Forum*, *26*, 333–44.

Tracy, K. (1998). Analysing context: Framing the discussion. *Research in Language and Social Interaction*, *31* (1), 1–28.

Turk, M. J. (2007). Self-referential gestures in conversation. *Discourse and Society*, *9*, 561–9.

Uchida, A. (1992). When 'difference' is 'dominance': A critique of the 'anti-power-based' cultural approach to sex differences. *Language and Society*, *21*, 547–68.

Velody, I., & Williams, R. (1998). Introduction. In I. Velody & R. Williams (eds.), *The Politics of Constructionism*. London: Sage.

Wall, J. A. (1981). Mediation: An analysis, review, and proposed research. *Journal of Conflict Resolution*, *16*, 51–65.

Walsh, C. (2001). *Gender and Discourse: Language and Power in Politics, the Church and Organizations*. Harlow: Pearson Education.

Watson, D. R. (1978). Categorization, authorization and blame negotiation in conversation. *Sociology*, *5*, 105–13.

Watson, D. R., & Weinberg, T. S. (1982). Interviews and the interactional construction of accounts of homosexual identity. *Social Analysis*, *11*, 56–78.

Weatherall, A. (2000). Gender relevance in talk-in-interaction and discourse. *Discourse and Society*, *11* (2), 286–8.

(2002a). *Gender, Language and Discourse*. London: Routledge.

(2002b). Towards understanding gender and talk-in-interaction. *Discourse and Society*, *13* (6), 767–81.

West, C. (1984). Not just 'doctor's orders': Directive–response sequences in patients' visits to women and men physicians. *Discourse and Society*, *1*, 85–112.

(1995). Women's competence in conversation. *Discourse and Society*, 6 (1), 107–31.

West, C., & Fenstermaker, S. (1993). Power, inequality, and the accomplishment of gender: An ethnomethodological view. In P. England (ed.), *Theory on Gender/ Feminism on Theory*. New York: Aldine de Gruyter.

(1995). Doing difference. *Gender and Society*, 9 (1), 8–37.

(2002a). Accountability in action: The accomplishment of gender, race and class in a University of California Board of Regents. *Discourse and Society*, 13 (4), 537–63.

(2002b). Accountability and affirmative action: The accomplishment of gender, race, and class in a University of California Board of Regents Meeting. In S. Fenstermaker & C. West (eds.), *Doing Gender, Doing Difference: Inequality, Power, and Institutional Change*. London: Routledge.

West, C., & Garcia, A. (1988). Conversational shift work: A study of topical transitions between women and men. *Social Problems*, 35, 551–75.

West, C., & Zimmerman, D. H. (1987). Doing gender. *Gender and Society*, 1, 125–51.

(2009). Account for doing gender. *Gender and Society*, 23 (1), 112–22.

Wetherell, M. (1998). Positioning and interpretative repertoires: Conversation analysis and post-structuralism in dialogue. *Discourse and Society*, 9 (3), 431–56.

(2007). A step too far: Discursive psychology, linguistic ethnography and questions of identity. *Journal of Sociolinguistics*, 11 (5), 661–81.

Wetherell, M., & Edley, N. (1999). Negotiating hegemonic masculinity: Imaginary positions and psycho-discursive practices. *Feminism and Psychology*, 9, 335–56.

Whalen, J., Zimmerman, D. H., & Whalen, M. (1988). When words fail: A single case analysis. *Social Problems*, 35 (4), 335–62.

White, S. (2002). 'Accomplishing the case' in pediatrics and child health: Medicine and morality in inter-professional talk. *Sociology of Health and Illness*, 24 (4), 409–35.

Whitehead, K. A., & Lerner, G. H. (2009). When are persons 'white'? On some practical asymmetries of racial reference in talk-in-interaction. *Discourse and Society*, 20 (5), 613–41.

Wickes, R., & Emmison, M. (2007). They are all 'doing gender' but are they all passing? A case study of the appropriation of a sociological concept. *Sociological Review*, 55 (2), 311–30.

Widdicombe, S. (1998). 'But you don't class yourself': The interactional management of membership and non-membership. In C. Antaki & S. Widdicombe (eds.), *Identities in Talk*. London: Sage.

Wilkinson, S., & Kitzinger, C. (2003). Constructing identities: A feminist conversation analytic approach to positioning in action. In R. Harré & F. Moghaddam (eds.), *The Self and Others: Positioning Individuals and Groups in Personal, Political, and Cultural Contexts*. Westpost, CT: Praeger.

(2006). Surprise as an interactional achievement: Reaction tokens in conversation. *Social Psychology Quarterly*, 69 (2), 150–82.

(2007). Conversation analysis, gender and sexuality. In A. Weatherall, B. Watson, & C. Gallios (eds.), *Language, Discourse and Social Psychology*. London: Palgrave Macmillan.

Williams, J. (2000). *Unbending Gender: Why Work and Family Conflict and What To Do About It*. Oxford: Oxford University Press.

Wodak, R. (ed.). (1997). *Gender and Discourse*. London: Sage.

(2001). The discourse-historical approach. In R. Wodak & M. Meyer (eds.), *Methods of Critical Discourse Analysis*. London: Sage.

Wooffitt, R. (2005). *Conversation Analysis and Discourse Analysis: A Comparative and Critical Introduction*. London: Sage.

Wowk, M. T. (1984). Blame allocation, sex and gender in a murder interrogation. *Women's Studies International Forum, 7* (1), 75–82.

(2007). Kitzinger's feminist conversation analysis: Critical observations. *Human Studies, 30,* 131–55.

Wu, R. (2004). *Stance in Talk: A Conversation Analysis of Mandarin Final Particles*. Amsterdam: John Benjamins.

Zimmerman, D. H. (1992a). They were all doing gender, but they weren't all passing: Comment on Rogers. *Gender and Society, 6* (2), 192–8.

(1992b). The interactional organization of calls for emergency assistance. In P. Drew & J. Heritage (eds.), *Talk at Work: Interaction in Institutional Settings*. Cambridge: Cambridge University Press.

(1998). Identity, context, and interaction. In C. Antaki and S. Widdicombe (eds.), *Identities in Talk*. London: Sage.

Zimmerman, D. H., & West, C. (1975). Sex roles, interruptions and silences in conversation. In B. Thorne & N. Henley (eds.), *Language and Sex: Difference and Dominance*. Rowley, MA: Newbury House.

Author index

Subject index

action formation 21–2, 158, 160
action relevance 18–19, 64, 66–1, 74, 78, 80,
  81, 141, 145, 150
address terms 204–5, 240–3
  gender-neutral 15, 17, 32, 45, 58, 75, 78,
    99, 107, 242, 279–81, 288–9
  gendered 17, 58, 99, 252, 263–8, 274,
    279–81, 288–9, 296
A-event statement 168
age categorizations 45–6, 245
age norm 45–6
'Agnes' case 5, 64, 231, 244, 245, 249, 274
apologies 99, 101, 102
'auto discussion' (film) 184

B-event statement 42, 138, 139, 141, 142,
  144–5, 151, 170, 174, 176, 179, 180
body orientation 22, 184, 185, 190–4,
  198–200, 204, 206, 208–9
bragging 21, 158, 163–6, 180, 181

categorization 11, 48–63, 295–96
  first person 18, 49–63
  multiple set 68–9
  non-present third party 48
  person reference and 65–6, 68
  of self 17–19, 49–63
  see also gender categorization
category-bound activities 92, 109, 244,
  253–5, 262, 296–7, 298, 301, 303, 305
category-formed errors 19, 87–8
category membership 18, 55, 73, 76, 198,
  234, 244–8, 273
  cross-gender 23
  inferential order of 296–7
  multiple 34–6, 40–1, 45–7, 48–63
  see also membership categorization
children
  girls' and boys' competitive play 23,
    257–9, 270
  language 250–1
  person formulations 23, 251–2

play and gender categorization 24, 295–7,
  299–309
  see also parenting
compliments 161 see also third party
  compliments
consecutive reference 90–2
constructionism 5–8
conversation, male–female differences 85–6,
  207–9
conversation analysis 8–13, 25, 85–7, 250n2
  criticisms of/debates 12, 15–16
  and epistemics of self-praise 160–6
  feminist 13–17, 26, 31–2, 297
  policy relevance 27–7
  procedural consequentiality 10–12
  and self-reference 32–8
correction
  embedded 90–2
  exposed 96–102
cross-gender identity 22–3, 231–49 see also
  transsexualism
cross-gender play 296–7

dirty jokes 21, 183, 184, 185–209
discourse 4–7, 20, 89, 102, 185n2, 298
  analysis 10–11, 25, 308
  gendered 12
  identities 252n9
  interview 169, 178, 181
  and iterability 260
Discourse Studies 33
discursive psychology 17, 20, 48, 298
divorce mediation 23, 272–93
dominance 10–11, 12, 266
  model 3
  theory 258

economy rule 88
embodied conduct 1, 9, 15, 20, 22, 25, 98,
  164 see also body orientation;
  eye gaze
endearment terms 204–5